explo[illegible]

CRETE

Christopher Somerville

AA Publishing

Essential

Written by Christopher Somerville
Original photography by Ken Patterson

Edited, designed and produced by AA Publishing
Maps © The Automobile Association 1995

Distributed in the United Kingdom by AA Publishing, Norfolk House, Priestley Road, Basingstoke, Hampshire, RG24 9NY.

The contents of this publication are believed correct at the time of printing. Nevertheless, the publishers cannot be held responsible for any errors or omissions or for changes in the details given in this guide or for the consequences of any reliance on the information provided by the same. Assessments of attractions, hotels, restaurants and so forth are based upon the author's own personal experience and, therefore, descriptions given in this guide necessarily contain an element of subjective opinion which may not reflect the publishers' opinion or dictate a reader's own experiences on another occasion. We have tried to ensure accuracy in this guide, but things do change and we would be grateful if readers would advise us of any inaccuracies they may encounter.

A CIP catalogue record for this book is available from the British Library. ISBN 0 7495 1026 9

Published by AA Publishing (a trading name of Automobile Association Developments Limited, whose registered office is Norfolk House, Priestley Road, Basingstoke, Hampshire RG24 9NY. Registered number 1878835).

Colour separation by LC Repro & Sons, Aldermaston
Printed and bound in Italy by Printers SRL, Trento

A tamed and rather benign dragon – whose foot has become part of the decorative foliage below – graces its new home on this house in Margarítes

Cover picture: Voríza
Page 4: Réthimnon harbour
Page 5 (top): from the Minoan palace of Ayía Triádha, now in Gallery XIV, Iráklio Archaeological Museum
Page 5 (left): Cretan haversacks from Anóyia
Page 5 (right): a monk from Ayíos Nikólaos Monastery, near Zarós
Pages 6 and 7 (top): Cretan shepherd
Page 7: a quiet street in Mírtos
Page 9: view from Préveli Monastery
Page 23: Poseidon and Anemone, Khaniá Archaeological Museum
Page 255: between Ayíos Nikólaos and Sitiá
Page 273: Hotel Doma, Khaniá

Contents

Quick reference

This quick-reference guide highlights the features of the book you will use most often: the maps; the introductory features; the Focus-on articles; the walks; and the drives.

Níkos Psilákis
Born in 1955, Níkos Psilákis hosts a daily programme on Radio Crete. His broadcasting career has seen him contribute to over 1,500 radio transmissions and 70 television documentaries on the island's history.

His books include two collections of poems, and the latest of his publications about his native island, *Monasteries and Hermitages of Crete*, was given an award by the Academy of Athens in 1994.

My Crete

by Níkos Psilákis

I was born in Crete – and have never thought to leave. It's not the sun and the light, nor the coast and the mountains which keep me on my island; nor is it solely history and antiquities. What fascinates me in Crete is continuity; words that Homer spoke live on in the conversation of today's shepherds and fishermen, while many Cretan customs – themselves almost a way of life – speak to us from the Minoan period.

Four thousand years ago the Minoans would kneel in front of a tree which they held sacred. I have seen people doing just the same, not because they are heathens, but because they have heard their ancestors' secret voice and are worshipping not the tree but, through it, Christ himself. I have seen farmers offering the first grapes of the season to Christ, whilst others pour a few drops of the new wine on to the dry earth, as if presenting it to the Great Mother.

My Crete is the island of gods. I see Zeus emerging from the sea in the guise of a white bull, carrying his beloved Europa, who was to give her name to a whole continent. And it is Apollo's island; in the wild gorge of Samariá I imagine him hugging the beautiful nymph Akali.

And it is the island which gave the Apostle Paul landfall on its southern shores, the island which stood out against the Ottomans, the island which fought with stones and wood against Hitler's paratroops.

My Crete is an amalgam of all these, but I don't search for it in the busy streets or the frequented beaches. I find it in the far off villages, on the mountains, in the shepherds' stockyards and in the fishermen's huts...

Alexándra Karétzou
A graduate in history and archaeology from the University of Athens, Alexándra Karétzou has worked in the archaeological museums in Iráklio, Ayíos Nikólaos and Réthimnon. Since 1993 she has been the Director of the Iráklio Museum. For over 20 years she has had a fascination for matters Minoan and has worked on an excavation of a temple on Mount Yioúchtas for most of that period.

My Crete

by Alexandra Karétzou

The Crete I love lies beyond the northern highway, far from the commercial drudgery of tourist towns. The Crete I love is near Dreros, in a small, enclosed, upland plain called Dryvaxonas (from the word meaning to protect or surround). The Crete I love lies in the mountains, in the open-air sanctuaries of the Minoans. Here nothing is silent. All is rock, thirst and danger, and all, having seen generations prosper and vanish, cry out in the same voice, 'Don't leave anything until tomorrow. Perhaps we shall live; perhaps we shall die.'

The Crete I love and have deep within my heart is found in the island's sacred places where worship continues to this day with the same devotion on the part of the believers – even though we say times have changed. In the Amári Valley, nestling in the cave of the Patsos Gorge, in the same spot where Hermes was worshipped, is the shrine of the Christian Ayíos Antónios. And here, as in so many places in Crete, time seems to stand still. Offerings hang from a rope on the rock, and with them the hopes and despairs of mankind; wedding wreaths, a faded robe, plaited hair. At the foot of the rock, two pairs of Cretan boots, a goat-skin bag, votive gifts which go back to the earliest times of Cretan civilisation.

CRETE IS

An island of contrasts

■ **Crete is not a large island, being only 250km long and just 12km across at its narrowest point. But within its shores there is an astonishing variety of landscape, activities and atmospheres of old and new worlds.....■**

Contrasts The old and the new, the sophisticated and the simple, rub shoulders in Crete. The long-established harbour towns of Iráklio, Réthimnon and Khaniá have Venetian houses and waterfronts of golden stone, but there are also areas of rowdy nightclubs where modern tourism comes abruptly into focus. There are popular, crowded beaches in the north, and secluded sandy coves on the more inaccessible coasts. You can stay in a bland and expensive luxury hotel, or take your chances in a rough-and-ready village taverna. Archaeological sites range from the world-famous and thronged Minoan palaces of Knosós, Faistós, Mália and Zákros to unfrequented classical Greek country houses and Roman temples, quietly crumbling away on obscure hillsides.

People Cretan people, too, exhibit a mercurial mix of temperaments – fiery and nonchalant, eager and laissez-faire, formal and impulsive. But what you can always rely upon is their unfailing courtesy and their instant, unrestrained hospitality, a hospitality which the stranger can never repay, but only enjoy and appreciate.

❑ Make use of the EOT (Greek Tourist Organisation) offices in Iráklio, Réthimnon, Khaniá, Ayíos Nikólaos, Sitiá and other towns. They are always busy, but they have comprehensive information on regular and special events and celebrations. ❑

Landscape Crete's landscape is marvellously varied, with four great mountain ranges. From west to east these are: Levká Óri or the White Mountains in the far west, Psiloritis or the Ída range south of Réthimnon, the Dhíkti Mountains between Iráklio and Ayíos Nikólaos, and the Thriptís or Sitiá range out to the east. These are limestone mountains, the end of a great chain which runs down from the Balkans. The bare peaks, pale grey in summer or white with snow in winter, dominate the island. Below the peaks, the rocks are sunbaked to brown, purple and orange. Remnants of once-extensive pine and cypress forests clothe the upper ranges; below are skirts of

The fertile Lasíthiou plain lies below dramatic mountains

Scented, flowering herbs clothe the mountainsides of much of the island and are particularly fine in the Cretan spring

prickly scrub, giving off an entrancing scent in the hot Cretan sunshine.

Lowlands Below the mountains spread the richer and more lush lowlands, strongholds of the olive grove and vineyard, cornfield and vegetable plot, orchard and nut grove. Country roads undulate from one village and small town to the next, through a green landscape scarcely visited by holidaymakers but with its own soft, easy-going atmosphere. Typical of these pleasant lowlands are the lovely Amári valley south of Réthimnon, the fertile length of the Mesarás plain in the south of the island, and the wide country behind Khaniá and Iráklio.

Coasts The lowlands dip to flat plains along the north coast, lush and damp in the far west, sandy of

❑ As little as only 30 years ago it was often extremely difficult to reach the mountain villages of central Crete. Most journeys had to be made either on mule-back or on foot. The road system has greatly improved since then, but journeys on many Cretan dirt roads are still a challenge, even to experienced drivers. ❑

❑ Astivítha has pride of place among the prickly scrub plants of the mountains. It is a low, cushion-shaped bush with hexagonally arranged spikes and deep red flowers... and when you brush against a clump it releases a delicious, spicy smell. ❑

beach and rocky of headland further east. Between Iráklio and Ayíos Nikólaos the shoreline is largely built up, but out to the east there are many lonely stretches of rocky coastline. The south coast is far less frequented, and long stretches of it – such as the rugged emptiness of Asteroúsia and the dramatic splendour of the White Mountains as they rear abruptly out of the Libyan Sea – are roadless.

Climate No matter what climate suits you, Crete can provide it. Owing to the mountains' barrier, there may be beautiful sunshine on the south coast while rain is sweeping the north. From January to March there is snow in the mountains and generally wild weather. April and May are warm and fresh, with flowers everywhere. June is hot, July and August hotter still, with dust and uncomfortable winds always possible. From September to October the island slowly cools down, lovely clear days bringing a second flowering of the Cretan flora, before the gales and snow begin once again in November.

Evidence of history

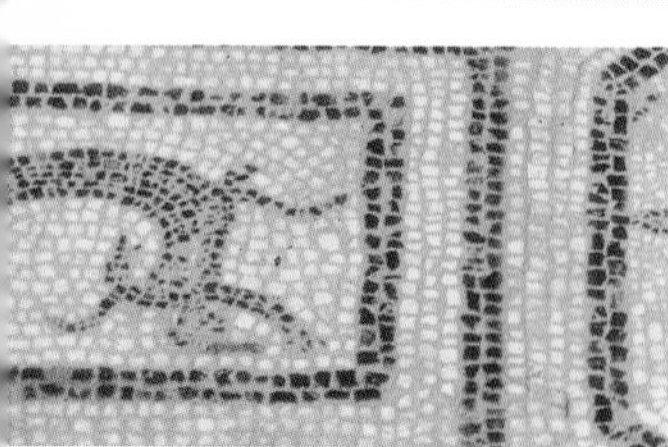

■ Crete's history is long, dramatic, bloody and heroic, and it has left its mark throughout the island. The world-famous sites attract the crowds, but elsewhere you will stumble across tiny painted churches, fragments of mosaics, two-thousand-year-old houses, a Minoan jug handle under a stone, or a Roman column lying in a field.....■

Invaded island Situated as it is, at the crossroads of sea communications between Europe, North Africa and the Middle East, Crete has always been a tempting plum, ripe for picking by invaders, colonisers and traders. Some have coveted the island for its natural riches of timber and fertile agricultural land; some have wanted to use it as a buffer between themselves and aggressors, others as a base for attacking enemies or as a departure-point for invasions. Crete's history is inextricably bound up with invasion, resistance, battle and bloodshed, interspersed with periods of calm and prosperity under a succession of rulers. At times the island has seen such prosperity that it has been known as the jewel of the Mediterranean. At other times it has sunk into the misery of neglect and cruelty so deep that it looked as if it would never rise again. Each succeeding culture, beneficial or destructive, has left its stamp. There are relics and remains of every period in the town streets and on lonely hillsides, among which the present-day Cretans lead their lives unconcernedly while visitors probe and puzzle among the ruins.

Relics of the rulers The great Minoan civilisation that rose and fell in Crete between 2600 and 1400BC left palaces at Knosós, Faistós, Mália and Zákros which are magnets for hundreds of thousands of visitors. Another is the hilltop town at Gourniá, but there are hundreds of lesser, and less crowded, sites to enjoy, like the little oval house at Khamezi, domestic and intimate on a lonely hill. The Dorians, who ruled Crete after the Minoans, built small city-states, such as Polirrínia and

❑ Crete's steep hillsides are terraced to create level fields for cultivation. Some of the walls still in use are extremely old, dating back hundreds of years. They are patched and patched again, with stones that lie conveniently to hand, perhaps first used in Minoan times. ❑

Village life often still revolves around the church, many of which are rich with ancient decoration

The magnificent Minoan palace of Faistós

Ítanos, in the hills and by the shore, and their house and temple ruins lie mostly unvisited. The enormous sprawling Roman city at Górtina, where the olive groves are strewn with marble columns and fragments of pottery, also has a large basilica which was built by the Byzantines, the next rulers of Crete. Byzantine artists decorated the church of Ayíos Nikólaos with geometric frescoes which display thousand-year-old colours that are still bright. From 1204 for the next 450 years the Venetians held the island and their magnificent, solid architecture is still widespread, and can best be seen in Khaniá and Réthimnon. The Turks drove the Venetians out in 1669, and stayed until 1898. They built fountains and minarets, and added their own style of doors, windows and arches to the Venetian houses. War memorials, newly built mountain villages and recent rebuilding in the bigger towns are reminders of the destruction wrought in the island during World War II.

❑ The Church has a powerful influence on all generations of Cretans today. Young and old, even in towns, will cross themselves when they pass a church during religious festivals. The priest's teenage daughter at Méronas in the Amári Valley says, tenderly, of the 14th-century icon of the Virgin in the village church: 'We look after her, because she looks after us'. ❑

Cause for concern The best-known historic sites are suffering from the huge numbers of people who tramp through them causing damage and erosion. Less famous sites are unprotected from the elements and have been pillaged for building stone over the years. Souvenir and treasure hunters have also been at work for countless centuries, and the threat continues today.

A bronze goddess from 700BC

Town life and country life

■ **There are two separate and distinct atmospheres to savour on the island. There is the lively bustle of the Cretan towns, where traditional courtesies and hospitality mingle with commercial vigour and street sharpness. And there is the slower pace of the villages, where the old way of life is gradually changing.....**■

Thriving towns At first acquaintance, the towns seem thronged and disorderly, a muddle of lorry-jammed streets and dusty shops. However, you quickly begin to distinguish the individual character of each place you visit. Each is distinctive, each in its own way worth lingering over to catch the full flavour of the island's thriving town life. Some, like Ayíos Nikólaos and the north coast resorts nearer to Iráklio, are essentially tourist towns, given over to servicing the visitor trade, dependent on the hotels, beaches, restaurants and night spots. Khaniá and Réthimnon, with a wealth of well-preserved Venetian architecture and a strong sense of historical and regional identity, operate a successful mixture: a thriving visitor-oriented economy and a social and cultural life that revolves around local people and affairs. In Ierápetra, the agricultural centre of the south coast, it appears that the separation of tourism and commercial activity is wider. In Iráklio, the full-to-bursting capital, business takes precedence over the desires of visitors.

These are all coastal towns with historic commercial links to the sea, currently making the most of the seaside resort trade. Inland, in towns such as Pérama near Réthimnon, or Moíres in the Mesarás plain, you will discover a wholly rural, rough and ready, unselfconscious way of life that can be a refreshing change. It is worth stopping a day or two away from the coast to absorb this atmosphere, quite unaffected by the north European visitor.

❑ In a car hire office in Odós Idomíneos, Iráklio, the man behind the desk whiles away his long afternoons by playing the dance tunes of his native village on his *bouzouki* – a lifeline in a sea of noisy streets and querulous customers. ❑

The streets of Iráklio are hectic

Little seems to change in the countryside

Village change and tradition

Though many Cretans have left their villages in recent years to seek work and a broader outlook in the towns, the social and economic lifeblood of the island continues to pulse strongly and with heartening vigour in its hundreds of small rural villages. Each region has its own character, acknowledged almost to the point of caricature by the islanders themselves. There are the laid back qualities of the Sitiá folk in the east, the commercially minded Mesarás farmers, and the proud and ferocious Sfakiots of the west. Perhaps these regional temperaments have something to do with the landscape, reflecting the gentler gradients of the east, the prosperous fertility of Mesarás, and the harsh bleakness of the mountainous west.

In the villages people work hard at basic agriculture with their bare hands and unsophisticated tools. Relaxation is found in a glass of *rakí,* with prolonged discussion of local affairs, and maybe a glance at the television which mutters incessantly in the corner. And it is here that you can still enjoy undiluted Cretan hospitality, see men and women going about their everyday lives in traditional dress, watch a potter creating a jar or a woman weaving a rug, in the same way that such things have been done for centuries.

❑ One side effect of the flight of young people from the villages to the towns has been to deprive the old people of much of their conversational fodder... the scandalous way young folk go on. Many of the men too old to work spend a good deal of the day nodding off outside the *kafeníon.* ❑

❑ In contrast to the old men sitting outside the village *kafeníon* in magnificent idleness, the elderly women are seemingly always occupied, hobbling to and fro with buckets, toting bundles of firewood on their backs, scrubbing clothes at the trough, peeling potatoes at their doors. ❑

Traditional dress is still a matter of pride for older men

■ One characteristic that all the islanders share is a love of celebration. All solemn religious occasions, full-blooded local festivals and village family gatherings are an excuse for singing, dancing, eating and drinking on a grand scale, accompanied by a fusillade of firecrackers.....■

Loud and long In his excellent book, *Crete: Its Past, Present and People,* Adam Hopkins tells of a British pilot during the last days of World War II who was shocked to encounter prolonged anti-aircraft fire over Iráklio some time after the Germans had withdrawn from the town. Subsequent investigation revealed the identity of the gunners to be a party of carousing wedding guests, joyfully letting off their weapons at the sky. This story sums up the Cretan attitude to celebration: make it loud and make it long. In a society where life is, on the whole, still hard and demanding, celebrations when they come are eagerly welcomed, and pursued remorselessly to the end.

Lamb is frequently eaten at festivals

❑ At midnight, as Easter Saturday becomes Easter Sunday, many villages celebrate with the ritual burning of the traitor Judas Iscariot. The effigy may take the form of a stuffed dummy, or appear symbolically as a floral wreath, swinging from a gallows or blazing on top of a bonfire.

After the midnight ceremonies at the church, families and friends return to their houses for a ceremonial meal. The main dish is usually lamb stewed with vegetables and herbs gathered from the mountainside. ❑

Religious festivals Most Cretans subscribe to the Greek Orthodox faith, with its very practical attitude to worship and its strong roots in everyday life and the local community. Orthodox priests are not demi-gods; they are married men who live and work with their parishioners, and play their full part in island life. In the past this has included resistance to oppressors. This special and central rôle of the church helps to explain why the islanders, even modern young people who may have turned their backs on church-going, flock to the many religious celebrations that take place through the year.

By far the most important of the church festivals is Easter, when Cretans will make every effort to return to their home villages from the towns and even from overseas to join in the ceremonies. On Good Friday evening the churches and

The Greek tradition of decorating the church for Easter lives on in Crete, as here outside Khaniá

streets are packed for the procession of the *epitáphios* or flower-decked bier. On Easter Saturday night everyone gathers at the church to pass on the candle flame that symbolises the Risen Christ. They greet each other with cries of '*Christós Anésti!*', 'Christ is Risen!', to be answered with '*Alíthos Anésti!*', 'Truly Risen!' Returning home, the master of the house will bless his threshold by making a smoky cross on the lintel with a lighted candle, after which the family celebrations can begin.

Other religious celebrations include the *paniyíria,* or saint's day, of the village church; name days when all those with the same name will gather to baptise the next generation to bear that name; and christenings at which the rôle of godparent is undertaken as a serious lifetime commitment.

Other celebrations Nowadays many towns have their own festivals. Réthimnon has a Wine Festival in July, Iráklio Festival is held in high summer, Sitiá holds a Sultana Festival in mid-August, and the Chestnut Festival at Élos occurs every year in October.

Other celebrations include Independence Day (March 25); Battle of Crete Week (May 20–27); *Óhi* or No Day (October 28) which recalls the single-word reply that the Greek leader General Metáxas gave in 1940 to Mussolini's ultimatum for a Greek alliance with Italy or invasion; and November 7–9 when fireworks at Arkádhi Monastery commemorate the devastating explosion of 1866 (see pages 258–9).

❑ A great tradition of Easter is the battle of the red eggs. Hardboiled eggs in red-painted shells are handed round, then the contestants pair off. A player enfolds an egg in his fist and presents one end to his opponent, who brings his own egg down on it with subtle force. The egg that stays uncracked is the winner. Then the eggs are reversed, and the loser can try to gain an honourable draw. ❑

Pride in independence

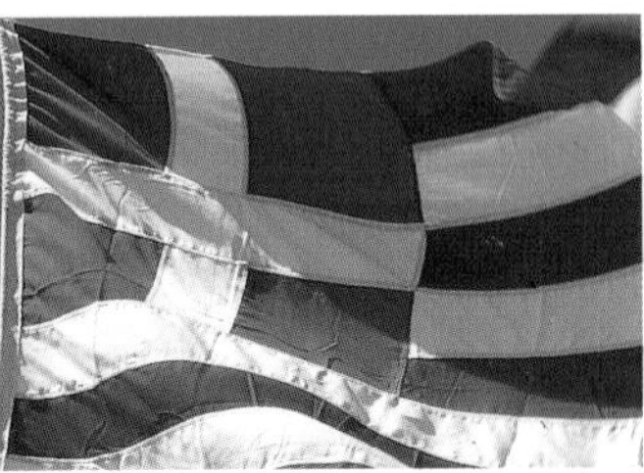

■ Crete's population fought, suffered and died for many years to attain political union with mainland Greece which, was only finally gained in 1913. Yet the single, most obvious, unifying characteristic of the islanders is their fierce pride in being Cretan, an independent people beholden to nobody. Crete is a land apart, as every visitor quickly discovers.....■

Fighting and freedom 'Freedom or Death!' cried the old *palikáres,* the mountain freedom fighters, as they leapt down to do battle with their Turkish rulers. 'I believe in nothing. I hope for nothing. I am free', runs the inscription on the grave of Crete's great novelist, Níkos Kazantzákis. Freedom has always been the watchword of the islanders. It is something that they have both believed in and hoped for, a mighty aspiration that has brought countless imprisonments, exiles and deaths. For three thousand years they sought freedom from succeeding conquerors. After the Turks withdrew in 1898 they pressed relentlessly for the freedom to unite with Greece. They fought bitterly and with enormous courage to free themselves once more during World War II. And they united again in the late 1960s for freedom from the Greek military dictatorship.

Fighting and the search for freedom are two aspects of the character of the Cretan population which, even when constrained in calmer times, refuse to lie down. Cretans bend the knee to nobody. They may be part of a modern conservative Greece, but by instinct they are republican and liberal, not much inclined to take Athens and her regulations too seriously – still less Brussels and hers. Cretans first, and the Greeks second, is how the islanders explain themselves to outsiders.

Independence of spirit Cretan traditions of work and social life, and even the shape of the island itself, have played an important part in fostering this notable independence of spirit. Small-scale farmers and shepherds work either alone or in

❑ The Cretan passion for the discussion of politics gets a chance to flourish during elections. In every village rival party headquarters are plastered with posters and festooned with flags, and people bring chairs into the *platía* to listen to visiting politicians. ❑

Political elections are taken very seriously in Crete

small groups, at a pace dictated by seasons and weather rather than by a boss or commercial considerations. The villages are small, close-knit, and isolated in a mountainous landscape. In the past, communications were so poor and the distances so great that natural geographical divisions created pockets of individuality, not only locally but throughout the island.

The trend of modern life may be softening these hard conditions, but the pride in independence remains. When the chips are down, as they have so often been during the island's history, Cretans display an admirable steadfastness. But there is mercury in the iron. Cretans seem more colourful and more highly flavoured than other Greeks. 'All Cretans are liars', as the islanders themselves are fond of quoting; it is a crude way of saying that a Cretan can be charming and maddening, warmly concerned and shruggingly indifferent, solid as a rock and a seemingly casual breaker of appointments, all within an hour.

❑ *Kafeníon* owners fear for their television sets at election time. Tempers are quickly roused and party allegiances forcefully asserted during the party political advertisements and debates that interrupt the regular programmes. ❑

❑ One of the most powerful novels produced by Crete's best-known writer, Níkos Kazantzákis, dealt with the bloody struggle of the *palikáres* or freedom fighters against Turkish rule. As a title Kazantzákis chose the rallying cry of the Cretan patriots, 'Freedom or Death!', but changed the 'or' to 'and' to reflect the actual theme of Cretan history, *Freedom and Death*. ❑

'Ware politics! International affairs may not appear to loom large in everyday life, but watch out for thumped tables and raised voices when politics and *rakí* mingle. You should perhaps steer clear of this territory, as outsiders do not have much of a right to a say in Cretan or Greek politics!

Politics is the meat of café talk

A tourist take-over?

■ Any visitor to the north coast between Iráklio and Mália will be unable to ignore the changes that mass tourism has brought to Crete. But the island is trying to turn the tide, with ambitious plans for green tourism that will introduce a much-needed balance between the need for foreign currency and the ravages that low-budget tourism brings to the island's ecology and social life.....■

Mistakes and remedies Package tours to Crete only began in the late 1960s. Many mistakes were made in those early years. Big parcels of prime seaside land were bought up by speculators, shady hotels were run up by the score, there were non-existent or unenforced planning regulations, unsupervised jobs for the boys. Shoals of bars and discos sprang up, mostly superimposed on the northern coastline with its under-developed infrastructure.

Evidence of poor planning and building control is still to be seen today, but the authorities, under the long-range direction of Athens, have woken up to the potential disaster they have been inflicting on their lovely island. Regulations concerning the design, spacing and servicing of buildings, the layout and planning of resorts, sanitation and the hiring of seasonal staff have been tightened up. The road system has been greatly improved, especially with the construction of the modern highway between Ayíos Nikólaos and Khaniá. The development of the south coast fishing villages has come under scrutiny for the first time, and there is a reluctance to grant planning permission in areas of conservation value or great natural beauty.

❑ Topless sunbathing for women has become a commonplace feature of most western European beaches, and Crete is no exception. There are many secluded spots for whole-hog nudists; but visitors are well advised to behave with some sensitivity as many older Cretans do not care for the trend. As a rule, toplessness is all right on secluded tourist beaches, but should be avoided on public stretches of the town beach. ❑

At Mália, every last patch of sand can be taken

Green tourism Many holidaymakers these days are exploring the island, rather than simply frying on the beach. Unfortunately, at present, this means driving in open-topped four-wheel-drive hire cars. But the advent of green tourism will perhaps see more visitors taking to the countryside on foot. The old shepherds' paths are being waymarked, better maps are in preparation, and more information is being made available. A long-distance path now runs the full length of the island, some 250km from end to end. Conservation of Crete's wildlife is slowly becoming recognised as a priority, and villagers are being encouraged to provide accommodation for visitors who want to stay with a family and discover more about community life.

Surviving the changes The islanders' way of life has inevitably changed in the last 25 years. With improvements to the roads, tourists have taken to the hills in hire cars and have destroyed the village peace and solitude. Youngsters have left the remote villages for work in the city, in tourist centres and abroad. Most villagers now have electricity, running water, television, cars and aspirations. Demand for consumer goods is growing. Social divisions between the haves and the have-nots, professional and manual workers, have widened. Perceptions of wealth and glamour arrived with the tourists and with the television, changing forever the quiet acceptance of fate. Somehow, though, the essential Cretan virtues of kindness, courtesy, hospitality and interest in the stranger, continue to survive the onslaughts of tourism, the latest and perhaps the most invidious in a long line of foreign invaders.

❑ Nothing reflects the raw incompatibility of tourism more than the brightness of its colours. Multi-hued nylon jogging suits, fluorescent orange shorts, lipstick pink and luminous green motor bikes jar with the subdued grey, brown, green and black of the Cretan landscape and the village dwellers' clothing. ❑

❑ Old customs, thank goodness, die hard in Crete. The Greek authorities have recently tried to stamp out two traditions they felt reflected badly on the country as a modern nation: firstly, the enlivening of religious celebrations with a burst of firecrackers, and, secondly, the keeping open of *kafenía* and bars until the early hours. Cretans have simply turned broad backs and deaf ears to these edicts from across the sea. ❑

Crete's long monastic tradition is now under threat from dwindling numbers of novices

■ A characteristic that marks out Cretans, and a virtue for which they are rightly well known, is their unstinting hospitality to friend and stranger alike. This is a feature of island life that has withstood all recent changes.....■

Philoxénia The Greek word for this trait is *philoxénia,* love of the stranger. In Crete *philoxénia* is a social, almost a religious, obligation. The poorer the giver, the greater the pleasure in giving. There may be a return in the form of news, entertaining topics of conversation or a fresh ear to bend, but that is not the point. The impulse is a pure one.

Coffee and apples Cretan hospitality takes many forms. An Iráklio shopkeeper, resigning herself to having failed to sell you a handbag, will still offer a cup of coffee. An old woman, peeling apples on her doorstep, will hand you one as you walk by. You give a lift in your car to a homegoing boy, and his family will probably invite you in for a meal. You are benighted on the mountain, and a shepherd may offer to put you up for the night in his hut.

Water with a smile These customs have been abused by freeloaders from time to time, and in the bigger hotels and smarter restaurants *philoxénia* may by now have shrunk to a complimentary *rakí,* whose price you will find buried in your bill. But out in the country it still flourishes. Perhaps the best expression of Cretan hospitality is the simple glass of cold spring water, offered with a smile to the thirsty walker.

❑ One aspect of Cretan hospitality that visitors usually find embarrassing is the taboo on any payback gesture by the guest. You must know your host well and judge your moment before you can stand your round without causing offence. Smiles and signs of appreciation are the best way to return hospitality. Attempts at Greek will be received with pleasure: *efharistó polí* is thank you very much, *issi-yian* is good health, *polí kaló* is very good. ❑

A welcoming glass of soumadha

CRETE WAS

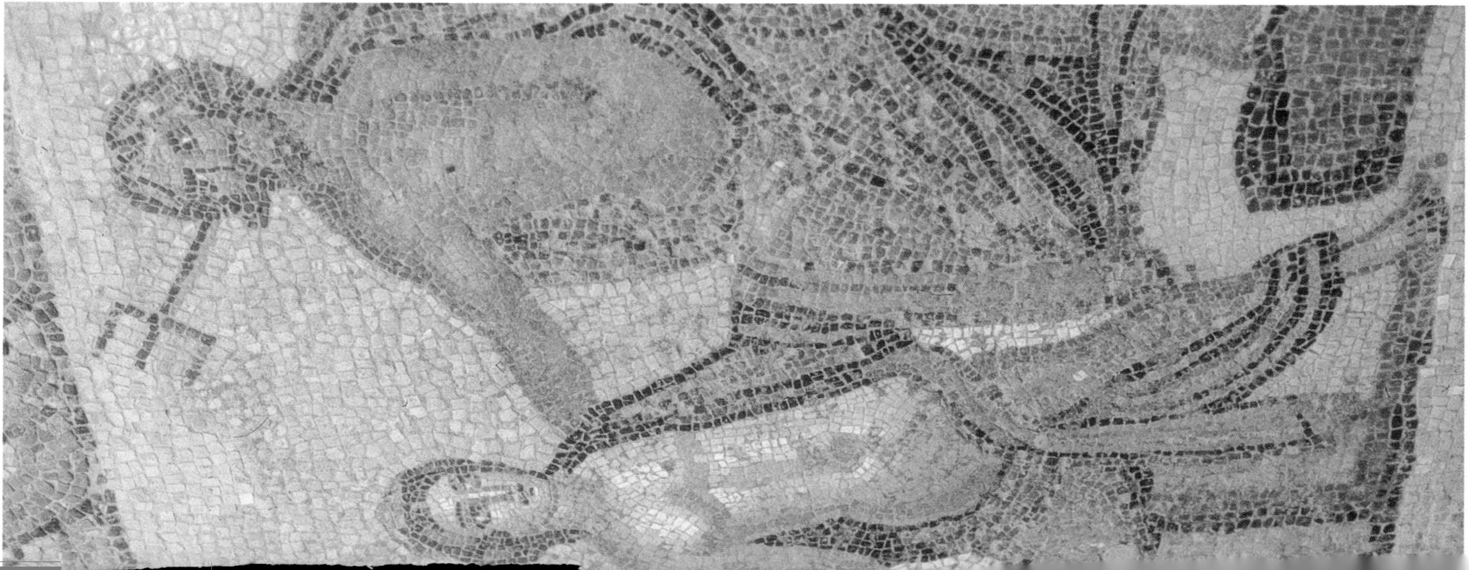

Myth and legend

■ Early civilisations, searching for an explanation of their origins in an unrecorded past, invested Crete with a fabulous and dramatic history. The stories make compelling entertainment; believe as much as you like.....■

Kronos Kronos, ruler of the gods, married his sister Rhea and begat five children whom he ate, fearing a prophesy which suggested he would be overthrown by his son. To protect her unborn sixth child, Rhea fled to Crete and gave birth to Zeus in the Dhíktaean cave above Lasíthiou. The infant was reared in the Ídaean cave on Psiloritis. You can visit these caves and imagine for yourself how the stories came into being.

Later, Zeus, perhaps in the guise of an eagle, lay with Europa at Górtina, and they had three sons together: Sarpedon, Rhadamanthys the law-giver, and the mighty king, Minos. When Zeus died he was buried on Mount Yioúchtas.

❑ The bull was the gathering-point for many strands of Greek mythology. The bull was the favourite animal of Poseidon the earth-shaker, it was the symbol and plaything of King Minos and the civilisation he ruled, and it was the *alter ego* of Zeus when the god of gods wished to dally with mortal maidens. It is a shame that bulls are such a rare sight in Crete these days; rams and billy-goats seem to have taken over. ❑

Minos Some have said that Minos was a just and fair king, others that he was a cruel tyrant. Certainly he was loved by his father Zeus, who would summon him every nine years to the Dhíktaean cave to relearn the art of kingship. But Minos was foolish enough to try to trick Poseidon, god of the sea, who had sent him a magnificent white bull as a gift. Minos should have returned the bull as a sacrifice, but offered instead a lesser animal. In revenge, the sea god caused the king's hot-blooded wife Pasiphae to fall in love with the bull. Pasiphae enlisted the help of the master-craftsman Daedalus, who had built a wonderful, maze-like palace at Knosós for the king. Daedalus constructed a model cow, in which the libidinous queen concealed herself to be mounted by the bull. She gave birth to the Minotaur, a bull-headed monster whom King Minos consigned to the labyrinth beneath the palace, where the beast devoured consignments of youths and maidens shipped in from Athens.

Theseus and the Minotaur

Theseus and the Minotaur
Theseus, son of the king of Athens, volunteered to join a shipment of victims, enlisted the help of Ariadne, the daughter of Minos, and managed to kill the Minotaur. Theseus escaped with the princess, but apparently abandoned her after a night of passion on the island of Naxos.

Daedalus and his son Icarus fled the wrath of King Minos on homemade wings of wax and feathers. Icarus flew too near the sun, the wax of his wings melted and he fell to his death. His father went into hiding at the court of King Kokalos of Sicily. Minos followed him there to exact revenge, but was scalded to death in his bath by the daughters of the Sicilian king.

❑ Amaltheia, the resident of Mount Ída who suckled the infant Zeus and nursed him through his Cretan babyhood, is one goat at least that has made it into the annals of mythology. In some versions of the legend, Amaltheia appears as half goat and half nymph, an adoptive mother for the infant god, after his own mother Rhea had given birth to him in the secrecy of the Dhíktaean cave to save him from the jaws of his bloodthirsty father Kronos. ❑

❑ For sheer enjoyment and pace, *The King Must Die* by Mary Renault still remains the best and most accessible retelling of the legend of Theseus and the Minotaur. ❑

Daedalus and Icarus

Pre-Minoans and Minoans

■ Elaborate palaces and huddled hilltop towns, priests intoning in the depths of caves, snakes wrapped round the arms of bare-breasted priestesses, golden bees hanging from a necklace, a clay jar decorated with goats and an octopus, a doe-eyed girl pouting from a wall painting, the uplifted horns of a bull – the Minoans.....■

Legend and fact The fame of Crete rests largely on the remains of an obscure Bronze Age civilisation unearthed at the turn of this century by a short-sighted Englishman. When Sir Arthur Evans discovered and excavated the palace at Knosós in 1900 (see pages 90–3), he brought to light one of history's most fabulous treasures, that had lain forgotten under the earth for 2,000 years and more. Evans named the palace-builders Minoans, after the mythical King of Crete (see pages 24–5), for this discovery brought together mythology and history, legend and fact. Other excavations at Faistós (pages 82–3) and Ayía Triádha (pages 80–1), Mália (pages 131–3) and Gourniá (pages 122–3), were to confirm what Evans suspected – that the ancient legends of Crete were founded in reality. Folk memories existed of a sophisticated, creative, artistic and powerful society that had once flourished on the island. The excavations early this century were not the end of the story. As late as 1962 the splendid Minoan palace at Zákros (pages 158–9) was unearthed, and new discoveries are still being made in caves and on hillsides all over Crete. Libation jugs, votive figurines, statues, pots and gold ornaments are among the treasures brought to the surface in recent years. Hundreds of Minoan houses, storerooms, streets and sanctuaries lie concealed, some known to archaeologists, others unremembered and perhaps never to be rediscovered.

❑ The neolithic, pre-Minoan people (6000–3500BC) who first settled in Crete were largely preoccupied with internal affairs. But when the island's civilisation flowered into the Minoan period or Bronze Age of Crete, the island was perfectly placed – right at the heart of the trade routes north and south, east and west, across the Mediterranean – to become an outward-going, vigorously trading and widely influential nation. ❑

Snake goddesses from the palace at Knosós

Early days (c. 6000–2000 BC) Late Stone Age people first arrived in Crete from the east around 6000BC, and made their homes in the numerous caves of the island. As confidence grew

The queen's megaron at the palace of Knosós

they moved down towards the sea, establishing a settlement where Knosós was later built and quickly developing social contacts and trade with other islands and countries across the Mediterranean. Around 3000BC a new wave of settlers arrived from the north and east, lively-minded and energetic people who had the skills of working copper and using the potter's wheel. From 2400BC onwards they made beautiful pottery using swirling colours and created jars carved from stone using the natural patterns of the material to harmonise with their flowing designs. These craftsmen made clay seals to mark their individuality, and built massively walled stone houses across the island beside the land they cultivated. They brought votive offerings of clay figures and worshipped their gods in the darkness of the mountain caves.

❑ Sir Arthur Evans stamped his name on Cretan archaeological history with his discovery and reconstruction of the palace of King Minos at Knosós in 1900. But another archaeologist, the Italian Federico Halbherr, deserves to be equally well remembered. He had been in Crete for ten years when Evans arrived in search of King Minos, and had excavated a large number of sites. The discoveries at Górtina, Faistós, the Dhíktaean cave at Psikhró and many other places were made by Halbherr, who cut a dash in the Cretan countryside astride a galloping black horse. ❑

❑ If the appearance of a typical Minoan woman was that shown in the celebrated fresco of *La Parisienne* from the palace of Knosós – large dark eyes, full red lips and a nose with a bump in the middle – then the old Cretan physiognomy lives on in the face of one of the guides currently showing visitors around Knosós. ❑

Minoan splendour

■ Around 2000BC the Minoans began to build palaces on carefully selected sites, enormous sprawls of interconnected rooms and passages, two storeys high, cleverly lit by light wells and equipped with sanitation. The rooms clustered around great open courtyards. There were shrines, treasuries, bedrooms, dining halls, store-rooms, hallways, and the throne rooms of the priest-kings who ruled the surrounding lands.....■

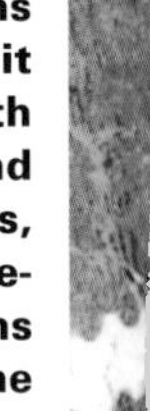

Outside the palace walls grew towns of narrow cobbled streets and tiny, box-like stone houses where the smiths and carpenters, potters and jewellers lived. Knosós was the mightiest of these palatial settlements.

All seemed secure, but Crete was then a land of frequent earthquakes. Around 1700BC every palace, every town and street in the island was flattened by catastrophic earth tremors. But within a hundred years the palaces had been rebuilt and the towns restored, and Minoan society entered a yet more splendid and sophisticated phase.

People of Minos From infinitely careful excavation of the Minoan palaces and towns, historians have learned a good deal about the way of life of these people. The frescoes they painted on their walls show elegant, wasp-waisted princes crowned with flowers, chains of dark-eyed dancing girls, cats stalking wild birds, and solemn priests. In the most famous, from the palace at Knosós, a graceful acrobat somersaults over the back of a charging bull towards the outstretched arms of a girl. The stone vases are carved with rejoicing harvesters, boxers and wrestlers. Sea creatures swim around their elaborate jugs and long-horned wild goats are hunted across their clay coffins.

Bulls were worshipped, fêted, and danced with. The bulls'-horn symbol occurs again and again, as does the sacred, double-bladed *labrys* or axe. Their kings, probably named Minos in succession, were gods, monarchs and politicians. Priestesses in bell-bottomed dresses had snakes as their familiars, poured libations from bulls'-head vessels, and may have been the power behind the throne of Minos.

The Minoans ate cheese, fish, wild fruit and olives, drank goats' milk and

The magnificent bull's head rhyton *from Knosós*

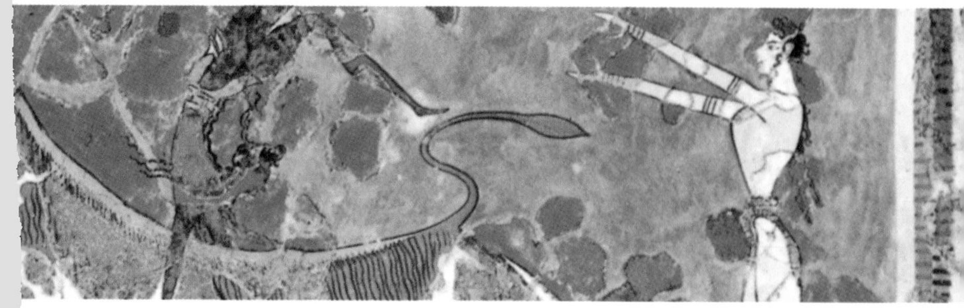

❑ On some late Minoan pottery, made after the cataclysm of 1450BC, a design of rearing, toppling waves appears. Some observers point to the sinister distortion of animal figures that appears on seals, and to an expression of horror on the faces of clay goddesses made during this period. Fanciful nonsense? Or echoes of the disaster that destroyed all the palaces and towns of Crete at a single stroke? ❑

wine, sweetened their palates with honey and sharpened them with salt and wild herbs. They kept domestic records using hieroglyphs incised into clay tablets. They took wine, corn, olive oil and timber to their trading partners and subject islands around the Mediterranean in square-sailed ships, bringing back all kinds of metal and stone for building and ornamentation.

❑ The skills of the early Minoan artist-craftsmen are shown in the symmetrical vases carved and smoothed out of solid stone, employing the natural patterns of the material to enhance the beauty of the product. All this was achieved with tools of bronze, stone and bone, sand to rub the rough article smooth, and endless time and patience. ❑

Part of Iráklio Museum's excellent ceramics collection

Civilisation and catastrophe

■ **The end came around 1450BC. Once again the palaces and towns came crashing down, felled by a disaster so sudden that the Minoans dropped whatever they were doing and ran for their lives. Was it a volcanic eruption across the sea, a tidal wave, another cataclysmic earthquake or sudden attack by invaders? Nobody knows for certain. All the palaces burned and were abandoned, except Knosós which lived on as a declining remnant of the golden civilisation of the Minoans.....** ■

MINOAN ERA	DEVELOPMENTS IN CRETE	DEVELOPMENTS ELSEWHERE
Pre-Palace c.2600–1900BC	Country villas with plastered stone walls. Hieroglyphs appearing. Delicate handmade pottery, long-spouted jugs. 'Vasilíki ware' pottery, mottled. Fine miniature work on seals. Gold necklaces and pins. Copper, then bronze.	c. 2800BC: **Egypt:** hieroglyphs and first stone building, the step pyramid. **Mesopotamia:** potter's wheel. c.2200BC: **Egypt:** copper, then bronze. **Iran:** reversion to plain pottery. **Scandinavia:** primitive pottery. **Northwestern Europe:** megalithic tombs; copper produced in France.
Old Palace c.1900–1700BC	Structured society, villas and towns. Great multi-storey palaces at Knosós, Faistós, Mália, Zákros. Frescoes, drainage, road-building, irrigation. 'Kamáres ware': exquisite, painted, moulded, eggshell thin. Stone vases, metalwork, jewellery to high art. Linear A script developing. c.1700 BC: Earthquake destroys all palaces.	**Egypt:** Golden Age of Middle Kingdom. Bronze well established. **Europe:** bronze spreading, but still not reached northwest. Copper throughout. Beaker Folk taking sophistication northwest.
New Palace c.1700–1450BC	Palaces and towns rebuilt, all services refined. Gourniá and Palaikastro towns flourishing. Powerful god-kings, Minos dynasty. Elaboration of frescoes, jewellery, gold work, bronze and silver, stone vases. Superb 'marine' decoration of pottery, but general formalisation of style. Linear A and Linear B script. Faistós Disc (only example of printing for next two millennia).	c.1670BC: **Egypt:** invaded by Hyskos who introduced chariot. c.1650BC: **Anatolia (Turkey):** all-conquering Hittite Empire established. Cities walled with huge stone blocks. c.1550BC: Egypt expels Hyskos, starts aggressive expansion, devises 365-day calendar; towns with houses up to five storeys high, built of mud bricks. c.1500BC: **Britain:** Stonehenge completed.
Post-Palace c.1450–1100BC	c.1450 BC: Fire partially destroys palaces and towns. Knosós and Gourniá reoccupied. Most other palaces and towns not rebuilt. Invading Mycenaeans take control. Native Minoan society in decline.	**Egypt:** civilisation in decline after death of Rameses III (1198–1166BC). **Europe:** bronze throughout. **India:** Sanskrit script developing. **China:** entering Bronze Age.

What actually happened in 1450BC? Theories abound as to what may have occurred in c.1450BC and which destroyed the Minoan palaces and towns on Crete.

The one link is fire, which left scorch marks at every one of the devastated palaces, villas and town streets. A tidal wave large enough to overwhelm inland as well as coastal sites would surely have extinguished fires, however widespread the inferno may have been. An earthquake would have trapped people in the ruins, but there is an almost complete absence of human remains. A combination of earth tremors, wave and ash smother would have followed a cataclysmic volcanic explosion. One such natural disaster occurred only 150km away when the whole island of Théra (Santorini) exploded, but this event probably took place some 50 years or so before the destruction in Crete. And in any event, why did Knosós escape the demolition that all the other Minoan towns and palaces suffered?

What about an overwhelming attack, perhaps by massed Mycenaean invaders taking advantage of their favourable position? The Mycenaeans had recently usurped the Minoan Cretans, so perhaps they turned on their former oppressors and destroyed the occupied palaces and towns. But, again, why are there no bodies to be found? And could the huge, multi-storey Minoan palaces possibly have been physically flattened in such attacks?

Another mystery surrounds the whereabouts of migrating Cretans after the mysterious disaster. The Minoans were expert seafarers. Were they, perhaps, the Sea People who all but overthrew Egypt in 1180BC before eventually settling in Palestine and later adopting the name Philistines? Philistine and Late Minoan pottery have strong similarities, and the Philistines always maintained that they had indeed originated in Crete. Or were the fleeing Minoans the forerunners of the Phoenicians, the Canaanite merchants who traded in exquisite coloured glass and in murex dyes manufactured from Cretan shellfish? And was it Minoans-turned-Phoenicians who incised a double-headed axe, a sacred *labrys* of Knosós, on one of the Stonehenge pillars in far-off, misty Britain?

A Kamarés ware krater *used for the mixing of wine and water*

Greeks and Romans

■ **What could follow the glories of the Minoan civilisation but a steady decline? From that high peak of achievement Crete slipped slowly down, until it began to rise again towards the peaceful prosperity of the Romans.....■**

Mycenaeans (c. 1500–1100BC) Around 1500–1400BC Mycenaeans arrived in Crete from the north – a warlike people, bent on expansion. Swords and spears were buried with their dead, and helmeted warriors in chariots appear on their pottery. Did they themselves destroy the palaces of their hosts? At all events they re-inhabited the ruined Minoans towns, but the Cretan society that had been so well ordered now began to fragment.

Dorians (c. 1100–67BC) In about 1100BC the Mycenaeans were displaced by Dorian Greeks from further north, efficient warriors who divided Greece into 1,500 city states. Several were established in Crete in the following centuries, among them Lató above Kritsá, Polirrínia in the far northwest, and Praisós in the east. Down in the south Górtina became the most powerful settlement on the island, while the city states feuded with each other and traded on their own account across the Mediterranean.

On the Greek mainland Athens grew to eminence, while Egypt still dominated North Africa. From the one came classical influences of building and sculpture; from the other, the grim and formal Archaic style which was far removed from the Minoan lightness of touch.

❑ The decline in craftsmanship after the end of the Minoan civilisation can be seen clearly in the clumsy wheeled animal toy of the 7th century BC on display in Khaniá's Archaeological Museum. A Roman statue of Aphrodite teaching Eros to play the guitar, very warmly and expressively sculpted in the 1st century AD, shows how far, and in how different a direction, it rose again. ❑

Roman (67BC–c. AD337) Then came the invading Romans, who built new temples, theatres, villas and aqueducts. Górtina flourished, and peace came to the island. St Paul arrived briefly in AD59, and St Titus followed, bringing Christianity and its attendant martyrdoms.

A bearded philosopher from Górtina

■ One ordered empire succeeded another as Rome gave way to Byzantium. This was healthy for Crete, until the savage Saracens came with fire and sword. There followed more than a century of brigandage, before a return to further prosperity under renewed Byzantine rule.....■

First Byzantine occupation (c. AD337–824) On 11 May AD330, King Constantine declared a Byzantine empire which he promised would last a thousand years. The stronghold of the empire was Constantinople, renamed New Rome, and within seven years it had control of the Mediterranean. The Roman Empire tottered on until AD395, when it was carved up by the triumphant Byzantines who were, by this time, well established in Crete. The Byzantines ran the island as a very tight ship, rigidly controlled from Constantinople. They built round-apsed basilica churches throughout Crete, the greatest of which was Ayíos Títos at Górtina. Much of this church still stands. The island's agriculture prospered and trade increased, but trouble began to brew to the south during the 7th century as the Arabs moved steadily northwards, threatening Christian Constantinople at the heart of the Byzantine empire.

Saracens (AD824–961) The Saracens invaded from Alexandria in AD824, intending to use Crete as a pirate base. This they did, to great and deadly effect, attacking shipping far into the Aegean. The port below Knosós, present day Iráklio, was known as Rabdh-el-Khandak, and was the Mediterranean's most notorious slave market. Górtina and many of the island's basilicas were destroyed. The island lay neglected, and its Christian inhabitants were mercilessly persecuted.

❑ Crete in this era was a veritable nest of pirates and slavers, whose ships menaced the whole of the Mediterranean. Perhaps this was when Cretans got their reputation for being both ferocious and cunning. ❑

Constantine, fourth-century ruler of the Byzantine Empire

Second Byzantine occupation (AD961–1204) Crete was recaptured by the Byzantines in AD961 after a horrific siege of Rabdh-el-Khandak, during which Saracen heads were catapulted among the defenders. Byzantine landowners arrived and restored agricultural and trading prosperity; more churches were built and enhanced with frescoes.

Under Venetian rule

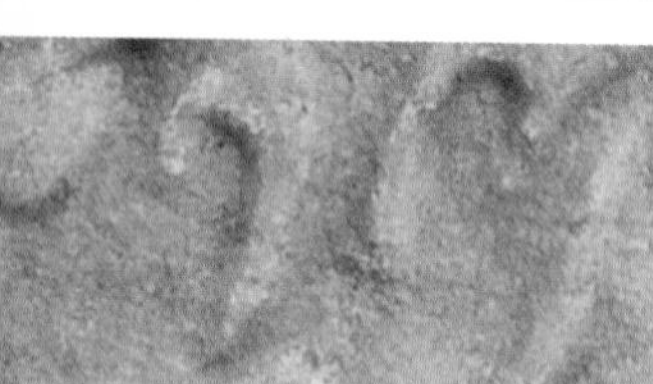

■ Elegant and cultured, the Venetians ruled Crete for almost 450 years, bringing unrivalled prosperity to the island. They built solidly and handsomely in golden stone, and carved their symbol, the winged lion of St. Mark, on fortress walls, staring seawards towards both friend and foe.....■

Sold for silver By the beginning of the 13th century the Byzantine empire was in disarray, over-stretched and rotting from the core. In 1204 the Fourth Crusade, composed not so much of ardent warriors of Christ as of freebooters with an eye to the main chance, took and sacked Constantinople. As the Byzantine empire had carved up the Roman empire 850 years before, so it was itself now divided up. Crete was allotted to Prince Boniface of Montferrat, leader of the Crusade, and he swiftly sold it on to Venice for 1000 pieces of silver. Crete was to remain under Venetian rule for the next 435 years.

Prosperity and culture Venetian nobles, like the Byzantines before them, were granted estates through-out the island, and ran them feudally under the overall control of the Doge who ruled from Candia, the name by which the capital city, and soon the whole island, came to be known. The Candy of which Shakespeare wrote was famed for its beauty and its productivity. Agriculture flourished and wine, grain, fruit and olive oil left the ports of Khaniá, Réthimnon and Candia, along with timber felled across the island. The Venetians were masters of communication and trade, and Crete benefited from their commercial acumen.

Along with increased prosperity came another flowering of Cretan culture. The Orthodox religion of the island was supplanted by Roman Catholicism, and many fine monasteries and churches, large and small, were built. Byzantine culture was still strong in Crete, and its traditions began a long fusion with emerging Renaissance expertise and a certain native Cretan energy to produce a new artistry, culminating in the superb 16th-century icon painting of Mikháil Dhamaskínos and the supreme master El Greco. Drama and poetry had a fresh impetus, too – a highlight being *Erotókritos*, an epic poem of courtly love written by Vinzétzos Kornáros towards the end of the period of Venetian rule.

❑ Cretan mythology depicts the Turks as the most irredeemable villains of all the island's invaders. This view throws rather too favourable a light on the Venetians who carried out mass executions, torture and other atrocities, and were heartily disliked and implacably opposed by most Cretans. ❑

Proud Venetian lions guard the fortress at Iráklio

Rebellions All was not sweetness and light under the Venetians, however. The feudal system imposed obligations of service, penalties and taxes, and put legal limitations on the old Byzantine families and peasants, and resentment against these was strong. Rebellions began not long after the new rulers came to power on the island. After an uprising in 1263 was snuffed out by reinforcements from Venice, the Lasíthiou plateau was cleared of its inhabitants as a punishment for their rôle in the revolt, and left uncultivated for the following two centuries. Rumblings continued with a rising in about 1527 which saw the leader, a Sfakiot named Kandanóleon, executed along with his family and many supporters. The Venetians built castles on the coastal plains, the rebels gathering and raiding from the mountains. Periods of truce were followed by rebellions, and this uneasy state of affairs was worsened by frequent Arab pirate raids on the coastal towns. In 1538 the buccaneering Barbarossa sacked Réthimnon, after which the main towns of Réthimnon, Khaniá and Candia were walled and refortified.

❑ The barren nakedness of the mountains is one of Crete's most striking features. This sad stripping away of the native pine forests, exacerbated these days by the teeth of sheep and goats, was started by the Venetians who cut down enormous numbers of trees for shipbuilding and the maintenance of their great galley fleet. ❑

The Venetian walls of Réthimnon

CRETE WAS *Turkish, then Greek*

■ Under Turkish rule, Crete entered a period of resentful decline and neglect. Rebellions grew in number and strength, and reprisals grew in ferocity, until the Turks were forced to leave. The island then entered the last straight on the long road to freedom and enosis, union with Greece.....■

Turkish victory

The Turks attacked Crete in 1645, at a time when the Venetian empire was losing control of the Mediterranean and the vigorously expanding Ottoman empire was pushing westward. With the first momentum of their invasion they captured Khaniá, and Réthimnon fell the following year. By 1647 only Candia was still in Venetian hands, along with a handful of fortified islets. As Europe stood by and wrung its hands, the Turkish noose tightened around the Cretan capital, and the epic Great Siege of Candia got under way. In 1667 they began the attack in earnest.On 5 September 1669 the defenders of Candia finally surrendered, and Venetian rule was over.

Decline and neglect

Cretans see the period of Turkish rule as the nadir of their island's fortunes. Certainly great injustices and cruelties were perpetrated on

❑ Any reader of Níkos Kazantzákis's great novel set during the Turkish occupation of Crete, *Freedom and Death,* will doubtless be familiar with the *narghile* or Turkish hubblebubble pipe. The tobacco fumes are cooled as they are drawn through water into the lungs of the smoker, or smokers, since *narghiles* can have multiple stems and be enjoyed by several friends at the same time. Every now and then, though only rarely nowadays, one is lit in a city men's club or on some devotee's balcony. ❑

The Turkish fleet off Candia

Mosque and fountain in Ierápetra

the population. The Turks were not interested in the humdrum affairs of trade and agriculture, and never actively promoted them. They taxed the Christian islanders on the fruits of their labour and, not unnaturally, the fruit began to wither on the vine. The Christian Cretans started to convert in large numbers to Islam, for safety and to ease their burden of taxes and penalties. The new rulers preferred town to country life, but apart from converting the churches to mosques by adding minarets, erecting fountains, altering doors and windows to Islamic designs and building a few town houses, they did little to maintain the towns. Pashas or overlords ruled the three districts into which Crete was now divided, leaving law enforcement to an increasingly undisciplined and vicious soldiery. Art and literature declined, and the rich gloss of prosperity departed from the island.

❑ Protruding belts of stone run horizontally around the walls of many churches and schools built during the Turkish occupation. They were added as a reminder that Christian worship and teaching might be permitted, but only within the jurisdiction of Ottoman and the all-embracing grip of Islam. ❑

❑ Perhaps the best thing the Turks left behind was the art of the pastry cook. Try *baklavá*, a pastry triangle packed with honey and nuts, and *kataífi*, a kind of shredded wheat, also soaked with honey and filled with nuts, for a tooth-tingling, sweet and glutinous treat. ❑

From rebellion to *enosis*

Conditions like these created a hot-house for rebellion. While lowlanders lived cheek by jowl with the Turks and had to learn to get along with them, the mountain dwellers, particularly the proud Sfakiots of the west, took up arms. The heroic tales of the *palikáres* or freedom fighters were bred here. Daskaloyiánnis was flayed alive in 1770 by the Pasha at Megálo Kástro (Iráklio), and Hatzimicháli Daliánis and his followers were slaughtered at Frangokástello in 1828. Rebels were hanged, impaled and shot. 2,000 Cretans and Turks died in an explosion at Arkádhi Monastery in 1866. There were uprisings in 1878, 1889 and 1896. Finally, in 1898, the Great Powers of Britain, Russia, France and Italy imposed a settlement. The Turks left the island, and after further unrest and civil disobedience the people of Crete at last achieved their dream in 1913 – independence within a union with Greece.

The gunpowder room of the Arkádhi Monastery; *see pages 171–2*

■ **History had yet another invasion in store for Crete. The German capture of the island in 1941 was followed by four years of resistance, and many horrific episodes of ambush and reprisal, a further grim chapter in Crete's bloody story.....■**

Above: war memorial in Réthimnon

Valuable prize Between the wars, Greece was torn by struggles for power between monarchists and republicans. These quarrels were temporarily set aside in October 1940 when the Italians invaded mainland Greece, closely followed by the Germans. By spring the following year 32,000 Allied troops were in Crete, but they failed to create the impregnable fortress that Churchill had demanded. Crete was a valuable prize. The Germans wanted it as a staging post for attacks on the Royal Navy in the Mediterranean, and on Allied troops in North Africa. General Bernard Freyberg, VC, the New Zealander in command of the Cretan defences, was convinced that a German attack would come mainly from the sea. But, when it came, it was from the air.

The Battle of Crete At dawn on 20 May 1941, German paratroopers and gliders began to descend on Crete. Thousands were killed before they even reached the ground. By the end of the day the Germans had a toehold near the vital airfield at Máleme, west of Khaniá, but had mostly been contained. But due to confusion, broken communications

❑ One of the best-known figures from the World War II resistance movement still living in Crete today is George Psychoundákis. He earned international and literary fame with his 1955 account of his wartime experiences, *The Cretan Runner*, and his later translations of Homer into Cretan dialect. He is also remembered for the legendary stamina, toughness, humour and courage he displayed as a young man during his epic solo journeys on foot, at the double, across scores of miles of harsh mountain, plateau and ravine, carrying messages between the scattered resistance bands. ❑

Cretan heroes from World War II were numerous and are well remembered

In 1941 British soldiers work hurriedly to prepare for the air defence of Crete

and a lack of reinforcements, the New Zealanders holding Máleme airfield withdrew from their positions. Soon the Germans were pouring in fresh troops and supplies. Gradually the Allies were pushed back, and the balance of the battle swung the Germans' way. British and Australian troops were hurriedly evacuated from Iráklio by the Royal Navy. Réthimnon was captured from the Australians and Greeks on 31 May. The south coast port of Khora Sfakion saw the further shambolic evacuation of troops (see page 229). At the cost of 6,530 young lives, the Germans captured Crete.

Resistance After the Battle of Crete, many of the soldiers who had escaped to the mountains were taken off the island by submarines and small boats. Allied organisers and wireless operators were landed, to help the Cretan resistance bands that soon formed. The years of determined resistance which followed form one of the most heroic chapters in the history of Crete – pages stained with blood and tears.

Sabotage, ambushes and clandestine wireless transmissions drew down reprisals in which civilians were shot and villages were burnt. As always, the mountains became the stronghold of the resistance movement. Supplies were dropped by parachute or landed on the coast. Hunted men departed for North Africa, and replacements arrived to fill the gaps. Many Cretans went hungry and in fear, but they were also implacably opposed to the occupation.

By 1944 the Germans knew there was no future for them in Crete. In October that year they barricaded themselves in an enclave around Khaniá, and by June 1945 they had left the island.

❑ The Paterákis brothers from Kostoyérako, in the southwest fringes of the White Mountains, belong to one of the most celebrated of the resistance families. Mention of the Paterákis clan anywhere in the Sfakiá district will still bring out stories about the brothers: Manoli and the abduction of General Kreipe, Antoni and the pothole incident, Costis and the miraculous shot that saved a village. ❑

Life before tourism

■ **After the war, Crete picked itself up and set out on the road to recovery. Old ways of life resumed their measured course with traditions of work and culture that can still be encountered today by the explorer who makes a point of getting off the beaten track.....■**

Revival In the late 1940s Crete was lucky not to be drawn into the bitter civil war that tore mainland Greece in two. There had been the potential for internecine fighting on the island between communists and non-communists, but somehow everyone held back or was prevented from initiating conflict. Gradually life returned to normal. Agriculture revived, and the burned, bombed and neglected towns and villages underwent a massive and long-drawn-out scheme of reconstruction.

Village life In the early 1950s, returning to Crete to pay a call on his wartime resistance colleague and good friend George Psychoundákis, the writer Patrick Leigh Fermor embarked on the long uphill mule-back journey to reach the White

❑ You do not have to venture far from the north coast beach-and-hotel strip between Iráklio and Ayíos Nikólaos to find many aspects of life going on much as they did before tourism invaded the island. House ovens still produce home-baked bread, homemade wine and *rakí* are on sale, cheese-makers stir boiling cauldrons of sheep's milk in lonely huts, and black-cowled women are out on the mountainside gathering wild herbs. Such traditional activities, still very much the mainstay of local village life, give Crete its unique and enchanting flavour. ❑

Mountain village of Asigoniá where Psychoundákis lived. Much of rural Crete was inaccessible to motor cars then, with poor roads to upland settlements and the majority of the population living in small, remote settlements without electricity, tap water or modern sanitation.

Donkeys are still hard at work in the country

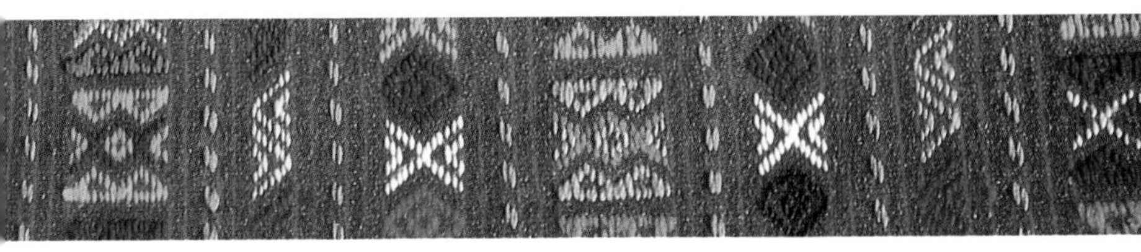

Away from the towns of the north coast, people lived in a silence only occasionally interrupted by the click of a donkey's hooves, the tinkle of a spoon, or the scratch of a hoe. Village agriculture predominated, much of it subsistence gardening, but the Cretans ate simply and well on a diet of tomatoes, green stuff, potatoes, and onions grown on their own *kipos* or patch of ground. They grew their own wheat, ground their own flour, baked their own bread, pressed their own olive oil, drank homemade wine and *rakí*. Village houses had earth floors, smoke-blackened beamed ceilings under earth-on-plank roofs, an open fireplace, a storeroom with oil, wine and dried fruit in big earthenware jars unchanged in design since Minoan times. Furniture was sparse, and water came from the well or stream. Almost everyone over 30 wore traditional dress: the older women in head-to-toe black, old men in knee-boots and baggy breeches, younger men in cavalry-style jodhpurs. Most youngsters got a decent primary education in the village schools, but very few from rural backgrounds went on to secondary level. There was a basic equality of income and aspirations among the rural poor, and that meant most Cretans. Medical care was traditional and herb-based, and superstition, cruelty, generosity and realism were the mix of every day life.

Change of character? But of course better communications, motor cars, money, television, modern facilities and the onrush of mass tourism were only just around the corner. Have they eroded the Cretan character since those days before tourists arrived on the island? Are

This simple open-air oven is a remnant of a vanishing way of life

the Cretans still volatile, warm-hearted, hospitable, infuriating, easy-going, fierce, capricious, independent-minded and blackly humorous? You will have to judge that for yourself.

❑ The earnest backpacker, tottering through a village on his way to the mountains wearing gigantic hiking boots and with a camel's load on his back, will both amuse and baffle watching villagers. Cretans take to the hills burdened only with a stick and a pair of battered old shoes, and then only for purely practical reasons such as shepherding or visiting friends in remote places – seldom for the perverse pleasure of taking exercise in the open air. ❑

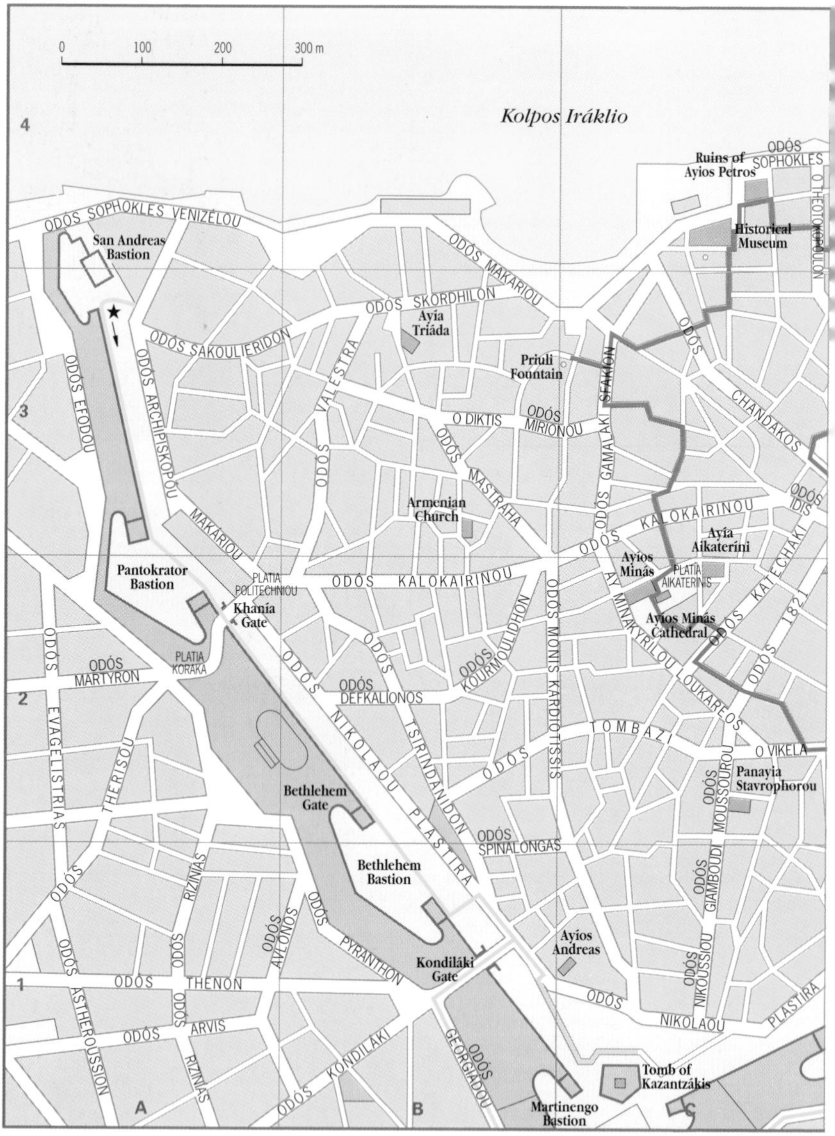

0 100 200 300 m

Kolpos Iráklio

Ruins of Ayios Petros

Historical Museum

San Andreas Bastion

Ayía Triáda

Priuli Fountain

Armenian Church

Ayía Aikateríni

Ayios Minás

PLATIA AIKATERINIS

Ayios Minás Cathedral

Pantokrator Bastion

PLATIA POLITECHNIOU

Khanía Gate

PLATIA KORAKA

Bethlehem Gate

Bethlehem Bastion

Panayia Stavrophorou

Ayíos Andreas

Kondiláki Gate

Martinengo Bastion

Tomb of Kazantzákis

ODÓS SOPHOKLES VENIZÉLOU

ODÓS SOPHOKLES

ODÓS MAKARIOU

ODÓS SKORDHILON

ODÓS SAKOULIERIDON

ODÓS EFODOU

ODÓS ARCHIPISKOPÓU MAKÁRIOU

ODÓS VALESTRA

O DIKTIS

ODÓS MIRIONOU

ODÓS MASTRAHA

ODÓS GAMALAKI SFAKION

CHANDAKOS

ODÓS KALOKAIRINOU

ODÓS IDIS

ODÓS KATECHAKI

ODÓS 1821

AY MINA KYRILOU LOUKAREOS

ODÓS MARTYRON

EVAGELISTRIAS

THERISOU

ODÓS DEFKALIONOS

ODÓS KOURMOULIDHON

ODÓS MONIS KARDIOTISSIS

ODÓS TOMBAZI

O VIKELA

ODÓS NIKOLAOU PLASTIRA

TSIRINDANIDON

ODÓS SPINALONGAS

ODÓS MOUSSOUROU

ODÓS GIAMBOUDI

ODÓS NIKOUSSIOU

ODÓS NIKOLAOU PLASTIRA

ODÓS RIZINIAS

ODÓS AVLONOS

ODÓS PYRANTHON

ODÓS THENON

ODÓS ASTHEROUSSION

ODÓS ARVIS

ODÓS KONDILAKI

ODÓS GEORGIADOU

A B C

1 2 3 4

42

Right: Iráklio's busy harbour
Far right: Nikós Kazantzákis

IRÁKLIO

Venetian Fort
Harbour
VENIZÉLOU
Arsenali
Arsenali
Ayíos Demetriós
Roman Catholic Church
PLATIA KOUNTORYOTON
ODÓS EPIMENIDOU
ODÓS 25 AVGOÚSTOU
ODÓS EPIMENIDOU
El Greco Park
Ayíos Títos
O AY TITOU
ODÓS MALIKOUTI
Sabionera Bastion
PLATIA VENIZÉLOU
Morosini Fountain
Loggia (City Hall)
Ayíos Marcos
MERAMBELON
ODÓS MERAMBELON
ODÓS IDOMÍNEOS
Archaeological Museum
ODÓS BEAUFORT
PLAN PHOKA
ODÓS DAIDÁLOS
ODÓS DIKAIOSÍNIS
Street Market
Tourist Police
PLATIA DAKALOGIANI
PLATIA ELEFTHERIAS
St George's Gate
ODÓS IKAROU
ODÓS ANTHEMIOU
ODÓS ARPHIMIDOUS
ODÓS 1866
ODÓS EVANS
ODÓS AVÉROF
ODÓS PEPHIADOS
L DIMOKRATIAS
Bembo Fountain
PLATIA KORNAROU
Public Gardens
ODÓS EVANS
ODÓS PEDIAKOS
St George's Bastion
DIMOKRATIAS
ODÓS GERONIMAKI
Jesus Gate
L HARILAOU TRIKOUPI
PLATIA KIPROU
Jesus Bastion
ODÓS DRAKONTOPOULOU
ODÓS MISSONOS
ODÓS KASTRINAKI
GEORGIADOU
ODÓS
D
E

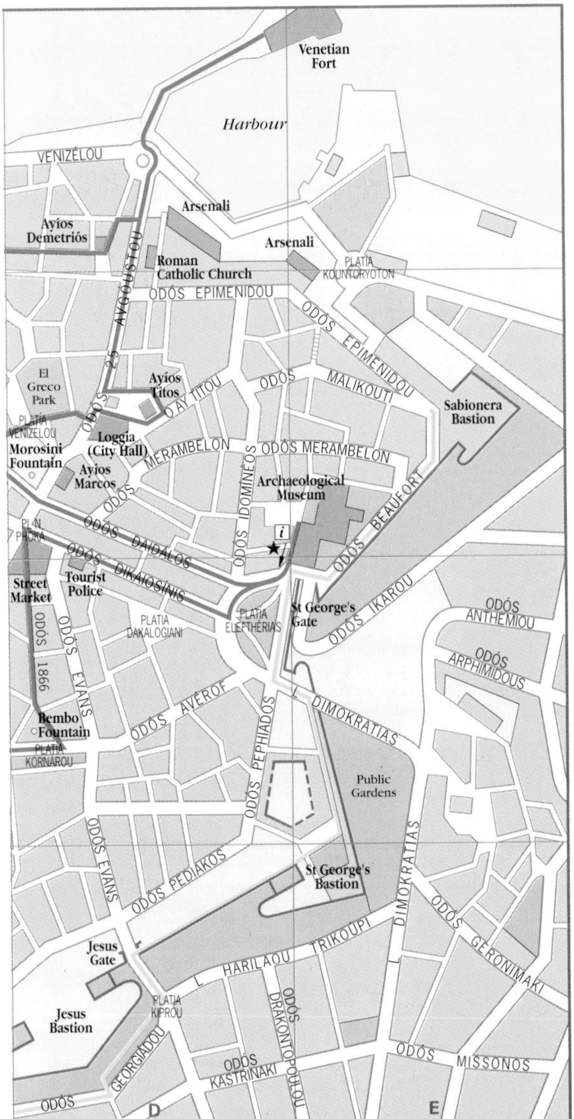

Kiosks
In Iráklio you will not take long to spot your first cigarette kiosk. An omnipresent feature of Cretan towns and villages, it is usually a little hut on the pavement, every wall and window jam-packed with goods, in whose dark interior skulks the owner. Many have a public telephone with a meter which clicks up the charge, and you pay after your call. As well as cigarettes the kiosk will probably sell postcards, stamps, sweets, books, magazines, newspapers, worry beads, souvenirs, lottery tickets...

Iráklio Iráklio lies midway along the northern coast, and is the centre of Crete's commercial and cultural life. It is a bustling modern city with 130,000 inhabitants, that strikes the arriving visitor as the very antithesis of everything that Crete is famous for – peace, quiet, a relaxing atmosphere, and getting away from it all. Iráklio is the first experience of Crete for almost every holidaymaker who drives in from the airport or steps off the ferry. Faced with the roar of traffic, the constant mess and clangour of new construction works, the heat and dust of crowded pavements, the understandable reaction of most visitors is to get away from the city as soon and as quickly as possible.

Windows on history Yet even here, as in every great and historic city, there are many delights and revelations, many windows on the history and character of Crete, waiting to be discovered and enjoyed. Iráklio has an Archaeological Museum that many claim is the finest in Europe; superb Venetian squares and a massive fortress on the waterfront; notable churches, including Ayía Aikateríni on Platía Aikaterínis which has an unparalleled collection of icons; a famous market where you can enjoy the atmosphere of a genuine, jam-packed bazaar. All this and much more is encircled by the most outstanding medieval city walls of any Mediterranean country. There are first-class restaurants, and obscure but entirely Cretan backstreet tavernas; thumping discos and traditional music of *lýra* and *bouzoúki*; international standard luxury hotels and inexpensive rooms to rent; sophisticated

The carefully restored Venetian Loggia

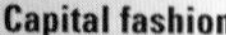

Capital fashion
Iráklio's young people are intensely fashion-conscious, and the latest European clothing trends appear on the city's streets almost as soon as they do in London, Paris or Berlin. One of the many striking contrasts of Iráklio is the sight of a gleaming fashion-plate of a young man or woman inspecting a market stall shoulder to shoulder with an elderly man from a mountain village in traditional knee-boots, wide drab breeches and black shirt.

Áyios Títos church

vintage wines, tear-jerking local *rakí* and rough village wine from the barrel; bland modern shopping thoroughfares and twisting side streets where a domed Turkish doorway or a tottering Venetian town house will sharpen your focus on Cretan history.

Welcoming gestures Iráklio people may shout, gesticulate, bluster and roar, for self-effacement is not the style here. Many are recent arrivals in the city themselves. Young Cretans in particular are drawn to Iráklio from their native villages in search of work, fun and a lively time. Many are on their way up in business or in the service industries which are so thick on the ground in the island capital. Some seem to have little time for the visitor in search of advice or directions. But summon up a few introductory words of Greek such as *kaliméra* (good morning), *kalispéra* (good afternoon), *signómi* (excuse me), *parakoló* (please), *efharistó* (thank you), *adío* (goodbye) and you will soon break through the city sharpness to genuine politeness and a desire to help the stranger.

Take a walk It would be a great shame to hurry away from Iráklio without giving this cosmopolitan and vigorous city a chance to captivate you. This process will take a bit longer, and demand a little more effort on your part, than in Réthimnon or Khaniá, with their cosier and more instantly attractive atmosphere. A walk around the city will introduce you to the most important and well-known features of Iráklio, and show you many uncelebrated but intriguing nooks and corners. Here, as in all extensive and ancient cities, there is always something waiting to surprise, perhaps to shock, perhaps to delight, but always to interest you, just around the corner. Exploration of Crete begins here, in the heart of the island's least-explored and most underrated location.

Backstreet craftsmen
Iráklio may seem like a big, impatient city that has thrown off its former provincialism, but first impressions can be deceptive. In tiny workshops tucked away down side streets the tradition of craftsmanship is alive and well. Opposite the church of Ayíos Demétrios between Odos Kosma Zoton and Odos Thalita, a cooper still turns out wooden barrels made by hand, exactly as his father and grandfather did.

Booking office
It is a good idea to take something to read with you when you visit the tourist information office opposite the Archaeological Museum. Understaffed and overstretched, especially in the summer season, they take their time to get to you. Eventually your turn will come and then you can expect undivided and enthusiastic attention.

There are many good views to be had from the old walls

From the Stone Age to the Saracens Neolithic people were the first to settle in the area to the east of modern Iráklio. In Minoan times there was a thriving harbour on the same site, which served the settlement at Knosós, 5km inland. The Roman port of Herakleium grew up on the site of the present-day harbour, trading with the southern and eastern parts of the Roman Empire. Knosós became a Roman colony during the 1st century BC. After the overthrow and partition of the Roman Empire during the 4th century AD, Herakleium continued to prosper under Byzantine rule, though Górtina to the south had become the island's capital. In 824 the Saracens invaded and conquered Crete, destroyed Górtina and established their power centre at Herakleium. They fortified their new settlement with a mighty ditch, and renamed the town Rabdh-el-Khandak, the castle of the ditch. Throughout the following century the port was a base for pirate raids across the Mediterranean, but in 960 the grim Byzantine general Nikephóros Phokás landed with a polyglot army and laid siege to Rabdh-el-Khandak, underlining his determination by catapulting the heads of Saracen prisoners into the town. The siege lasted ten months, and ended with victory for the Byzantine invaders and widespread destruction of the town.

The Byzantines and Venetians After the departure of the Saracens, Rabdh-el-Khandak was renamed Khándakas, and reverted from piracy to relatively peaceful trading with the Byzantine empire for the next 250 years. At the beginning of the 13th century the empire of Byzantium in its turn collapsed and with the arrival of the Venetians the capital city, and subsequently the whole island, gained yet another name – Candia. The city now enjoyed a Golden Age which lasted for 450 years. Fine Venetian town houses and a ducal palace were built, new churches were erected, the harbour was massively fortified, sanitation and efficient water supplies were introduced, enormous and cunningly-engineered walls were built around the city, and trade with Europe, North Africa and the Middle East brought renewed prosperity to Candia.

Sin city
Iráklio people were noted in Venetian and Turkish times for their decadence, idleness, love of luxury, fondness for drink and addiction to the pleasures of both board and bed. *Plus ça change...!*

Turkish rule All this came to an end on 5 September 1669, when the gates of the city were opened to allow the last Venetians on mainland Crete to leave the island. The city gates had been closed for 21 years during the epic Great Siege of Candia, while the Turks who had invaded and conquered the rest of Crete were prevented from picking this last and juiciest plum. The city started a long, dark journey of decline and tension which lasted some 250 years. Venetian churches were converted to mosques, a pasha was brought in to govern the capital and its dependent province, and the city itself received its fifth name since Roman times, Megálo Kástro, the Great Fort. Pogroms of the city's Christians, the indifference of the Turks to trade, and clandestine support within the capital for the frequent rebellions in other parts of the island all contributed to the unhappiness of Megálo Kástro. At the end of the 19th century the murder in the city of 14 British soldiers and their consul finally focused the minds of the European Powers upon Crete. The Turks were ousted, and the capital received yet another name, though one with echoes of the distant past – Herákleion, or Iráklio as it is known today.

Big Castle
Megálo Kástro, the Big Castle, was the name by which Iráklio was known under Turkish rule. Níkos Kazantzákis retained the old name when writing of the city, both in his novels and in his long and vivid autobiographical book *Report to Greco.*

The 19th-century Cathedral of Áyios Mínas

World War II During the Battle of Crete in May 1941 Iráklio was badly bombed as the Germans tried to dislodge the British, Greek and Australian defenders of the city. House-to-house fighting, and the bombardment of the port to harrass the evacuation of Allied troops, reduced much of the city to ruins. During the years of occupation Iráklio became a hotbed of resistance. Towards the end of 1944 the Germans withdrew from the city, and the partisans and Allied resistance workers came down from the mountains. After the war, reconstruction began to change the face and character of the old city, work that has continued to the present day. In 1971 Iráklio took over from the ancient stronghold of Khaniá as the official capital city of Crete.

Backstreet architecture
There are many modest delights of architecture to be spotted and enjoyed among Iráklio's blocks of flats and lines of modern shops. Tottering Venetian town house façades, gracefully curved Turkish window frames, ornate old doorways and curlicued iron balconies suggest that history has not departed from Iráklio, but has shifted from the main thoroughfares into the side streets and more obscure parts of town.

Town mosaic
The blueprint for much of the reconstruction of the Palace of Knosós lies in Case 25, Room II. Here you will see a set of beautiful small glazed earthenware plaques, richly decorated with colour, in the shape of Minoan house-fronts, some of them two or three storeys high. Known as the Town Mosaic, they are complete with doors and windows, and probably originally fitted together with others in one composite display.

Mother's milk
Case 55 in Room IV holds two of the small masterpieces of Minoan art: a cow giving suck to her calf, and a wild goat with great curled horns nuzzling her kids.

▶▶▶ Archaeological Museum *43E3*

Platía Elefthérias (entrance on Odós Xanthoudídou)
Open 8–7 summer, 8–3 winter; 8:30–3 on Sundays; 10:30–7 Mondays.
This is one of the world's great archaeological museums, rather unimaginatively laid out, but giving a unique and very moving insight into the daily lives, worship, dreams and laughter of the Minoans. Visit it twice, once as soon as you arrive, and then again after you have explored the sites, to put the exhibits in their proper context.

Room I (c. 6000BC–c. 1900BC) These are some of the earliest artefacts discovered in Crete. There are idols, stone axe heads and bone scrapers as well as early examples of the mottled, semi-fired patterns of Vasilikí ware, notably jugs with the extended, upward pointing spouts so characteristic of early Minoan pottery, combining grace and practicality. In Case 12 is a crudely fashioned little clay bull with an acrobat curled around his left horn, and in Case 16 some exquisitely worked seal-stone carvings that include a tiny fly and dove.

Room II (c. 1900BC–c. 1700BC) Finds from Knosós include scores of votive figurines of people and animals. Case 21 contains a two-headed push-me-pull-you. There are also pottery *taxímata* (diseased arms, legs and feet) very like those stamped on silver plaques and affixed to church icons by sufferers today. Swirly decorations on great thick jars and basins in Case 27 are a complete contrast to the Kamáres pottery in Case 23, eggshell delicate and as thin as fine porcelain.

Room III (c. 2000BC–c. 1700 BC) The Old Palace at Faistós contributed most of the items here, including some delicate Kamáres ware with black, red and white decorations. Pride of the room, however, is the Faistós Disc in Case 41, a flat clay disc 16cm in diameter, stamped with as yet undeciphered pictorial characters incorporating fish, shells, a ship, tools, running figures and flowers which spiral in towards the centre.

Room IV (c. 1700BC–c. 1450BC) The fine flowering of Minoan art is represented here, from the period after the palaces had been rebuilt following their destruction c. 1700BC. Nature is the main influence here, with few abstract designs. Among well-known exhibits are the two bare-breasted snake goddesses (Case 50); the intricate design of reeds on a jug (Case 49); the bull's-head *rhyton* or libation jug

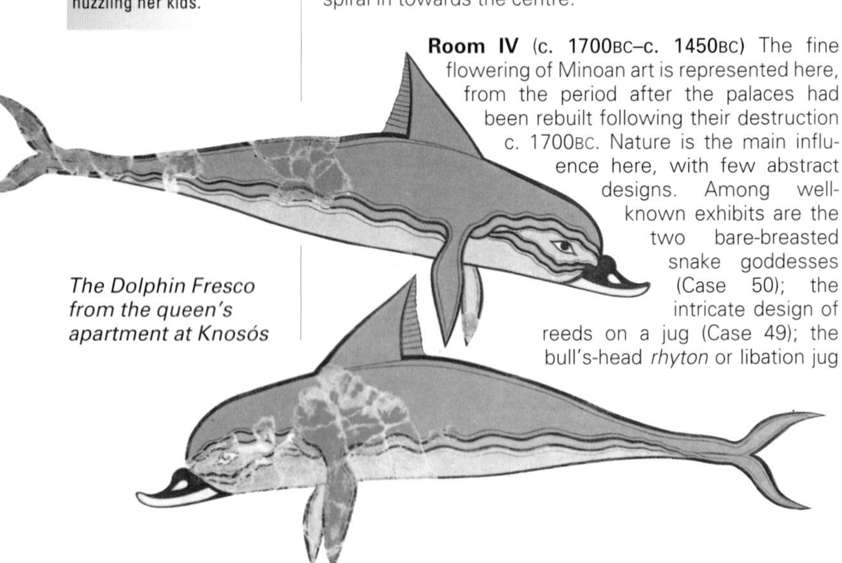

The Dolphin Fresco from the queen's apartment at Knosós

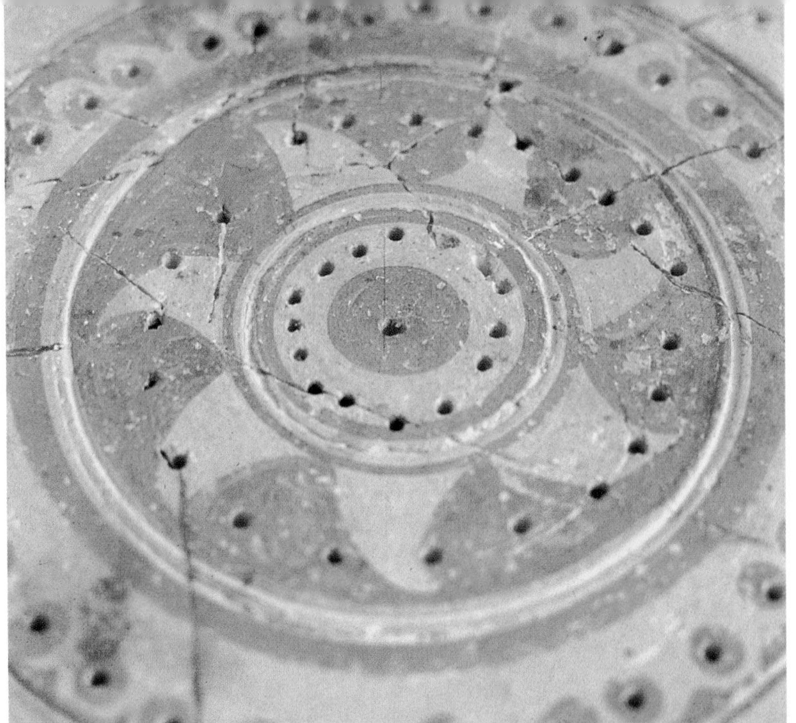

with mother-of-pearl nostrils and rock crystal eyes (Case 51); another *rhyton* shaped like the head of a lioness; a leopard's-head axe from Mália (Case 47); an ivory acrobat caught in mid-leap (Case 56); and a very complicated and unfathomed gaming board (Case 57).

Iráklio's Archaeological Museum holds a fine collection of pottery from Knosós

Room V (c. 1450BC–c. 1400BC) Finds here are chiefly from Knosós, dating from the period immediately after the cataclysm of c. 1450BC. The decoration on pottery is beginning to turn away from naturalistic designs to something more formal and stylised. Seal stones are still beautifully carved; helpful drawings show enlarged subjects. In Case 69 are examples of Minoan scripts.

Room VI (c. 1450BC–c. 1400BC) Finds from cemeteries including Knosós, Faistós and Arkhánes on display here include helmets and weapons, reflecting the advent of a more aggressive, military society. There are also some fine clay figures dancing in a circle (Case 71); elaborate jellyfish on amphorae in Case 82; and beautiful jewellery in Cases 86–8, including a ring decorated with women dancing amongst flowers, and another with figures mourning the annual death of the god of vegetation.

Room VII (c. 1600BC–c. 1450BC) Treasures here include three black steatite vases from Ayía Triádha palace: the Chieftain Cup (a Minoan potentate accepting animal skins); the Harvester Vase (wildly singing harvesters with flat caps bearing home sheaves of corn); and the Boxer Vase (a boxer knocked flat with his heels in the air, a wrestling match and bull-leaping). Case 101 contains the famous gold pendant from Mália showing a pair of bees with a honeycomb.

Linear mystery
In Room V you will find examples of the two types of hieroglyphs found at many Cretan sites. The Linear A of the Minoans is as yet undeciphered, but the Linear B, that was brought to the island by the Mycenaean Greeks shortly after the widespread destruction c. 1450BC, is reasonably well understood. How exciting it will be when someone succeeds in interpreting the secrets of Linear A, and opens a new window on the Minoan world.

Attitude problem
The bronze and terracotta figures of men and women praying probably show the actual attitude that Minoans adopted in prayer with one hand on the breast and the spine arched backwards, a most uncomfortable stance. Try standing like this for two minutes!

Room VIII (c. 1700BC–c. 1450BC) This room contains finds from the great palace at Zákros at the eastern end of the island such as tools and weapons, including big saws and a wonderful variety of *rhytons* or jugs. Case 111 contains a green chlorite *rhyton* burned into variegated colours, showing a long-horned wild goat. Case 109 holds a delicate and beautiful rock crystal *rhyton* reassembled from over 300 pieces.

Room IX (c. 1700BC–c. 1450BC) Finds here are from the lesser sites in the east, and include terracotta figures in ordinary dress; tools and weapons from Gourniá (Case 127); amphorae with staring octopuses (Case 128); and marvellous seal stones with beasts, gods, thistles, goats and bull leapers (Cases 124, 128).

Minoan pottery from the palace of Knosós

Room X (c. 1350BC–c. 1100BC) Artistic decline and a loss of vitality and originality become apparent after the destruction of the great palaces c. 1450BC. Decorations are mostly geometric and stylised with the octopus motif being reduced to a formulaic squiggle.

Room XI (c. 1100BC–c. 800BC) There are pottery goddesses here with raised hands, stiff and crude. Case 158 has Egyptian jewellery; Case 153 shows evidence that iron was taking over from bronze. Cretan society was now changing, but old and vigorous influences were still at play. In Case 149 there are figurines of copulating couples and pregnant women, which were probably votive offerings to the goddess of childbirth.

Uplifted
In contrast to the backward-bending devotees, the goddesses themselves, perhaps priestesses, were shown by artists through the Minoan era standing with upraised arms, reaching skyward or maybe passing on a blessing.

Room XII (c. 800BC–c. 650BC) Foreign artistic influences are becoming stronger, with winged griffons and sphinx-like Egyptian figures, and eastern-looking flower motifs resembling the lotus. Case 163 has Theseus and Ariadne embracing on the neck of a vessel, a beautiful snarling lioness and a wise old horned owl.

Room XIII This is a collection of *larnakes* or clay sarcophagi, some with gabled tops; others may have been used as bathtubs and are complete with plug holes. Decorations include flowers, water birds, octopuses, geometric patterns, and red and black sacred axes.

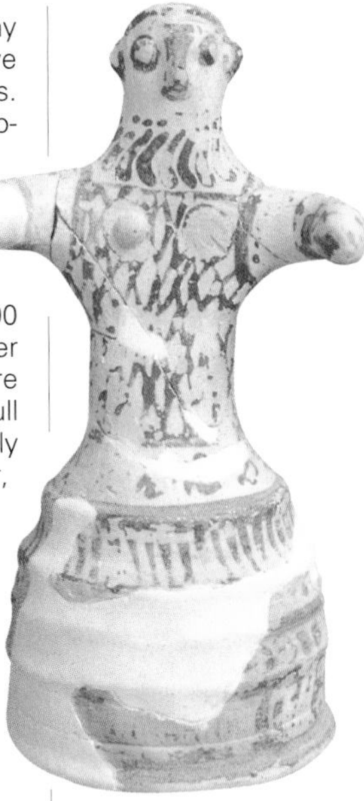

Rooms XIV, XV and XVI These upstairs rooms contain restored frescoes illustrating the light, graceful and airy quality of Minoan life. Most are from the palace at Knosós and date from between 1600 and 1400BC. They were painted directly onto wet plaster with vegetable, mineral and shellfish dyes. Men are depicted with red skin, women with white. There are bull frescoes, griffons from the palace throne room, lively dolphins from the queen's room, and the bull-leaper, somersaulting backwards over a charging bull. *La Parisienne*, a doe-eyed, carmine-lipped, carefully coiffed priestess; the saffron-gatherer; a Minoan officer and two black-skinned soldiers are all here. Others from Ayía Triádha are even more vividly coloured: long-eared wild cats with bob tails watch oblivious birds feeding; a marine floor fresco shows wildly cavorting fish; a stunningly decorated sarcophagus from Ayía Triádha has a bull being sacrificed while two terrified calves look on awaiting their turn.

One of several small votive offerings from Knosós

Room XVII The wide-ranging collection of the late Dr S. Giamalákis includes a chubby-thighed neolithic goddess seated in the lotus position, gold jewellery, figurines with smiling faces, and a little clay shrine with two men and a dog on the roof, peering or perhaps speaking down a central shaft.

Room XVIII (c. 650BC–c. AD400) Classical, Hellenistic, Greek and Roman cultures mingle here with wild dancers, winged figures, hunters, figures from Classical mythology, coins of bronze, silver and gold.

Room XIX (c. 700BC–c. 500BC) There are big, clumsy, solid sculptures here, in contrast with the worked bronze shields from the Ídaean Cave with projecting bosses and splendid decoration in the form of a hawk, a lion, embattled men and gods.

Room XX
Graeco–Roman sculpture lines the walls of this room, sculpture executed with a technical skill that the Minoans never approached, but they are pale and cold, devoid of the Minoan delight in the natural world. Only no. 153, a rather endearing and shaggy-thighed Pan blowing his pipes, gives an echo of those warm, light-hearted people.

Model palace
For those who have visited the palace site at Knosós, and have come away unable to visualise the Minoan reality of that great jumble of stone, there is an excellent model in the Hall of the Frescoes upstairs, showing the palace as King Minos must have known it.

A bronze shepherd and his rather canine sheep

Walk Iráklio's highlights

As the capital city of the island, and the site of its main airport and ferry terminals, Iráklio may well be your first taste of Crete. Arriving tired and tense from your journey, a sense of let-down is almost inevitable. It is probably best, from a scenic point of view, to arrive by ferry. Seen from the sea the city benefits from its cradle of mountains, with the Dhíktaean range rising inland snow-capped or dramatically bare according to season. Entering Iráklio this way, you will be spared the concrete reality of the dreary suburbs with their uncompromising blocks of flats and dusty streets. Either way, it is likely that your first emotions will be confusion and a mild but definite disillusion. Iráklio is not an easy place to fall in love with. Thanks to extensive rebuilding after the destruction of World War II, and constant development during the commercial boom of recent decades. The city seems initially to have little of the historic charm that characterises Réthimnon and Khaniá, its smaller and less frenetic north coast neighbours.

Bear in mind that 130,000 people live and work in Iráklio, making it a noisy, hasty and crowded place. In the high summer season you can add hundreds of thousands of tourists *en passage* to this number. Iráklio is in many ways entirely untypical of the Crete you have come to explore, but in its grimy, roaring heart the basic Cretan virtues still flourish: warmth, vibrancy, time for the stranger, an inexhaustible curiosity as to who you are and what you are up to. Many of the city's inhabitants are only first or second generation Iráklio people, and so they look to their native villages in the mountains or out along the coast for their roots and manners. Village mentality and traditions are still strong in the city. Most people in Iráklio will go out of their way to help, direct and advise you, particularly if you approach them with a few simple phrases in Greek.

The restful courtyard of the Venetian Loggia

In spite of comprehensive restructuring and development, Iráklio is full of odd corners and reminders of its rich, violent history. A rambling walk through the old city will introduce you to the strong and idiosyncratic flavours of Iráklio past and present, which mingle to great effect inside its encircling Venetian walls. The Iráklio chapter lists the sights of the city in the order that you will encounter them on the walk. Allow a full day, or at least 5–6 hours. See the map on pages 42–3.

Start outside the Archaeological Museum on Odós Xanthoudídou with the tourist information office opposite you. Turn left into **Platía Elefthérias**.

Cross Odós Xanthoudídou and keep left, then bear right around the end of the cinema block. Odós Idomíneos runs at the back of the block, parallel to Odós Xanthoudídou. Wander downhill for a detour here past dark shops in crumbling Turkish houses. The main walk follows the pedestrianised Odós Daidálos which branches off left immediately after you round the cinema, sloping past souvenir shops, bars and restaurants down to **Platía Venizélos**. Walk through the square and the covered passage between the restaurants, taking first right and right again to reach **El Greco Park**, and beyond, on the corner of Platía Kallergou, the **Venetian Loggia**. Walk through here to the **City Hall** and the church of **Ayíos Títos.** Cross the *platía* and turn right down Odós 25 Avgoústou to reach the **harbour** and the **Venetian fort.**

From the landward end of the breakwater cross the roundabout back to Odós 25 Avgoústou. First right (Odós Kosma Zotou) leads to a *platía* with cafés. Turn left here to find the Church of **Ayíos Demétrios**, decorated with fine modern frescoes. Continue along Odós Thalita, crossing Odós Laxana. Turn right at the T-junction, left down Odós Kalokairinou, past the ruined Venetian Church of St Peter which is gradually being restored, and find the **Historical Museum**.

From the museum continue up Odós Grevenou. Take the second right down Kalimeraki, left into Chortatsou, immediately right across Chandakos and on down Vistaki. At the end turn right, then left along Giamalaki and first right down Kazantzáki to the **Priuli fountain** on the left. From the fountain return up Kazantzáki. Turn right, then first left up Apokoronou, a twisting little alleyway. Keep dog-legging right and left. Odós 1770 is the next right turn; follow it round, bearing left by a tottering old building with curly iron brackets supporting its overhanging upper storey. Take the first right down Ioánnou Moirelou, cross wide Kalokairinou into Ayíon Déka, to reach **Platía Aikaterínis**, a wide paved square with three churches to explore.

From the steps of the Cathedral of **Ayíos Minás** bear left round the corner of the building. Turn right up Karterou, crossing Katechaki, and take first right down pedestrianised Amisou. Turn left at the bottom, cross Odós 1821 and go up Pizaniou. Bear right at the tree, and left along busy Vikela into **Platía Kornárou**.

Leave Platía Kornárou and head straight up **Odós 1866,** Market Street, opposite the Turkish fountaincafé. At the top of Market Street is Platía Nikephórou Phoká. Turn right at the traffic lights along Dikaiosínis Street, lined with shops ranging from tacky souvenir stalls to smart dress and jewellery emporia, and finish the walk back in Platía Elefthérias.

Platía Kornárou

Modern ceiling frescoes in the church of St Mary, located between Iráklio's Historical Museum and Ayíos Demetriós

▶▶ Platía Elefthérias *43D2*

Elefthérias means freedom, and as an expression of the traditional Cretan spirit of fortitude and resistance it is the perfect name for the square where the Iráklio walk begins, Platía Elefthérias. A mass of traffic swirls around the dusty little gardens shaded by acacias and palm trees. This used to be the city's main meeting and gossiping centre, and despite the cars and buses is still reckoned by most Iráklio people to be at the heart of their city. Cafés, hotels, cigarette kiosks and a cinema line the wide square, which at night swaps its motorised traffic, to a certain extent, for the two-legged variety.

▶▶ Platía Venizélos *43D3*

Nearby Platía Venizélos, better known to visitors as Lion Square, has become the hub of the tourists' Iráklion, and it is certainly a pleasant place to sit and watch the world

Sadly the Morosini Fountain rarely plays

go by. Lion Square is traffic-free, and is peppered with cafés and restaurants as well as bakers' shops where you can buy a cheese pie or *boúgatsa,* a pastry filled with cinnamon-spiced custard to enjoy with a cup of coffee. The focal point of the square is the celebrated **Morosini fountain▶▶▶** constructed in 1628 by Francesco Morosini, the Venetian governor of Candia, as Iráklio was then known. A 10-mile-long aqueduct was built to bring water from Mount Yioúchtas to the fountain, which incorporated four stone lions carved three centuries earlier. They still roar (under rather human noses) above a maritime frieze of mermaids, nymphs, tritons and winged cherubs, though the marble statue of Neptune that once surmounted them has long gone, destroyed during the Turkish occupation. Opposite the fountain stands the colonnaded porch of the **Basilica of St Mark▶.** Founded in 1239, twice rebuilt after earthquake damage, and later converted by the Turks into a mosque, the basilica contains a superb marble doorway decorated with clusters of grapes.

▶ El Greco Park *43D3*

A bust of the great Cretan painter stares over tree-shaded flower beds and a children's playground with swings and slides in El Greco Park. Beyond the park on the corner of Platía Kallergou stands the tall, rectangular **Venetian Loggia▶▶.** This is a reconstruction, after earthquake and war damage, of the original which was built in 1626 by Francesco Morosini as a pleasant gathering place for the great and good of Venetian Iráklio. The open ground floor arches are duplicated above in the window frames, and the top is balustraded and pinnacled. Inside the loggia is an open, D-shaped courtyard from which you walk through a door into the **City Hall▶** or Dimarkheíon, formerly the Venetian city's armoury, a massive construction whose far side faces the **Church of Ayíos Títos▶▶▶** across a little court.

Coffee break
As midday approaches the street waiters emerge, carrying cups of sweet Greek coffee and glasses of water from the cafés through the crowded streets to the office workers. Some carry trays balanced on one hand, others swing a pyramid-shaped tin cradle.

■ Iráklio possesses a number of statues and memorials to Cretan heroes. Most striking of all, in sheer size and gloominess, is the larger-than-life statue of Crete's greatest statesman, Elefthérios Venizélos, that stands at the southeastern corner of Platía Elefthérias.....■

Above: the plaque on the grave of Níkos Kazantzákis

Demon Turks
In icons painted during the Turkish occupation of Crete, the Roman or Barbarian soldiers shown martyring the saints are generally of unmistakably Turkish mien, with pointed hats, chin beards, pantaloons, curved sabres and slippers with upturned toes.

Street heroes
Cretan heroes of various wars and campaigns of resistance are frequently commemorated in street names. Among the most common are Venizélos, Daskaloyiánnis, Kandanóleon (leader of a 16th-century revolt against the Venetians), Daliánis (a mainland Greek leader who occupied Frangokástello in 1828 and was killed when the Turks retook it) and Gabriel Arkádiou, the Abbot of Arkádi Monastery who blew up the building and everyone in it on 9 November 1866 rather than be taken by the besieging Turks.

Elefthérios Venizélos The likeness of Venizélos's statue to Lenin is often remarked on, probably less a matter of individual features than the stiffness and aloofness of the pose. Venizélos (1864–1936) is seen, not only by Cretans, as the founding father of modern Greece. Cretans revere him as the local boy from Mourniés near Khaniá who played his part as a young man in the struggle against Turkish rule, organised the 1897 protest that led to the raising of the Greek flag, convened the Revolutionary Assembly in 1905 which prompted the resignation of Prince George of Greece as High Commissioner of Crete, became the Prime Minister of Greece in 1910, and three years later saw his and his island's dream of *enosis*, union with Greece, at last realised. After the Great War, Venizélos had his share of ups and downs, including long periods in opposition, the survival of an assassination attempt, the bloody failure of his attempt to establish a New Byzantium in Turkey which culminated in his resignation as Prime Minister in 1932, exile when the short-lived Greek Republic collapsed, and a sentence of death *in absentia* when a coup failed. He was pardoned

Eleftheríos Venizélos brought union with Greece in 1913

by the newly restored King George II, but never came back to Greece, dying in France in 1936. In Crete, though, the failures of his later years are disregarded. What counts is the dynamism and cool competence of the young Venizélos who brought about *enosis*.

A well-armed Daskaloyiánnis

Ioánnis Daskaloyiánnis A few hundred metres to the west stands the statue of **Ioánnis Daskaloyiánnis,** in the *platía* of the same name. The 18th-century rebel leader was born Ioánnis Vláhos in Anópolis, on the southern coast of Sfakiot country in the southwest of the island. He embodies all the Cretan heroic attributes: he was learned (Daskaloyiánnis means John the Teacher), he was charismatic and brave, and he died a particularly nasty death. His 1770 rebellion against the Turks started brilliantly, but when support from the Russians melted away he went down to Frangokástello on the south coast to give himself up. The ruling pasha in Iráklion, having treated him most hospitably, took umbrage at Daskaloyiánnis's assertion that he had rebelled to set right the wrongs of all Cretans and Christians, and ordered the unfortunate hero to be flayed alive.

Nikephóros Phokás Just south of the Archaeological Museum, and outside the medieval town walls, a column beside Dimokratías Avenue commemorates a hero with an even more bloody story attached to his name. **Nikephóros Phokás** was not a Cretan but a ruthless Byzantine general who was charged with recapturing Rabdh-el-Khandak from the Saracens in AD961. He ensured success by catapulting the heads of captured Saracens into the city, where they fell among the understandably demoralised defenders.

Heroes of arts and letters In El Greco Park, the small public gardens just off Platía Venizélos, stands the bust of the celebrated painter, who was born Doménico Theotokópoulos, probably at Fodhéle near Iráklio. Theotokópoulos (c. 1541–1614) found widespread fame under the pseudonym of **El Greco**. He was an acknowledged master at marrying the spirit of the old and new, the Byzantine and Renaissance worlds.

The painter El Greco

At the southernmost tip of the medieval walls, massively simple in its setting on top of the Martinengo Bastion, is the tomb of Crete's most celebrated writer, the very widely admired **Níkos Kazantzákis** (1883–1957). 'I hope for nothing; I fear nothing; I am free' reads the inscription. The Iráklio-born writer became internationally famous when his novel *Zorba the Greek* was filmed. Today his other work attracts equal interest. Only *Zorba* and his superb *Freedom and Death* were set in Crete, but Kazantzákis drew on his roots throughout his unorthodox, wandering life.

Big-head
The story goes that a visitor, on being shown the skull of St Titus, remarked that he had been shown the saint's skull, rather smaller than this one, the day before in a distant monastery. The custodian, not taken aback in the slightest, hastened to explain that that must have been the skull of the saint as a boy.

The Church of Ayíos Títos

▶▶ **The Church of Ayíos Títos** *43D3*

The church was rebuilt as a mosque following an earthquake in 1856 which destroyed the Byzantine original. The interior is capped by a galleried dome and has a modern iconostasis. Paintings of Cretan martyrs and scenes from the life of St Titus hang on the walls, and a shrine contains a reliquary that holds the skull of the saint.

Titus was sent by St Paul to convert the Cretans, and he became the first bishop of the island. His body was brought to the newly built church at Iráklio in AD962. In 1669 the Venetians, evacuating Candia after its capture by

Fishing boats line the harbour in Iráklio

The magnificent Venetian fortress still dominates the harbour

the Turks, took the relics to Venice. They were returned to Ayíos Títos in 1966. A gold reliquary holds the skull of the saint and a little brown dome of bone is just visible through a hole in the top of the container.

► Odós 25 Avgoústou *43D3*

Odós 25 Avgoústou is one of Iráklio's chief commercial streets, named after the day in 1898 when several Cretans were killed by Turkish soldiers just before the Great Powers enforced their withdrawal agreement on the Turks. Big, crumbling buildings at the bottom of the street, fronted in Turkish style, overlook the **harbour►►**. Iráklio's harbour has seen many centuries of fighting, destruction and bloodshed along with the steady flow of commerce that has made it the most significant place in Crete's history. One look at the enormous stone fort on the breakwater tells you the importance that the Venetians attached to securing this gateway to the island. But this harbour has been the commercial nerve-centre of Crete since it was named Herakleium by the Romans. During the Battle of Crete in 1941 the port was heavily bombed, and the British forces around Iráklio were evacuated from the mole by Royal Navy ships at dead of night on 28–9 May. Nowadays the harbour scene is a lively one, with visitors crowding the quays and breakwater while fishermen unconcernedly continue to mend their nets and transfer their catches to the battered pick-up trucks of the fish dealers. Caïques take parties of tourists on fishing trips and out to the island of Día, whose long bulk lies offshore. Ferries from Piraeus and other islands dock at a big modern terminal to the east, so there is little to spoil the attractive old harbour.

►►► Venetian fort *43E4*

The Venetian fort (open 8–4, Sunday 10-3), a few hundred metres out along the breakwater, is an obvious magnet for visitors. Step over a metal barrier and walk into the shadow of its massive walls, and a wide view opens to the west as far as the Psiloritis mountains, which are snow-capped for much of the year. The walls of the fort are many metres thick, built of enormous blocks of yellow stone eroded and rounded by centuries of wind, weather and attack. The Venetians called it Rocca al Mare, the Rock in the Sea, a name which perfectly expresses its air of grim defiance.

Pride of lions

As a symbol of their eternal vigilance, and their pride and swiftness in retribution, the Venetians set up marble statues of the winged lion of St Mark in the walls and over the gateways of the forts they built across Crete. These Venetian lions still look seaward in poignant defiance. Many Cretan churches also bear the winged lion in tympanum carvings.

Raging bull
The Romans named their port of Herakleium after the Greek hero Heracles, in commemoration of the seventh labour set him by King Eurystheus of Mycenae. Heracles was sent to Crete to tame a white bull that was ravaging the island. Its owner, King Minos, had refused to sacrifice it to Poseidon as the god of the sea had demanded, and Poseidon had driven it mad in revenge. Needless to say, Heracles soon had the bull in a half-Nelson and brought it triumphantly to the astounded Eurystheus.

The Saracens built a fort on this tiny rock opposite the harbour, as did Genoese adventurers when they briefly took control of the north coast towns early in the 13th century. The Venetians, who succeeded them, constructed a stronger fortification, but this was wrecked in the earthquake of 1303, and was again rebuilt. A rocky breakwater connected it to the mainland, and another fort stood at the mouth of the harbour. After destructive raids in the 1530s by the much feared Ottoman pirate-admiral Khaireddin Barbarossa, Rocca al Mare was refortified and strengthened yet again, work that came into its own a century later during the epic Great Siege by the Turks.

There are three imposing marble winged lions of St Mark in the north, east and south walls of the fort. The best preserved of these faces out to sea, threatening all-comers with snarling jaws and upraised wings. This sculpture, gazing out above the clicking cameras, speaks eloquently of the pride and power of medieval Venice, and of the subjugation of the island to so many succeeding conquerors. Entering the fort by the southern door, you wander through shadowy stone chambers among rusty, ancient cannon and piles of dusty cannon balls. A roughly paved stone ramp rises to the upper storey which is laid out with a small open-air theatre and from which you can reach the crenellated ramparts. Climb up the lookout tower for a superb view over Iráklio and the mountains behind. A lower-level but even wider panorama can be enjoyed from the seaward tip of the mole beyond the fort, a pleasant ten-minute stroll from here.

▶ Arsenali *43D4*

Around the east side of the harbour a number of tall, hollow, stone arches rise above the offices, shops and cars. These were *arsenali*, or sheds for the construction and repair of ships, which were built in the 16th century, around the same time as the re-strengthening of the fort, to service the Venetian galley fleet.

A 17th-century icon from the Historical Museum

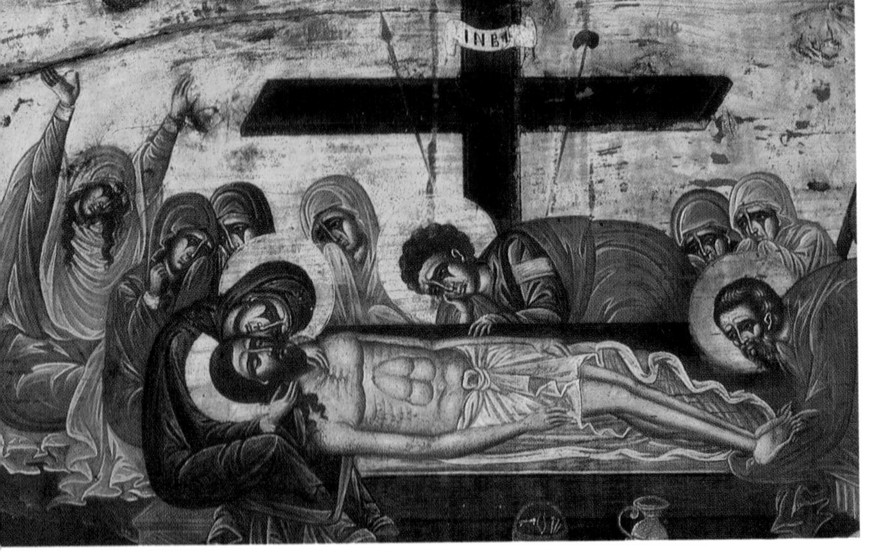

►► Historical Museum 42C4

The Historical Museum (open 9:30–4:30, Saturday 9:30–2:30, closed Sunday) is in a dignified Venetian town house with a Turkish fountain outside the door, opposite the Hotel Xenia. This excellent museum is worth at least an hour's visit. Compare the intriguing 17th-century Venetian prints of Candia in the entrance hall with the modern map before descending to the basement, where Venetian wealth and industry are beautifully illustrated in the stonemasons' craft. There are also some 18th-century Turkish mural scenes of Iráklion, rescued from the house of Fasil Bey. On the ground floor there are icons and a beautifully restored 13th-century church fresco of a tousle-haired and heavy-eyed John the Baptist. Red-capped Sfakiot partisan chiefs line the stairs leading to the upper floor and to reconstructions of the studies of Crete's pre-eminent novelist Níkos Kazantzákis and the Crete-born wartime prime minister of Greece, Emmanuel Tsouderós. Also here are exhibitions of wartime photographs, while on the top floor there are examples of traditional Cretan weaving and embroidery, and the recreation of a peasant house.

► Priuli Fountain 42B3

The nearby Priuli fountain was built in 1666 by Antonio Priuli during the Great Siege of Candia, and embellished with Corinthian columns, a pediment, ornate side scrolls and an inscription. It stands today in the shadow of a workaday block of flats, but is still a poignant monument to the gracious living of the past.

The quiet courtyard of the Historical Museum

El Greco

The painter El Greco was a native Cretan, born Domenico Theotokópoulos in the village of Fódhele near Iráklio in 1541. The Historical Museum contains one early painting of his, on display by itself in a room on the ground floor. This depiction of travellers on their way to the monastery of St Catherine on Mount Sinai was painted in about 1570, when El Greco had just left Crete to pursue his studies in Rome. Deep rooted Byzantine formality and discipline show in the stiffly posed figures, but there is an altogether Renaissance depth and realism to the mountainous setting.

Ornate ceilings and candelabra in Áyios Minás cathedral

The Last Supper
Note the two dogs contesting ownership of a bone under the table; a little black-skinned slave bringing three bowls up from the cellar on a tray; the ornate benches which have lions' feet; and a heavy, embroidered rug which covers the table under the linen tablecloth. St John's head is on the table, cradled on his arms, a picture of dejection. Another disciple bends intently forward on one elbow, while a red-capped man leans through a curtained archway, giving a meaningful now's-the-time look to the stealthily departing Judas.

► Platía Aikaterínis *42C2*

Platía Aikaterínis is a wide paved square with three churches to explore: **Ayía Aikateríni;** the **Cathedral of Ayíos Minás**; and the **Church of Ayíos Minás**. All three are described below, but the first of these is the most notable.

►►► Ayía Aikateríni *42C2*

Ayía Aikateríni is on your left as you enter Platía Aikaterínis. This barn-like church was built in 1555. Apart from the elaborately carved Venetian doorway at the west end, there is nothing particularly special about Ayía Aikateríni from the outside, but once inside the church (open 10–1, and 4–6 on Thursday and Friday; it may be closed out of season) you will be dazzled by the fabulous collection of Byzantine and Renaissance icons, religious texts and precious ceremonial items from churches and monasteries all over Crete.

El Greco and Mikhaíl Damaskinós A college attached to Ayía Aikateríni, an outpost of a great monastery of the same name on Mount Sinai, became Crete's most influential centre for religious and philosophical education and teaching of the arts in late Venetian times. A small painting of the mother monastery by El Greco hangs in the Historical Museum.

El Greco, born and raised in Crete, was rivalled only by his contemporary Mikhaíl Damaskinós, who studied here before going abroad to make a living and nurture his talent in Venice. Returning to Crete, Damaskinós painted a series of six superb icons in 1582–91 for the monastery at Vrondísi (see pages 190–1). They were brought to Iráklio in 1800 to save them from the Turks, and now hang here in Ayía Aikateríni. They are the *Adoration of the Magi;* the *Last Supper;* the *Burning Bush* with a sublime Virgin; *Noli Me Tangere,* with the resurrected Christ astonishing the two Marys; a semi-circle of bearded and haloed bishops at the *First Ecumenical Synod at Nicaea;* and adoring angels cluster round Christ celebrating *Holy Mass.* Brilliantly executed, wonderfully detailed and full of life and expression, these icons deserve closer study than they sometimes receive.

► Cathedral of Ayíos Minás *42C2*

The big 19th-century Cathedral of Ayíos Minás dominates Platía Aikaterínis. Inside there is a profusion of frescoes from floor to roof, and in the centre hang fantastically elaborate chandeliers. In the shadow of the cathedral lies the little **Church of Ayíos Minás**► with twin apses and bellcote. It is usually kept locked, but the custodian of the cathedral may rouse himself sufficiently to hunt out the key so that you can go in and admire the beautiful carved and painted iconostasis.

► Platía Kornárou *43D2*

In Platía Kornárou there is a modern sculpture of a three-headed, multi-legged horse carrying two warriors, approaching a pre-Raphaelite maiden. This is an interpretation of a stirring scene from the famous Cretan epic poem *Erotókritos* in which the eponymous peasant hero meets his nobly born lover Aretoúsa.

▶ Fountains 43D2

Below and across Platía Kornárou are two historic fountains, close together. The octagonal stone **kiosk▶** was erected by the Turks to house one of the many fountains they provided around Iráklion and the other major cities of Crete, reflecting the Islamic reverence for water, so often in short supply in the religion's Middle Eastern homelands. Nowadays the graceful little building with its projecting eaves contains a very hospitable café, a welcome break on the walk. With a drink and a snack to hand you can contrast the Turkish fountain-building style with the nearby Venetian **Bembo fountain▶**, assembled in 1588 from an odd collection of antiquities including the torso of a Roman statue from Ierápetra, various columns and carved slabs.

▶▶ Odós 1866 43D2

Odós 1866 opposite the Turkish fountain-café is one of the city's most famous, and correspondingly crowded, thoroughfares, better known as Market Street. Iráklio's present-day commercial activity is concentrated near the freight docks beyond the ferry terminal, but in Market Street, tourist-orientated though it is, you can still catch the flavour of what the bazaar must have been like in Turkish and Venetian days. Little shops line each side of the street, many of them selling souvenirs that are likely to be over-priced and of poor quality. But there are also butchers with carcasses swinging from hooks, savoury-smelling bakers, fruit shops, vendors of olives, shops crammed with leather belts and bags, and shops hung with flapping festoons of brightly coloured woven rugs and embroidered linen, some produced on village looms and needles, others definitely not. Slacken your pace or stare for more than a second, and you will invite entreaties to step inside. Haggle over the price, if you can, but don't expect to buy a genuine piece of Cretan folk art at a discount. You should find better value at the tavernas in the side lanes to the right as you walk up the street. Fotíou Theodosáki is said to have suffered a recent decline in standard and rise in prices, but it is still an atmospheric little street in which to sit at a pavement table and eat as the shopkeepers shout in Market Street a few paces away.

Adoration
An especially tender aspect of Damaskinós's *Adoration of the Magi* is the humility with which the long-bearded, ermine-collared king bows his head to the touch of the infant Christ's chubby fingers on his bald pate.

Cheese, please
Be sure to sample the cheeses before you buy. Stallholders will expect you to do so, and will be pleased to tell you the village where each variety was made. You will find soft *feta* cheese, waxy fat cheese and hard crumbly goat and sheep's cheeses with a mould-blue rind and a thick musky tang in the mouth.

Lively markets sell food and souvenirs

Taking your time

■ It is tempting, but a great mistake, to set yourself a punishing schedule during your holiday in Crete. There are many attractions here, the Minoan sites, the Venetian towns, the remote villages, the beaches and islands, the back-country drives and mountain hikes. But anyone who tries to hurry through timeless Crete ends up hurrying nowhere.....■

Making it last
Nothing better illustrates the theory and practice of taking one's time than the Cretan ability, incredible to those from gobble-and-go cultures, to make 3cm of thick coffee and a glass of water last as long as the conversation that goes with them. Well over an hour is nothing.

The best plan is to have one or two objectives at most each day, earmarking a good number of days for aimless wandering. You won't see everything this way, but what you do see, taken at leisure with no pressure of time forcing you onwards, will mean far more when you look back. It will be remarkable if a day of unplanned driving or walking does not lead you to a wealth of hospitality and conversation, to beaches and hilltops, villages and view-points that no guidebook could discover for you.

In the bigger towns, make for the market streets and the waterfront, and idle there, or cut up a side street into the quarters where ordinary life goes on. If a shopkeeper beckons you inside for a cup of coffee, or a glass of *rakí* is offered by someone, accept the invitation and don't hurry off. You'll learn more of Cretan life, customs and history this way than from any book or lecture. In the evening, don't eat too early; any music or dancing that takes place will probably not reach its climax until the small hours of the morning. And if you make an appointment with a Cretan, treat the agreed time as a statement of intention rather than as a fixed certainty, especially with regard to getting away again. In short, when in Crete, do what the Cretans do, and take your time. You won't regret it.

Shady café tables by the Bembo Fountain

Walk Around Iráklio's Venetian city walls

This is a 4km stroll along the line of the old Venetian walls, with lovely rooftop views into the old city, particularly enjoyable at sunset. Allow about two hours. See map on pages 42–3.

Almost the whole semi-circle of the medieval city walls has survived the ravages of time, war and development. Straight stretches of massively thick wall, 40m wide in some places, are interspersed with even thicker defensive bastions and pierced by corresponding gates. These were the strongest city walls anywhere around the Mediterranean, built from 1462 onwards on the foundations of the previous Byzantine walls, and strengthened from 1538 by the great Venetian engineer Michele Sanmichele. At present only the first kilometre can be walked on top of the walls, but there are plans to extend this path right round the circuit.

Start at the stout, square San Andreas Bastion on the northwestern corner of the walls at the seaward end of Odós Archipiskopóu Makáriou. This is most easily reached by taking a taxi from Platía Elefthérias. Steps lead up to the wall-top path which runs south towards the great stone bulge of the Pantokrator Bastion. Note that the steps down to the left just before the bastion lead to a good ground-level view of the arched Pantokrator or Khaniá Gate. Continue on the wall past the Bethlehem Bastion, looking inland to shadowy streets and across to the red dome of the cathedral. Descend to ground level by the Bethlehem Gate and continue at street level, climbing again to the top of the wall at the enormous Martinengo Bastion where you will find the simple tomb of Níkos Kazantzákis.

Return to and pass through the Bethlehem Gate and continue outside the walls for 1km, noting their enormous size and strength. Beyond the busy Knosós road junction, walk through the Jesus gate. Steps inside and to the right climb to another short wall-top section, and then descend to a road which leads to Platía Elefthérias. A final short stretch, sickeningly high as you look over, runs downhill from the Archaeological Museum towards the harbour.

The imposing Bethlehem Bastion

Accommodation

Sour notes
It is a thousand pities that piped music of the blandest international kind is invading a number of Cretan hotels, including some upmarket enough to know better. Why not have traditional Cretan music, if they must have music at all? Who wants to drink rakí, eat stuffed vine leaves or read about Crete to an irritating background of character-free, could-be-anywhere rock?

As previously noted, visitors to Crete tend not to base themselves in Iráklio for their holiday. It is a town where an overnight stay might be forced on you at the beginning or end of a holiday by the exigencies of air or sea timetables. Since most people like to travel to and from Crete during the daytime, a demand for one-night beds has grown here, and you are more likely to find unbooked, short-stay accommodation in Iráklio than elsewhere on the island. Ask at the helpful tourist information office opposite the Archaeological Museum, but be sure to arrive well before 2:30pm when they close.

Accommodation will probably be in D and E class hotels (see page 274 for an explanation of these categories). A good number are too basic and uncompromisingly bare to be properly comfortable, but beggars can't be choosers if they are stuck for a bed! Around the two parallel streets of Hándakos and Hortátson, which run northwest from Platía Venizélos down towards the waterfront, there is a big selection of inexpensive rooms and pensions, along with unofficial youth hostels at Vironos and Hándakos.

Reasonable, moderately priced hotels can be found to the east of Odós 25 Avgoústou, the commercial artery of Iráklio which runs up from the harbour. There are also plenty outside the walls of the old city, a cheap taxi ride away from Platía Elefthérias and the centre of Iráklio. Taxi drivers themselves can often recommend a hotel, and remember that you don't have to take the room if you don't like the look of it.

Generally speaking, the hotels nearer Platía Elefthérias, the centre of Iráklio life, will be more comfortable, better appointed and more expensive. The Astoria, right on the square, is a good example of a very comfortable, expensive but central hotel. However, if you are aiming this high, book well in advance.

A typical budget pension in Iráklio

Food and drink

If you have just arrived in Iráklio, the chances are the city will be offering you your first taste of Cretan food and drink. If you are passing through at the end of your visit, this will be your last chance to eat and drink Cretan. So forget international cuisine and the predictable tourist restaurants around Platía Eleftherías, and forage among the side streets for something more local in flavour.

The little restaurants in narrow Fotíou Theodosáki, between Odós 1866 and Odós Evans, are always good value, especially during the day when the market stallholders are eating there. Odós Daidálos, which links Platía Eleftherías and Platía Venizélos, is lined with unexciting restaurants, but two streets to the north, in Odós Mílatou, is the small and atmospheric *Taverna Aplo,* run by the genial Byron, where *bouzoúkis* may be playing at two in the morning, and where Byron's cooking is fine, even if the service may lack five-star polish.

More expensive restaurants, but not wildly so, can be found in Odós Kórai, parallel to Daidálos and Mílatou, where *Giovanni's* and *Loukoulos* will offer you plenty of variety and substance.

Down by the Venetian harbour prices tend to rise, since you pay for the view. The fish restaurants are ranged here, and a stroll into the kitchen to lift lids and sniff pots is not only expected but is a wise move if you want to try out something entirely new.

It is also worthwhile taking a taxi, or walking for about 20 minutes from Platía Eleftherías, outside the city walls to Odós Dimokrátias, where restaurants such as *Kiriákos* specialise in Cretan food. Irákliots eat here.

Cheaper and more basic, but extremely good value, are the *ouzéri* or small-scale tavernas. And then there are the takeaway *souvláki* or kebab stalls, and the doughnut, pastry and pie shops around Platía Eleftherías and Platía Venizélos, all quite safe, very nourishing and quite impossible to walk past if you are hungry.

Tirópitta
Tirópitta are little round or oval pies, their flaky brown pastry cases filled with hot, soft *feta* cheese. A handful of these, eaten fresh from the counter of a *zakharoplasteío* or pastry shop, makes a sustaining and toothsome snack.

Shopping

Nuts on a street stall

Glass that cheers
If you linger more than a few minutes in a shop or at a market stall, you may well be offered a cup of coffee or a glass of something stronger by the owner. This is a pleasant gesture still occasionally met with in Iráklio, but very likely to sweeten business in the smaller towns and villages.

Iráklio offers a greater number and variety of shops than any other Cretan town. Being the capital of the island, however, many of these sell everyday goods that are not especially appealing to visitors. There are plenty of rather expensive dress and jewellery shops in the streets that radiate from Platía Elefthérias. Daidálos has stolen the crown of Leophóros Dikaiosíni in this regard, but fashion often changes from one year to the next.

For souvenirs and presents, the top end of Odós 25 Avgoústou is crammed with small shops, as is Odós Idoméneos where it joins Platía Elefthérias behind the Astoria cinema. Pavement stalls push the same sort of things: 'Minoan' chess sets, jars of perfumed creams, reproductions of classical statues and Byzantine icons. Inside the shops you will find woven and embroidered rugs, blankets, bags and tablecloths. Look for rough stitching and weaving on the reverse of the work if you want handmade goods, which will be more expensive. Pottery, modern jewellery and leatherwear, along with decorated daggers, are other favourites. If you are looking for genuine antiques, try Odós Kórai, parallel with Daidálos. For knives that will actually cut, try the side streets off Odós 25 Avgoústou.

The sounds of Cretan traditional music will bring the island to your armchair back home. Tapes and CDs are widely available: try the shop on the right halfway down Daidálos. Vasilis Skoulas is a master of both *lýra* and *bouzoúki*.

By far the best place for shopping, for both fun and colour, is Market Street (Odós 1866) that runs north–south between Platía Nikephórou Phoká and Platía Kornárou. In between the food stalls there are souvenir shops, and one or two leather goods places with reasonable, and negotiable, prices. From the food stalls you can taste and buy fresh cheese from the mountains, delicious Cretan honey, and packets of herbs including the famous dittany.

Pottery is often a good buy in Crete

Iráklio is a sophisticated modern city with a variety of nightlife on offer. There are plenty of discos along the streets south and north of the Archaeological Museum. The *Trapeza* and *Atrium*, in Bofor Street towards the harbour, are good examples, but they are disco-bars rather than the non-stop music and light show variety that you will find in the resorts to the east. There is an older-style disco at *Flou* on Platía Daskaloyiánnis. Outmoded but excellent R&B and rock'n'roll accompany your drinks here, and dancing depends on who feels like it. The atmosphere is just the right side of tongue-in-cheek.

Traditional music and dancing are strong in Iráklion, owing to the large number of first-generation city dwellers who hark back to their roots. Byron's excellent *Taverna Aplo* on Odós Mílatou often has music and singing in the early hours, and everyone joins in. There is no tabletop-dancing or plate-smashing; this is the real McCoy. Other good restaurants with stages and dance halls which put on Cretan music, singing and dancing are *Avisínos,* Odós Skalani; *Delína,* Odós Ikárou; *Kástro,* Avenue Bofor; *Kritíko Konáki,* Odos Karteros; *Aposperítis,* Leofóros Knossóu.

At present there are four enclosed cinemas, with the Astoria on Platía Eleftherias offering pretty standard Hollywood fare, and several open-air ones in the vicinity of Iráklio. Those in the eastern suburbs at Néa Alikarnassós are good fun, with a party atmosphere often developing among the audience.

As in all Cretan towns, the chief evening occupation is simply strolling or sitting around watching the world go by. The *voltá* or evening perambulation is still a feature of Platía Eleftherias's shady gardens away from the traffic, and also of the Venetian harbour. Sitting outside a café or bar, commenting on passers-by over a *rakí* and dish of nuts, is *the* Iráklio evening pastime. On the waterfront you get a wonderful view as well.

Drinker's delights

'When I drink and get drunk
I don't bother anyone.
I only celebrate my youth
And have a lot of fun.'

'Would the sea were wine
And the ships were dishes,
And the masts of the ships
Were fried fishes!'

Cretan Mantinádes

Cleopatra – or at least her modern Greek counterpart – is still to be found in Iráklio...

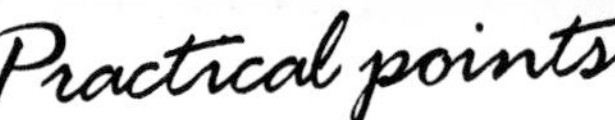

Practical points

Junk the Jeep
At most car-hire places you'll see four-wheel-drive jeeps for rent. Unless you are planning some extremely bold off-road motoring, it is not worth paying extra for this kind of transport. A good hire car will cope with all but the very worst road conditions on the island, but remember that insurance may not cover the underside of the vehicle or the tyres, so check first.

Airport The airport is 4km east of Iráklio (information tel: 081–228426). The No. 1 bus connects the airport with the Olympic Airways office in Platía Elefthérias (tel: 081–229191). Fixed price taxis run between airport and Platía Elefthérias.

Banks Most banks, including the Commercial, Ionian and the National Bank of Greece, are represented on Odós 25 Avgoústou, due south of the harbour.

Bicycle hire Odós 25 Avgoústou is a good bet. Try Candia Motor at No. 48 (tel: 081–221227), and Nikos at No. 14 Bofor Street between the Archaeological Museum and the harbour (tel: 081–226425).

Bus stations Information on tel: 081–221765. Station A, opposite the ferry terminal, for buses to Ayíos Nikólaos, Sitiá and the east. Station B, immediately outside the Khaniá Gate, for Faistós, Mesarás, Ayía Galíni and the southwest. Across the road from Station A, for Réthimnon, Khaniá and the northwest. Platía Kíprou on Knosós road just outside Jesus Gate for Ierápetra and the southeast.

Car hire Odós 25 Avgoústou has all the well-known companies: Hertz, No. 44 (tel: 081–229802); Holiday Autos, No. 38 (tel: 081–289497/284438); Budget, No. 34 (tel: 081–221315/243918); Eurodollar, No. 24 (tel: 081–243237).

Car parking It is wise to park only in official parking bays between 8am and 8pm (Sundays are free). The best car park for the city centre is on Ikaroú (the airport road), 200 metres from the Archaeological Museum.

Consulates Germany: 7 Odós Zografoú (tel: 081–226228)
UK: 16 Odós Papalexándrou (tel: 081–224012)
Netherlands: 23 Odós 25 Avgoústou (tel: 081–246202)
Norway: 24 Platí Agíos Dimítrou (tel: 081–220536).

Those signposts that do exist are often 'bilingual'

Ferries To Piraeus (Athens), Italian ports and many Greek islands, from terminal east of Venetian harbour. Book through shipping agencies in Odós 25 Avgoústou. Try Paleológos at No. 5 (tel: 081–246185/246208).

Festival Late June to mid-September; music, plays, exhibitions, cultural events.

Foreign newspapers Try the shops on Odós Daidálos and Platía Venizélos.

Gardens Platía Elefthérias; El Greco

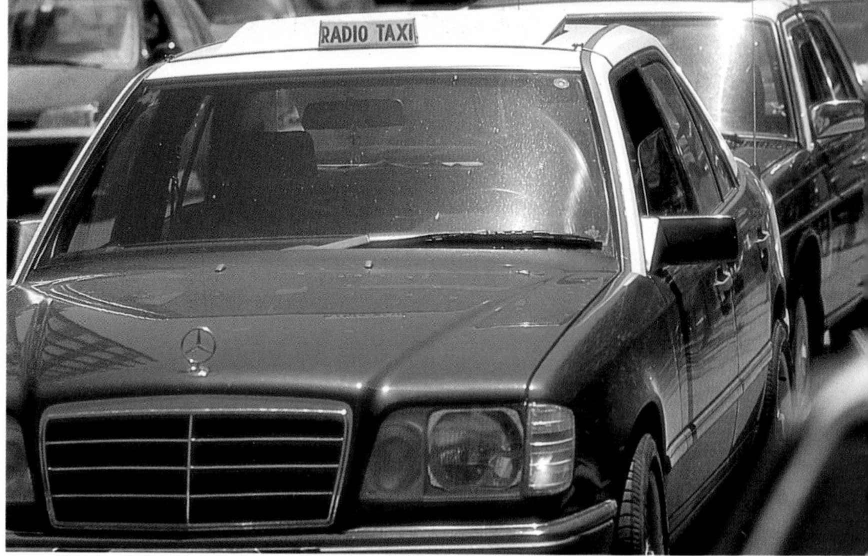

Park; there is an extensive stretch of gardens in the 'ditch' of the old city wall.

Hospitals Venizélos Hospital (tel: 081–237580) Apollónion Hospital (tel: 081–287411).

Launderette Odós Mirabéllo at the first T-junction toward the harbour on Odós Xanthoudídou.

Police 10 Odós Dikeossínis (tel: 081–283190/282031).

Post office Platía Daskaloyiánnis (7:30am–7:30pm Monday–Friday; money change 7:30–1:30). Mobile Post Office in El Greco Park and by Bus Station A, 8am–8pm (9–6 Sunday).

Roman Catholic Church On P. Adóniou, parallel and to the east of Odós 25 Avgoústou.

Taxis Many wait in Platía Elefthérias.

Telephones (OTE) Area code is 081. Main OTE office is beside El Greco Park (7:30am–11pm).

Toilets Platía Elefthérias, opposite statue of Elefthérios Venizélos; El Greco Park.

Tourist information National Tourist Organisation of Greece (EOT) office is at 1 Odós Xanthoudídou, opposite the Archaeological Museum. It is best to visit early in the morning. Open 8–2:30; Monday–Friday (tel: 081–228825/ 244462).

Tour operators Many in Odós 25 Avgoústou. Also try Christopher Travel at 18 Odós Malikoúti (tel: 081–71202); Cretan Holidays at 36 Odós Daidálos (tel: 081–242106).

Walking For all advice on walking contact the Greek Mountaineering Club, 53 Odós Dikeosínis (tel: 081–227609).

Blue Mercedes taxis vary from ancient to modern

Taxi!
If you are caught up in a blast of Greek and it appears that a taxi service is being forced on you, or one is being arranged for you on the telephone, don't panic. It is probably only excessive use of the much-loved Greek word for OK – *endáksi*.

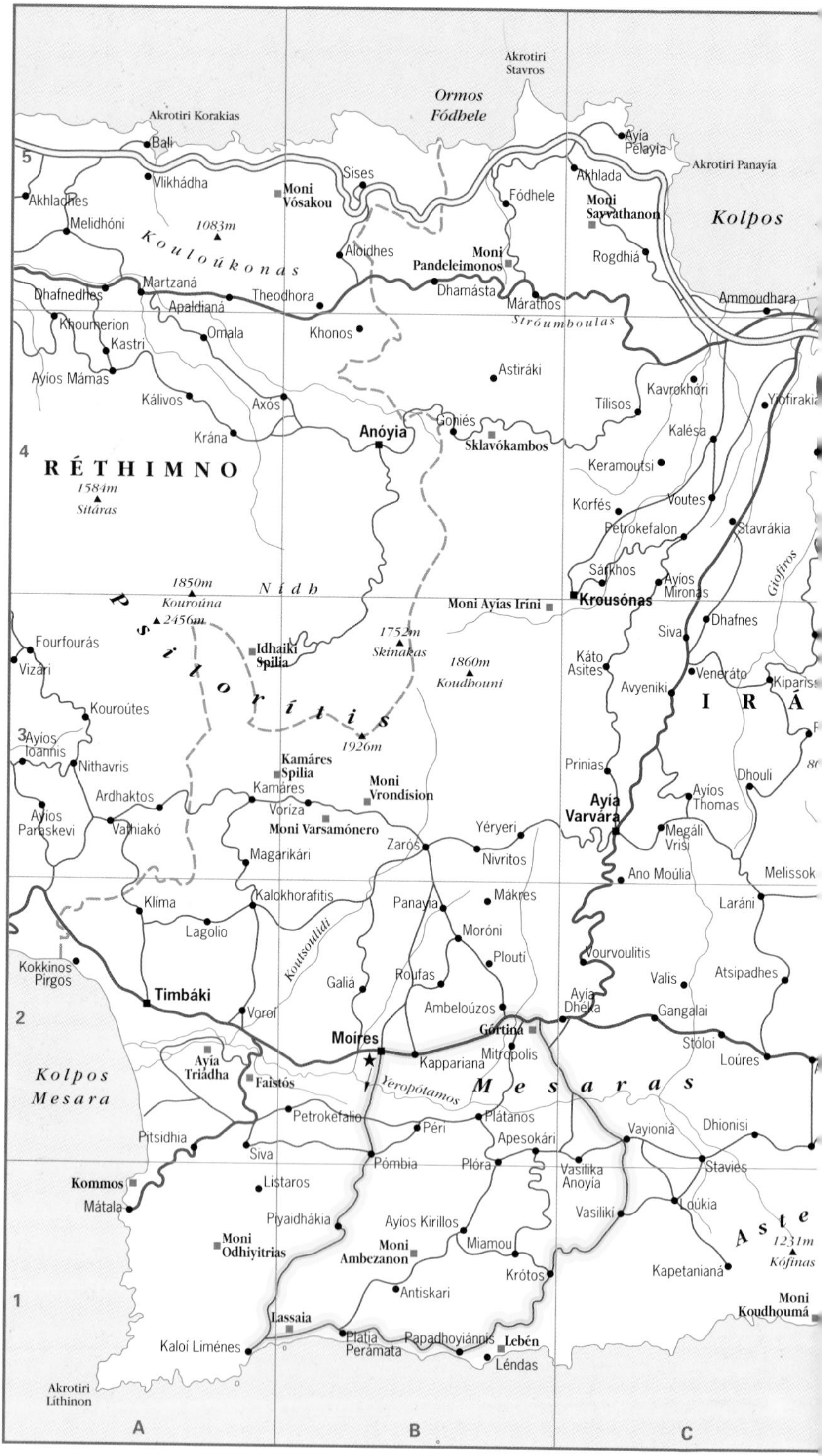

Akrotiri Stavros
Ormos Fódbele
Akrotiri Korakias
Bali
Ayía Pelayía
Akrotiri Panayía
Vlikhádha
Sises
Moni Vósakou
Akhladhes
Akhlada
Fódhele
Moni Savvathanon
Kolpos
Melidhóni
1083m
Kouloúkonas
Aloidhes
Moni Pandeleimonos
Rogdhiá
Dhafnedhes
Martzaná
Theodhora
Dhamásta
Márathos
Ammoudhara
Apaldianá
Khoumerion
Omala
Khonos
Stróumboulas
Kastri
Ayíos Mámas
Astiráki
Kálivos
Axós
Tílisos
Kavrokhóri
Yiofirakia
Goniés
Kalésa
Kránа
Anóyia
Sklavókambos
Keramoutsi
RÉTHIMNO
1584m
Sitáras
Korfés
Voutes
Petrokefalon
Stavrákia
Sárkhos
Ayíos Mironas
Giofiros
1850m
Nídh
Kouroúna
Moni Ayías Iríni
Krousónas
2456m
Psilorítis
1752m
Skinakas
Dhafnes
Fourfourás
Idhaiki Spilia
Siva
Vizári
1860m
Koudhouni
Káto Asites
Venеráto
Kiparis
Avyeniki
IRÁ
Kouroútes
Ayíos Ioannis
1926m
Nithavris
Kamáres Spilia
Prinias
Kamáres
Moni Vrondísion
Dhouli
Ardhaktos
Ayía Varvára
Ayíos Thomas
Ayíos Paraskevi
Vathiakó
Vóriza
Moni Varsamónero
Yéryeri
Megáli Vrisi
Zarós
Nivritos
Magarikári
Ano Moúlia
Melissok
Kalokhorafitis
Klíma
Panayia
Mákres
Laráni
Lagolio
Koutsoulidi
Moróni
Ploutí
Vourvoulitis
Kokkinos Pirgos
Galiá
Roufas
Valis
Atsipadhes
Timbáki
Ambeloúzos
Ayía Dhéka
Gangalai
Voroí
Górtina
Moíres
Stóloi
Mitropolis
Ayía Triádha
Kappariana
Loúres
Faistós
Kolpos Mesara
Yeropótamos
Mesaras
Petrokefalio
Plátanos
Péri
Vayioniá
Dhionisi
Pitsidhia
Apesokári
Siva
Pómbia
Plóra
Vasilika Anoyia
Stavies
Kommos
Listaros
Mátala
Loúkia
Vasilikí
Piyaidhákia
Ayíos Kirillos
Asterousia
1231m
Kófinas
Moni Odhiyitrias
Moni Ambezanon
Miamou
Kapetaniana
Krótos
Antiskari
Moni Koudhoumá
Lassaia
Kaloí Liménes
Platia Perámata
Papadhoyiánnis
Lebén
Léndas
Akrotiri Líthinon
A
B
C
1
2
3
4
5

FROM IRÁKLIO TO THE MESARÁS PLAIN

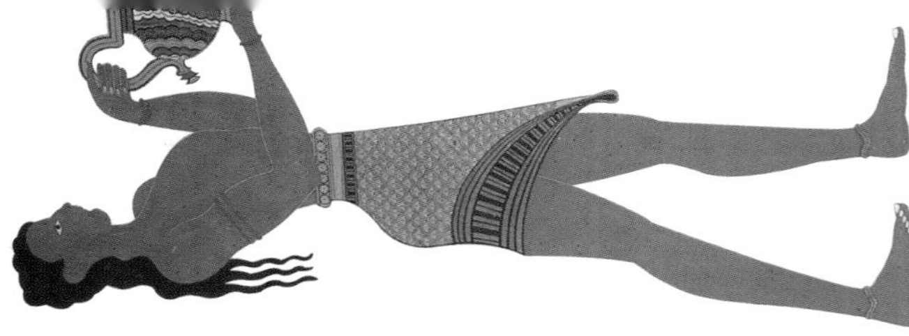

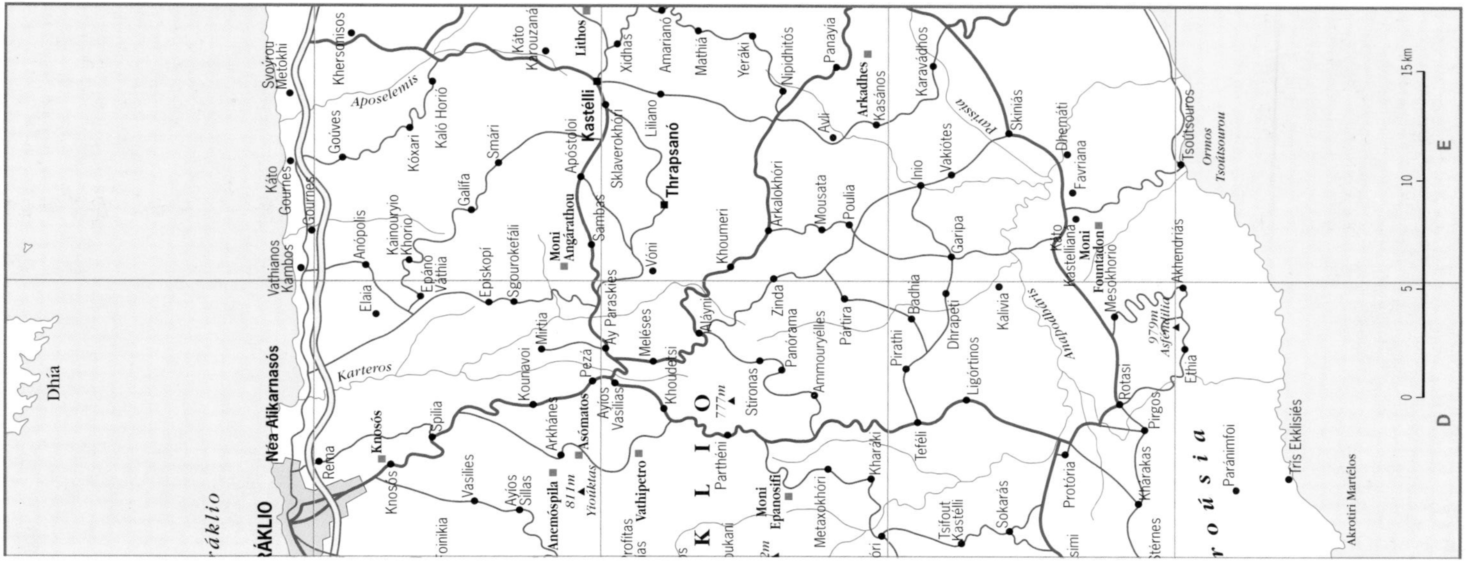

Looking back to Iráklio

From Iráklio to the Mesarás Plain There are more dramatic parts of Crete than this central section of the island. The west, for example, has the stark dignity of the White Mountains; the Réthimnon area looks south to Psiloritis and the higher peaks in Crete; Ayíos Nikólaos, bustling with holiday life, backs on to the wildly beautiful Dhíkti Mountains with the 10,000 windmills of the Lasíthiou Plateau at their heart. The big V-shaped slice of land that lies between Iráklio and the lonely coast south of the Mesarás plain has none of these striking features. This is a relatively low-lying landscape with attractive hills, a tract of pleasant, fertile country 40km wide and about the same deep, shouldered by the great mountain ranges of Psiloritis to the west and Dhíkti to the east. Only in the south does the land rise significantly. Here the long, narrow barrier of the Asteroúsia Mountains stands between the green fertility of the Mesarás olive and fruit groves, and the rocky solitude of the south coast with its terrible dirt roads, isolated hamlets and stretches of rarely visited beaches and bays. There is nothing particularly awe-inspiring about any of this, but the region works a subtle magic on anyone who idles here for a few days. This spell is composed of the crowd-free south coast, the smells of fruit and flowers, the unsophisticated pleasures of good local wine, easy-paced villages, vineyards and potato fields. Cretan life and landscape here is not much concerned with holidaymaking and caters mainly for local tastes and needs.

The region abounds in these unspecific delights of atmosphere and ambience. But there are particular archaeological and historical attractions to seek out. Crete's two best-known excavations of Minoan palaces are here: the seat of fabled King Minos and lair of the bull-headed Minotaur at Knosós is just south of Iráklio, and sprawling Faistós in its beautiful position above the Mesarás plain looks up the southern rise of the Psiloritis range to the dark mouth of the Kamáres cave. A mile or so from Faistós is the excavation of the Minoan summer palace at Ayía Triádha. And not far away are the extensive remains of the

Cicadas
The shrill, zithering sound of the cicada permeates all the country districts of Crete. If you can spot one of these greyish, long-bodied insects with its big wings folded like a tent across its back, notice that it doesn't, as many people believe, rub its legs together to produce that monotonous, soporific sound. In fact the noise comes from two tiny echo-chambers on the abdomen. Each contains a membrane, which the cicada vibrates with muscle spasms, thousands per minute. This is nature's own kazoo.

Dorian city of Górtina, where the olive groves are littered with fragments of columns and shards of pottery more than 2,000 years old. Further north is the Minoan country villa at Vathípetro where the winemaking equipment still survives intact, and the high and lovely peak sanctuary on the summit of Mount Yioúchtas is just outside Arkhánes. Near here, too, are wonderfully lively and intense early 14th-century frescoes in the little church of Ayíos Mikhaíl Arkhángelos, tucked away among the vineyards.

Iráklio city, of course, is the focus of the north coast of the region, along with the built-up holiday coast to the east with a seemingly unending ribbon of hotel and apartment, disco and beach bar development. But drive half an hour south and you will find yourself in the most peaceful and relaxing of landscapes, where traditional small-scale farming is carried on alongside local industries of pottery (around Thrapsanó) and winemaking (Arkhánes and Dhafnés).

The Mesarás plain runs parallel to the south coast, just north of the Asteroúsia Mountains, a fertile, well-watered and productive green basin, 48km from east to west where it reaches the Gulf of Mesarás. This is Crete's best agricultural land, with unattractive plastic greenhouses and the unmemorable towns of Moíres and Timbáki. The old saying that 'you can't eat scenery' applies hereabouts. Mesarás farmers are well-to-do and hardworking, and their landscape reflects their priorities.

As for the Asteroúsia Mountains – in all of Crete there are no lonelier hills, no rougher roads, no wilder stretches of coastline, no mountain more satisfying to climb than Kófinas, and no monastery more welcoming in its isolation than Koudhoumá.

Simple delights
Anything elaborate or delicate that you take on a picnic is liable to be melted or mashed after it has been bumped over dirt roads or mountain tracks. It is better to take a Cretan picnic: olives, cheese, hard bread, an orange and some water. You could dine more richly, but never with more relish than on these simple ingredients in their proper outdoor setting.

Uncommon seals
Sir Arthur Evans stumbled upon the secret of Knosós in truly romantic fashion. In an antiquarian shop in Athens in 1893 he bought some seals, inscribed with hieroglyphs, which had been dug up from the still-hidden palace site in Crete. Evans had recently inspected inscribed seals discovered during the excavation of Mycenae nearly 20 years before, and immediately saw the similarities in the two sets of inscriptions. The Mycenaean seals had come from an ancient civilisation, thought to be mythical but now proved by excavation to have actually existed, so might not Crete, too, be holding similarly exciting secrets?

Lifts
When you stop your car in a village, someone may well ask you for a lift a few miles up the road. If you agree to take them, don't be surprised if hospitality is offered at the other end.

The Mesarás plain

Olives, sheep and goats

■ **Plastic hothouses have proliferated along Crete's south coast in recent years, forcing vegetables for the export market. Most of Crete's agriculture is, however, still village-based, and a fair proportion of it is still carried out in traditional fashion: broadcasting seed by hand, horse-ploughing, irrigating with a bucket and hard labour.....■**

From extra virgin to blended, olive oil comes in many forms

Olives Of all Crete's agricultural produce the olive is clearly pre-eminent. As soon as you reach the countryside you will notice the olive groves: young trees dot the hillsides in regular rows, older groves spread their dull green cushions of foliage across valley floors and up the slopes. Olive oil and edible olives are a multi-billion-drachma

export operation, yet still a business that relies upon thousands of experienced individual village farmers. These people know each tree, its age, its bearing capacity and its state of health. Olives have been farmed here in Crete for over three thousand years, and in some of the remoter villages there are stone presses and storage jars still being used that a Mycenaean grower would recognise.

The tree is grown from olive stones or bits of root, and it may be 15 years before it produces fruit, but the tree may then bear fruit for many hundreds of years. A mature tree flowers in April, and the hard green olives appear in early summer. Tradition says that the oil starts to form on 20 May, the feast day of Profítas Ilías. In autumn, when the olives are black and becoming plump, large nets are laid out under the trees to catch windfalls. At Christmas the harvest begins, with sophisticated blowing or combing machines, or in the traditional way with the whole family beating and shaking the trees.

Wild olives
The original wild olive (*agría eliá*), forerunner of the present-day plump black fruit, is still to be found growing on Crete's hillsides, as it has done since before Minoan times. The wild olive's leaves are like little slips of privet, its fruit tiny and scarcely palatable. But it is a particular thrill to find it among Minoan remains, on a site where its ancestors may well have been cultivated by the Bronze Age bull-leapers.

At the oil mill, or in the family's stone press, the fruit is crushed, then pressed with hot water which runs off as a horrible black goo to pollute nearby streams. The first pressing goes for edible and cooking oil, and the second is turned into soap or fed to animals. What is left can be dried and burned as a pungent-smelling fuel. Excess wood from the tree itself is burned, or goes to the wood carver. Olive farming is virtually waste-free.

Sheep and goats Olive trees cannot be profitably grown on the higher slopes of the mountains. These wilder places are where the Cretan sheep and goats come into their own. They are hardy, skinny foragers, nimble climbers, voracious nibblers of anything tender and green, including the shoots of the sadly depleted native trees, which would regenerate quickly if there were no grazers on the mountains. But sheep and goats are the backbone of the Cretan upland economy. Shepherds still migrate to the high mountain pastures in early summer, living up there in *mitátos* or stone huts, in spartan and lonely conditions. In more fertile spots, such as on the Katharó plateau in the Dhíkti Mountains, they may be joined from time to time by their wives and children.

Lamb is the staple meat dish of Crete; goat is far less frequently on the menu. The best of the wool fetches high prices; the milk is turned into cheese, either in the stone huts by boiling in huge cauldrons and subsequent pressing in wicker baskets, or mechanically in the cheese factories of the lowlands. The crumbly white *féta* is familiar as a garnish on Greek salads, but each region has its own speciality, hard or soft, tangy or sweet.

Sheep or goats?
At first sight you may be hard put to it to distinguish between the Cretan goats and their mountain companions, the ragged-fleeced, bony sheep. Identification is easier at siesta time when the sun is high. However intermingled the two species become on the hillside, they separate into two distinct camps when the time comes to lie down and rest in the shade of the trees.

New residents take over an abandoned village

The belltower of the Church of Our Lady

► **Arkhánes** *73D4*

Arkhánes, 20km south of Iráklio, is the most important winemaking centre in the nome (administrative region) of Iráklio. The big wine-producing and bottling plant on the west side of Arkhánes employs most of the villagers. The vineyard-owners have formed themselves into the very effective Minos Co-operative, which dominates the economic life of the area. There is no industrial grimness or indifference about Arkhánes, however. This is a friendly place, proud of its excellent product, with most of its social life revolving around the *platía* at the southern end of the village where you can sample the Arkhánes wine by the bottle, or more cheaply by the jugful.

The snack bar Myriophytó, on the right as you go south through the square, holds the key to the **Church of Ayíos Mikhaíl Arkhángelos►►►** at Asómatos, whose beautiful 14th-century frescoes are a treat not to be missed. Your passport will be requested as a deposit. After 1km on the Vathípetro road, turn left halfway along a straight stretch between vineyards, onto a rough road. In 1.5km the road dips and bends left over a watercourse. The church is down to the left under two tall trees. A vivid Archangel Michael stands with drawn sword on the south wall; old men blow trumpets to demolish the walls of Jericho; demons ride beasts among severed limbs; an agonising Crucifixion has the angels covering their eyes and St John cupping his hanging head with one hand in a gesture of ineffable sorrow.

A further 3km along the Vathípetro road, a right turn, signposted to Yioúchtas, leads by a rough zigzag road to the 811m summit of **Mount Yioúchtas**▶▶ and a wide view over the mountains of the Psiloritis and Dhíkti ranges, the whole of Iráklio, a vast tract of wrinkled countryside, and a patchwork of olive groves and vineyards. A ridge connects two spurs at the summit of the mountain, and local legend suggests that Zeus may have been buried here. On the southern peak are the Church of Aféndis Christós with four apses and numerous icons of varying solemnity, and a tall wooden cross studded with electric lights. A paved path leads to the northern summit, where a radar station stands beside the fenced and locked site of a Minoan peak sanctuary. Big squared stone blocks form the walls that support several layers of terracing. There is a ceremonial space below a hollow in the rocks spanned by the massive slabs of an altar. Hundreds of items offered to the gods by Minoan pilgrims and priests, and by later worshippers, have been unearthed from the space beneath the altar, including figures of humans and animals, bones of sacrifices and fragments of ceremonial vessels. It is a pity that the wire fence and padlocked gates prevent visitors from exploring this site at closer quarters.

To the northwest of Arkhánes, on the lower northeastern slopes of Mount Yioúchtas, lie the remains of the temple at **Anemóspila**, whose excavation brought to light remains that have raised the possibility of human sacrifice among the Minoans. An earthquake around 1700BC entombed four bodies here: a priest and priestess, a man curled up on an altar with an inscribed bronze knife on top of his body, and another man who had been carrying a ritual vessel. Was it full of the blood of the man on the altar, shed to propitiate the earthquake spirit that buried the celebrants at the same time as it wrecked the old palaces of the Minoans all over the island?

Locked out
Many of Crete's historic sites are kept locked, even those as relatively unvisited as the peak sanctuary on Mount Yioúchtas. Finding a padlock between you and your objective is frustrating, particularly after a long, hot climb. But it is worth remembering that excavation and exploration are still taking place periodically on most sites, work which can be ruined by a carelessly placed boot or the unthinking pocketing of ancient fragments as souvenirs.

▶ Arkalokhóri *73E3*

Southwest of Arkhánes, Arkalokhóri is a large, busy and friendly village, the centre of a widespread country district of vineyards, olive groves and vegetable fields. The village is also the gateway to the Dhíkti mountain range which rises dramatically to the east.

Looking back to Arkhánes from Mount Yioúchtas

Ayía Triádha Minoan Summer Palace

Key to the map
1 shops
2 bastion/warehouse
3 Minoan house
4 shrine
5 eastern forecourt
6 reception rooms
7 *Rampa del Mare*
8 storerooms
9 loggia
10 treasury
11 archives/fresco room
12 hall

▶▶▶ Ayía Triádha Minoan Summer Palace *72A2*

Ayiá Triádha, open daily 8:30–3, stands 3km west of the Minoan palace of Faistós (see pages 82–3), looking down over the Gulf of Mesarás where the Yeropótamos River empties into the sea between long headlands. This wonderful view may have been even better around 1570BC when the Minoans were building here, for then the sea probably came much nearer to the rise of ground where Ayiá Triádha stands. Ayiá Triádha was an important complex. It may well have been a summer or alternative residence for the rulers or chief priests of Faistós, and was certainly an influential centre of administration in southern Crete.

The Minoans built a road to connect Faistós with Ayiá Triádha. Technically this is in use as a footpath today, running around the north side of the hill between the two sites, but obscure signposting and locked gates make it a doubtful proposition.

The palace (actually something between a minor palace and an extremely grand villa) was built as a number of linked areas, connected but able to function independently. It probably only stood intact for about 120 years, before being flattened in the 1450BC disaster – earthquake, tidal wave, insurrection, volcanic eruption or some cataclysmic combination of these – that destroyed the great palaces at Faistós, Mália and Zákros. But Ayía Triádha was reoccupied a couple of hundred years later,

The Minoan Palace of Ayía Triádha – still popular in summer

the town on the slopes below was rebuilt and large new buildings were put up among the ruins of the Minoan palace. In Dorian times, during the first millennium BC, there were successive shrines here. Later the Byzantine church and associated village of Ayía Triádha occupied a site just to the southwest of the palace remains.

Walk down steps from the car park, through the site gate and down more steps, then bear left to the open space of the upper courtyard just below the 14th-century church of Ayíos Yeóryios at the top of the site. From here there is a good overview of the palace layout in front of you with the northeast wing of the palace to your right, the west wing to the left, kitchens and storerooms further round to the west. Beyond the east wing the ruins of the town lie down the slope.

Pass the west end of the church, noting the variety of crucifix forms inscribed in its walls, and bear right through the shells of the storerooms to reach the grand apartments in the northwestern corner of the palace, enjoying a fine sea view and cool sea breezes. Right in the centre is the room where excavators disinterred the superb frescoes, including the famous one of cats concealing themselves in bushes to stalk birds, which are now in the Iráklio Archaeological Museum. The inner angle of the palace here had two storeys and was probably used for entertaining visitors. This was where the brilliantly carved black steatite vases and libation vessels of the elated harvesters, the flattened boxer, and the haughty chieftain were found. They are now in Room VII of the Iráklio Archaeological Museum.

The paved Minoan roadway dubbed *Rampa del Mare*, the Sea Road, by the Italian excavators of Ayiá Triádha ran to the north of the palace wall. To the east, under the modern roof, is a group of rooms where you can sit and appreciate the coolness of the alabaster and gypsum lining slabs, and consider the ingenuity of the post-catastrophe rebuilders of Ayía Triádha who supplied water and took away sewage through a remarkable spillway of grooved stone between the floors of the palace.

There were no such refinements in the town, though there were basins with outlets in some of the houses which lie to the west of the market place with its pillars and portico. You can walk on the walls, above a maze of dark alleyways, speculating on the cramped, dirty, smelly, noisy and intimate lives they must have seen.

Fine frescoes
The fresco painters of Ayía Triádha seem to have developed the science of preserving paint to a higher level than those at Knosós. The blues, yellows and reds in the *Cat and Birds* and the *Lady in the Garden* still look astonishingly rich, while the pictures themselves are just about the finest yet unearthed for detail and subtlety of execution. The remaining fragments are on view in Room XIV of the Iráklio Archaeological Museum.

The carved black soapstone Harvester Vase

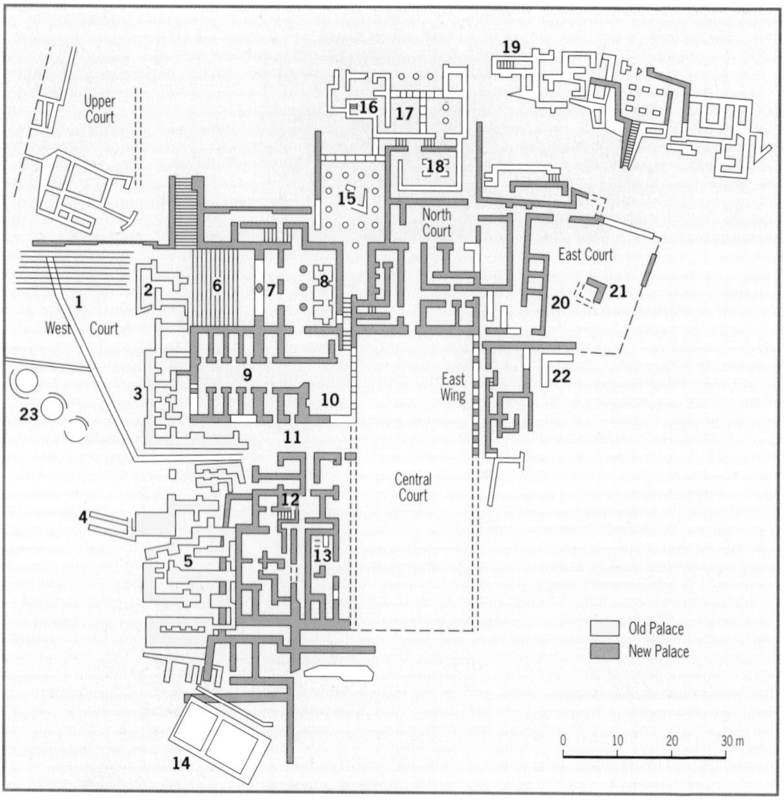

Upper Court
West Court
North Court
East Court
East Wing
Central Court
1 2 3 4 5 6 7 8 9 10 11 12 13 14 15 16 17 18 19 20 21 22 23
Old Palace
New Palace
0 10 20 30 m

The Minoan palace of Faistós

The Faistós Disc, now in Iráklio's Archaeological Museum

▶▶▶ Faistós 72A1

The Minoan palace of Faistós (open 8–7, Saturdays and Sundays 8:30–7) lies just south of the Iráklio–Timbáki road, 8km west of Moíres. It is badly signposted, but when you reach the top of the side road you won't mistake the sight, which is visible from the main road. It sits on a great knoll, overlooking the fertile green valley of Mesarás covered with the grey squares and rectangles of stone walling. Faistós is the most dramatically sited of Crete's Minoan palaces, looking across the plain to the distant blue outlines of the Psiloritis mountain range and the dark hole of the Kamáres cave which can be seen clearly between two horn-like peaks.

Homer mentioned Faistós in the *Iliad* as a populous city, but it had declined a long way by then from the power it had wielded over southern Crete when the palace was in its heyday around 1500BC. The New Palace, the remains of which are largely what you see on the hilltop, was built in c. 1700BC on the original foundations of an older palace which had been three times destroyed by earthquakes, and three times rebuilt. The New Palace, in its turn, was flattened c. 1450BC, in the calamity that destroyed

the settlements at nearby Ayía Triádha, at Gourniá, Zákros and the other major Minoan sites on Crete.

The layout of Faistós is confusing to the uninitiated, the difficulties compounded by the absence of labelling or explanatory notices. As with all these Minoan palatial sites the best plan is to make for the big central court, from which you can get your bearings without too much trouble. To start your tour, however, descend the steps from the entrance gate and bear diagonally left across an uneven area, then down more steps, to turn right into the west court. Cross the court and turn round to face the Psiloritis mountains. To your left are circular storage pits, and to your right the grand stairway, up which you walk into the *propylon*, a verandah-style porchway and light well once supported on columns, the round bases of which are still there.

Go diagonally right and down some steps, then turn right into a square office room where records would have been kept of the goods held in the long, narrow storerooms beyond. These are provided with hollowed out receptacles which would have held differently-shaped storage vessels. In the first chamber stands a dusty *píthos,* which looks as if it could very easily crumble into its component shards.

Now walk back through the office room into the central court, savouring the views of Psiloritis to the north, and the far range of the Asteroúsia Mountains to the south beyond the Mesarás plain. The Kamáres cave is clearly visible on the upper flanks of Psiloritis, and the fields of Mesarás look green and well-watered, contrasting with the dark spires of poplars standing alongside the white and dusty roads.

Two *píthoi* stand next to the pillars that mark the north doorway of the central court. Walk through the doorway and along a cool stone passage to pass the colonnaded peristyle hall on your left, then descend stairs to the king's and queen's apartments on the left, sheltered by modern roofs of concrete and plastic. The hall and apartments were sited to catch the best views, and the cool mountain breezes.

Reaching the trees at the northern edge of the site, turn right and walk along the palace walls, past a run of tiny chambers built of mud brick. In 1903 the excavators found the Faistós Disc in one of them. A little flat circle of baked clay only 16cm across and dating from about 1700BC, it is stamped with a spiral pattern of symbols half pictorial and half geometric, obviously writing of some kind, which has yet to be deciphered. It is now in Room III of Iráklio Archaeological Museum.

Turn right at the end across the pillared court of a house and walk up the steps, bearing right in order to return to the central court.

Key to the map on page 82
1 theatre area
2 shrine complex
3 west façade
4 ramp
5 shops
6 grand stairway
7 propylaeum
8 lightwell
9 storeroom block
10 pillared hall
11 corridor
12 lustral basin
13 pillar crypt
14 temple of Rhea
15 peristyle hall
16 lustral basin
17 king's apartments
18 queen's apartments
19 archives
20 workshops
21 furnace
22 colonnaded court
23 storage pits (cisterns)

Faistós wit
Faistós people were reputed to be the wittiest in Crete. Unfortunately none of their gems has come down to us. Perhaps, when the Faistós Disc is finally deciphered, a few rib-ticklers will be brought to light. The oldest jokes, they say, are the best ones, and these will have been maturing for 3,500 years.

Wise judge
King Mínos is said to have installed his brother Rhadamanthys, revered for his wisdom and honesty, as ruler of Faistós. Rhadamanthys was also appointed arbitrator of all legal wrangles among Minos's subjects, and travelled to Knosós to exercise these judgements.

■ Cretans like to drink, at the right time and in the right company, though they are fairly abstemious during the day. Not every glass of colourless liquid on a *kafeníon* table contains a killer dose of ferocious local spirit, as some travellers' tales would have you believe.....■

***Rakí* rub**
Rakí, also known as *tsikoudhiá,* is not only the drink that holds social life together in Crete, it is also recommended by the wise men and women of the mountains as a specific for chest colds, liberally applied as an external rub, and internally in the usual way.

Aqua pura In fact, the taller the glass the more likely it is to contain nothing more heady than water. Spring water from the mountains is probably the most delicious drink on the island. Places like Záros have made a good living out of bottling and selling their water, which is exported far and wide. A glass of water comes *gratis* with meals and coffee. A compliment on the local water is usually received with pleasure.

Alcohol For the harder stuff Cretans tend to stick to three tried and tested drinks: wine, beer and *rakí.* The further inland and the higher you go, the more courtesies will accompany drinking. There is likely to be a clinking of glasses together or knocking them on the table, accompanied by '*iss-i-yián*', 'your health', or '*iss-i-yámas*', 'health to us'. Elaborate *mezédes* or nibbles may well be served too. Taking a drink with a friend or casual acquaintance is an unhurried affair, as much a matter of social ritual as of refreshment.

Wine Cretan wine has been celebrated for many centuries. Minoan, Mycenaean and Hellenic winemaking equipment has been found at several archaeological sites in the island. The press, vat and cleaning apparatus at the villa at Vathípetro near Arkhánes is particularly well preserved. When the Portuguese planted Madeira with vines in the 15th century, it was to Crete that they turned for their supplies. The Malmsey wine that was drunk across medieval Europe came from Crete.

The Greek for wine is *krasí.* There are three varieties: *mávro* (red), *áspro* (white), and *kókkino* (rosé). *Retsína*, the Greek white wine flavoured with resin that tastes to the uninitiated like a distillation of old violin bows, is not traditionally a Cretan drink, though it has been making a steady advance in recent years in response to the expectations of tourists. There are several decent bottled wines available on the island. Mínos is the most widely distributed thanks to the power of the well-organised co-operative, based at Arkhánes, that produces it.

Mínos, one of the best known of Cretan wines

However, the ordinary village wine is cheaper, stronger, much more characterful and complementary to the heavy, oily taste of Cretan cooking. Traditionally it is sold by weight rather than volume, the customer ordering a half-kilo or kilo rather than a half-litre or litre. This, too, is changing as international standards and manners invade the island, and most restaurants now sell it by volume. It comes either in glass *carafes* or in metallic-pink jugs. A request for red usually produces a thick, cloudy, rose-tinted wine, drawn from a plastic barrel, with a heavy, sherry-like taste. It is unsophisticated, but effective. Restaurant owners are proud of their local wines which often originate in their own village. Wines from Dhafnés, south of Iráklio, and from the Moulianá villages just west of Sitiá, are especially well thought of.

Beer and *rakí* Beer-drinking is a recent, imported fashion. There are no specially recommended brews, but Henninger and Amstel, brewed under licence in Greece, are worth a try as a variation from the universal Heineken.

Oúzo is the traditional Greek spirit, a distillation from the mush of skin, pips and stalks left behind after wine-making, flavoured with aniseed, and drunk either neat or with water. Cretans prefer *rakí*, the same spirit without the aniseed and with more power, drunk neat from tiny glasses. In the west of Crete it is known as *tsikoudiá*. Cretans claim many beneficial properties for *rakí*, as an aphrodisiac, a soothing rub and a specific against all ills. The taste is hard to describe, but quite unmistakable. It burns all the way down, and one glass leads to another.

Rough wine
Wine (*krasí*) made locally and sold from the barrel was traditionally ordered by the kilo and half-kilo, rather than by the litre and half-litre, although the word *carafe* is nearly universally understood in today's tavernas. In any case, it will probably come to the table in a battered, pink tin jug, the official wine measure of Crete.

Neat spirit
Rakí and Greek coffee compliment each other as felicitously as do brandy and French coffee, but Cretans tend to take them separately. A *rakí*, on-the-house, at the end of a restaurant meal is a very pleasant and widespread custom.

Many Cretan wine barrels are made from oak; retsína, made using pine casks, is more of a mainland tradition

Fruitful plane
One of the plane trees at Górtina is reputed never to shed its leaves. If you visit in midwinter and find it, you will not be the first. Legend has it that under this tree, Zeus disguised as an eagle had his lordly way with Europa, a union that produced three sons: Rhadamanthys, Sarpedon and Minos.

Waterworks
The *praetorium* was the terminus of the great aqueduct system that brought water to Górtina all the way from the mountain springs at present-day Záros, 10km to the north, a notable feat of engineering.

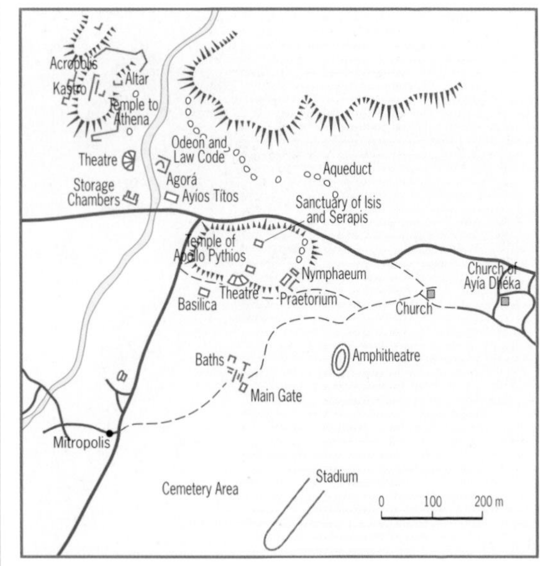

▶▶▶ Górtina *72B2*

Your imagination will work overtime as you wander around the enormous, rambling site where the mighty city of Górtina (open 8:30–3, closed Monday) once stood. Walls, columns, pavements, baths, a theatre and even basilicas bear witness to Górtina's influence over the best part of 2,000 years. Who knows what may still lie under the bean fields and olive groves?

The site lies 6km east of Míres, about half way along the northern edge of the Mesarás plain, on the main road from Iráklio. The fertility of Mesarás made it the natural location for an important city, and by the 5th century BC what had been a small Minoan settlement had expanded into a flourishing city under Dorian rule. By 200BC Górtina had usurped the rôle of Faistós as the most influential city in southern Crete, and after the Roman invasion of 65BC it became the capital of the island and the centre of power for much of Egypt and North Africa. St Titus, despatched by St Paul to Crete to convert the islanders to Christianity, set up his bishopric here. During the first Byzantine occupation of the island Górtina continued to expand and prosper, right up until 824 when invading Saracens sacked the city. Partial reoccupation followed and some rebuilding, notably of the 6th-century basilica of Ayíos Títos, where the saint was buried, but most of the city remained a ruin.

A good way to explore the site is to start in the village of Ayía Dhéka, just east of Górtina. The church contains a magnificent old icon of the martyrdom of ten Cretan Christians in AD250. Below it is the stone slab on which they were executed, deeply

A tangled toga or a sling?

The once-roofed theatre at Górtina

indented with the imprints of their knees. From the west end of the church a lane leads to a low-walled footpath. Bear right to reach a red-domed chapel. Under the west end, in a gated crypt, are the tombs of the martyrs. Continue through the olive groves among fallen stone columns and outlines of walls, to pass the fenced site of the Roman governor's palace or *praetorium* with fluted, smooth or elaborately carved columns, and great walls of Roman brickwork.

Continue around the perimeter of the site, and at the first right bend keep straight on, south, through the olive groves for five minutes to find the Roman amphitheatre, big blocks of masonry around a hollow depression. Pottery shards lie all around: jug rims and handles, curves and discs of broken vessels. Returning, you pass the big, tiled heating chambers and stone-built rooms of the Roman baths, and the temple of Apollo Pythios with its welter of fallen columns. Make due north to reach the main road, turn left for 300m, and pay a small fee to enter the part of the site that lies north of the road.

The big *bema* or apse of the 6th-century AD basilica of Ayíos Títos stands here, beautifully preserved. From the northwest corner of the church foundations follow the fence through the *agora* or forum, now thickly grown with olive trees, to the odeon, once a roofed theatre, with encircling square pillars of brick and a semicircle of bevelled benches. Beyond stands a modern, crescent-shaped building that protects the most important of Górtina's many remains, a series of big stone blocks inscribed in about 500BC with amendments to Dorian law. Written in script that runs left to right, then right to left in succeeding lines, the laws deal with rape, inheritance arrangements, divorce, allocation of property, adultery, assault and the rights of adopted children. The blocks were found by chance in 1884, when the nearby mill stream was drained.

Above and behind the odeon is the acropolis of Górtina, with the remains of a Dorian temple to Athena, a Roman hall or *kastro*, and a mass of retaining walls.

Pocket history?
To pocket or not to pocket the shards of Cretan history? Temptation is never stronger than at Górtina, where millions of pieces of pottery, most of it clumsy workaday stuff of no particular merit, lie tumbled across the fields and olive groves. But only experts can distinguish the extraordinary from the ordinary. The jug handle or piece of bowl rim that you take away with you might just be the fragment that, in other hands, could unlock a door to greater understanding.

Walk Ambeloúzos to Zarós

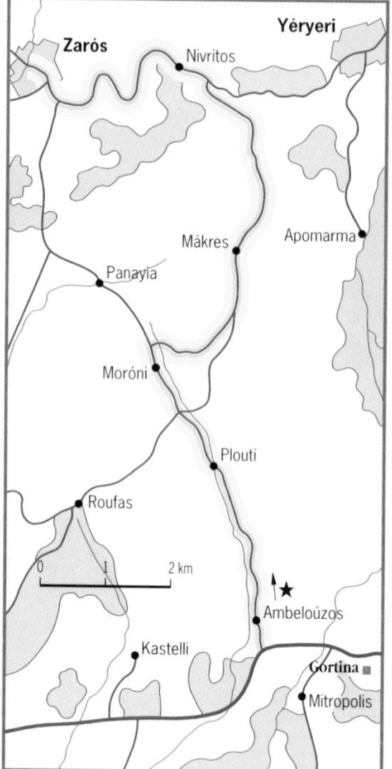

This is quite an easy walk from the Mesarás plain to Zarós in the foothills of Psiloritis, following a dirt road through a slowly changing landscape (11 km, allow 2½–3 hours).

Many of Crete's old dirt roads, recently by-passed by new tarmac highways, have become ideal, traffic-free footpaths. This walk takes you from the Mesarás plain up through a string of seldom visited villages to Zarós below the majestic upsweep of Psilorítis, following a wide but stony old route that has been superseded by the new road which rushes directly from Moíres to Zarós.

The walk begins in the village of Ambeloúzos, reached by a turning to the right off the main Moíres road 1km to the west of Górtina. Ambeloúzos is a typical small Mesarás village, with farmers' motorised tricycle pick-ups parked along its streets. Turn right half-way through the village onto the Zarós road, which quickly sheds its tarmac in favour of stones and dust. You soon leave the fruit and vegetable lushness of Mesarás behind, and climb gently into a less well-regulated landscape of rock, scrub and olive groves. Flocks of grazing sheep and goats make their appearance, and you can practice your Greek greetings on the shepherds who use the road, their crooked sticks cradled behind their necks.

The road climbs for 4km through Ploutí and Moróní, tiny villages where your arrival will provoke stares and nodded acknowledgement. At Moróni you can join the new road for a fast but busy 4km to Zarós. A better alternative is to turn right here for 4km more of rough road though Mákres to the Ayía Varvára–Zarós road at Nivritos, where you turn right to reach Zarós. The big village at the foot of the mountains has plenty of tavernas. Try the local trout, and the water which has been famous since it supplied Górtina 2,000 years ago, now bottled and exported all over Greece.

The mountain village of Kapetanianá – see opposite

►► Kapetanianá 73C1

Kapetanianá, lodged high in the Asteroúsia Mountains southeast of Moíres, is certainly nobody's idea of a tourist village. The dirt road leading up to it from the Mesarás plain, rough and winding, seems to emphasise its isolation from the better-favoured villages lower down. The Kapetanianá villagers rely on sheep and small vegetable plots for their living. The houses, most of them one-roomed, slope downhill along narrow footways to the church of Panayía. The key is kept at one of the nearby houses. The frescoes of 1401 include, on the north wall, one of Christ bending to help Adam out of the grave, and another of a calm and dignified Saviour entering Jerusalem on a donkey. On the south wall, with graffiti dating back to 1589, there is a Baptism. And from the dome of the apse the Virgin stares down gravely.

The black-garbed older women of Kapetanianá could have stepped out of one of these frescoes. In the evening their menfolk in head fringes sit in the *kafeníon*. Kapetanianá, however, has not been wholly deserted by its younger people, unlike many of Crete's mountain villages.

The village is the starting point for the strenuous walk to the 1,231m summit of Mount Kófinas (see pages 106–7).

Place names
An enquiry into the meanings of place names will often throw interesting light on a locality. For example, Mount Kófinas near Kapetanianá means 'big basket mountain'. The mountain does look like a basket upside down. And the name of the whole mountain range, Asteroúsia, reflects the clear atmosphere above these tall peaks. It means 'near the stars'.

►► Koudhoumá Monastery 73C1

Many of Crete's monasteries are on lonely parts of the coast, but Koudhoumá must be one of the loneliest. The Asteroúsia Mountains rear inland of Koudhoumá, cutting it off from contact with the populous Mesarás plain. You can drop down to it on foot in two hours from Mount Kófinas, or drive down the tortuous and primitive road from Paránimfoi and Trís Ekklisiés.

At the base of the mountain there is a cluster of red-roofed buildings, a 19th-century church of no particular merit, the hospitable abbot (his *rakí* bites hard) and a few monks in blue, working overalls. A small sandy beach, sheltered by the rocky headland of Akrotíri Martélos, lies just beyond.

The lonely monastery of Koudhoumá

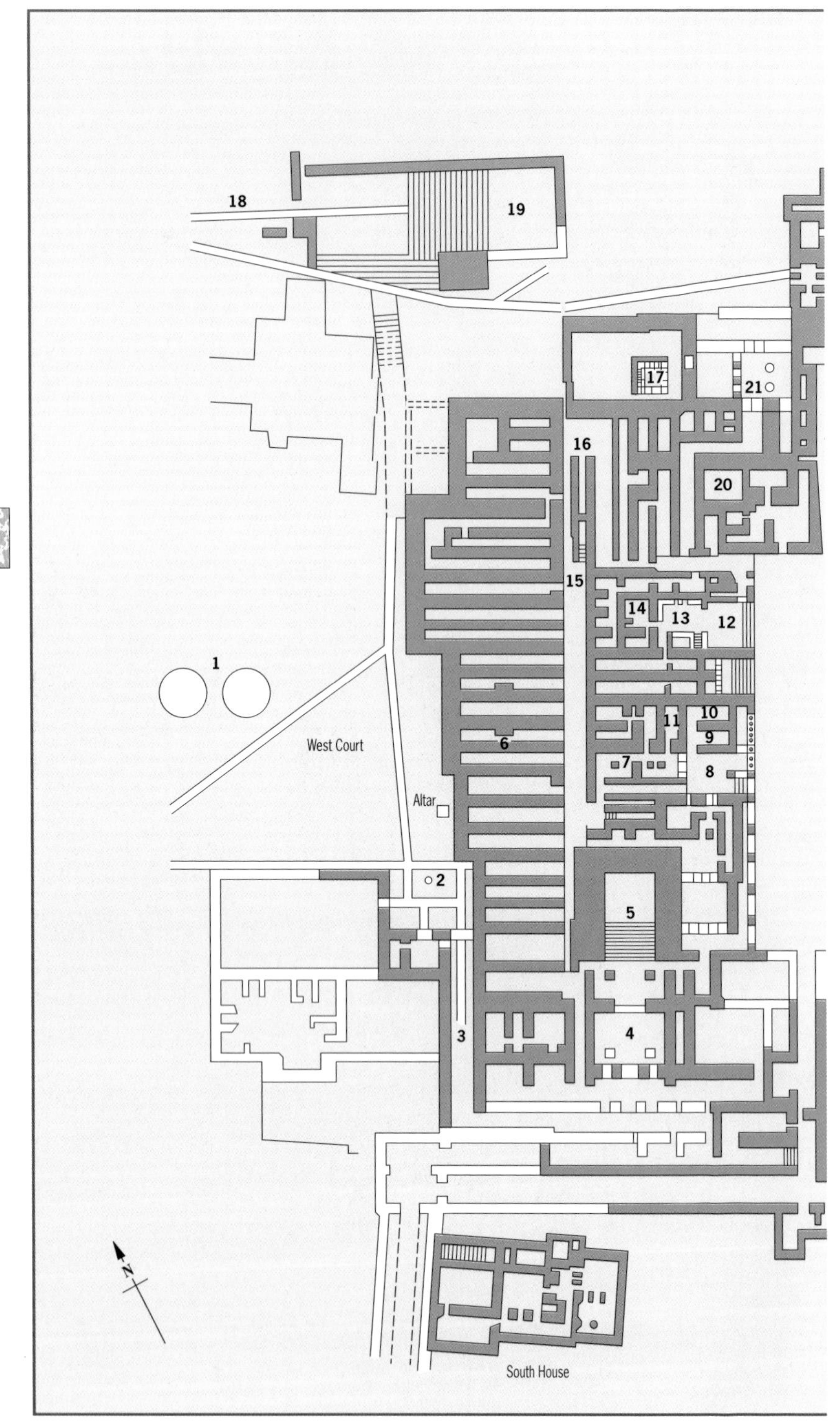
18
19
17
21
16
20
15
14
13
12
1
11
10
9
West Court
6
7
8
Altar
2
5
4
3
N
South House

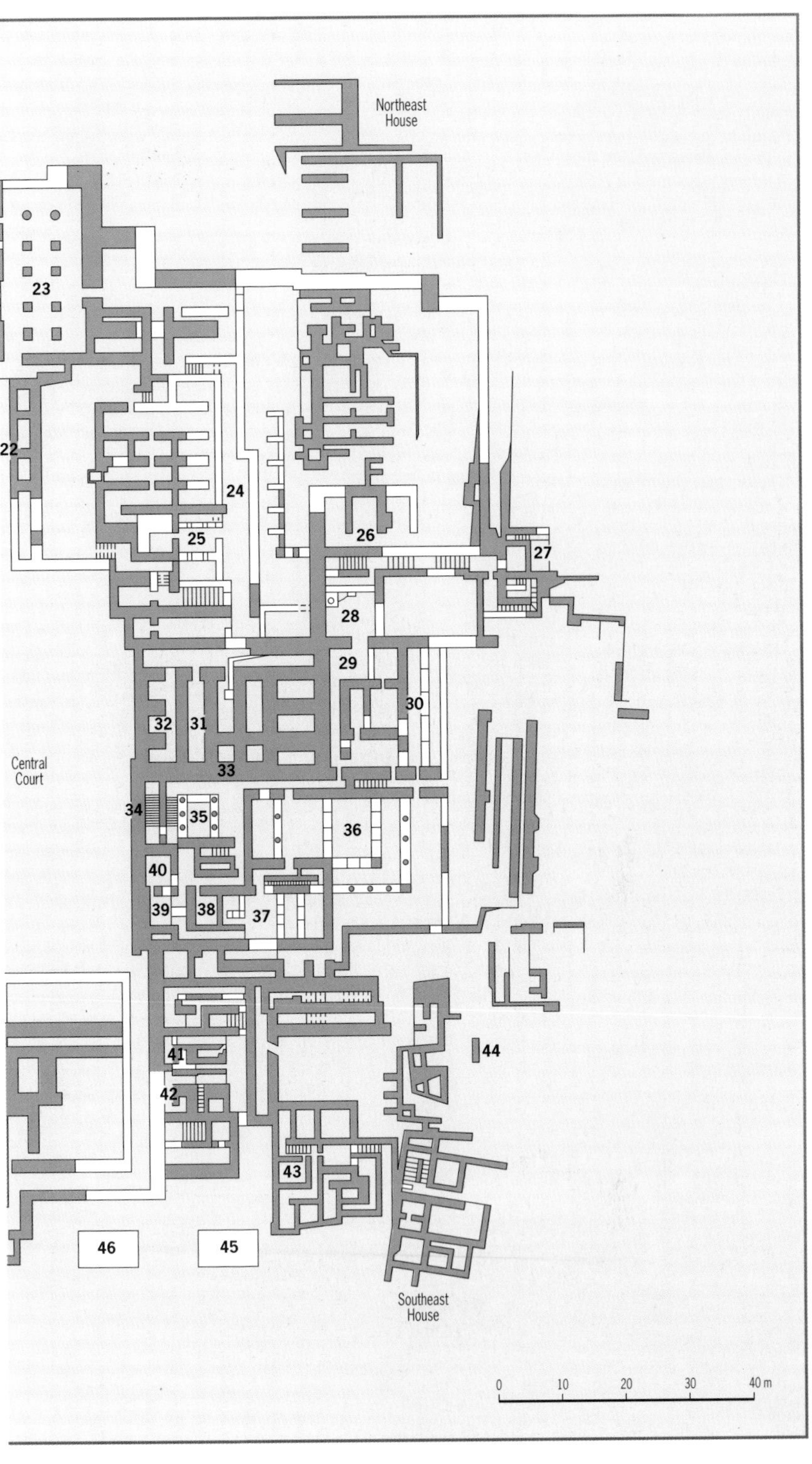

Northeast House
23
22
24
25
26
27
28
29
30
Central Court
32
31
33
34
35
36
40
39
38
37
44
41
42
43
46
45
Southeast House
0
10
20
30
40 m

Key to map on pages 90–1
1 walled pits
2 west porch
3 corridor of the procession fresco
4 south propylaeum
5 staircase to *piano nobile*
6 lower storeroom block
7 pillar crypts
8 room of the column bases
9 room of the tall *pithos*
10 temple repository
11 vat room
12 antechamber
13 throne room
14 inner sanctuary
15 lower long corridor
16 deposit of tablets
17 lustral basin
18 royal road
19 theatre area
20 old keep
21 northwest portico
22 north entrance passage
23 pillar hall
24 corridor of the draughts board
25 northeast hall
26 magazines of giant *pithoi*
27 east bastion
28 court of the stork spout
29 craftsman's workshop
30 east portico
31 magazine of the medallion *pithoi*
32 corridor of the bays
33 east–west corridor
34 grand staircase
35 hall of the colonnades
36 hall of the double axes (king's megaron)
37 queen's megaron
38 bathroom
39 toilet
40 court of the distaffs
41 shrine of the double axes
42 corridor of sword tablets
43 house of chancel screen
44 Minoan kiln
45 house of the fallen blocks
46 house of sacrificed oxen

Tall píthoi

▶▶▶ (Palace of) Knosós *73D4*

The Minoan palace at Knosós is deservedly Crete's premier tourist attraction, the one place that even a day visitor to the island will be certain not to miss. This is not to say that the site pleases everyone. It is often unpleasantly crowded with guided tours. As with all the well-known Minoan sites, an early morning visit is recommended. Controversy still rumbles on over the partial rebuilding of the palace by its original excavator, the English archaeologist Sir Arthur Evans, using conjecture to shore up research. But a tour of Knosós (open Monday–Friday 8–7; Saturday, Sunday and holidays 8:30–3; winter 10–sunset) is essential for a better understanding of the other great Minoan palaces of Crete, which can seem to be a wilderness of unlabelled stone walls if you have not first had your imagination tuned in here. The best-known of Cretan myths is focused on this little knoll above the olive groves. The desperate adventure of Prince Theseus took place in the labyrinth beneath the palace of cruel King Minos, as the hero fought and conquered the bull-headed Minotaur.

When Sir Arthur Evans unearthed the palace at the turn of the century, what had been a fantasy was suddenly seen to be rooted in fact. A vast and intricate maze of rooms and passageways came to light. Bull's-head vases, bull's-horn roof decorations, a royal throne room, a fabulous treasure of jewellery, and brilliantly coloured and executed frescoes showed a vibrant, warm-blooded and sophisticated society in full flourish. Evans, who had long suspected that something special lay underground at Knosós, bought the site as soon as Turkish occupation of Crete ended in 1898, and struck the palace ruins immediately after beginning excavations in 1900.

The problem Evans had to solve was how to preserve material that was liable to fall apart after having been interred for the best part of 3,000 years. As he owned the site, and was using his own money to finance the excavations, he felt he had the right to do as he thought best. Reconstruction would at least put everything roughly where he thought it had originally stood, and would give a fair picture of how the palace had probably looked. Authenticity undoubtedly suffered from Evans's over-liberal use of concrete and perhaps over-optimistic shaping of some of the upper storeys. But better, surely, that so much should have been preserved this way than that it should have disappeared altogether.

What one sees today, fragmentary though it is with upper rooms opening onto air, flights of stairs ending nowhere, roofless halls and stark, empty chambers, is chiefly the remains of the second or new palace, constructed around 1700BC after an earthquake had destroyed the old palace, itself built three hundred years earlier. Knosós was the powerful capital of Crete in those days, the nerve centre of a Bronze Age civilisation which Evans named 'Minoan' after its most famous king. The disastrous event of c. 1450BC – experts disagree as to whether it was another earthquake, a tidal wave or an attack

The fresco of the coquettish Ladies in Blue

by invaders or insurrectionists – that destroyed most of the other Minoan palaces and settlements on the island seems to have affected the palace at Knosós only marginally. There was a fire and extensive damage, but the palace and its associated town continued to be used and to be a centre of influence throughout Crete for at least another seven or eight hundred years.

A tour of the palace begins at the entrance kiosk on the well-signposted road 5km south of Iráklio. Here you can join one of the continuous guided tours which is a good idea if you want to be sure not to miss anything. But a couple of hours wandering around the site on your own will give you an excellent idea of the sheer scale and sophistication of the layout.

From the entrance gate you approach the palace across the wide west court, an open area for public markets or meetings in Minoan days. Just beyond the statue of Sir Arthur Evans, bear left to walk through the palace entrance and on into the enormous central court, some 55m by 30m, a feature of all Minoan palaces and a focus for the entire complex. The view down the valley from here is a fine one. Far below are the remains of what may have been an arena where the famous Minoan bull-leaping displays took place.

At the northwestern corner of the court is the throne room, where Minos and the other priest-kings of Knosós would have performed their rituals. Just inside is a stone throne above a sunken lustral or purification basin, and in an inner chamber a copy of the wooden throne supposed to have been used by Minos himself. Stairs nearby lead to the upper storey rather speculatively reconstructed by Evans and named by him the *piano nobile*, where you will find reproductions of some of the best-known Knosós frescoes, including the celebrated bull-leaping scene now in the Iráklio Archaeological Museum.

From the east side of the central court the grand staircase leads down to the austere king's apartments, and below them the queen's apartments where excavators found a magnificent fresco of leaping dolphins, a bath tub and a lavatory, flushed by jars of water. The queen probably bathed in a glutinous mixture of ass's milk and honey. From here you can work your way north around the edge of the palace, past rows of workshops full of enormous *píthoi* or storage jars, and back along the top of the complex to tread the paved royal road that runs in a stone-sided gully past the massive walls of houses and the huge cut blocks of the palace foundations.

Light in the dark

Knosós would have been a dark and dismal place to live, huddled together as it was in massed clusters of small rooms built of heavy, cold stone, if it had not been for the ingenuity of the Minoan architects in bringing in light from the outside by way of the many light-wells which reflected daylight into dark corners. All the same, the palace's chief source of internal light was the naked flame of torch and lamp, with all the attendant risks of disastrous fires which did, indeed, devastate Knosós and every other Minoan palace.

Palace that grew

The labyrinthine construction of Knosós, notwithstanding the Minos legend, was the result not of planning but of centuries of gradual growth as rooms, courtyards, workshops and houses were added. Nikos Kazantzákis declared that Knosós was a place where fantasy and creativity were expressed, a palace which 'grew like a living organism, like a tree'. A very apt description.

Development is creeping round the bay at Léndas

►► Léndas *72B1*

From Górtina, on the main Moíres–Ayía Dhéka road through the Mesarás plain, a good tarmac road brings you south towards Léndas. From Apesokári it wriggles and twists 23km down to a little holiday village, which appears below you as a sprinkle of white and peach-coloured buildings packed into a recess of the coastline under the eastern flank of the bulbous, craggy Cape Léndas, the Cape of the Lion. The other routes into Léndas are rough and difficult dirt tracks but now that this road has been improved the village is gradually growing into one of the better-known small resorts on the south coast of Crete. There are plenty of rooms to rent and a number of restaurants along the pebbly beach. Léndas is a ramshackle kind of place, with nothing smart about it, and it is too remote to attract large numbers of visitors to stay, though there are plenty of day trippers in high summer. It is at its best early or late in the season. There are excellent beaches a short but boneshaking drive to the west, at and beyond Papadhoyiánnis, and more within walking distance along the roadless coast to the east. The slanting heights of the Asteroúsia mountains behind the resort add drama to its setting.

It must have been a long and difficult journey carrying goods inland to Górtina from this remote bit of coast two thousand years ago, when Léndas, then called Lebéna, was the port for the flourishing Graeco–Roman city in the Mesarás. But Lebéna had been well-known for hundreds of years by then, thanks to the healing properties of its mineral springs. A Hellenistic sanctuary, with temple and baths, was built around one of the springs on the hillside just east of the harbour around the 4th century BC, and it was an important enough curative centre to be comprehensively restored several centuries later by craftsmen from Górtina.

The fenced site (open 8–3) stands on the left of the road just before it reaches Léndas. Down the hill from the gate is a square excavation, paved with slabs, its original walls of stone blocks lined by the Górtina restorers with flat red

Paximádhia
Taking bread on a picnic is usually a bad move. By the time it emerges from the rucksack at lunchtime it is squashed, stale and unappetising. Not so in Crete. Buy *paximádhia*, hunks or rings of hard-baked bread, and soften it with water to release its subtle, rather nutty flavour.

Roman tiles. This was the Hellenistic temple to Asklepios, the god of healing. A cluster of stones at the bottom of the inner wall is all that remains of the base of a statue of the god. Two tall granite pillars rise from the temple floor, their capitals now broken off. A few metres nearer the gate the square foundations of the sanctuary treasury contain a really striking Hellenistic mosaic, showing a prancing seahorse with a rippling tail. The shapes of the muscles under his white pebble skin are outlined in black, his mane and the spines along his back are picked out in red, and round his joyfully cavorting form is a frame of curling waves. The exuberance of the artist, perhaps inspired by the vivid turquoise of the sea in view from the hill, comes clearly across two and a half thousand years. Just to the east, among deep excavation trenches, stands the little brick arch that spanned the healing spring, a source resorted to by Cretans with stomach troubles until very recently.

▶ Mátala *72A1*

Mátala, on the Gulf of Mesarás a 15km drive southwest of Moíres, is one of those places everyone has heard of, chiefly in lurid or Utopian tales of the hippies who established themselves in the caves above the beach during the 1960s. These caves, originally Roman rock-cut burial chambers, are now empty, and the village has swapped its Shangri-la aura for modern prosperity as a full-blown resort. Mátala does have plenty of places to stay, an excellent sandy beach and famously clear, fish-filled waters. But if you don't care for crowds and night-time noise, this is not the place for you.

Souvláki
Beach taverna cuisine is simple, predictable and nearly always reliable. *Souvláki*, kebabs of lamb, pork or fish, grilled over charcoal and served with chips or salad, are the mainstay. Try swordfish or tuna *souvláki*. Eat them gazing out to sea and you will find that the flavour intensifies, magically.

Holiday traffic at Mátala Bay

■ For lovers of wildlife, Crete is a paradise. Within this comparatively small island there is an astonishing variety of habitat, from the caves, marshes and plains of the coast through scrubby hillsides and fertile lowlands to the plateaux and peaks of the high mountains. A pair of binoculars and a few good Mediterranean reference books on birds, trees, flowers and butterflies are all you need.....■

Name of the beast
What should you properly call the Cretan ibex? 'Wild goat' is the most commonly used term, but incorrect; *agríma*, often heard, can refer to other animals; *kri-kri* is an abominable Americanism, say the purists who prefer *égagros* (pronounced with soft, rolled g's) from the beast's Latin name *Capra aegagrus cretensis.*

Popular pelicans
In spite of all the ornithological delights of Crete's wildest mountains and coasts, the island's most sought-after birds remain Níkos and Pédros, the half-tame pelicans that terrorise the waterfront at Sitiá.

Golden eagles can be seen throughout the year – if you are lucky

Between March and May Crete bursts into bloom, with carpets of wild flowers from shore to summit. Many species are indigenous to the island and, given that traditional farming practices are still so widespread, the flowers bloom extravagantly. A second flowering in the late autumn makes a visit in October very worthwhile. Crete is sited on the bird migration routes between Europe and Africa, and is an important landfall in spring and autumn for many species.

There are areas of coastal wetland around Tavronítis in the northwest, and at Yeoryióupouli, west of Réthimnon which have not been drained. There are others near Frangokástello and around the Gulf of Mesarás west of Timbáki. These are fine sites to look for waders such as sandpipers and avocets during the migration seasons, and you will find herons, terns and marsh harriers there all year round. Feathery tamarisk trees are widespread along the coasts and beaches, and there are orchids in the sand dunes.

On higher ground Above the agricultural lowlands, scrubby hillsides rise to 1000m where a *maquis* of prickly, sun-dried scrub gives way to *phrígana*, a mixture of scrub and low shrubs dense with herbs such as Jerusalem sage, oregano and thyme. Pink and white rock roses, white and yellow asphodels and midnight-blue Cretan iris can be found here in spring, along with prickly cushions of red-flowered *astivítha*, its yellow-flowered cousin *astamnágathos*, and the Judas tree with striking pink flowers. In the shady gorges between the mountains there are cypress, pine and wild fig trees. Songbirds are plentiful around the villages and gardens, the hayfields and olive groves.

Up in the high mountain gorges you will find saxifrage and peonies, and in autumn crocuses glow in the remaining pine woods. Orchids thrive around Omalós, Lasíthiou, Katharó and other upland plateaux. Dittany shows its hairy

round leaves on rock ledges. Griffon vultures, pine choughs, buzzards, golden eagles and ravens haunt the peaks. In the northeast you might enjoy a rare sighting of an Eleanora's falcon, or a big Lammergeier vulture. Even rarer is the Cretan ibex, almost entirely confined now to special reserves on the offshore islands, but keep an eye open in the White Mountains, especially around the head of the Samariá Gorge. You may be lucky.

The Mediterranean pine is now far less common than it once was

Under threat However, all is not rosy in the Cretan wildlife garden. Pollution of watercourses by runoff from olive oil factories, use of herbicides, fouling of shores with fuel oil and rubbish, disturbance of birds and animals by increased numbers of visitors, are making themselves felt. The most serious problem, though, is that of erosion. The visitor cannot fail to be struck by the harsh grey nakedness of the peaks and ridges. The pine and cypress forests that once covered them have been cut down over the centuries, most rigorously by the Venetians for timber to build and repair their great fleets of galleys. The forests helped to create clouds and rainfall; their roots bound the soil which retained moisture, slowly releasing it to lower levels and their watercourses. Now, with the disappearance of tree cover, waterlessness has become Crete's most pressing ecological and economic concern. Herds of goats and sheep, nibbling their way unchecked across the island, allow tree seedlings no chance to grow. A recent spate of forest fires has destroyed a significant proportion of the remaining native trees. These problems need to be addressed, and sooner rather than later.

Mandrake
Beside paths through the olive groves you may find a big flat rosette of crinkled leaves sporting purple flowers with five pointed petals. Orange berries will show in the autumn. This is the fabled mandrake with its forked, man-shaped root, so potent in inducing sleep, dreams and desires. And it is said to shriek pitifully when pulled out of the ground.

The fruits of the prickly pear are edible

The Mesarás plain is surrounded by mountains

Busy buggies
A familiar sight of the Mesarás plain is the farmer's motorised buggy, sometimes a three-wheeler, sometimes with two front wheels set perilously close together. Powered by a noisy, fume-rich engine and steered with handlebars or with a tiller, the Mesarás buggies take farm produce or passengers slowly along the road in their open trailers, passed by all other transport save the even slower but more environmentally friendly donkey.

►► Mesarás *72B2*

Three mountain ranges hem in the 29km length of the Mesarás plain: Psiloritis to the north, the Dhíktaean range to the east, and the lower Asteroúsia mountains to the south. Streams from the three ranges pour down to join the two great rivers of the plain, Yeropótamos and Anapodháris. Mesarás itself is an alluvial basin flush with rich soil thousands of years old, well watered by streams and rivers directed into manmade irrigation channels, sheltered by the mountains and warmed by the Cretan south coast climate, making the Mesarás plain the most productive agricultural area in Crete.

Older civilisations were well aware of the fertility of Mesarás. The Minoans sited their palaces of Faistós and Ayía Triádha on the ridge north of the plain, and the Dorian Greeks, and later the Romans, built extensively on the old Minoan village site of Górtina further to the east.

Descending into the Mesarás plain, you are immediately aware of its prosperity and productivity. Where Roman wheat grew, there now flourish melons, cucumbers, watermelons, tomatoes and other fruits and vegetables that thrive on plenty of sun and water. Though you might not guess it from the very ordinary-looking, rather down-at-heel buildings of the Mesarás towns, the farms here are among the most prosperous in the island, with lively markets at Moirés and Timbáki. But a price has been paid. Wherever you look, you will see the tattered, shiny, reflective surfaces of the hothouses, and windblown shreds of plastic seem almost as ubiquitous as the Mesarás wild flowers.

▶ **Moirés** *72B2*

Moirés stands at the centre of the Mesarás plain, the chief town and the only place with a bus terminus and eateries to attract the lorry drivers who park up here, and local farmers who flood in on donkeys, motorised tricycle trucks and in battered pick-ups with their produce for sale at the rowdy, thronged street market on Saturday morning. Moirés has little of elegance or physical attraction, but as the largest Mesarás town it has plenty of shops, cafés, tavernas and all the facilities needed by locals and visitors alike. There are a number of cheapish rooms to rent, too, though few are attracted to the idea of staying in such a workaday place.

If that is the case, you will certainly avoid **Timbáki**▶, 10km to the west and only a couple of kilometres from the shore of the Gulf of Mesarás. Guide books do not have a good word to say for Timbáki. It is an unprepossessing place, for sure, with shabby streets of run-down, post-war flats and houses each side of a long, traffic-choked main street where the tavernas reek of cooking oil and the customers roar at the youths racing their motorbikes outside. But the village square just off the main drag is overarched with big, shady trees and surrounded by *kafenía* where you will almost certainly be the only foreigner. Here, as elsewhere off the Cretan tourist routes, a few words of Greek will be repayed by instant friendliness, interest and hospitality. Timbáki's Friday morning market is even louder and fiercer than that at Moirés. The frustrated lorry drivers honk more furiously among the crowds, the stallholders urge and coerce passionately over ranks of cheap clothes and shoes, and counters packed with fresh fruit and vegetables. A night in Timbáki will not be *grande luxe* by any stretch of the imagination (the hotels are pretty basic), but a short stay here can show you a side of Crete that you will experience in very few other places – commercial, everyday, loud and unadornedly vital.

Mesarás hothouses

Watering the groves

Walking through the olive and orange groves of the plain, you will come across the complicated network of irrigation channels that bring water from the Yeropótamos and Anapodháris rivers, helped by snaking miles of black hosepipe connected to spurting multiple valves – a reminder that even in this naturally lush and fertile region, Crete's shortage of water is only overcome by constant hard work and ingenuity.

Meandering in Mesarás

With such an abundance of dramatic mountain and coastal scenery attracting visitors to other parts of Crete, Mesarás is a relatively unexplored area. Nobody will mind you walking around their fields, orchards and groves provided you bear in mind that these are their places of work. For ramblers who prefer not to encounter other ramblers, enjoyment is guaranteed.

Drive The western Asteroúsia Mountains

This is an exciting and lonely 75km round drive in one of the least-visited corners of southern Crete, through the tumbled valleys and hills of the western Asteroúsia Mountains, and the rough but perfectly driveable coast road that skirts them between Kaloí Liménes and Léndas.

The drive explores the isolated country between the popular west-facing resort of Mátala on the Gulf of Mesarás and the emerging one of Léndas on the south coast. It is important to fill up with petrol and check your tyres at Moíres before setting off, since there are very few garages *en route*. The south coast road is rough and rutted, but presents no problems that the average Cretan hire car cannot tackle if driven with care. See map on pages 72–3.

Your road turns south in the centre of **Moíres** before setting off, signposted Pómbia and Mátala, towards the green and grey wall of the Asteroúsia Mountains and the big farming village of **Pómbia** cradled in the foothills. In the village fork right uphill by the church, and right again at a Kaloí Liménes sign. Soon you are above Pómbia, heading up into the hills, with enormous views opening northwards over the fruit farms of the Mesarás plain towards the massive, fissured bulk of Psiloritis. Suddenly you crest a saddle of ground to see the Libyan Sea in front of you between the hills. At the square in **Piyaidhákia**, follow the Kaloí Liménes sign to descend through the wild Asteroúsia hills, brilliant with wild flowers in springtime. A good tarmac road takes you to within a couple of kilometres of Kaloí Liménes and then the dirt returns.

Kaloí Liménes is one of the few sheltered anchorages on Crete's south coast, guarded by three small islets offshore. This was the 'fair haven' where St Paul landed in about AD60, a captive on his way to Rome: his first contact with European soil. Paul wanted to spend the winter here, but was overruled by the centurion in charge of him, and by the ship's owner and captain; a fatal error of judgement, since they went on to shipwreck in Malta. Today there are huge cylindrical oil storage tanks on one of the islets, and a clutch of hotels and tavernas on the grey sand beach, but Kaloí Liménes is still a peaceful fishing harbour with a local life of its own.

Back-track from the end of the road, and in a couple of kilometres turn right downhill past a hotel on a poor dirt road that soon improves. It clings to the puce-coloured cliffs above the half-built hotels of tiny **Platía Perámata**. At a T-junction in the valley beyond, turn right onto a short bad

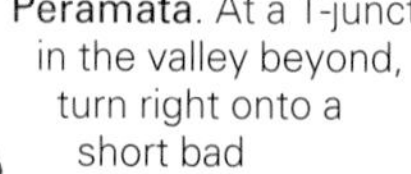

stretch and then go left, winding in and out of little clefts in the skirts of the shore, full of greenhouses and fruit and vegetable plots. There are no signposts; just keep to the cliff road and ask the horticultural workers if in doubt.

At a T-junction above the little beach at **Papadhoyiánnis**, turn right to pass tavernas and drive on towards the craggy headland of **Cape Léndas**. The name means lion, and you can make out a roughly leonine shape if you try hard enough! **Léndas** (see pages 94–5), on its little bay of green sea and grey-yellow beach, is developing year by year as a resort.

The road is now tarmac again, which will come as a welcome respite for your suspension, and climbs away north into the mountains. Yellow gorse splashes the scrubby slopes, and you will probably spot eagles floating overhead. This is marvellously lonely country, where the village of **Krótos** sits in isolation. Fork right by the church beyond the village on a bad dirt road to Vasilikí. Keep straight on at the junction and on through the Mesarás vineyards and olive groves to Vayioniá, Ayía Dhéka and the road to Moíres.

The Asteroúsia Mountains are bare and lonely

Left: shepherds' huts dot the slopes of the Asteroúsia Mountains
Below: even this sparse settlement has its own church

Driving in Crete

■ Crete's road system has improved out of all recognition during the last twenty years. The new road from Iráklio west to Khaniá and east to Ayíos Nikólaos has provided the north of the island with an excellent modern highway, some of it dual carriageway. Other good roads, slower but still negotiable, criss-cross the island between the larger towns, most running north–south in obedience to the lie of the land.....■

Shrines often denote accident blackspots

Shrines

As soon as you embark on the Cretan roads you will notice roadside shrines erected by the families of accident victims on the fatal spot. These vary from modest tin boxes to really elaborate miniature churches. Inside are icons, flowers, lamps, candles and bottles of olive oil. At night the lighted lamps and candles in the shrines of recent victims flicker a warning as you pass.

Open tops give a good view – but mind the sun

Up in the mountains, however, and along the south coast, road conditions can still be very primitive. Tarmac can suddenly degenerate into a dirt surface, and in the more remote areas you may come across surfaces so cracked by landslips, so narrow and rocky, that you may have no alternative but to turn around and seek another route.

Maps The road maps of Crete are not much help. Freytag & Berndt's 1:200,000 map (Sheet 14 of the Greek series) is probably the best general map, and it is fairly accurate, but the colour-coded depiction of the varying surface qualities is already out of date. The Harms-ic-Verlag 1:80,000 map in five sheets is more detailed, but contains more inaccuracies. A combination of the two is probably your best bet, but be prepared for unwelcome surprises.

Vehicles Hire cars can cope with most of the dirt roads, and there are hundreds of rental companies all over the island. On the whole it is advisable to choose one of the reputable international firms. Four-wheel-drives are essentially for image value rather than practical necessity. Motorcycles are cheaper, mopeds and scooters cheaper still, but these can be very dangerous on the loose dirt surfaces and the lower engine capacity machines may not be able to climb the steeper hills, especially with two up. Bring your own helmet to be sure of having one.

Rules of the road In Crete you drive on the righthand side of the road. Town drivers tend to be hasty of speed and judgement. Traffic lights flick straight from red to green, and drivers behind will beep impatiently if you do not react instantly. Motorcycles and commercial vehicles do not always respect oneway streets. Mediterranean insouciance does not extend to the traffic police in the big towns, so it is wise to park in official parking areas.

Out in the country, white lines mark major roads. An unbroken white line in the centre of the road means no overtaking, though most local drivers ignore this. Another

white line on the nearside marks a crawler lane into which you are expected to move when being overtaken or when an overtaking vehicle is coming at you. But beware! There may be a donkey, bicycle or parked vehicle just around the corner.

Potholes feature on all roads, and you must learn early on to watch out for them. Roadworks are frequent and rarely signposted in advance. Garages are usually to be found around the larger towns, but they are few and far between elsewhere, so it is a good idea to fill up when you have the opportunity. Unleaded petrol and diesel are widely available. Garages rarely accept credit cards.

Traffic signs are standard continental when they exist. Some major sites, for example Faistós and Fournaróu Korifí, are poorly signposted. On main roads, signs are usually given in Greek followed by English. It is useful to know that the letters X, H, Ch and Kh are interchangeable, as in Xaniá, Haniá, Chaniá or Khaniá. On minor roads signs may be in Greek only, and on dirt roads they are often tiny and handmade, and very hard to spot. On the south coast and up in the mountains, dirt roads are often entirely unsignposted at forks and crossroads, so keep a wary eye on the map and be willing to backtrack and ask directions.

There are two basic rules. Firstly, for any journey on back roads, allow half as long again or even twice as long, as you normally would. And, secondly, be patient.

Roadworks
Drivers are unlikely to have advance warning of roadworks on minor and dirt roads. If you come round a corner and find the road blocked by a mound of stones or a digger, don't despair. Within a few minutes the obstruction may well be cleared. If it looks as if work is due to go on for any length of time, ask the workmen for help and someone will direct you through the obstacle course.

Uses of the Cretan car horn 1
Greeting friends; venting rage at street blockages; summoning or repelling oncoming traffic (hard to say which, until it is too late!); calling attention to what the blarer judges to be poor driving; attracting the attention of pretty girls; announcing mounting impatience while waiting for a dilatory passenger; occupying the fingers of restless children; and dispersing sheep.

Uses of the Cretan car horn 2
Never, but never, to alert other drivers to the immediate appearance of the onrushing owner around the next hairpin bend, on the wrong side of the road!

Mountain roads are narrow and winding

Píthoi
Enormous earthenware *píthoi* or storage jars, some standing up to shoulder height, are still to be seen in use in village storerooms, and as rubbish receptacles in the back streets. But the days of the *píthos* in everyday use are numbered. Modern fridges store more, keep their contents cooler and don't break when bashed into. But *píthoi* don't consume electricity, or flood the floor, or hum at night. A secondary use for *píthoi*, and one you'll see in many villages, is as chimney pots. The smaller jars are the perfect size, shape and material for the job.

Remember your hand luggage limit before you buy!

▶▶ Thrapsanó *73E3*

Thrapsanó is well signposted to the right off the Iráklio–Kastélli road. The village straggles along the side of a wide valley of olive groves, a rambling place of side turnings and narrow lanes. Thrapsanó has been famous for centuries for its pottery, and today the tradition is as strong as ever. There are many small workshops in and around Thrapsanó, turning out every kind of pottery from souvenirs through practical household crockery to enormous *píthoi,* waist-high earthenware storage jars whose design has scarcely changed since Minoan times. The first pottery you come to on your approach from Iráklio is that of Ioánnis Moutzákis, and this is as good a place as any to watch the skill of the potters. One turns the wheel by hand while his colleague teases and coaxes the sinuous shape of a jar or bowl out of a lump of inert grey clay. Fired in a white-hot kiln, the pottery flushes a rich orange colour.

▶ Tsoútsouros *73E1*

This little coastal settlement is signposted in Káto Kastellianá, off the main Ierápetra–Áno Viánnos road. 11km of spiralling, rough road through a landscape of purple rocks and dizzying drops brings you down to Tsoútsouros. There are signs of blasting and widening along this road, perhaps omens of upgrading. If so, and

the big tourist coaches are tempted to try this route to the coast, an awful lot of reversing on blind hairpin bends is in prospect.

Tsoútsouros is a lonely little place. The isolation of this part of Crete's southern coast made it ideal for the daring, clandestine landings of members of the Allied resistance movement during World War II. The village itself is no more than a clutch of white-painted tavernas and rooms to rent, along with a couple of small hotels. The grey shells of half-built speculative constructions, grey cliffs and the grey sand beach add up to a rather gloomy atmosphere, but the setting, between rocky headlands, is peaceful and lovely.

Tsoútsouros straggles along a grey strand

► Vathípetro *73D3*

Following the road south out of Arkhánes, you reach the site of Vathípetro in 5km, signposted just off the road to the right and reached by a short dirt track. Vathípetro (open mornings only, but *may* be open at other times; ask at Café Ioúktas in Arkhánes) is a well-preserved example of a Minoan country villa. Everything was home-produced on the big agricultural estates, and the inhabitants of Vathípetro were kept busy weaving, making pottery, pressing olive oil and producing wine.

You enter the site past a shrine on your right. Continue forward to reach a low-roofed building. This may be locked, but the curator will open it for you. Inside is uniquely well-preserved winemaking equipment. You can see a big round earthenware grape press with a spout, a receptacle for the grape juice, and in the stone-flagged floor a circular basin and drainage channel for washing the feet after treading grapes.

To the right (westnorthwest) of the building is the villa's main room, with a wonderful view over a wide valley covered by a patchwork of vineyards, fields and olive groves, with snow-capped Psiloritis beyond. To the right again stands a roofed storeroom, containing fragments of big *píthoi*. Return to the entrance by way of the villa's thick-walled living rooms.

Vathípetro was built on a spectacular site

Walk Kapetanianá to Mount Kófinas

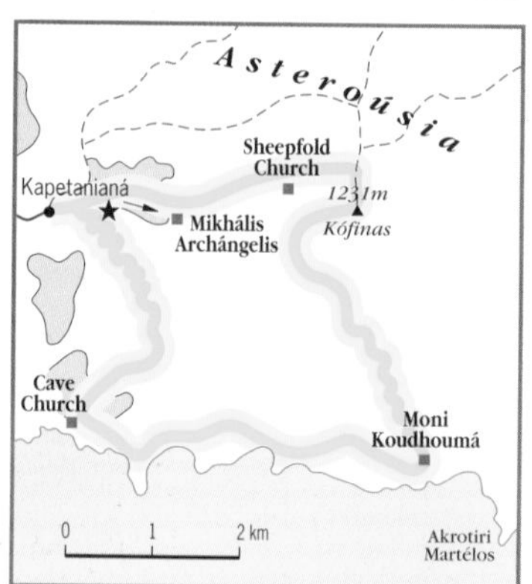

This walk is in one of the wildest parts of southern Crete, from a remote mountain village to the highest peak of the Asteroúsia Mountains, passing churches with frescoes along the way (allow about 4–5 hours). A very tough and precipitous extension (add at least 5 hours) leads down to the isolated monastery of Koudhoumá on the coast, and up again!

The walk starts at the top of a rough, twisting dirt road in the high, lonely village of Kapetanianá, reached from the Moíres–Iráklio road in the Mesarás plain. Turn right in Ayía Dhéka through Vayioniá and Loúkia, where you begin the ascent to Kapetanianá. Park beside the first buildings you come to. The church of Panayía, in the lower part of the village, has faded frescoes dating from 1401.

You could follow the dirt road directly from the car to the chapel below the peak of Mount Kófinas, but for a more interesting walk take the path that descends from the church, forking right downhill past the cemetery, for 1km, to pass the church of Mikhális Arkhángelis on the right. This, too, contains faded frescoes, some dating as far back as the 13th century, slowly dissolving through rainwater damage.

200m past the church on a right-hand bend, hairpin left on a path between wire fences. Soon the left-hand fence bears off uphill to the left, but keep straight on here downhill to pass through a shepherd's gate. Scramble over the wire fence ahead and climb the hillside, crossing a dirt road on the way. You will see above you a dry stone wall across the mouth of a cave, a shepherd's rough dwelling-place.

The domed peak of Kófinas is your aiming point as you climb to a dirt road and pass a wired sheepfold. The saddle-roofed hut inside the fence, with a white cross painted on the wall, was a church built by John the Honest, a 14th-century hermit. There are traces of fresco inside, around the base of the ruined apse. Half a kilometre beyond, an orange scar on the hillside shows the route of a short cut. Aim directly for the saddle of ground to the left of the mountain which will take you across the windings of the

The extension will take you to Koudhoumá Monastery

dirt road, to reach the little chapel on the saddle. From here climb towards the biggest of the conifers above, and follow the red dots and arrows of waymarks as you scramble up among the rocks for 15 minutes to reach the chapel on the summit of Mount Kófinas (1231m). The view from here is superb, with Psiloritis and the Dhíkti Mountains to the north, and the south coast a head-spinning drop below.

The return route to Kapetanianá is back the way you came. But the very strenuous extension to Koudhoumá Monastery is highly recommended to strong and experienced walkers with plenty of stamina. Note, however, that it will require a further five to six hours, and involves a steep descent of 1200m, and a correspondingly steep ascent of 500m. So check your watch, and your state of fitness, before tackling it.

Extension to Koudhoumá

Return to the chapel on the saddle, bearing left downhill to the water

The wild and rocky south coast overlooking the Libyan Sea

trough. Head westnorthwest down the gully, which curves left. In ten minutes look for a stubby tree on your left, pass it and cross the scree slope on the path high on the left bank of the gully. Continue curving left under the crags of Kófinas; you will soon be heading due south with a deep gorge on your right. Descend across a stony plateau, bearing left of a wooden post on the skyline, to find red waymarks. Soon the red roofs of Koudhoumá monastery will appear below. Follow the steep zigzag waymarked descent through the pines to the monastery.

From the monastery turn west, keeping close to the coast, for 2km to the settlement of Ayíos Ioánnis. There is a church with frescoes in the cliffs, 1km to the west. A zigzag track is clearly in view above. Follow it, or climb directly up, a very steep ascent taking a minimum of two hours, to Kapetanianá.

4
Káto Gournes
Svoýrou Metókhi
Akrotiri Khersonisos
Limin Khersonisou
Kolpos Málion
Sisi
Goúves
Aposelemis
Khersonisos
Stalidha
Mália
Mália
Kóxari
Kaló Horió
818m
Mokhós
Potamiés
Smári
Selena Oros
Sfendhili
Krasi
1599m
1487m Makhaira
3
Káto Karouzaná
Avdoú
Kera
Apóstoloi
Askoi
Mesa Potamoi
Kastélli
Lithos
Exo Potamoi
Sklaverokhóri
Xidhas
Moni Vidhianis
Tzermiádho
Pinakiano
Liliano
Amarianó
Lasíthiou
Mésa Lasíthi
Mathiá
Pláti
Psikhró
Ayíos Yeóryios
Dhiktaio Andro
Avrakóndes
Kath
Yeráki
Nipidhitós
1414m Viryiomeno
Órosira Dhíkti
2148m
2
Avli
Panayia
Arkadhes
Kasános
2141m Afendis Khristos
Katofini
Thomadhiano
Inio
Karavádhos
Vakiótes
1783m Madhára
Parissia
Áno Viánnos
Kefalovrisi
Skiniás
Káto Viánnos
Amirás
Ay Vasilios
Dhemáti
Favriana
Khóndros
Sikólogos
1
Keratókambos
Tértsa
Árvi
Faflangos
Ormos Keratokambou
Akrotiri Sidhonia
Tsoútsouros
Ormos Tsoútsourou
A
B

Anastasia and St John take a rest in Ayíos Nikólaos harbour

AYÍOS NIKÓLAOS AND THE DHÍKTI MOUNTAINS

Akrotiri Dhrepani
Akrotiri Ayíos Ioánnis
Vlikhadhia
Mironikitas
Amigdhalea
Finokalia
Selles
Paralia Milatos
Milatos
Anoyía
Dhilakos
Váltos
Vroukhas
Epano Loúmas
Nofaliás
Spinalónga
Agoroi
Karidhio
Pláka
Moni Xera Xila
Dhoriai
Spinalónga
Kourounes
Vrakhasi
Latsídha
Dhriros
Pines
Mavrimianon
Kolokithia
Fourni
Eloúndha
Voulisméni
Kastélli
Oloús
Neápoli
Limnes
Kalós Lammos
Vríses
Ay Pelayia
Lenika
Ayíos Konstandinos
Katsikia
Zénia
Amigdhaloi
Karteridhes
Xirokambos
Roussapidhia
Ay Pándes
Skisma
Tápes
Flamouriana
Ayíos Nikólaos
1664m Katharó Tsivi
Lató
Kolpos Mirambellou
Mardhati
Kritsá
Ammoudhára
Avdheliakos
Kroustas
1485m Platía Korifí
Ístro
Pakhiá Ammos
Pírgos
Kalo Khorio
Gourniá
Moni Faneroménis
Prina
Vasiliki
1141m
Meseléroi
Khristós
Máles
Kalamávka
Moni Pan Exakoustis
Stavros
Papadhiana
Metaxokhori
Makrilia
Episkopí
951m
Káto Khorió
Anatoli
Kendrí
Miloi
Vainia
Riza
Kaloyeroi
Bramiana
Ayiasmenos
Mírtos Pyrgos
Fournoú Korifi
Mournies
Stómio
Gra Liyia
Ammoudháres
Mírtos
Neos Mírtos
Ierápetra
0 5 10 15 km
C
D

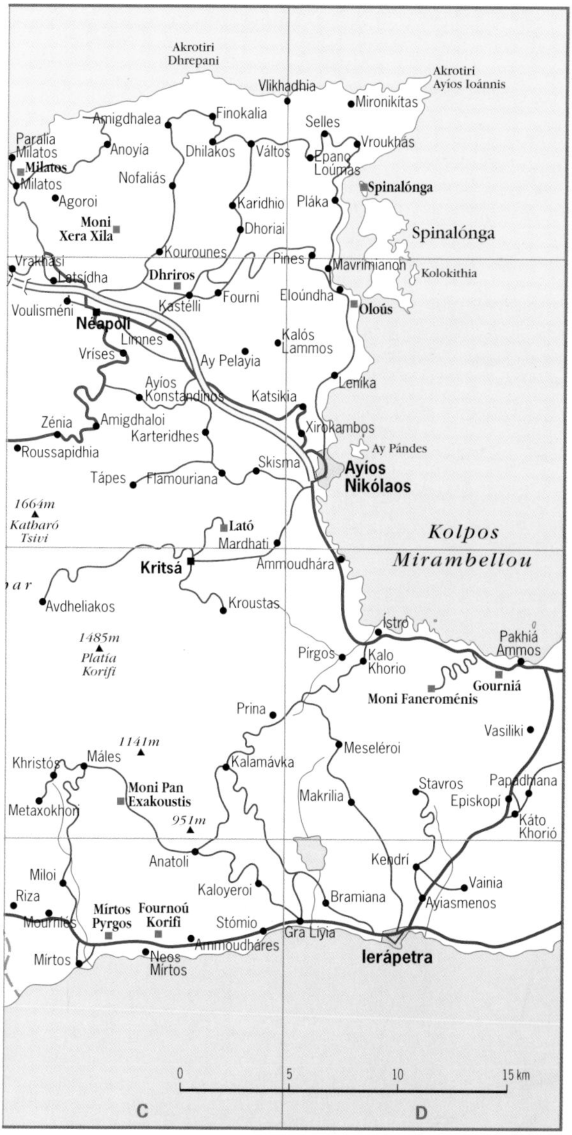

Sash with a dash
While many items of traditional dress, such as wide-cut breeches and knee-boots, have been retained by the older men of the hill villages, the old-style cummerbund has largely disappeared. Perhaps this is because there is no call nowadays for the silver-hilted pistols and daggers that were so dashingly thrust into it by the *palikáres* of yore.

Shepherds' gates
The gates that shepherds install in their stock fences are flimsy grids of wire, held to the posts with a single loop. These gates are strong enough to deter sheep and goats, but will not withstand rough handling. Do remember, when you encounter one on a walk, to open it with care, and to close it securely behind you.

Ayíos Nikólaos and the Dhíkti Mountains Between Iráklio and Ayíos Nikólaos is a long stretch of northern coastline and a hinterland that rises to the tremendous rocky ranges of the Dhíkti Mountains. There is no more varied a region in Crete.

The mountains surround Lasíthiou, the best-known upland plateau in Crete, with its whirling white windmills that have launched a thousand postcards, and Katharó, equally delightful but very little visited. The mountains themselves see only the occasional walker; solitude and face-to-face enjoyment of Cretan wildlife are guaranteed. In the flanks of the mountains quiet green valleys rise through olive groves to harsh, stony heights. Yet only a few kilometres north across the foothills is an almost continuously built-up, developed and over-exploited strip of coastline 40km long where the world is at your elbow, if not occupying your sunbed.

All roads hereabouts lead to Ayíos Nikólaos, the one town of any size in the region, and all excursions begin here. The town is the administrative capital of Crete's easternmost quarter, the nome of Lasíthiou. The region south and east of Iráklio is drawn towards Ayíos Nikólaos for its services, commercial life and entertainment. Ayíos Nikólaos has become the island's premier seaside resort, perhaps because it feels free of the weight of Byzantine, Venetian and Turkish architecture that anchor Khaniá and Réthimnon to the past, and it is more centrally placed than Sitiá. It is not a dignified town, nor a staid one, and it is certainly not quiet. But Ayíos Nikólaos is lively and has everything for the holidaymaker: buses leave for the inland towns and villages, boats depart for islands and beaches, traditional music and dancing displays break out like a rash in summer, and discos batter the night air along the restaurant-lined waterfront. Some modest and some very plush and correspondingly expensive hotels have spread along the coast to the north of the town, to cater for the hundreds of thousands of visitors who base themselves each year in Ayíos Nikólaos.

The happy holiday town of Ayíos Nikólaos

The excellent new road to Iráklio runs northwest from Ayíos Nikólaos, and where it meets the coast the built-up strip begins. There are hotels, restaurants, apartment blocks, complete new holiday villages, gift shops, bars, discos, sports complexes and packed beaches where bodies grill flank to flank. Many Cretans will tell you of their disillusionment with this new world, which has gobbled up most of the coastline in the last 15 years with much unregulated, crass and ugly building. On the positive side, it has produced a livelihood for many local people, and it has concentrated much of Crete's more brash tourism in a clearly defined area. But welcome change is in the air. The Cretan tourist authorities, contemplating the rapacity of this brand of holidaymaking, have begun to edge towards a greener and gentler view of the future of tourism in their island, refreshing thinking that is still working its way towards action.

Away from the strip there are treasures on every side for the explorer who takes a little trouble to look for them: the breathtaking frescoes at hospitable Kritsá; Spinalónga Island with its haunting history; the unfrequented shores of the northeastern peninsula and the south coast; the wriggling mountain roads up to the Lasíthiou plateau; great caves and their legends; high and lovely Katharó; and the wild and stony beauty of the valleys and peaks of the Dhíkti Mountains.

The Dhíkti backdrop

Waymarks
Waymarking of footpaths in Crete is an uncertain science, even though the OYK (Long Distance Club of Crete, tel. 081 228225, President Cháris Kakoulákis) has done a competent job in recent years. Splashes of red, or occasionally orange, on wayside rocks show the route, but they have a nasty habit of disappearing when most needed. A good point to bear in mind in the mountains is that waymarks easily visible on the way up may be tricky to spot when descending. Take a reliable bearing on a landmark you'll recognise again, if you think a waymark may be of this awkward type.

Tamarisk
The feathery tamarisk with its pale green fronds and dangling, catkin-like white or delicate pink flowers is the tree you will see most frequently in seaside towns and villages, planted to throw its whispering shade over the café terraces and nearest beach.

Greasy but good
As a change from *souvláki* and Greek salad, invite yourself into the kitchen of your restaurant or taverna and see if they are offering *arní tis katsarólas me patátes* – lamb casserole, cooked with potatoes. With luck, or good judgement, you will be served a plateful of this greasy delight.

▶▶▶ Ayíos Nikólaos *109D3*

Thanks to its vigorous tourist trade and bustling atmosphere, Ayíos Nikólaos ranks as one of Crete's Big Four towns. But the town as it stands today is very much a younger sister to Iráklio, Réthimnon and Khaniá, having developed its harbour and surrounding buildings only since the 19th century. You won't find in Ayíos Nikólaos the glories of Venetian architecture that characterise the other three towns of the north coast. There are no strong fortifications of golden stone around the harbour, no mighty castle frowning down from a promontory, no impressive stretches of ancient city wall. Ayíos Nikólaos is a town absorbed in modern tourism, whose discos, bars and hotels have been grafted in the last 30 years onto the framework of a commercial centre that grew from almost nothing to become the capital of the Lasíthiou nome of Crete. But take the town on its own terms as a prettily sited tourist resort with all modern facilities and a lively flavour, surprisingly resilient under its enormous weight of summertime visitors, and you will find it is an excellent base for exploration of the Dhíkti Mountains, the coastline and the lush lowlands between Iráklio and the eastern end of the island.

Early port There was a flourishing town in Hellenistic times on the headland just south of the modern harbour which served as the port for the Dorian city of Lató (see page 131), high in the hills 6km to the west. The town

Ayíos Nikólaos

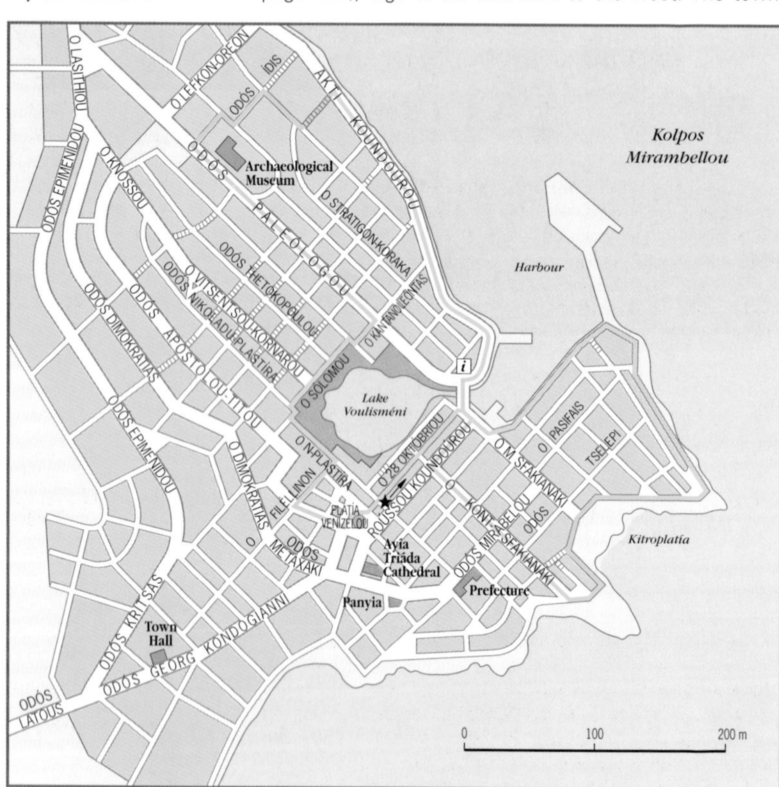

Small fishing boats supply the many restaurants

continued to thrive during the Roman occupation, but went into a decline shortly after the Byzantine takeover of the island. The Venetians later revived it, building their fortress at Mirabéllo inland of the old port to guard the harbour of Porto di San Nicolo, in the shelter of the headland to the north where the Byzantine church of Ayíos Nikólaos stood. Nothing remains today of the fort, and very little to bear witness to either Venetian or Turkish rule, but by the late 19th century a new harbour nearer to the ancient port had revitalised the town.

Tourist town After the union of Crete with mainland Greece in 1913, Ayíos Nikólaos became the capital of the nome of Lasíthiou, and continued its modest prosperity as a trading centre. In the early 1960s tourists began to arrive, attracted by the picturesque position of the town above the harbour and by its convenient location close to the Lasíthiou Plateau (see pages 130–1) and to nearby beaches just a short boat ride away. Since then, package holidays have filled the town with visitors, and smart hotels and apartment blocks have begun to stretch away along the coast in both directions. But, remarkably, this is not eyesore territory. Ayíos Nikólaos people are relaxed and welcoming by nature, and even the most modern hotels benefit from the hilly landscape and the ever-visible sea with its backdrop of mountains.

Beach charges
Charging people for the use of a municipal beach has turned out to be a good system. Those who pay appreciate the cleanness of the sand and water, and the absence of semi-permanent colonies of campers. Those who object to paying have not far to go out of town before they find a free beach of their own.

Walk Ayíos Nikólaos

Allow about two or three hours. See the map on page 112.

The walk begins in Platía Venizélos▶, the little square just inland from the harbour to which tired holidaymakers climb from the shopping streets, to relax and watch the world go by at a pavement café table. The tiny, circular central gardens with their feathery sentinel palm trees lend a green and pleasant atmosphere to the square. On the south side, at the top of Odós Elefthérias Venizélos, is the **Cathedral of Ayía Triádha▶**, with its interior entirely covered with vigorous and expressive modern frescoes, a testimony to the still flourishing tradition of Byzantine-style church painting. An old icon in faded gold and red records the adventures of St Paul in several vivid scenes.

From the north side of the square, walk down Odós 28 Októbriou▶, lined with shops selling all manner of tourist goods and souvenirs. At the bottom of the street turn right and right again up tamarisk-shaded **Odós Koundoúrou▶**, a similar, parallel street. Everyone comes to shop in these two crowded thoroughfares and, as elsewhere in Crete, you get what you pay for. Half-way up Koundoúrou, turn left up Odós Sfakianáki. Here, you are at once out of the bustle and into a quiet street between flats, each with a caged bird singing from the balcony. At the crest of the street a grand view opens up over the hill-encircled Gulf of Mirambéllou to the south and east of the town. A new marina and breakwater lie immediately below. At the bottom of the street turn left up steps, then descend to turn left along the long promenade that stretches right round the waterfront of Ayíos Nikólaos.

The sandy beach of **Kitroplatía▶** is fringed with tamarisk trees, and the headland where the port of ancient Lató stood gives a wide view of the **harbour of Agíos Nikólaos▶▶**, scenically the chief attraction of the

Ayíos Nikólaos caters for a large number of British visitors

town. Pale, colourwashed houses lined with balconies are piled above the narrow harbour where fishing boats and ferries lie at their moorings. Beyond stretch the swooping ridges of the hills behind the town, running down to the sea in the distance. Cafés and restaurants, gift shops and excursion boat agencies stand shoulder to shoulder around the harbour. From here you can take a boat to nearby beaches, to pirate caves and to the spectacular former leper colony of Spinalónga Island. Crowds jostle, boat touts implore, buses roar and belch fumes. Tourism is writ large and loud here. Walk on northwards along the seafront promenade and after 300m you will come to steep Odós Salamínos on your left. Climb the steps of Odós Salamínos. Turn right along Odós Stavrou, second left up Odós Ídis, right at the top and first left to reach Odós Paleólogou and the **Archaeological Museum▶▶** (open Tuesday–Sunday 8:30–3).

The Archaeological Museum is clearly laid out in chronological order through seven rooms:

Room 1 contains pre- and early Minoan finds such as stone axe heads, fish hooks, bone scrapers, some elaborate pottery from Gourniá and some clumsy pottery from Aghía Fotiá. In a centrally placed case of her own in **Room 2** stands the Goddess of Mírtos, a libation vessel made between 2600 and 2150BC in the shape of a fat-bodied woman with a long neck rising to a tiny face. Her thin arms cradle a high-spouted jug from which the libations were poured. Grid patterns in faded red, squares and triangles, decorate her body. This is a wonderfully ingenious and imaginative piece of work, testimony to the already highly developed culture of the early Minoans. Vasilikí ware and beautifully cut stone jugs are here too, and flat gold jewellery.

Room 3 contains more jewellery, some earthenware sarcophagi with

The skull from Potamós with its wreath of golden leaves

marine decorations, one still housing a skeleton, and a superb green-black steatite vase in the form of a conch shell, on which two carved demons pour libations. In **Room 4** is a funerary urn with a child's remains inside. In **Room 5** the post-Minoan artefacts show a decline from Minoan skill with stiff votive figurines, some in Egyptian style headdresses.

Room 6 sees a return to the more expressive work of the Dorian period (6th to 5th centuries BC) such as tall figures with firm chins and graceful folds in their clothing, votive figures of wild boar, lions and tortoises, and some Buddha-like seated figures in various states of sexual arousal. **Room 7** contains more finds from the same period: a smiling, ample-bosomed goddess, a remarkable vase with 70 light holes, tiny decorated seal stones and, to cap the exhibition, the squashed and grinning skull of a Roman, his brows encircled with a victor's gold laurel leaves, and a silver coin to pay Charon the Ferryman beside his long teeth.

From the museum, descend Odós Paleólogou, and just before the bottom turn right along Odós Kantanoleóntas, then up steep Sólomou to walk among pines and tamarisks above **Lake Voulisméni▶▶**.This remarkable deep-water lake is reputed to be bottomless, though unromantic science has fixed its depth at 64m. Did the goddesses Artemis and Athena bathe here? Is the lake connected by a submarine channel to the volcanic island of Santorini, causing a sulphurous steaming of its waters from time to time? Local legend says so, and you are free to believe it.

Bear left from the cliff overlooking the lake down Odós Plastíra. Halfway down turn right along Odós Filéllinon and take third left down narrow Odós Daskaloyiánni to return to Platía Venizélos.

The steep streets of Áno Viánnos wind up the hill

Torn to shreds
Most visitors find the proliferation of plastic greenhouses along the coastal plains of Crete unsightly, particularly on the south coast whose beauty derives from the unspoiled wildness. The sea winds make merry with such easily ripped and dispersed material, and where the tatters of plastic descend after their flight, they stick on fences, on bushes and on beaches. A comprehensive clear-up would seem to be in order...

▶▶ Áno Viánnos *108B1*

The small town of Áno Viánnos lies 40km east of Ierápetra on the main road to the Mesarás plain. This is a really delightful place. The people display an interest in and hospitality towards the stranger that is a feature of Cretan hill villages. There is usually a cool breeze blowing through the streets from the mountains. Not that Áno Viánnos is truly a mountain settlement. It stands with its back to the southern foothills of the Dhíkti range, looking south over a beautifully green plateau. The site is superb, and the village huddles attractively at the foot of the slopes in a tight pile of white and colourwashed houses.

There is a hint of Mesarás fertility in the olive groves and vineyards that spread around the village on three sides. Áno Viánnos has always been a prosperous place as the centre for the countryside east and south of Mesarás. These days its influence has diminished, especially since the development of the south coast villages west of Ierápetra into a chain of ever-expanding tourist resorts. Few visitors choose to stay in Áno Viánnos, which is a pity, since this is a characterful, friendly and inquisitive village, where tiny stepped alleyways lead up the hillside into a maze of traffic-free back lanes where conversation and glimpses into other people's lives are guaranteed.

Take any of the side lanes that rise from the main road. An easy one to identify is the one that starts opposite a gigantic plane tree in the village centre. You will soon find yourself in labyrinthine lanes. Two churches are worth seeking out. Ask directions of anyone you meet. Ayíos Yióryios has fine 14th-century frescoes, but even better is Ayía Pelayía near the top of the village. Ask for Papa Lech or Maria Moulach, either of whom may have the key.

The church was built around 1300, and its frescoes are wonderfully well preserved in spite of eye-gouging, face-scratching and fire damage by Turkish zealots. Some of the figures have tenderly expressive faces and graceful hands. The Passion scenes on the northwest wall are particularly moving. Other scenes are savage: harlots being embraced by snakes, and St Bartholomew, blood-red after his martyrdom by flaying, standing with his skin flung over one shoulder.

► Arví *108B1*

You can reach Arví in comfort along the tarmac road that leaves the Áno Viánnos–Ierápetra road in the village of Amirás, or you can arrive adventurously from the west by way of the rough dirt road along the coast from Keratókambos. Arví itself is not particularly attractive. There are rather too many abandoned vehicles about, and the landscape is festooned with strips of plastic torn by the wind from the proliferating greenhouses. But there are plenty of tavernas and rooms to rent, a couple of hotels, some shops and a pebbly beach shaded in part by tamarisks.

Just to the east is the Arví gorge, 300m deep, a narrow and dramatic rip in the mountain wall said to have been created when the god Zeus Arvios struck the hillside. These bare grey hills attract and radiate solar heat, and Arví is famous for its warm climate which allows the local farmers to cultivate oranges, pineapples and bananas as well as the usual beans, potatoes, tomatoes and olives.

In spite of the stony nature of the beach, Arví is an excellent spot to spend a couple of days if you are looking for sunbathing and an enjoyably lazy time. And when your energy returns you can stroll up to the monastery that clings to the mountainside near the eastern flank of the gorge (see page 127).

►►► Ayíos Nikólaos *109D3*

See pages 112–15.

Venerable trees
Many of the trees that grace the village *platía* grow to enormous size and are several centuries old, objects of pride to the inhabitants and handy points of reference when arranging to meet someone or when giving directions. Acacia, fig and plane are the species that seem most prone to this spectacular growth.

The monastery of Ayios Andónios above Arví

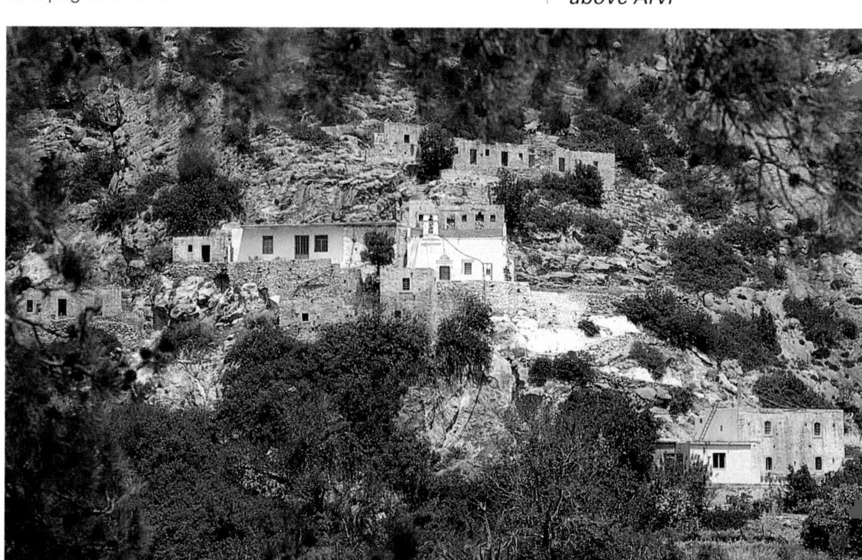

The easy way to the Dhíktaean cave

Saddle up
If you decide to hire a mule for the ascent to the cave, don't be alarmed to see a hard wooden saddle across your beast's back. Padded with a blanket, it is surprisingly comfortable.

Note the traditional wooden saddle

▶▶▶ Dhíktaean Cave *108B2*

The Dhíktaean Cave (marked Dhíktaio Andro on several maps, open 10:30–5) is one of Crete's most popular tourist attractions and the source of many highly coloured legends. It lies a short walk or donkey ride above the village of Psikhró on the western edge of the Lasíthiou Plateau. A turning at the west end of the village points up a side road to the car park where you begin the climb to the cave. There is tourist clutter here at its most intensive, though this being Crete the vendors are not unsmiling if you essay a few words of Greek. If you enjoy the spectacle of cursing bus drivers jammed among cars, and being part of an endless, slow-moving snake of people, then visit the cave at midday in the height of the tourist season. Otherwise, early morning, out of season if possible, is definitely the best time.

Just above the car park you come to the departure point for donkey rides and guided tours. A guide will point out features associated with the cave legends that you may miss if you go unaccompanied. Take a torch and wear shoes with non-slip soles, as the descent into the cave is very slippery and steep.

There is a climb of about 15 minutes from here up a zigzag pathway of smooth cobbles to reach the kiosk where you pay your entrance fee and have another opportunity to hire a guide. Just beyond, the cave mouth opens in the hillside, a big dark hole in the rock that plunges very steeply down some 65m to pitch-black depths. The descent is by way of a stone-cobbled path with a handrail. You will need its support, as moss, damp, and the passing of thousands of feet have polished the stones to a skidpan surface.

As visitors inch their way down, the dank air catches at throats and brings steam from bodies sweaty from the climb to the cave. Mosses and ferns cover the walls and below in the gloom you can make out the organ-pipe shapes of stalactites hanging from the roof, and the stumpy, knobbed towers of the much larger stalagmites below them. The cave mouth diminishes to a rectangular slit of daylight, and the guides light their gas lamps as they near the floor of the cavern. Down here it is easy to understand why the Dhíktaean Cave, overwhelmingly dark and other-worldly, was the focus of religious worship long before Minoan times, and continued to play that rôle for thousands of years.

As you reach the bottom of the cave, a side chamber on the left,which is easy to miss, holds the chief element of the legend of the Dhíktaean Cave, cited as the birthplace of Zeus, god of gods. Rhea, the mother of Zeus, came here to conceal the birth of her son from her jealous husband, Kronos, who had eaten all five of his previous offspring after an oracle warned him that he would be overthrown by his son. Kronos seems not to have been overburdened with intelligence, as he readily swallowed the stone wrapped in swaddling clothes that Rhea gave him in lieu of her baby. The guides flash their torches on a stalactite with the leering face of Kronos, a stalagmite shaped like a mother and child, the ledge where Zeus was born and the nipples of rock which gave him suck.

Excavators in 1899 and 1900 discovered hundreds of pottery and bronze offerings in this little chamber. Many more were subsequently retrieved by local boys diving in the dark pool at the bottom of the cave. Local religions embraced the Zeus legend wholeheartedly, adapting it to fit with other and older gods of the cave. Echoes of these ancient devotions still reverberate among the stones in these cold depths.

Needlework
Among the festoons of embroidery and weaving on sale in Psikhró are genuine treasures of antique needlework. Best of all are the exquisitely worked pillow and cushion covers with patterns so small they must have consumed eyesight at a terrible rate. Many were sewn together out of strips of material saved from even older covers. Look inside to admire the clever stitching that joined them, so that they appear seamless from the outside. Let price be your guide. Unless you are being duped, which is unlikely, the real thing will probably cost you four or five times as much as modern work.

Strange formations drip in the dark

The Dhíkti Mountains

■ Also known as the Lasíthiou Mountains, the Dhíkti range rises to the southeast of Iráklio and continues to the west of Ayíos Nikólaos. The border that separates the nomes or administrative districts of Iráklio and Lasíthiou zigzags from north to south across the mountains and links up the three highest peaks of the range, Lázaros (2,085m), Aféndis Kristós (2,141m) and Mount Dhíkti itself (2,148 m).....■

Hilltop churches are scattered through the mountains

The Dhíkti Mountains are impressive from wherever you see them. To the west of the main Sitiá to Ierápetra road, as it cuts between the wall of Thriptís and the sloping foothills of Dhíkti, they loom gradually from far in the distance. To the east of the Áno Viánnos to Iráklio road they appear more abruptly. And most dramatic of all is the view to the north of the road from Ierápetra to Áno Viánnos, where weathering has cut the foothills into rounded kops, their slopes terraced both by man and by water erosion, with the bare and dry hills behind.

The central uplands of Dhíkti are almost entirely devoid of roads. In this barren, rocky heart of the mountains you can walk the cobbled *kalderími* and the unpaved shepherds' tracks. Or you can make the adventurous and strenuous climb to the peak of Mount Dhíkti, with its stupendous views. Ayíos Yeóryios on the southern edge of the Lasíthiou plateau is the best place to find a guide and to stock up with water and supplies if you are going to attempt this expedition.

The Lasíthiou plateau with its world-famous white-sailed windpumps (see page 130) is the destination of one road that does penetrate the mountains. This wriggling route climbs southwards from the north coast just west of Mália to the pass of Selí Ambélou at 900m, where it suddenly gives a full view of the plain and the high mountains beyond it to the south. The road circumnavigates the green fields and orchards of the plateau, passing Psikhró and the start of the climb to the legend-haunted Dhíktaean Cave (see pages 118–19) before plunging off the eastern side of the plain to wind its way down to Ayíos Nikólaos.

Hippo teeth
Search along the silty banks of the Lasíthiou River where it winds across the Katharó plateau high in the Dhíkti Mountains, and you may come across the fossilised bones and teeth of hippopotamuses that roamed the plain many thousands of years ago.

Self-flavoured
The mountains are rich in wild herbs such as thyme, oregano, mint, rosemary and dittany – a pink-flowered herb that is native to Crete. Cretan sheep have the agreeable and convenient habit of flavouring their own meat as they graze.

There are other, lesser-known but equally delightful upland plateaux in the Dhíkti range, notably Katharó high above the village of Kritsá (see page 124). There are also tiny plains south of Ayíos Yeóryios on the path to the summit of Mount Dhíkti, and northeast of Áno Viánnos towards the southwest corner of the mountains. These little plateaux, with a solitary church and a scattering of stone-built huts, are the focus of summer migrations of shepherds and their flocks from the foothill villages. The heights of Dhíkti are inhospitable, though usually blessed with a cool breeze in summer. Snow blocks them during the winter months, there is a general lack of water and vegetation, and nowhere to stay overnight unless you happen upon a shepherd's hut. This is one of the chief strongholds of the much-sought-after herb, dittany, whose Latin name, *Origanum dictamnus,* came from these mountains. This species of small marjoram gives a subtle flavour to stews, and an infusion makes a highly prized mountain tea. It is also said to have wonderful medicinal properties. Wounded and sick animals seek it out, as do lovesick swains for the potency it bestows.

During World War II one of Crete's most ferocious and autocratic resistance leaders, Manóli Bándouvas, had his hideout on one of the isolated upland plateaux, guarded by piratically dressed partisans. Patrick Leigh Fermor, in charge of resistance planning in eastern Crete, had numerous lairs all over Dhíkti, and in September 1943 smuggled the Italian commander General Angelo Carta across these mountains to the coast, whence the general was removed to Cairo.

Kalderími

The cobbled footpaths or *kalderími* that crisscross the mountains were laboriously laid down by shepherds and packmen to guarantee passable routes through these remote uplands at all times of the year. Largely unwaymarked, unused by all but a few local shepherds, the *kalderími* still offer hundreds of miles of well-surfaced walking to anyone who takes the time to enquire and seek them out.

Stone-walled sheep corral and shepherd's hut

The well-kept village church in Eloúndha

► Eloúndha *109D3*

Eloúndha is a pleasant little seaside resort 7km north of Ayíos Nikólaos. Surrounded by hills, it faces a beautiful sheltered bay. Short boat trips go to Spinalónga Island (see pages 136–7).

Towards the southern end of the village a side road, on the right as you come from Ayíos Nikólaos, leads past a lagoon with remnants of Venetian salt pans, over an isthmus and bridge to the uninhabited **Spinalónga peninsula►►**. In the water on the right of the isthmus are walls of buildings, the remains of the Graeco–Roman city state of **Oloús►**. Beyond the taverna across the causeway is a 4th-century **Byzantine mosaic►** of lively fish and geometric patterns, enclosed in the foundations of an early Christian basilica.

►►► Gourniá Minoan Town *109D2*

As with all Crete's archaeological sites, a bird's-eye view of the overall layout greatly increases understanding and enjoyment. As the road descends towards the site from Sitiá, the view over the Minoan town of Gourniá will help you appreciate the help this excavation has been in shedding light on everyday Minoan life (8:30–3, closed Monday).

From the entrance you climb a cobbled street between box-like houses, with external walls constructed of great lumps of stone which rise to shoulder height. Inside are tiny rooms, storage chambers, outlines of doorways and passages. Many of these are the basements of long-gone houses that stood above. Alleyways a metre or so wide wind among the houses and workshops, and if you have recently wandered around the back streets of a Cretan mountain village your imagination will not have to work too hard to visualise the original town. Gourniá was

Cats
Wherever fish is eaten, there are cats. They prowl in and out of the taverna terraces, watching and waiting for their chance to pounce on discarded fish heads, tails and bones. Cat-lovers, comparing the street cats of Crete with their own pampered pets at home, may be upset by the patchy fur, rickety legs and protruding ribs of the scavengers around their tables. This, unfortunately, is one of the tougher realities of everyday Crete.

destroyed and burned around 1450BC in the same cataclysmic event that overwhelmed the other Minoan towns and palaces. It was excavated in 1901–4 by a young American archaeologist, Harriet Boyd Hawes, at the time of the unearthing of the famous sites of Knosós, Faistós and Ayía Triádha.

At the top of the long cobbled street, bear left by a tree to reach the wide, flat town court and market place which was the focal point of this prosperous trading centre. Gourniá traded widely from its harbour to the north, and with Ierápetra and the other south coast settlements. The town controlled the northern end of the narrow isthmus that connects easternmost Crete with the rest of the island, and goods could be moved south by land without exposing them to the risk of the dangerous sea route round the eastern end of Crete.

From the northwestern corner of the town court steps lead into the maze of square rooms that make up the palace of Gourniá which covers the top of the hill. This was probably the seat of a local ruler who dominated the northeast of Crete. On your left are the west and south wings of the palace, with a sacrificial slab – pierced to allow the blood to drain away. There are storerooms, open halls, and a cobbled west court with a corridor running south to another room with an altar. To the north there is another court lined with square and round column bases, and beyond, on the seaward slope of the hill, there is a shrine where animal, bird, snake and human figurines were found. Descending the hill you walk amongst more houses and workshops, including those of a carpenter and a potter.

Some of the items found at Gourniá are in the Archaeological Museum at Sitía; many more are in Gallery IX of the Iráklio Archaeological Museum.

Hidden town
What you see at Gourniá represents only a quarter of the town as it stood at the height of its prosperity. The land that slopes north from the hill of Gourniá towards the sea hides the remains of three times as many buildings, unlikely to be excavated now that the official site has been so clearly defined on and around the acropolis.

Part of the impressive stairway to the palace at Gourniá

Death watch
In the more traditional villages, death is accompanied by a prescribed set of rituals. A light is kept burning for 40 days and nights after the death, followed by a church memorial service every three months until the first anniversary. After that the dead person will be commemorated once a year, perhaps for many decades.

▶ Kalamávka *109C2*

High on a winding mountain road between Ierápetra and the north coast road at Ístro, Kalamávka clings between bluffs of naked rock streaked orange and black, looking south down a deep cleft over terraced lowland hills towards the Libyan Sea. This is a spectacularly sited farming and sheep-rearing village with some of the facilities you might expect of a small town. A couple of kilometres north, you reach a saddle of ground with views forward and back over both Cretan and Libyan Seas.

▶▶▶ Katharó Plateau *109C2*

The Katharó plateau is scarcely marked on most maps, and has no picturesque cloth-sailed windmills, which is probably the reason why this delectable saucer of green ground high at the eastern edge of the Dhíkti Mountains has escaped the tourist interest that centres on Lasíthiou (see pages 130–1). The plateau has no shops or other facilities, apart from a couple of tavernas which open only in summer, and is uninhabited between November and May. Yet this is one of Crete's most delightful hidden treasures, a circle of fertile land ringed by remote mountain peaks and filled with grasslands, orchards and vegetable plots, through which snakes the Lasíthiou River, a dry gully for most of the year that rushes with water during the spring snow melt.

A good dirt road climbs west from Kritsá for 11km to reach the plateau. Houses which dot the slopes above the fields are occupied from 20 May each year when the vegetable and fruit growers, and the wine and *rakí* makers of Kritsá settle here for the summer months. Katharó produce has a flavour unlike any other.

▶ Keratókambos *108A1*

Isolated on the south coast on a dirt road between Tsoútsouros and Árvi, Keratókambos is dignified with a strip of tarmac along its single line of tavernas, rooms to rent and village houses above a narrow but sandy beach. Marvellously clear green water lies in front, and behind rears the great jagged rock tooth of Keratό mountain. This is a peaceful place, unaffected by tourism.

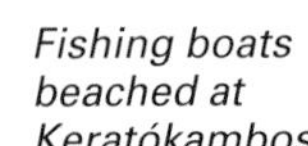

Fishing boats beached at Keratókambos

Walk Lasíthiou Plateau

It would be a pity to visit the Lasíthiou plateau and not venture out into the the middle of the plain among the fields and fruit orchards. Those who stick to the road that encircles the plateau see little of the traditional methods of farming that have survived here virtually unchanged by 20th-century technology. This is an easy stroll on flat roads with little possibility of getting lost, since your objective, the village of Tzermiádho, is in view all the way. This is a good way to complement your visit to the Dhíktaean Cave (see pages 118–19). The walk starts at Psikhró, is about 6.5km long, and you should allow 2 hours.

Just to the right of the entrance to the cave car park is a stepped, paved path. Turn left at the road below and keep on down to the main road into Psikhró by the Hotel Zeus. Cross the road and take the concrete track opposite. Soon it bears left. Turn right just beyond the bend and continue for 2km to the outskirts of Ayíos Yeóryios, walking between apple trees and corn fields. The distant mountains ring the plain and on the far side you can see Tzermiádho village under a hill crowned by a white chapel.

Hand and machine knitting, crocheting and weaving for sale in Tzermiádho

Turn left at a tarred road just outside Ayíos Yeóryios on to a wide dirt road that leads out into the middle of the plain. Here you'll see men and women breaking the ground with mattocks, ploughing with wooden horse-drawn ploughs and sowing seed from buckets – hard, primitive labour. The remaining cloth-sailed windpumps whirl round, raising water for the irrigation channels that criss-cross the plain, while the skeletons of abandoned pumps lie beside their wells.

After 2km turn right and immediately left at a T-junction, and follow the road round bends and over cross-roads to the road in Tzermiádho. Turn right, and bear left at the resistance memorial to reach the Taverna Kronion in the village, where you can catch the bus back to Psikhró.

Drive Coast road from Tsoútsouros to Arví

This is a very challenging 75km drive along the south coast, in beautiful wild scenery between mountains and the sea, featuring two lonely resorts and a spectacular monastery clinging to a hillside next to one of Crete's most dramatic gorges.

This is emphatically not a drive for the impatient. You should give half a day to it, and be prepared to stay in second, if not first, gear for much of the way. Sections of the road surface are very rough indeed, and there are some steep and narrow descents which can be slippery after rain; some of these roads do not appear on several island maps, including that on pages 108–9. Your reward will be the discovery of a stretch of coastline travelled by few, with wonderful views all the way. Plans are said to be under consideration to widen and improve the road. This may remove some of the heart-in-mouth moments, but will inevitably attract the day-trippers who are conspicuous by their absence at present. Taste it in its virgin state while you still can! As always, check your tyres and petrol before you set out.

Driving east from Moíres on the Mesarás plain, bear right beyond Ayía Dékha through Yanyáles, Asími and Píryos, to leave the main road to Áno Viánnos in Káto Kastellianá, following the Tsoútsouros sign. The bumpy dirt road spirals into the hills above some dizzying drops, between slopes of florid purple rock, with views down plunging valleys. Soon you look down on the huddle of Tsoútsouros (see pages 104–5) on a lonely coast where deep water comes close inshore.

Swing left at the bottom of the descent on a rough road passing between greenhouses. Sheep graze on the flat, scrubby coastal strip, overlooked by yellow rock faces slit by narrow gorges. Keep right at a fork 3km beyond Tsoútsouros, and take great care on the steep descent that follows. You cross the River Anapodháris on a concrete bridge and continue through groves of olives, lemons and oranges, past lines of plastic greenhouses sheltering tomatoes and cucumbers – this is one

The wild coastal scenery between Tsoútsouros and Arví

The hillside village of Áno Viánnos

of the sunniest spots in Crete. The pointed peak of Mount Keratό towers above a sea of sublime turquoise and the sandy beach at Keratókambos (page 124), where the tarmac begins.

You are soon back on the dirt again, keep straight ahead, twisting round difficult hairpin bends above the yellow clay cliffs. The surface here is atrocious, and concentration on the driver's part is essential. Make time, though, to look around and appreciate the beauty of ravines, mountain slopes and purple rocks, and to notice the young shepherds on the hillsides tending their flocks with the same timeless air of monumental patience displayed by their fathers and grandfathers.

After three quarters of an hour you descend once more to the coast and a junction with a tarmac road, signed to Amirás, which runs off to the left. Keep straight on here for 0.5km beside the bay until you come to Arví (see page 117). Pass through the village and bear sharp right over a ford, signposted to St Antony's Monastery. After 200m another sign points left; park here for a walk up to the monastery.

Stroll

The rough road winds inland for 1km with superb views of the towering and exceptionally narrow gorge that widens to a Y-shape near the top, some 300m overhead. The buildings of Arví Monastery cling to the face of the mountain nearby. When you reach the monastery, climb the winding steps to the church which has frescoes and a beautiful painted iconostasis. Above the church you will find the abandoned cells which command a memorable view to the sea over a lush, tree-filled valley.

Return to the western end of Arví and bear right on the road to Amirás. Turn left at the junction in the village to reach Áno Viánnos, piled on the southern flanks of the Dhíkti Mountains. You should stop here and seek out the village churches which have rich frescoes (see pages 116–17), before continuing to Káto Kastellianá and on to Moíres.

Key words
Many churches are kept locked these days, for fear of the theft of icons and other irreplaceable treasures. Someone always has the key, but who? Most likely the village priest, perhaps a nearby householder, or a specially appointed custodian. Three useful words to help you in your search: *o papás* (the priest); *o filakás* (the custodian); *to klithí* (the key).

►►► Kritsá 109C2

Tucked into the eastern flanks of the Dhíkti Mountains 9km west of Ayíos Nikólaos, Kritsá stands for all that is best and most typical of Cretan village life. It is a large village which runs uphill towards a splendid backdrop of crags, with a wonderful eastward view downhill towards the Gulf of Mirambéllou. The vice-president of the Kritsá community is keen to encourage visitors to stay with local families and join in with village life. Many shops along the village's narrow streets sell woven and hand embroidered handicrafts. Easter here, celebrated with volleys of firecrackers, long processions and riotous parties, can be a memorable occasion. On 20 May each year a large proportion of the village men trek up to the lonely and beautiful Katharó plateau (see page 124) high in the mountains west of Kritsá, and stay there for the next six months tending their vegetable and corn fields and making wine and *rakí*. The mountainous country behind Kritsá is ideal for rough walking on *kalderími*, cobbled paths, and ancient roadways that date back to Minoan times, and for discovering half-forgotten Minoan houses and Dorian settlements.

There are several notable churches in Kritsá, of which the most striking is Panayía Kerá (open Monday–Saturday 9–3, Sunday 9–2) at the bottom of the village. Here the superbly restored frescoes demonstrate the glory of Cretan Byzantine art. A 13th-century Baptism in the dome swells with sails and fish; the central nave has Salome balancing the Baptist's head on her own; in the north aisle the white-hooded souls of the dead are packed into their communal grave like bobsleigh riders; in the south aisle a marvellously sympathetic Virgin sorrows beside her inconsolable husband. These are only a few of the treasures in this unique church. Another fine church is Ayiós Pnevma with its old icons in the iconostasis, including some lively lions and a sinuous, upward-looking St Peter.

The ancient church of Panayía Kerá in Kritsá

■ Icons or religious pictures were being painted in the vivid Cretan style as far back as the 14th century. Local painters infused the formal Byzantine tradition with their own delight in earthy realities: expressions range from the sorrowful to the ecstatic, limbs are attenuated and sinuous, vigorous trees and animals are set against rocky backdrops.....■

Top: a 14th-century depiction of the patriarchs in the Garden of Eden, from the church of Panayía Kerá in Kritsá

Icon painting for souvenirs and religious use

Gradually, however, the perspectives of mainland Europe's Renaissance crept in and took over. Often the icons were set in a richly carved iconostasis or wooden framework. There is a particularly superb example at Préveli Monastery. Cretans still treat their icons with reverence, kissing them on entry to the church, pushing flowers into the frames, hanging them with silver *taxímata* to solicit help and healing.

The frescoes painted on church walls and ceilings are equally lively, and a good deal more striking due to their size and subject matter. Humour, subtlety, cruelty and tenderness fill the best of the Cretan-school frescoes from the 15th and 16th centuries. They can be found in the most unexpected places: in a crumbling cave church on the coast, in a sheepfold hut that was once a hermit's chapel, or in a seldom visited plateau church hidden in the mountains.

The Byzantine fresco arrangement seldom varies. Christ Pantokrator, Lord of All, stares down from the rounded roof of the apse, above Evangelists and Holy Fathers. Across the roof of the nave scenes from His life are always present: Nativity, Baptism, Crucifixion and Resurrection. The west wall shows the Second Coming and the snake-ridden torments of the damned. Below the dado rail are military and secular saints, perhaps the founder of the church as well, and medallions on the vaulting ribs hold the heads of yet more saints.

There have been recent revivals in both icon and fresco painting, though modern treatment, rather sadly, seems to have reverted to a stiffer and more formal, and some say, less Cretan style.

Modern art
Do not turn up your nose at modern frescoes and icons. There has been a welcome revival of the art in recent times, and the best of the modern painting is exceptionally good. Some of these new icons easily stand comparison with ancient masterpieces.

St Joachim, also from the church of Panayía Kerá in Kritsá

Pumps preserved
There are plans afoot to restore all the 10,000 wind pumps of Lasíthiou, in recognition of their enduring appeal to visitors. This is a welcome move. The hundreds of gaunt, rusting skeletons of collapsed pumps that now lie across their wellheads in the fields of Lasíthiou are a melancholy sight in this uplifting landscape.

►►► Lasíthiou Plateau *109C2*

The Lasíthiou plateau is one of the most-visited of Crete's attractions. Nearly everyone makes the ascent to see the windmills in action, either from Ayíos Nikólaos or from the north coast road at Svoúrou Metókhi, which is nearer Iráklio and gives the more dramatic initial view of the plateau. In late summer, when these small windpumps are being driven by their whirling white-cloth sails, it is a breathtaking sight. Unfortunately, many of the wind-driven pumps now stand or lie inactive, and a lot of the working pumps are driven by electricity.

But the plateau has more to offer than the windpumps. This level plain of tiny green and brown fields lies between 817 and 950m above sea level, the only Cretan plateau at this height which is occupied all year round. The fertility of the soil, enriched by minerals leached down from the surrounding mountains and still worked largely by manual labour, is partly responsible; tourism has also brought some prosperity to the string of villages that lies round the perimeter road. There is the Dhíktaean Cave near Psikhró, the legendary birthplace of Zeus (see pages 118–19); the local weaving and embroidery that flutters on clothes-lines along the road; the wild flowers that carpet the plateau every spring; and the coolness of the mountain breeze. Tzermiádho is a fair-sized village with most facilities. Ayíos Yeóryios is another, with an excellent folklore museum (signposted, open 10–4). It is actually a village house furnished in traditional style with loom, bread oven, raised bed, and with a cool storeroom

Windpump sails, made traditionally of white cloth, are becoming increasingly rare

full of *píthoi*. There is a stable with hand ploughs, equipment for horses, a threshing board ferociously set with toothed iron blades, and three ludicrous stuffed chickens.

Lasíthiou people have always been tough resisters. The Venetians drove them out in 1263 in response to their seditious activities, and the plain lay uncultivated for 200 years. Paduan engineers later laid out the irrigation system still worked today by the windpumps.

The well-preserved Dorian city at Lató

▶▶ Lató *109C3*

This Dorian city site (7th–3rd century BC), 2km north of Kritsá, is surprisingly little visited, considering its good state of preservation (open 8:30–3, closed Monday). The city remains occupy twin hilltops, reached by way of a stepped and cobbled street that rises from the city gate, just north of the entrance to the site at the top of the road from Kritsá. Almost everything is massively built of great stone blocks: the entrance gateway itself, the guard towers on the left of the path, the deep workshops on the right with their wells, olive presses and corn-grinding querns.

At the top the street doglegs to reach the *agora* or open court on the saddle, with a rectangular shrine to Artemis and a deep cistern to the left, a little bench-lined square to the right. A wonderful view opens over a valley to Ayíos Nikólaos, the ancient port of Lató. Wide steps lead up to the northern acropolis, from which you look across to the temple of Apollo on the slope of the southern hill.

View from the hill
Even if you have only minimal interest in matters archaeological, it is always worth climbing to a Cretan hilltop site for the view. Ancient settlers invariably chose their dwelling places with an eye on a good clear outlook over what was going on around them. In Crete that means, in almost every case, a superb prospect of mountain, coast and sea.

▶▶▶ Mália Minoan Palace *108B4*

The Minoan palace (open 8:30–3, closed Monday) at Mália lacks the dramatic hilly surroundings of Faistós and Ayía Triádha, sited as it is on the scrubby north coast plain 37km to the east of Iráklio. But it has been superbly excavated by the French Archaeological School from Athens who are still at work here on outlying sections of the complex. The portions of the palace constructed of mud brick have been roofed over to prevent dissolution by wind and rain. There are stalls selling guide books by the entrance, but refreshments are confined to a van in the car park.

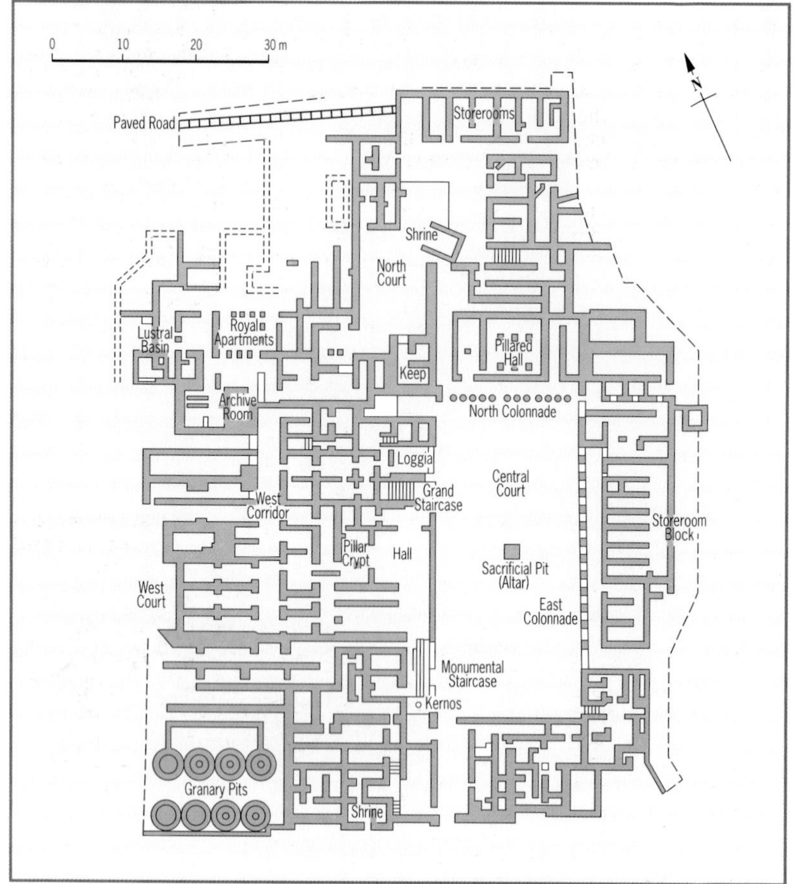

Mália Minoan palace

Gold pit
If you turn left just before the palace car park and follow the road to the shore, then bear right on a footpath along the coast for a few minutes, you will come to the fenced site of Khrysólakkos, where the famous and beautiful gold bee pendant was unearthed. Locals must have known of the treasures buried here long before the archaeologists came along. Khrysólakkos means 'gold pit', and the area has been so named for many years.

The old palace of Mália was originally built some time between 2000 and 1700BC on the site of a much earlier settlement. Around 1700BC it was demolished by the catastrophic event that flattened the other big Minoan palaces on Crete and, like them, it was rebuilt to enter a golden era of prosperity and influence. Then around 1450BC came the disaster that destroyed all the palaces, except Knosós, and most of the settlements of Minoan Crete. Mália was entirely destroyed in the catastrophe, and only a few individual houses on the site were ever occupied again.

Inside the gate, turn right and right again to reach the southwest corner of the palace beside eight cylindrical stone granary pits. Follow the enormously thick walls of blue-grey stone along the south side of the palace, past a little paved shrine, to a wide entrance and a passage flagged with big slabs. It leads to the central court, the hub around which this exploration revolves.

The central court is enormous (48m by 22m), big enough to hold thousands of people. Partially paved, it lies around a small central cavity, square-built of mud bricks, that might have supported an altar. Along the east side of the court runs a line of square pillar bases alternating with the round bases of marble columns, an arrangement echoed in many other Minoan palaces. East of here are storerooms, some uncovered and constructed of pebbles and red stone blocks, others roofed over and of crumbling yellow mud brick. The stone floors are provided with drainage canals running to sink holes, set between raised platforms grooved to channel away the spillage from wine and oil jars.

On the west side of the court a grand staircase rises and abruptly ends. It used to lead to the upper storey of the palace but only eleven steps remain. Just south of the staircase is the pillared hall of the west wing, and beyond it a flag-floored crypt whose square pillars are incised with the *labrys* or sacred, double-headed axe. North of the staircase, steps mount to a ceremonial platform behind which is the little room where excavators found the leopard-shaped axe and the crystal-hilted sword now in Gallery IV of the Archaeological Museum in Iráklio.

Along the north side of the central court runs a portico with ten columns, north of which is a hall with square pillars set close together. Beyond the northwest corner of the central court is the north court, with the massive wall of a *donjon* or stronghold on its south side. West of here, in a maze of rooms, were the apartments of the settlement's king and queen.

At the north edge of the palace two gigantic, finely decorated *píthoi* stand by a paved walkway. The more easterly jar is blackened by fire scorching, and dribbles of liquid carbonised in the final calamity still stain its sides. The walkway leads west to a roofed complex of sunken, thick-walled rooms, some with spillways and drain holes. The two most westerly rooms have stone benches round three sides. Palace notables may have gathered here to discuss, argue and legislate.

Body of evidence
A recent theory has gained a hearing, but certainly not respectability, by suggesting that the Minoan palaces were nothing of the sort, but were in fact giant necropoles or cemeteries. The almost complete absence of human remains in any of them presents something of a stumbling block to this hypothesis.

An intricate gold ornament found at Mália

▶▶ Mírtos *109C1*

There are two ancient sites to explore here. The first, Fournoú Korifí, lies just north of the south coast road at Néos Mírtos, 14km west of Ierápetra. This is an early Minoan hilltop site occupied well before 2000BC with a maze of tiny buildings from which, among many pottery finds, came the pot-bellied and slim-necked goddess of Mírtos (see page 115).

Mírtos Pýryos is also north of the road, 3km further on. At the east end of the bridge just before Mírtos village, turn right onto a dirt road. The path climbs right immediately. Walk clockwise round the summit of the hill past a deep cistern and scrub-smothered ruins, and climb a cobbled road up the east slope to the palace on the top. Destroyed by fire around 1450BC, but still visible, are a paved courtyard, a purple stone walkway, rooms and corridors, column bases and stairs.

A píthos, *also found at Mália*

Modern churches often contain modern frescoes

► Néapoli 109C3

A large, well-to-do market town 21km northwest of Ayíos Nikólaos, just off the new road to Iráklio, Néapoli was the birthplace in 1340 of Pétros Phílargos who was proclaimed Pope Alexander V in 1409, and it later became the administrative centre of its district under the Turks, a rôle it still performs. Today it is primarily a farming town. Pick-up trucks with bales of hay jolt along the streets, and workshops repair agricultural implements. Beside the tree-shaded gardens in the main square stands a big modern church with brightly coloured frescoes of stolid and expressionless saints. In its shadow is a little old church with a vivid icon of St John the Baptist. Stroll from the top right corner of the square into the back lanes of Néapoli to find more old churches. Ayíos Spirídon, Ayíos Demétrios, Ayía Varvára, and Ayíos Giórgios all have faded icons whose frames are stuffed with flowers and *taxímata*. Then find a café and idle over a glass of *soumádha*, a sweet and sherbet-tasting drink made locally of almonds.

► Pláka 109D4

A right turn 200m north of the harbour in Eloúndha (see page 122) brings you after 4km to Pláka, a strip of rooms to rent, village houses and tavernas, undeveloped and peaceful. From here you can catch a *caïque* out to Spinalónga Island, or you can just sit on the shady terrace of a taverna, enjoying the absence of bustle, as you admire a splendid view of the island over a plate of freshly caught fish.

►►► Spinalónga Island 109D4

See pages 136–7.

►► Tértsa 108B1

Tértsa goes unmentioned in most guide books, which is scarcely surprising since this tiny line of buildings is connected to the Ierápetra–Ano Viánnos road by 11km of seemingly endless dirt track. Turn off the main road at the Sikólogos sign. Where the track dips right into the village, keep left, and at a fork after 2km keep straight on by a concrete building, and persevere. Down on the coast at Tértsa you will find a tamarisk-shaded terrace overlooking a shingly beach, a few fishing boats, a taverna or two, strong homemade wine, and blissful peace, a real haven.

Loudspeakers
The advent of electricity has added a characteristic sound to the Cretan scene. The amplified human voice assails the ears of both willing and unwilling listeners: priests intone their prayers from belfries, politicians search for votes, music fans tune in to their local radio station, sellers of vegetables and fish call from their pick-up trucks. And all can be certain of a wider audience than hitherto, thanks to the power of the strategically-placed loudspeaker.

Tradition or tourism?

■ The village economy is still strong in Crete, and everywhere you go you will see people working in the groves and fields, and on the mountains. But they are almost all people over 50. Increasing numbers of Cretan youngsters are leaving the villages and land. There are two main reasons for this: tourism, and the power of the modern media, in particular television.....■

'Crete, why do you exile
Your brave young men?
Alien lands rejoice,
And you long for them.'

'Rise and say farewell
To your father's house;
You'll find a better one
Together with your
spouse.'

Cretan Mantinádes

Left and below: sheep and shepherding still form an important part of the island's agricultural economy

These are hard times for the slow-paced, traditional villages of Crete, though you might not think so when you see their neat white outlines among freshly watered fields and olive groves. The agricultural work of the villagers has always been hard manual labour: digging irrigation channels and fetching water, transporting tools and produce by donkey, pruning, harvesting and sowing with unsophisticated implements, tending sheep through long days in the heat of summer and the cold of winter on barren hillsides.

The tourist industry of the seaside towns absorbs a large amount of seasonal labour. Less well-educated youngsters can get work as bar staff, chamber maids, hotel porters and so on. They may return to their villages during the winter, or for festivals such as Easter, but they are often discontented, bored and unwilling to help out with what they see as low-grade work. This is even more true of the better-educated young people. The world is wider for them than it was for their parents, and they aim for office jobs in local government, administration and the professions, either in Iráklio or overseas, especially in Athens.

Some young people have returned to the villages, not to pick up their parents' tools, but to use their city know-how as entrepreneurs renting out rooms, running tavernas or souvenir shops, or in small-scale manufacturing. And they are keen to entice the tourist trade to their own doorstep. Fed by television images of wealth and success, they are vulnerable to economic difficulties and to disillusionment of a kind that their village forebears, for all the narrowness of their working lives, never had to face.

Venetian defences dominate Spinalónga Island

Pantiles
One note of beauty among the harshness and desolation of Spinalónga is the old pantiled roofing of the tumbledown houses, whose red baked clay has been faded by the sun and salt wind to the most delicate shades of peach and rose pink.

Quarries
From the crest of the island you can see sheer-sided scars on the blunt snout of the Spinalónga peninsula. These are the remains of the quarries from which the Venetians took the stone to build their fortifications on the island.

►►► Spinalónga Island *109D4*

The history of Spinalónga Island parallels that of Crete itself: a story of stoicism, hardship, refuge, persecution, compassion and cruelty, all in a setting of harsh beauty. The position of the island, at the entrance to the long bay that leads to Eloúndha, is a glorious one, and the approach to the grim fortress walls, the terraced slopes and the symmetrical, straight-spined shape of Spinalónga is one of Crete's most memorable experiences. Soon you see that the terraces are made of ruined houses invaded by pine trees and scrub bushes, and the boatman will begin to tell of Spinalónga's more recent history, a darkness that persisted until less than 40 years ago.

Boats run to Spinalónga Island from Ayíos Nikólaos, a long and fairly expensive cruise, and from Eloúndha and Pláka. You can join a guided tour. The earlier you get away the better, as crowds of visitors swarm over the island by midday, and the cruise boats pump out disco music and a tinnily amplified commentary.

On the summit of the island are the blurred ruins of an ancient stronghold. Spinalónga must always have been a prized possession, lying as it does in command of the entrance to the bay. The main fortifications that you see at the southern end as you approach, beetling stone walls, round-bellied bastions, stumpy guard towers and long runs of battlements, were built by the Venetians in 1579 when the rise of the Ottoman empire was beginning to threaten them. These fortifications were impregnable. After the Turks took Crete in 1646, a Venetian garrison remained on Spinalónga until it was ousted by treaty in 1715. Nearly three centuries later, when the Turks in their turn felt increasingly menaced by Cretan uprisings and world opinion, a town was built near the old fort as a refuge in case of trouble. After the Four Powers settlement of 1898 most Turks left Crete, but the town on Spinalónga continued to harbour several hundred until they, too, dispersed in 1903.

Then the island entered its dark days. Leprosy was still a virulent and dreaded disease in Crete at that time, and the position of Spinalónga made it the government's choice as a leper colony. It was near enough to shore to be supplied easily, but just far enough offshore for the contagion to be safely out of reach. The lepers were moved across to the island, housed in the old buildings of the Turkish town and left to their life of rejection and isolation. By all accounts they were initially treated more like criminals than victims of disease. The island was run with military strictness, and its inhabitants had to do almost everything for themselves.

But things did gradually improve. More doctors were sent to join the dedicated few who, with priests and nuns, had been doing their best for the lepers. A new medical centre was built, sanitation was improved and access was made easier for the sufferers' families. In 1957 the last of the lepers was evacuated, and soon Spinalónga became the tourist attraction that it is today.

After landing on the slipway, take a left turn through a long, vaulted tunnel which leads to the ruined town. Wooden doors hang open, roofless shells of houses are filled with collapsed floor joists. Ovens, cupboards, stove pipes and partitions made of fish boxes all stand as they were left when the island was evacuated. Cypresses, pines, prickly pears, olive trees and wild roses grow among the terraced ruins on the west slope. You pass a church and the concrete doctors' hall to come to a curved Venetian redoubt at the north end of the island. Just before this, a path doubles back to climb to the top of Spinalónga with bare grey rock, more crumbling fortifications, and a beautiful view of the mountains across the green, clear water that sealed the lepers into their island prison for half a century.

Island rebels
Not long after the Turks occupied Crete, a resistance movement was formed. Its members called themselves the *Khainides* and they operated from Spinalónga against the new rulers. Other branches were based on Nisos Soúdha and Gramvoúsa, as all three islands were still under Venetian control at the time.

Looking towards Eloúndha from the battlements of Spinalónga Island

Sitiá's Venetian fort was clearly built to last for centuries

SITIÁ AND THE EAST

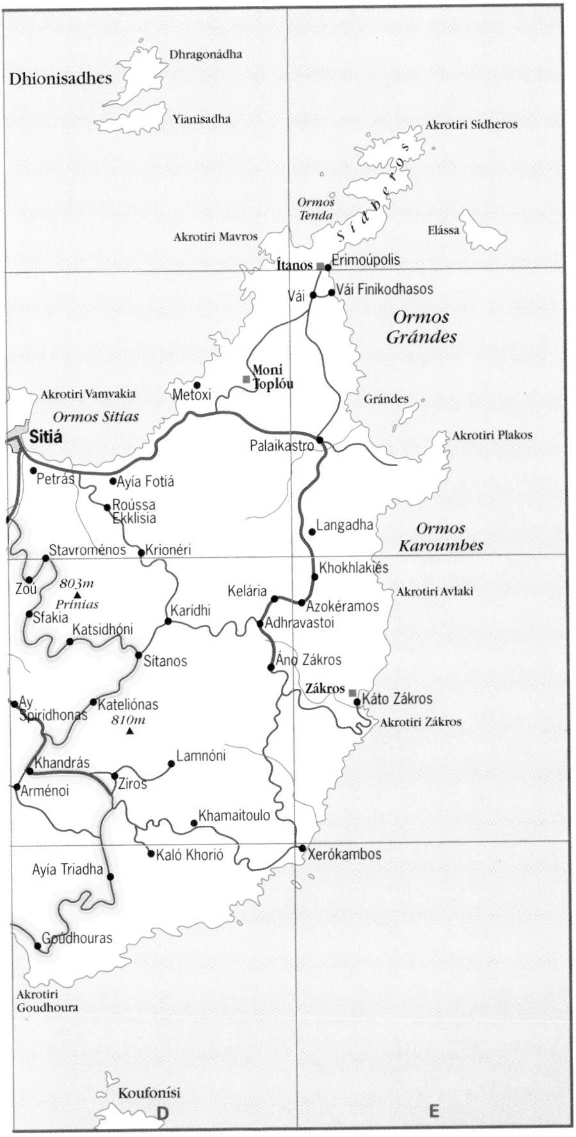

Dhionisadhes
Dhragonádha
Yianisadha
Akrotiri Sídheros
Sídheros
Ormos Tenda
Elássa
Akrotiri Mavros
Ítanos
Erimoúpolis
Vái
Vái Finikodhasos
Ormos Grándes
Moni Toplóu
Metoxi
Akrotiri Vamvakia
Grándes
Ormos Sitias
Sitiá
Palaikastro
Akrotiri Plakos
Petrás
Ayía Fotiá
Roússa Ekklisia
Langadha
Ormos Karoumbes
Stavroménos
Krionéri
Khokhlakiés
Zoú
803m
Prínias
Keléria
Akrotiri Avlaki
Azokéramos
Karídhi
Sfakia
Adhravastoi
Katsidhóni
Sítanos
Áno Zákros
Zákros
Káto Zákros
Ay Spirídhonas
Katelíónas
810m
Akrotiri Zákros
Lamnóni
Khandrás
Zíros
Arménoi
Khamaitoulo
Kaló Khorió
Xerókambos
Ayía Triadha
Goudhouras
Akrotiri Goudhoura
Koufonísi
D
E

Threshing floors
All over the Cretan uplands you will come across circular threshing floors built among the ruins of Minoan houses, Dorian temples and Byzantine basilicas. Constructed during the last few hundred years and with a concern for matters meteorological rather than archaeological, they are sited where winds funnel and concentrate to blow away the seed husks at winnowing time.

Three-in-one
In Greek Orthodox churches the devout cross themselves with the index and middle fingertips of the right hand touching the tip of the thumb. The three-in-one signifies the Holy Trinity.

Sitiá and the East Between Iráklio and Ayíos Nikólaos the north coast of Crete suffers from an exuberantly unplanned sprawl of recent development. But once you have passed through Ayíos Nikólaos everything improves: the landscape, the towns, the pace of life and the temper of the local people. Folk in the east of Crete pride themselves on their easygoing attitude to life, as much as the Sfakiots of the west congratulate themselves on their fierceness. The east has a landscape as dramatic as anywhere in Crete, and vast areas of mountain and coast with tiny, hospitable villages still very little visited by tourists. For a real sense of relaxation and of being truly welcome, this area is definitely the choice of the discerning explorer.

The two chief towns of the east are Sitiá on the north coast and Ierápetra on the south. There are few notable Venetian buildings in either town; both went into a long decline under Turkish rule and were allowed to fall into decay. But both have quarters where you can wander among tangled old alleyways, good hotels and excellent tavernas, lively waterfronts (especially at night), and busy harbours where brightly painted fishing boats disgorge freshly caught fish that you will eat in the evening. Sitiá is built on hills, giving far views over the town and harbour from the upper streets and squares. Ierápetra, by contrast, lies low on a fertile plain lined with long plastic greenhouses. These don't look pretty, but they have brought prosperity to this southeastern coast and their produce makes Ierápetra salad something to savour.

A narrow isthmus, 15km wide, connects the eastern end of Crete with the rest of the island. Immediately to the east rise two impressive mountain ranges, Thriptís to the south march north to join Ornó. The formidable western face of Thriptís is cut by one of Crete's most spectacular canyons, the narrow, plunging Monastiráki Gorge. The dirt roads up into these mountains are not for the faint-hearted nor those pressed for time, but venturers into the high places will be rewarded by the sight of villages piled house on house, clinging to bluffs above enormous drops, surrounded by pine forests and backed by jagged ridges

In the Sitiá Mountains

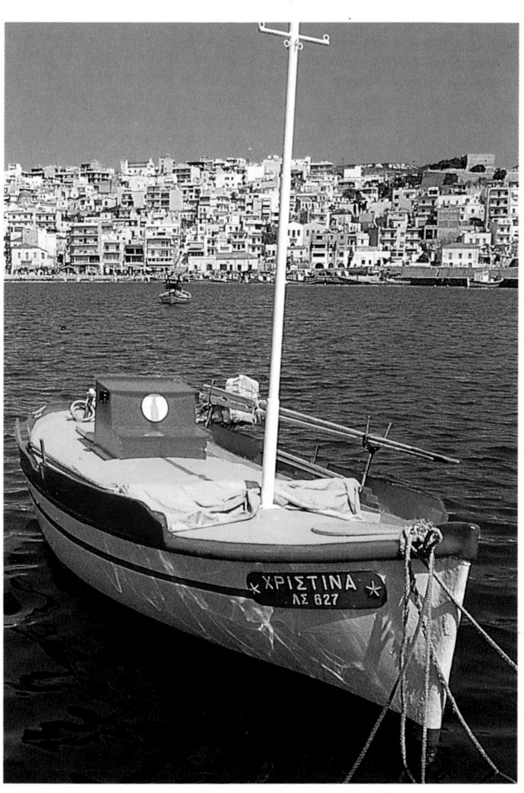

Sitiá is the main port of eastern Crete

Káto and _Áno_
When planning a day's excursion with a map, take note of *Káto* and *Áno*. *Káto* signifies the lower part of a village, *Áno* the upper part (sometimes also given as *Epáno* or simply *Ep.*). And although the village name will be shared between them, for example Káto Zákros and Áno Zákros, there is often a world of difference between the two halves, which could be several kilometres apart.

and peaks. Hospitality here is just as warming as the local wine, judged by most to be the best in Crete.

Another valley crosses the island to the east of Thriptís which carries the main road south from Sitiá to Ierápetra. Beyond this are the Sitiá Mountains which are lower than Thriptís and Ornó, but still impressive, forming a great block of high country, with farming villages such as Khandrás and Zíros making the most of the fertile highlands and very much the centre of local life. There are few concessions to tourism up here, but you'll find local people very interested in you, especially if you brave the stares and try out whatever Greek phrases you know.

The south coast is not all plastic greenhouses, though they are in evidence along much of the main road east of Ierápetra until it turns north for Sitiá. As the coast turns north around the end of the island the roads become fewer. Those that do descend to the sea end in excellent beaches with a few tavernas, for example Xerókambos, Káto Zákros where there is a superb Minoan palace, and Vái with its famous date palm forest. The wild peninsula of Síderos pokes out from the northeastern tip of Crete. This is, unfortunately, a forbidden paradise due to the presence of a NATO base.

There is no road along the north coast; the main highway runs inland. Little roads and tracks lead down to more isolated and delightful seaside hamlets, beaches and coves, looking out to islands a world away from the built-up coastline west of Ayíos Nikólaos.

The delightful Italianate church in Epáno Episkopí

▶ Ayía Fotiá

139D3

Six and a half kilometres east of Sitiá on the coast road, Ayía Fotiá spreads itself along the beach in a sprawl of flats and hotels, standard Cretan seaside development which you pass by with scarcely a glance. The old village lies inland of the road, and provides a pleasant half-hour stroll through the lanes and pathways among the houses. In 1971 archaeologists unearthed the largest Minoan cemetery yet discovered, on and around a little hill over-looking the beach. The dead were buried in dug-out cavities, and in chamber tombs cut into the rock of the hill. More than 250 burials were found, together with a vast number of vases, lead amulets, a large copper knife, other weapons, fish hooks and gold sheets sealed in a lead box, evidence of the Minoans' extensive trading in a variety of metals. Some of these finds are now in Sitiá's archaeolog-ical museum, others are in Iráklio.

► Epáno Episkopí 138C2

This village straddles the road south from Sitiá to Ierápetra. Above the road to the right stands the tall, graceful Italianate Church of the Panayía. The Catholic bishop of Sitiá based himself here when 16th-century pirate raids made the coast a dangerous place to live. Apart from the church, the main attraction of Epáno Episkopí lies in its fine view, south and east across the terraced hills, olive groves, rocky gorges and mountains of the dramatic Pantélis valley.

►►► Faneroménis Monastery (near Sitiá) 138C3

Not to be confused with the monastery of the same name near Gourniá, this Faneroménis is reached by a rough and winding road signposted to the left off the main road about 6.5km before you reach Sitiá from Ayíos Nikólaos. Inside the tiny church, to the left of the iconostasis, a square hatchway leads to a dark cavern. Light one of the church candles and you will see a heap of skulls and bones, and icons placed all around the cave. This was where an icon of the Virgin miraculously appeared in the 15th century and returned each time it was removed. The church frescoes were blackened in 1829 during an arson attempt by two Turks who were then stricken with fatal illnesses. Turkish bullets caused the holes in the face of the saint who sits reading a book in one of the few fresco medallions still discernible. Around the icon nearest the cave hatch are hundreds of *taxímata* or votive plaques requesting cures for illnesses, some tarnished and ancient, others shiny and new. Faneroménis offers an insight into Cretan suffering and faith, past and present, more striking than many of the island's better-preserved and more visited monasteries.

►►► Ierápetra 138A1

See pages 144–5.

►►► Ítanos 139E4

The local name for Ítanos is Erimoúpolis, the deserted city, and this is indeed a lonely place, a couple of kilometres north of Vái but far removed from its crowds and noise. Two little hills and the headland to the south across a tiny bay make up the site of the city that in post-Minoan times challenged Ierápetra (pages 144–5) and Praisós (page 148) for overall power in eastern Crete. The tablet in the wall of the church at Toploú Monastery (pages 154–5) records the settlement of a land dispute with Ierápetra in 132BC. Ítanos was the victor in this, but squabbles between the three had been frequent down the preceding centuries.

From the western or inland hill, with terrace walls dating from Hellenistic times well before the birth of Christ, you descend seawards into the valley before climbing the

[continued on page 146]

Mézedes

By tradition, Cretans only drink alcohol if it is accompanied by *mézedes* or nibbles. In larger towns *mézedes* may be reduced to a dish of olives, but the village *kafenía* usually offer a variety, sometimes almost a meal in itself. These might include sliced artichoke with lemon, fried squid, cubes of *feta* cheese, knobs of baked bread, lupin seeds like shiny butterbeans, sweet almond bread, slices of tomato, potato or peeled apple...

See and be seen

Few of Crete's inland settlements lie tucked away out of sight. From earliest times it was necessary to see and be seen. That way lay safety, an insurance against surprise attack. Villages and towns stand on the edges of bluffs and outcrops, with a good view all round, situations that lend an air of the spectacular to the most humble cluster of houses.

Faneroménis Monastery

Sandy shore
Ierápetra's beautiful marble-paved promenade was built over a fine sandy beach. This not only did away with the beach itself, but also caused a general shallowing of the water as the tides deposited sand in a wide area just offshore. In places, locals say, you can wade out for 300m and still only be up to your armpits in the sea.

Beachless
There is too much sand offshore, and not enough on the beaches to the west of Ierápetra. When the greenhouse building boom was at its height, and the search was on for sand to use as bedding for the greenhouse plants, these once excellent beaches became victims of countless scoop-and-grab raids, official and otherwise.

▶▶▶ Ierápetra *138A1*

Ierápetra is the largest town on the south coast of Crete, the southernmost town of Europe – and it gets more sunshine than anywhere else on the island. Superb mountain scenery forms a backdrop, and there is a long, sandy beach to the west of the town. The local people are friendly and relaxed, the local wine excellent, and there are any number of decent hotels and restaurants, and a lively night life.

Ierápetra is certainly somewhat overburdened with rather utilitarian modern architecture and it has a strongly commercial atmosphere as the centre of a large area of vegetable and fruit cultivation. But it is nevertheless a rewarding place to walk around, if you keep to the seafront and the old Turkish quarter. Its bustling and inquisitive character gives it an animated flavour unlike any other big Cretan town.

Ierápetra was the most influential town of post-Minoan Crete, trading with north Africa and the Aegean islands. The population of Ierápytna, as it was then known, had a belligerent attitude towards their neighbours, and in 155BC the inhabitants marched north to destroy their rival, Praisós. It was the last Cretan town to surrender to the invading Romans in 67BC. Under their rule it continued to prosper, as it did later after the Venetians had taken control. However, when the Turks captured the town in 1647, Ierápetra ran out of luck. The conquerors allowed the town to decay, and for centuries it gently declined. Now rebuilt, with rather more energy than style, and revitalised, Ierápetra enthusiastically cultivates oranges, beans, tomatoes and tourists.

Ierápetra

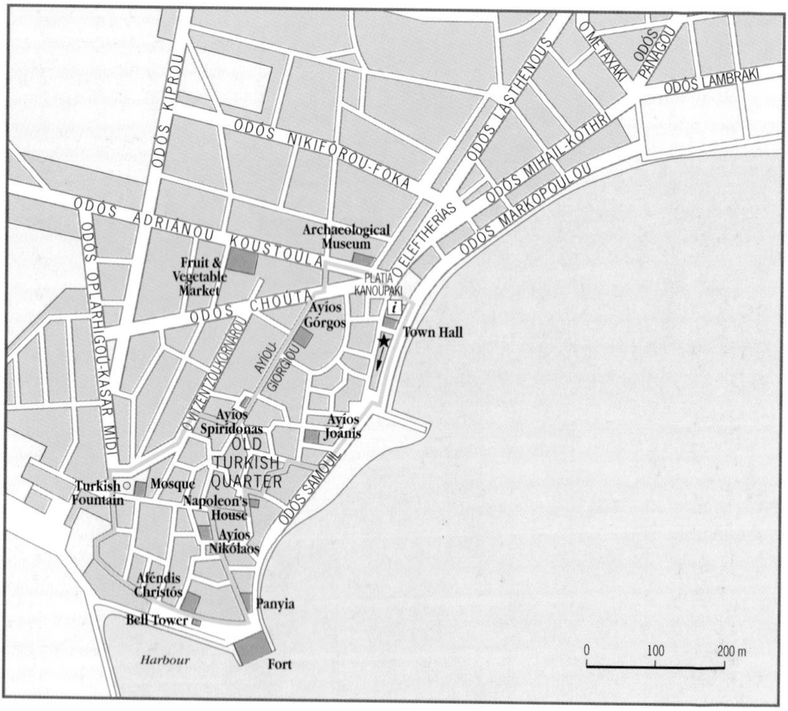

Walk Ierápetra

Allow two hours; see map opposite.

This leisurely walk on Ierápetra's waterfront starts at the square next to the town hall. From here turn right along the seafront promenade, past the jetty from which the ferries leave, and on down Odós Samouil. Any side turning to the right will take you into the narrow paved lanes of the **old Turkish quarter▶▶**, where modern blocks of flats and tottering, balconied old houses stand quietly side by side among the potted trees and flowers. It is easy to spend half an hour roaming here, and easier still to lose all sense of direction. Ask how to get to the fort, if you get lost, and you will come to the crenellated, slit-pierced old **castle▶** by the harbour. The Venetians rebuilt the uncompromising fortress after an earthquake in 1626, and the Turks later refortified it. Brightly painted fishing boats occupy the harbour inside a curved breakwater. A three-storey bell tower overlooks the scene, and across the road is the 14th-century church of Aféndis Christós with twin red-tiled domes.

Continue along the dusty road round a righthand bend to reach a **square▶** with a domed Turkish fountain which sports elaborate columns, dragonhead sculptures and an Arabic inscription. Beyond it stands a big Turkish mosque, with a capless minaret and inscriptions and symbols in marble.

In front of the mosque turn right along Odós Vitzéntzou Kornárou, and second right down Odós Mamounáki into the Turkish quarter. First left brings you to a square with a blue-painted church. Take top right, Ayíou Yióryiou, up to Odós Choúta. Ierápetra's **fruit and vegetable market▶** is opposite to the left and is well worth a visit in the early morning, when the artichokes, beans and aubergines are piled high. Cross Choúta and go up Odós Pagoménos, then turn right along Adriánou Koustoúla. Opposite, a few yards short of completing the walk, is the **Archaeological Museum▶**, rather dingy but with many Minoan, Doric and Graeco–Roman bits and pieces. The pride of the collection is the Minoan *larnax* or lidded clay coffin unearthed at Episkopí. It is decorated in vigorous, primitive fashion with octopus shapes, wild goat hunts and a long-tailed horse pulling a chariot.

Turkish mosque and fountain

Relief carvings at Ítanos

Fading black
Older village women dress almost invariably in black – black headscarf, black dress, black knee-socks. But it is becoming increasingly rare to see a woman under 50 dressed in this way. Uncovered hair, ordinary jumpers and even slacks are common among today's younger Cretan village women. Will the country streets and doorways be entirely empty of those nun-like, bent old figures in 30 years time?

Dress sense
The customary dress of the older men, however – tall knee-boots, drab-coloured wide breeches, black shirt, black head-fringe – is so practical, and so dashing, that its survival seems less in doubt.

[continued from page 143]
eastern hill. To your right, just below the summit, lies the outline of a basilica built in the 5th or 6th century AD. A very early Christian church, it has semicircular apses in the walls of the central aisle, which is flanked by side aisles and littered with sections of grey marble pillar, shaped stone blocks and scored and patterned stones. Looking south across the little beach with its feathery date palms, you can see other remains covering the slopes of the headland.

After Ierápetra attacked and destroyed Praisós in 155BC, Ítanos was the only other contender for control of eastern Crete. Ítanos remained influential until it, too, was destroyed, perhaps by north African or Middle Eastern pirates, well before the Venetians set foot on the island.

▶▶ Káto Zákros *139E2*

Káto Zákros lies at the foot of the Valley of the Dead (see page 153). Surrounded by carob and olive groves, fronted by a tiny fishing harbour and a fine pebbly beach between the hard-angled jaws of the headlands, the little strip of tavernas and rooms to rent has a spectacular setting. In summer it can be uncomfortably crowded with visitors to the nearby Minoan palace of Zákros (see pages 158–9). In winter (November to February) the place is largely unoccupied. There is occasional danger from floods down the gorge after heavy rain, but the main reason for the village's desertion is simply the absence of tourists. In early spring or late autumn, though, Káto Zákros is a delightful spot.

▶▶ Kavoúsi *138 B2*

Kavoúsi stands above the Ayíos Nikólaos–Sitiá road where it turns north to skirt the flanks of the Ornós Mountains. You won't see much of it from the road, but for those who leave their car and walk for half an hour through the tangle of lanes, up and down steps, under lemon trees and past flowers growing in wall cracks, the village provides rich rewards. There are pleasant cafés in the tree-shaded *platía,* and three Byzantine churches to seek out. The most interesting of the three is Apóstoli which is decorated with faded and blackened frescoes, and is reached by continuing along the narrowing lane which leads out of the square.

▶ Khandrás *139D2*

Khandrás, on the Zíros road from Epáno Episkopí, is a working village set in well-tilled fields at the western end of the fertile Zíros plateau. Turn left off the road just before entering Khandrás, on a dirt road signed to Stavroménos and

Colourful tavernas in Káto Zákros

The lanes of Kavoúsi

Karídhi. In 1km take another dirt road to reach the poignant ruins (smothered in grass and wild flowers) of the deserted village of **Voilá▶▶**. A brass tap still splashes water from a Turkish fountain; the remains of a Turkish tower stand on a bluff, with tessellated carvings around the doorway arch including two cypress trees – and cypresses still stand among the ruins. Above the village is the 15th-century church of Ayíos Yióryios; its twin aisles contain a faded fresco of the Madonna, and an icon of St George slaying a timid dragon

▶ Makríyialós *138B1*

The sprawling resort of Makríyialós has gobbled up the neighbouring village of Análipsi and is now a single agglomeration of hotels, shops, restaurants, car hire agents and the like. It makes a daunting introduction to the south coast when you arrive from Sitiá on the Ierápetra road. There are good views west along the coast and flanking mountains, however, and the beach is sandy and long. Little bays each side of the town are also sandy and can be less crowded.

Worry beads
Most Cretan men have them, but few women. They can be counted one by one, flicked from hand to hand, run through the fingers, whirled round like a propeller and clicked on a table top. Older sets are made of ornately carved wood or agate, polished from long use and handed down from father to son. Worry beads. Who knows what murder and mayhem would ensue if tension and anxiety were not dissipated by these secular rosaries?

Word puzzle
At Praisós three inscriptions were unearthed during excavations. They were written in Greek characters, but the language predated Greek. So far the inscriptions have not been deciphered, but there is speculation that they could be in the tongue used by the Eteocretans or true descendants of the Minoans, and might be a later version of the mysterious Linear A hieroglyphs found at several Minoan sites. If so, they may represent the best chance yet of one day receiving those unread messages from the dawn of European civilisation.

Mókhlos *138B3*

In Sfáka village, 40km east of Ayíos Nikólaos on the Sitiá road, you turn left, signposted, to descend towards the coast, and soon see Mókhlos below and to the left. The white houses of the village are sprinkled beside the sea, and Mókhlos island lies just offshore.

Mókhlos village is a pleasant place, not too crowded and with some friendly tavernas. You can get a boat here for the short crossing to the island which was a peninsula before a rise in sea level. You can explore the excavated remains of a Minoan harbour town on the landward side, or wander off to enjoy a peaceful hour or so to yourself, looking back for a lovely view of the village of Mókhlos and the mountains behind.

►►► Praisós *138C2*

Turn left in Epáno Episkopí, signposted to Zíros, some 11km from Sitiá on the south coast road to Ierápetra, and drop into the deep Pantélis valley. Then climb through Ayíos Spirídhonas, to enter Néa Praisós village on a left bend with a small *kafeníon* on the right. Go left where a small sign says 'To Antiquity Praisós', and follow a very bad dirt road with more handmade signs, to reach the three small hills of Praisós in about ten minutes.

The city of Praisós occupied these hills, and it was a powerful place from Doric times (c. 1000BC), through the Hellenistic period, until 155BC when it was destroyed by its jealous, and by now more powerful, neighbour Ierápytna, modern Ierápetra. The Eteocretans or Minoan descendants had their stronghold here on the middle hill or First Acropolis, and on the further one or Second Acropolis, while the nearest hill or Third Acropolis was topped by an altar, and later perhaps a temple.

Just beyond the ruined houses there is a gate on the left which leads to a footpath that winds clockwise to a saddle of ground between the First and Second Acropolis. Climb the slope of the First Acropolis to your left to find the rooms and storehouses of a 3rd-century BC house, its shaped stone blocks standing out from the rough terrace walling, facing a wonderful sea and mountain view.

Old Praisós occupied a commanding site

Islands of eastern Crete

■ A scattering of small offshore islands lies around the coastline of 'mainland' Crete. Some of these, such as Spinalónga, have shared in Crete's history and offer a microcosm of its beauty and its turbulent past. Others are more remote and difficult to reach, but they offer a valuable retreat – for both wildlife and their few visitors – from the pressures of modern life.....■

The first island that most visitors see is Diá, just off the harbour of Iráklio, and under the main flightpath of the airport. Diá was named after a nymph who was marooned on the island by Hera, the jealous sister and wife of Zeus, following a dalliance with the amorous god of gods. Diá is now one of the island sanctuaries of the *égagros* or Cretan ibex, and can be visited by boat from Iráklio.

To the east is the former leper colony of Spinalónga (see pages 136–7), and behind the adjacent peninsula lie the two Kolokithía islets with humped backs and long tail-like spits. Little Pándes, off Ayíos Nikólaos, is another *égagros* sanctuary. Psíra, in the Gulf of Mirambéllou, has a partly-excavated Minoan town and cemetery, and can be visited by boat from Ayíos Nikólaos and Mókhlos. Close to the coast is Mókhlos island (see opposite). Off the northeastern tip of Crete rise the three Dionysádes islands of Yianisádha, Dhragonádha and remote Paximádha where the rare Eleanora's falcon breeds.

Elássa lies 5km off Vaí beach and still offers a sheltered anchorage, as it has since Dorian times. Moving south to Xerókambos, there is a beautiful view out to tiny Kaválloi. Off the southernmost tip of Crete, Koufounísi lies low, deserted now, but with a long history. The island was handily placed on the sea route to North Africa and the Middle East, and the Romans established a sizeable settlement here. The Minoans had learned to crush the Murex sea snail to extract purple dye and the Romans developed the trade on Koufounísi by harvesting the extract from the living shellfish. The island can be visited by boat from Ierápetra.

Uninhabited Yaidouronísi, better known as Khrisí or Donkey Island, is 7km south of Ierápetra. With its wonderful beaches, the island makes the perfect getaway destination by boat from Ierápetra.

The island of Psíra

Untouched islands

Very few of the offshore islands of Crete can be reached easily and conveniently. Apart from the regular trips to Yávdos, Día, Yaidouronísi, Spinalónga and one or two others, private and often expensive arrangements have to be made with local boat owners or fishermen. While this is frustrating for lovers of small islands, it has preserved them in their untouched natural state, much to the benefit of their wildlife.

View from Mókhlos

'The fire that lightened me
Shines no more upon me.
A wind extinguished it, and
Now the darkness is on me

In the fullness of the moon,
A tree never takes root;
Only from the tree of love
Roots and branches shoot.'

Stanzas from *Erotókritos* by Vinzétzos Kornáros (1600–77) of Sitiá

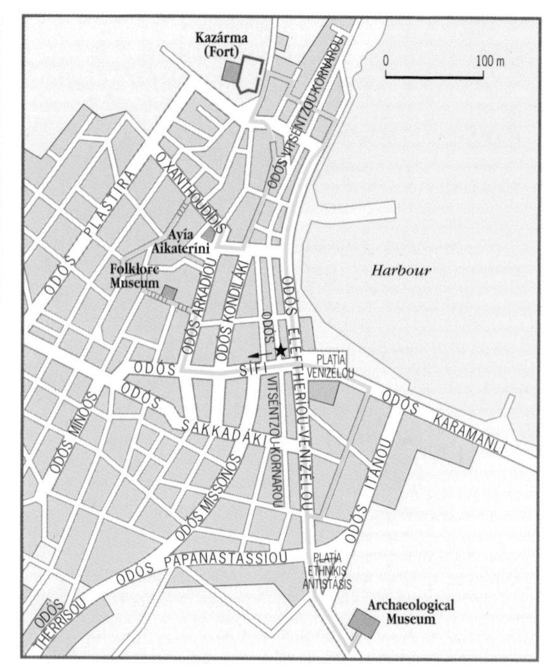

Sitiá

▶▶▶ Sitiá *139D3*

Sitiá, with its population of about 8,000, benefits from its relative isolation from the main tourist strip of Crete's northern coast. This is a friendly, relaxed place, ideal for visitors both in and out of season. There was a Minoan settlement at Petrás, 1km east of the present town, and many excavated items from here are in Sitiá's Archaeological Museum. The Venetians walled and fortified the town that they called La Sitiá, and it flourished as a trading port despite its partial destruction by two earthquakes. Apart from the castle there are few Venetian buildings to be seen. The Turks, who captured Sitiá in 1651 after a three-year sea blockade, laid it waste and left it in ruins for the following two centuries. In 1879 they established an administrative centre for eastern Crete here, and laid out a new town on a grid of streets, most of which survive.

Sitiá's houses look down upon its harbour

Walk Sitiá

Allow three or four hours; see map opposite.

Start at **Platía Venizélos▶▶**, the square just inland of the waterfront with formal gardens and which is the focal point of Sitiá. Head inland up Odós Sífi past the Krystal Hotel and take the fourth turning on the right into Odós Arkadíou, where the plain older houses contrast with the Moorish arches and elaborate ironwork of the modern, the reverse of Crete's usual architectural characteristics. Turn left up the steps of Odós Perogiamáki, looking back to see harbour, bay and mountains framed by houses. At the top turn right and first right again. Descend the steps at the foot of Odós Xanthoudídis and you come to the big church of Ayía Aikateríni. This is the heart of **Old Sitiá▶▶▶**, a network of stepped and cobbled streets where few cars or tourists venture.

Turn down the steps of the street in front of the church and bear left along Odós Kondiláki, which narrows and rises to reach a lane below the Venetian fort. Turn right, go almost to the end, then left up the steps of Odós Nikónos to come to the **fort▶▶**. Known to Sitíans as Kazárma, the House of Arms, the hollow square fort is used in summer as an open-air theatre and enjoys a fine view over the town, though a better one can be had by continuing eastward along the path to the church and **graveyard▶▶** beyond.

A number of stepped alleyways descend from the fort to the **waterfront▶▶**, where you turn right to reach the quay. There is usually a crowd here when the boats are in. Somewhere along the shore you are bound to catch sight of Nikos and Pédros, the tame pelicans of Sitiá who harass locals and visitors alike in their quest for titbits and attention. The beach runs east from the harbour, a long curve of sand with good bathing when the strong currents allow.

Pass Zorba's Restaurant to come to Platía Venizélos and turn left out of the square along shabby, bustling Odós Venizélos: a taste of workaday Sitiá, lined with cafés, bakeries, ironmongers, clothes stores and music shops. At the far end of the street cross the intersection of Platía Ethníkis Antistásis, and in 100m you will come to the **Archaeological Museum▶▶** on your left. This is a modern building, with clearly labelled cases of finds from many Minoan and later sites in eastern Crete. Work your way clockwise round the exhibits which include a bathtub-style coffin from Ayía Fotiá, slender conical vessels from Palaikastro, long-spouted jugs and a squat bull from Mókhlos. Finds from the palace at Káto Zákros (see pages 158–9) are the pride of the collection with jars, jugs, *píthoi*, cups, a wine press, and tablets inscribed with Linear A script.

Retrace your steps into Odós Venizélos. Take first right then first left down Odós 4 Septémbriou to regain the waterfront and Platía Venizélos.

Many watersports are available

Walk Episkopí to Triptí and back

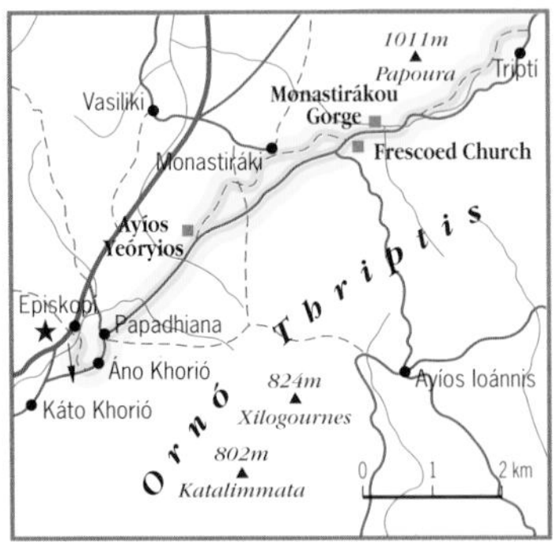

Allow nine hours for this demanding 20km walk which leads you into the Thriptís Mountains, with dramatic views down the Monastiráki Gorge and over both Cretan and Libyan seas.

Start in Episkopí village at a little Byzantine church on the right below the Ierápetra–Ayíos Nikólaos road. It has a 13th-century domed north nave and a Venetian south nave. A concrete road from the church crosses the bypass to reach a T-junction. Turn right here and after 0.5km you will come to Áno Khorió. Turn left and go up a concrete road, signposted to Triptí, to pass a silver-domed church and climb the mountainside on a dirt road past Ayíos Yióryios church. This will take about half an hour.

After 5km the road enters pine groves, and then forks. Go left to pass a church with faded frescoes on your right. A fine view soon opens down the cleft of Monastiráki Gorge. A kilometre beyond the church, you reach a balustraded house above a left bend. After 0.5km there are two concrete buildings below the road on the left. In 150m, before a right-hand bend, go left up a rough path. Keep going up and straight ahead until you reach Triptí village where both sustenance and a warm welcome are to be found.

Return to the church. The road bends right here. Turn right off the bend and go down on to a footpath. In 300m fork right at some electricity poles. After 0.5km keep right downhill to the bottom of the slope. Climb up the bank past a pine tree for 20m. Turn right along a rough, rising track to reach a saddle and a stirring view over both Cretan and Libyan seas. Bear right through the pines along a stony, sunken track, which descends in zigzags. In a rocky defile, hairpin right at some oleander bushes and continue downhill. You can see the track ahead by an electricity pole. In 10 minutes pass to the right of a wired enclosure and go right down a dirt road.

In another 10 minutes the road swings right at a stony outcrop. Go left here along the lower of the two paths which soon forks. Go uphill, following the vehicle tracks, and Ayíos Yióryios church can be seen ahead and below. The track divides at the top of a rocky valley and descends on the far side. After 10 minutes you will reach Ayíos Yióryios church and a dirt road down to Episkopí.

The sheer sides of Monastiráki Gorge

Walk Valley of the Dead (Áno Zákros to Káto Zákros)

The Valley of the Dead lies just beyond Káto Zákros

Allow five to six hours.

This is a deep and dramatic canyon, riddled with caves where the Minoans buried their dead, through which you wind your way down 11km to the Minoan palace at Káto Zákros.

Leave Áno Zákros on the tarmac road towards Káto Zákros. After 2km the road dips into a wide valley, with a conspicuous white house on the far hillside. After a straight stretch the road bends left. Just before this, near a concrete block building on your right, turn left at a red arrow waymark along a track which curves to the right between olive trees. After about five minutes bear left onto the track that descends sharply into the Valley of the Dead. There is a steep 10-minute scramble among rocks before you reach the floor of the gorge. Ford the river and follow the trail on its left bank, waymarked with red dashes. A rough but wonderful hour's walk under the towering and twisted orange walls of the gorge, with the burial caves showing as open black mouths on both sides, brings you to a concrete road. Red arrows point left to the palace of Zákros (see pages 158–9); Káto Zákros beach and a few tavernas are just beyond (page 146).

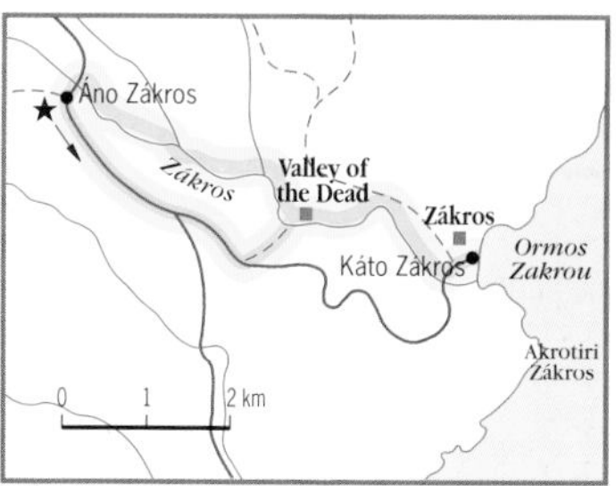

Return by the same route to the point where you scrambled down into the gorge. Continue along the right bank of the river until you come to a concrete irrigation channel, which guides you up for 20 minutes to where the gorge divides and the path is blocked by a wire fence. Cross the stream and go through a shepherd's gate with a pink cloth marker. A sign points left to Zákros. After a mile you reach olive groves. Go through a second cloth-marked gate and carry on uphill between trees to cross an unmarked fence and a field. Red way-marks will take you on towards Áno Zákros. Bear left at some stone sheds to cross the stream, then turn right along a dirt road and you will be back in the village.

Stone mills
Toploú has a well-preserved example of the thousands of stone-built windmills that served Cretans for hundreds of years until modern milling and the centralisation of bread supplies forced them into redundancy. They were sited on exposed saddles of ground, facing the prevailing wind, generally the southwest. They have the same sort of romantic appeal as the white-sailed working windpumps of Lasíthiou. There is something in their sturdy, uncomplicated lines, and the simple, graceful curve of their walls, which makes them highly attractive. And there is also a certain dignity in the usefulness that they embody. Technology has come full circle: a nearby hillside is now occupied by windmills of a new generation – a windfarm.

► Sídheros Peninsula *139E4*

This entry would undoubtedly rate three stars if the peninsula was open to the public. Unfortunately for all lovers of wild and remote places, there is strictly no admission to the outermost two of the three nodes of bare, rocky land that reach out into the sea from the north-eastern tip of Crete. NATO maintains a naval and military base here. After driving across the first of the three you will come to a checkpoint, where an unsmiling sentry will suggest unceremoniously that you return whence you came. This is a pity, since exploring the tracks above the cliffs, where falcons hover and only sheep and goats may venture, out to the lighthouse at the tip of the peninsula, would make one of the great wild walks of Crete.

►►► Toploú Monastery *139D3*

Arriving at the monastery you might well think you have come upon a Venetian fort. Toploú has had a violent history. Founded in the 14th and 15th centuries, it was

The now peaceful courtyard of Toplóu Monastery

sacked by pirates in 1498 and by the Knights of St John of Malta in 1530. It was ruined by an earthquake early in the 17th century and partially destroyed by the invading Turks in 1646. Successive rebuilding has given it a square, fortress-like appearance, with high walls pierced by tiny windows surrounding the tall bell tower. Resistance has always been a characteristic of Toploú. The name comes from the Turkish word for cannon, and during the 1821 uprising twelve monks were hanged at the monastery gate for succouring rebels. Toploú became a meeting place for British resistance fighters and Cretan partisans during World War II, and the abbot and several of his monks were shot in reprisal.

Toplóu's icon of the Virgin

Outside the main gate stands a stone windmill with its interior workings of wooden gears and driveshafts still intact. Inside the inner gateway the central courtyard is beautifully patterned with thousands of little oval pebbles, and the monks' cells and offices rise three storeys high on all sides. Toploú is reputed to be one of the richest monasteries in Crete, holding a vast area of land, and although the ground-floor cells are bare and plain, those higher up and still occupied are handsomely furnished and comfortable. Several stone tablets are set in the walls of the 14th-century Church of Panayía Akrotirianí, the monastery's proper name. One shows a Virgin and Child. Another, a large grey slab, dates from the 2nd century BC, and records the settlement by 'honest brokers', called in from Magnesia in Asia Minor in 132BC, of a land dispute between the cities of nearby Ítanos and Ierápytna (Ierápetra) on the south coast. Inside the church is a superb icon depicting 61 miniature scenes representing the Greek Orthodox prayer *Lord, Thou Art Great*, created in 1770 by Ioánnis Kornáros.

▶▶ Vái *139E3*

This famous beach, 6.5km northeast of Toploú, is *too* famous in summer, when hordes of sun-worshippers descend in cars and coaches to invade the white sands that lie seaward of the feathery forest of date palms (*Phoenix theophrasti*), the largest stand on Crete of this very rare, protected palm. Legend says they grew from date stones spat out by Phoenician traders – the fruit is bitter and inedible.

▶▶▶ Xerókambos *139E1*

Xerókambos has everything that Vái does not: peace, space to roam and dream, and an absence of crowds. Hidden away on the southern curve of the eastern end of the island, attainable only by a rough journey on a poor road, it offers heaven in the form of a long, unsullied beach and a couple of unhurried tavernas.

▶ (Áno) Zákros *139E2*

Áno Zákros is beginning to benefit from its proximity to the Minoan palace at Káto Zákros. The Hotel Zákros is plain but comfortable and friendly, and there are plenty of rooms to let in this big, unfussy village among olive groves overlooked by mountain ridges.

Early and late

Well-informed travellers, old Crete hands and most guidebooks will advise you to eschew Vái beach, citing it as a prime example of how tourism has spoiled a good thing. Don't be put off. Avoid the beach at peak times and, if you can, come here early on a breezy morning or on a starry evening in April or October. Lie in the shade of the whispering date palms and soak up the atmosphere of one of the island's most appealing spots.

Looking down on the clear waters off Vái beach

Drive Thriptís, Ornó and Sitiá Mountains

This is a circular drive of about 137km from Ierápetra through stunning mountain scenery, winding through villages where visitors are the exception rather than the rule. Be sure to check your tyres and fill up with petrol before you set off on this all-day drive through high, unfrequented mountain country. Some of the dirt roads are very rough and there are few garages along the way. This is emphatically not an excursion to be attempted in winter when the roughest of the roads may be cut by landslips. If in any doubt, check locally before you set off.

See the map on pages 138–9

Leave **Ierápetra** by the coast road towards Sitiá, and after 8km turn off left through **Koutsounári**, climbing into the wild and craggy Thriptís Mountains above plunging valleys to reach **Ayíos Ioánnis**, a village perched spectacularly below a crag. The road, now unsurfaced, hairpins along to **Skhinokápsala**, where it forks in the village square. Go left uphill through pine groves blackened by forest fires until you reach sleepy, whitewashed **Oríno**, a good place to idle over coffee. The dirt road rises beyond the village to a saddle. Immediately beyond, bear sharp right and after 0.5km turn left by an iron post to zigzag down to **Stavrokhóri**, a village spread on a ledge of rock and facing down a steep valley, overlooked by the tall bell tower of its church.

If this road is impassable, return from Oríno for 2km to a major fork, and keep left back down to the left turn on the coast road at Mávros Kólimbos. After 2km a signposted left turn at Koutsourás will bring you up to Stavrokhóri.

Continue northwards to **Khrisoniyí** and on through fertile upland valleys where marble outcrops shine white against the orange rocks. Beyond the side turning to **Dháfni** go left at an unsigned fork, to wind up and then zigzag down through **Paraspóri** and **Akhládhia**, perched, like all these villages, on bluffs, overlooking enormous views of the Ornó Mountains and the sea beyond the north coast.

At **Piskokéfalo** turn right on the Ierápetra road, and after 100m turn left opposite a garage. Fork right after 200m and continue to a T-junction. Go right here, and right again at a sign to Zoú. Keep straight ahead through **Káto Episkopí** for a diversion to the tiny, red-roofed 11th-century church of Ayíi Apóstoli. The route by way of Zoú, Sfakiá and Katsidhóni is winding but well surfaced to **Sítanos** in the heart of the Sitiá Mountains. Here you bear right on a rougher road past Kateliónas to turn left on a better surface through **Khandrás** (see pages 146–7) at the edge of the agricultural uplands of Zíros.

Zíros village is the centre for this hilly, largely unvisited district, and it is a place that exudes a wholly Cretan atmosphere, where the arrival of tourists is a real event. Stop and brace yourself at one of the tavernas for what follows: a very rough, wriggling track that drops for a difficult 13km to the south coast at **Goúdhouras**. You can relax here as the worst is over, and you join a tarmac road running west at the feet of the mountains.

Soon, though, the dirt surface takes over again as you come abreast of **Kápsa Monastery** at the mouth of a tremendous gorge. Bear right to climb to the monastery, a beautiful, peaceful eagle's nest, high against the cliff face, looking out to sea. During the 19th century Yerondoyiánnis, an illiterate monk from Kápsa who was a champion of the local people against the Turks and a miraculous healer, built much of the monastery himself. His remains are venerated in the dark church.

Back on the dirt road, continue through Kaló Neró to reach the highway, and turn left for Ierápetra.

Kavoúsi is dwarfed by the steep flanks of the Ornó Mountains

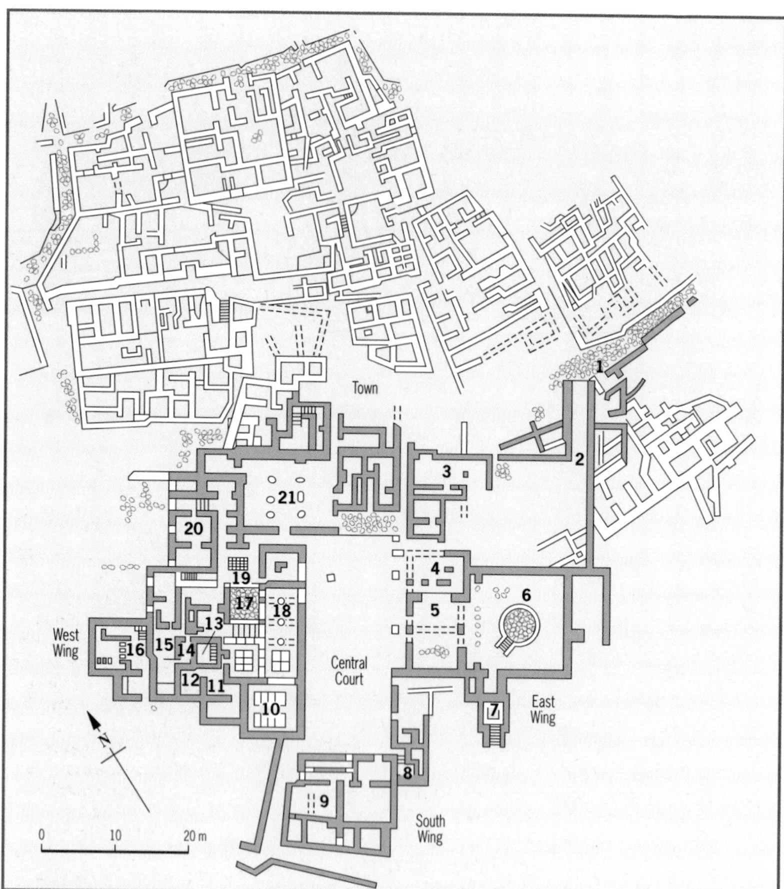

Key to the map
1 paved road
2 main gate
3 bath
4 queen's apartment
5 king's apartment
6 cistern hall
7 spring chamber
8 well
9 workshops
10 banqueting hall
11 workshop
12 treasury
13 lustral basin
14 central shrine
15 archives
16 workshops and dye-house
17 lightwell
18 main hall
19 lobby
20 storerooms
21 kitchen

▶▶▶ Zákros Minoan Palace *139E2*

The Minoan palace at Zákros (open 8:30–3, closed Monday) is the jewel in the crown of modern Cretan archaeology. The existence of a sizeable ancient settlement at the foot of the Valley of the Dead had been suspected since the middle of the 19th century. Federico Halbherr, who excavated Górtina, and Sir Arthur Evans, of Knosós fame, both made excavations here around the turn of the century. In 1901 the British archaeologist David Hogarth unearthed houses, pottery and implements from what he took to be a Minoan port. His dig came within feet of the palace itself, but the valley floor held onto its secret. In the 1930s a Cretan antiquarian, Dr Giamalákis, bought some gold items from a local farmer he had been treating, who said he had found them at Káto Zákros. The doctor's collection is now in Room XVII of Iráklio Archaeological Museum, and includes a bowl and a bull's-head pendant unearthed by the farmer. Suspicion was thus rekindled that there was something down there, but it was not until 1962 that a Greek archaeologist, Nikólaos Pláton, finally located the exact site.

Zákros differs in one important respect from the other sites: after its destruction in the mysterious disaster of

1450BC, the existence of the palace was forgotten. Nobody came to loot Zákros. The collapsed structure lay entire under the ground, exactly as it had been at the moment its inhabitants fled and it came crashing down on their belongings, tools, pots and sacred totems. Pláton's excavation revealed by far the most complete Minoan complex yet brought to light.

Once inside the gate, climb the hill through the streets and houses of the Minoan town of Zákros, to the ruined building at the summit with walls made of double-size boulders. From here you can look down on the palace remains and compare them with the plan. When you have got your bearings (to the east lie the flat, open rectangles of the cistern hall with its circular water tank; immediately below you is the central court of the palace) return to the entrance gate and walk along the paved roadway that led from the harbour into the palace complex.

The cistern hall, part of the east wing of the palace, lies south of the first courtyard that you step down into. The cistern may have been a swimming pool or a fish tank. Today it holds murky water and is full of green plants. Bear right past the king's and queen's apartments to the big central court. In the southeast corner is a waterlogged well where the excavators discovered a jar containing 3,500-year-old olives, perfectly preserved by the water. At the northwest corner of the central court is the base of an altar. Go through the entrance to the west wing of the palace. A beautiful stone vase decorated with wild goats and scenes of a peak sanctuary was found here and is now in Room VIII of the Iráklio Archaeological Museum. A surprisingly small banqueting hall lies two rooms south of the light well, and west of that is a huddle of rooms that includes the treasury. Stone jars, clay chests and the 300 separate pieces of the famous rock crystal *rhyton* or ceremonial jug were found here. The *rhyton*, now reassembled, can be seen in Room VIII of the Iráklio Archaeological Museum. The palace archive which consisted of wooden chests containing hundreds of clay tablets inscribed with Minoan Linear A hieroglyphs, was also found here, as was a tiny central shrine. On the western edge of the palace were a dye-house, and a latrine which emptied into a cesspit outside the walls.

Returning to the central court, walk north towards the hill to find the outlines of the kitchens and pantries which yielded animal bones, cooking pots and kitchen utensils, and a number of storerooms. Above lie the remains of the ancient town.

The water tank at Zákros Palace

Finds preserved

Most of the important finds from the palace of Zákros are on display in Room VIII of the Iráklio Archaeological Museum, and having wandered through the very rooms where they were found you may decide to go back to the museum to appreciate them afresh. There is the rock crystal *rhyton* from the treasury, the ceremonial vessel from the lustral basin with its gracefully curled twin handles and brilliant natural patterning, and the conical long jar from the central court well in which olives were found preserved by the water since the destruction of the palace.

Ha! Gorge

The dramatic gorge that cuts down through the hills to Káto Zákros was named the Valley of the Dead (see also the walk on page 153) after the Minoan cave burials which were discovered there. But local people have an equally apt name for it, 'Ha! Gorge'. Try shouting with all your might from the bottom of the canyon and you will soon appreciate why its other name arose.

Traditional music and dance

Africa, Europe and Asia all meet in the complex rhythms and haunting melodies of traditional Cretan music, which is currently enjoying a revival of popularity among the young. It is very much part of Cretan life, and can be seen and heard both in special performances devised for the tourists, and also as part of village life at weddings and festivals.....

Dancing and music for visitors

Musical moustaches
As much a part of the Cretan man's traditional dress as baggy breeches and fringed headband is the well-cultivated moustache – straggly, drooping, clipped or waxed. Some of the most luxuriant examples are seen under the noses of young musicians, the new heroes of the *lýra* and *bouzoúki*, who rightly feel themselves to be the guardians and ambassadors of Cretan tradition.

Music For an island so heavily invaded by the outside world during the last few decades, Crete enjoys a remarkably vigorous and lively tradition of music and dance. The discotheques of Iráklio, Khaniá, Réthimnon and Ayíos Nikólaos certainly claim plenty of custom from Cretan boys and girls in the evening, but it is both exciting and moving to walk into a bar or restaurant in the back streets of the same towns in the early hours of the morning and find the same youngsters singing their heads off, roaring out Cretan songs to the accompaniment of *bouzoúki* and guitar. There is a fierce enjoyment in such singing, an echo perhaps of the way their ancestors sang songs of defiance against the Venetians and Turks.

Singing and dancing are driven by the great triumvirate of Cretan music: the *lýra*, a three-stringed bowed fiddle that sobs and wails across the player's knee; the deep-bellied, eight-stringed *bouzoúki*; and the recorder-like flute. These days Cretans are developing a taste for their traditional tunes taken neat, without singing, but with plenty of *rakí* to fuel proceedings.

There are several parallels between the traditional cultures of Crete and rural Ireland: the hospitality, the enjoyment of the stranger, a willingness to take what the moment offers, and particularly the power of music as a social glue, an affirmation of local life and feeling. In Crete, as in the west of Ireland, musicians are well respected, and even revered. Here, too, the tradition is enjoying a revival, with plenty of excellent young musicians putting salt on the tails of their seniors. Children are encouraged to learn, and eager boys turn up, *lýra* under arm, for teaching sessions in the lobby of the Mosque of Nerantziés in Réthimnon. *Lýra* and *bouzoúki* playing have traditionally been a male preserve, but increasing numbers of Cretan girls

A bouzoúki

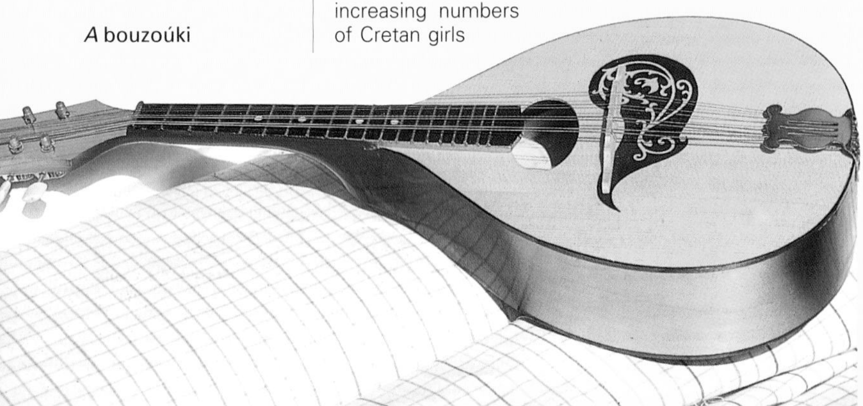

Traditional dress may be donned for a wedding

and young women are taking up the instruments these days, sharing prominence with men on the posters that announce music concerts. Many Cretan radio stations are devoted to the island's music, and Cretan television broadcasts live and recorded concerts.

This is wild music with wild rhythms, complicated and even formless to the uninitiated ear. It is music for dancing, fighting and lovemaking, a fiery meeting of North Africa, Europe and Asia. Time signatures can seem bizarre to outsiders, but once tuned in, the ears and feet suddenly find it easy to keep up. Singing can be roaring and tribal, or it can take the form of the subtle *mantináde*, a verse or series of verses in rhyming couplets, sometimes tossed to and fro between singers, often full of allusions to issues and personalities that only locals can fully appreciate. Another kind of singing is the chanted recitation of epic poems. The 17th-century *Erotókritos* of Vinzétzos Kornáros is widely known, in spite of its length, and some say that you can still hear old men recite the lament for the fallen heroes of Sfakiá, the *Song of Daskaloyiánnis*.

Dance and dress Dancing happens as and when Cretans feel moved. Nowadays, of course, it is also laid on for visitors as part of a plate-smashing, table-stomping evening out. These events will probably be your only chance to see the most spectacular dances where the men spring high in the air and slap both heels against a hand. There will be stunning costumes, too, with the women in beautifully embroidered velvet jackets looped with gold lace, white aprons, long dresses over voluminous pantaloons, and the men in baggy breeches, white boots and many metres of silver chains which clash on superbly engraved silver daggers tucked into red sashes. Such costumes are a cockatoo display, far removed from the other, sombre traditional dress still worn by many village men (knee boots, tasselled black head fringe, wide khaki breeches, black shirts) and women (head-to-foot, self effacing black for those that have suffered a bereavement).

Dances of delight
Cretan dances are at their most spectacular when performed by athletic young people in full traditional dress, most commonly seen these days at special displays put on for tourists. But there is a different, perhaps a purer, delight in witnessing, and joining in with, the dancing that goes on during festivals in village houses and courtyards. The participants may be in workaday clothes and some of them will be too old or too young or too stout to leap high. But this is where the tradition is still being passed on from one generation to the next.

Have a go
Don't be shy of asking to take part in a dance you like the look of, or asking to be shown how to play a traditional instrument. If you aren't embarrassed, the performers and onlookers certainly won't be. And delighted plaudits will be yours if you can carry it off!

Drive Gulf of Mirambéllou (Ayíos Nikólaos to Sitiá)

The coastline that fringes the Gulf of Mirambéllou has been nicknamed the Cretan Riviera. The road (72km) from Ayíos Nikólaos to Sitiá is its corniche, twisting and turning through villages that cling to the mountainsides, above bays of wonderfully clear, shallow water.

There are several excellent vantage points from which to look back as you drive south and east from **Ayíos Nikólaos** along the coast road. The town is the very picture of a Cretan resort, its houses in a graceful mound looking out on to a startlingly blue sea, which shades into green as it reaches the sandy little bays of the coastline. The road passes Ammoudára and Ístro, then after 5km a sign on your right to Faneroménis Monastery points up a very rough dirt road. This is a 6.5km diversion zigzagging up to **Faneroménis**. The monastery is built hard against a mountain cliff, facing a breathtaking view out over terraced hillsides to the Gulf of Mirambéllou. (There is a *different* Faneroménis Monastery on the coast just west of Sitiá; see page 143.)

Father Nikódemos is usually about; and if not, vigorous knocking and halloing may rouse him! He will guide you up the stairways of the canyon-like courtyard to the roof terrace, and unlock the door of the church built into a cave above the

The coast road offers spectacular views of the Gulf of Mirambéllou

monastery. There are some lovely old icons to see; and be sure to take a peep into the inner recess where the discovery of a mysterious icon of the Virgin led to the founding of the monastery in the 15th century.

Back on the main Sitiá road, another 5km brings you to a side-turning to the Minoan town site of **Gourniá** (see pages 122–3). Beyond the turning the road drops to the coast at **Pakhiá Ámmos**, a modest strip of shops, tavernas and hotels along a grey sand beach where a storm in 1914 exposed a Minoan cemetery, the incumbents buried in upturned *píthoi*. Now the grey, wrinkled wall of the Thriptís Mountains stands ahead, sliced by the dark crack of the Monastiráki Gorge. **Kavoúsi** village (see page 146) lies under the towering, bald peak of Mount Aféndis Stavroménos (1476m).

The road wriggles east across the foothills of Thriptís' northern neighbour, the Órno range, with memorable views over the sheer sides of Psíra Island (see page 149) and the whole gulf. Lástros, Sfáka and Tourlotí lie like heaps of white sugar cubes on the slopes. The side road down to **Mókhlos** (see page 148) branches off in Sfáka, another detour not to be missed.

Five kilometres beyond Tourlotí, at the entrance to **Mirsíni** village, a hand-painted sign wheedles passers-by to 'Come and visit most beautiful village in Creta'. Mirsíni is scarcely that, though the sign says a lot about local pride, but it is another tangle of old houses on tiny lanes, and the rather nondescript church encloses a far older one, of the 14th century, with some fine frescoes. The priest, if he is in the village, will let you in.

On the bar of the *kafeníon* in **Éxo Mouliná** there is always a bowl of sultanas, the main produce of the Sitiá district. They complement to perfection the much-praised local wine, sharp and fruity.

After a further tortuous 8km a sign on the right points to **Khamézi Middle Minoan House**, up a rough road for the last detour of this drive. You pass a group of abandoned stone windmills, and bear immediately right on a dirt track for about 2km to find the ruins of the house in front of you, on the crest of a conical hill. An oval wall encircles rooms, a tiny central court and a deep cistern. It was built around 2000BC and is the only one discovered of this shape.

Back on the road, an uneventful 11km will bring you down to Sitiá.

The Órno mountains rise up behind this village near Mókhlos

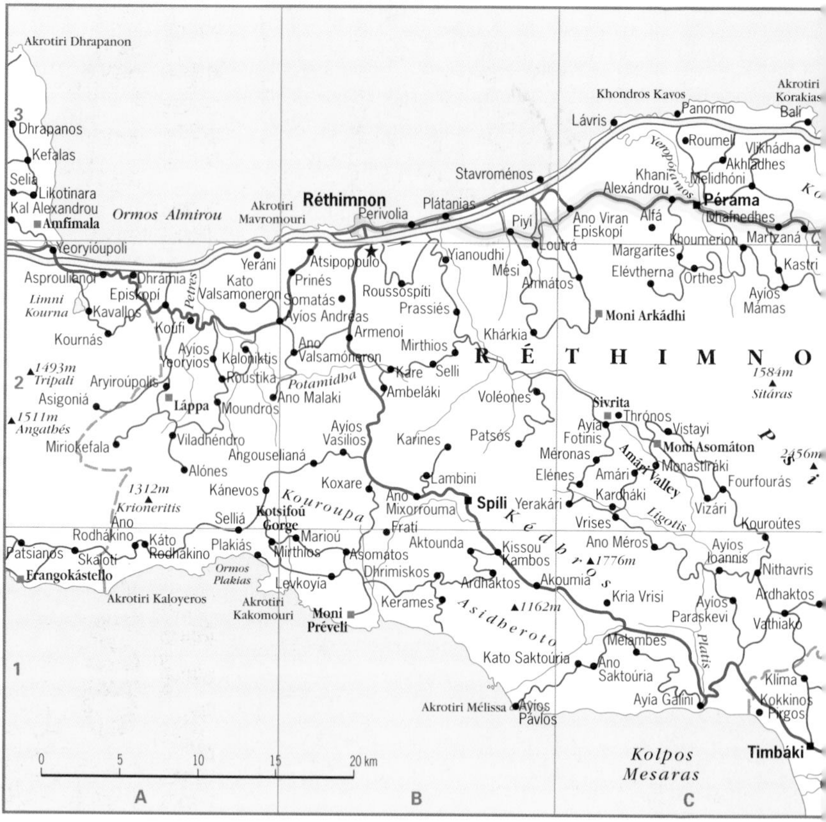

Below: Réthimnon harbour *Right: Amári church*

RÉTHIMNON AND THE ÍDA MOUNTAINS

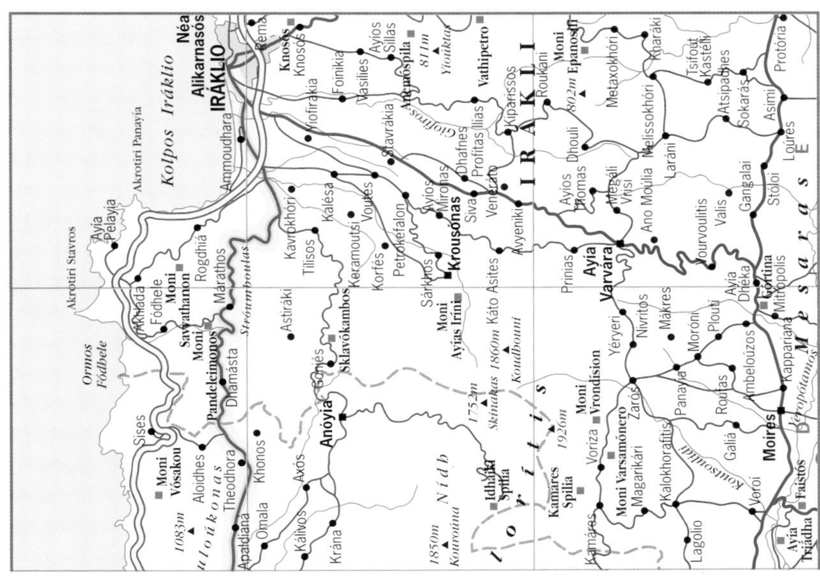

Painted relief work

Kotsifoú Gorge
One of the most ruggedly beautiful yet least visited gorges in Crete lies beside the road from Réthimnon to Frangokástello. This is the Kotsifoú Gorge, just north of Selliá, an echoing, sheer-sided chasm, snaking, thrillingly narrow, and offering a rough excursion on foot from its seaward end near Plakiás.

Old Réthimnon street

Réthimnon and the Ída Mountains This section of western central Crete extends along the north coast from Yioryiópoulis on the Gulf of Almiróu to Iráklio, and along the south coast from Frangokástello to Ayía Galíni. The eastern part of the region is dominated by the great ragged range of the Ída Mountains, better known in Crete these days as Psiloritis, too wild and steep to be crossed by any north-south road. In the centre lies the high and beautiful Amári valley. To the west the land runs in broken hill ranges and valleys towards the narrowing wrist of the island and the upthrust of Levká Óri, the White Mountains of westernmost Crete.

On the northern coast, out towards the west of the region, sits Réthimnon, the city towards which the entire area looks as its tourist and cultural capital. Like Crete's three other main centres, Khaniá, Iráklio and Ayiós Nikólaos, Réthimnon has its own particular character, a gentle and timeless one that seems to owe less to its rôle as a thriving holiday centre than to its Venetian and Turkish history, which surfaces everywhere in minarets, domes, ornate stonework, solid fortifications and sea defences. This is a town for idling away the days strolling the narrow streets and peering into shop windows, with a detail of architecture or everyday life to surprise you around every corner.

The new coastal highway which runs from Iráklio to Khaniá bypasses the town and takes most through-traffic straight past Réthimnon. Small resorts have begun to spring up seaward of the road, but the main ribbon development is still confined to a strip east of the city. Turn inland off the new road and you find yourself immediately in quiet olive groves, fruit orchards and tumbled hills, a world away from the bustle of the coast. The old road from Réthimnon to Iráklio, and the other roads further and higher inland, reveal this landscape in a leisurely way.

Above and behind these northern roads of the region towers the Psiloritis range, nearly 32km from east to west, formidable mountains that rise to 2,456m at the summit of Mount Psiloritis, the highest peak in Crete, that gives its name to the whole range. Shepherds' tracks crisscross the heights, a challenge for determined and well-prepared walkers. In the heart of these mountains lies the Nídha Plateau, from which you can reach the Ídaean Cave where, legend says, Zeus, chief among Greek gods, was raised. In the southern flank of Psiloritis is the Kamáres cave, a Minoan religious centre where delicate pottery and many other marvellous relics have been found.

Psiloritis has been a place of refuge for resistance fighters throughout the long history of struggle against invaders in Crete. The mountain village of Anóyia was razed during German reprisals in World War II, and there was more destruction along the Amári valley that lies west of the mountains. This is an area of Crete much written and talked about, a truly beautiful and peaceful upland which seems green, cool and fruitful even in the heat of high summer. Olive groves, cherry orchards, woods and wild flowers abound, dotted with tiny Byzantine churches rich in frescoes. A couple of days spent lazing along the two winding roads that flank the valley, east and west, will introduce you to a hospitable and largely unchanged way of life among the villages of Amári and the little-visited Kédros mountains to the west.

The south coast rises dramatically from the sea. There is as yet no coastal road to connect the square Venetian coastal fort of Frangokástello with the lively small resort of Ayía Galíni. But there are superbly sited villages to explore here – Rodhákino, Ayíos Pávlos, Selliá – and the historic monastery of Préveli in its peaceful cleft above the sea.

The Venetian fort at Réthimnon, perched on a bluff

Sea hue
An aspect of the Cretan coast commented on by all visitors from more northern climes is the superb colour of the sea, especially close inshore. There is nothing wine-dark about this southern Aegean or Cretan Sea. A combination of gently shelving sand below, strong sunlight above, and the wonderful clarity of the water gives a blue-green hue, a turquoise shimmer so vivid as to be indescribable, though many have tried.

Old Voríza
Driving the mountain road between Zarós and Voríza, glance down to your left about halfway between the two villages to see Old Voríza, a dozen roofless shells of houses, stone walls cracked and crumbling, blank windows facing down a lovely valley. These houses, now used as sheep pens, were destroyed in a wartime divebombing practice by Stukas in a reprisal gesture.

Choose your fish
In the fish restaurants on Réthimnon's waterfront, follow the general rule of eating out in Crete: don't order sight unseen, but walk through into the kitchen and choose something you like the look of.

Weary Lear
Edward Lear stayed at Réthimnon in 1864, during the course of what was evidently a rather wearisome and uncomfortable visit to Crete. Sketchy representations of the town appear among the illustrations in his diary of the trip, published as *The Cretan Journal*.

Amári valley memorial

Cretan haversacks
Traditional Cretan haversacks, woven of brightly dyed wool in geometric patterns that vary from village to village, are common items on souvenir stalls. If you keep your eyes open when walking in the mountains, you may see a shepherd carrying the day's provisions in one, slung by the side or dangling from the crook of a walking stick.

Amári shepherd

►► Amári 164C2

Amári is the capital of the beautiful high Amári valley (see below), under the western flank of the Psiloritis mountain range south of Réthimnon. Coming south, you turn off the road to the Mesarás plain at Moní Asomáton, to reach Amári 5km to the southwest. It is a typical mountain settlement of narrow lanes, farmyards and tiny white houses. During World War II Amári was a formidable centre of resistance to the Germans, and like its neighbouring villages paid in blood for its stance.

Leave your car by the Café-Bar Petrakakeion in the village square and turn right on foot up a lane which climbs to the Venetian clock tower. Spiral steps inside rise to a wonderful view from among the bells to the craggy wall of Psilorítis. The nearby church has good modern frescoes; there are ancient ones in the Church of Ayía Ánna (see below).

►►► Amári valley 164C2

Southeast of Réthimnon lies the beautiful Amári valley, filled with orange and cherry orchards, quiet villages and churches with frescoes. A selection of the valley's many treasures could begin with Thrónos at the northern end, where a well-preserved early Byzantine mosaic pavement underlies the Church of Panayía (key at the shop next door). Faces look down from faded 14th-century frescoes in the apse. The nave has 15th-century frescoes, including the body of Christ being tenderly caressed by his mother and St John. Just along the main road, the 15th-century Ayía Paraskeví, isolated among cypresses in a cornfield, contains the bones of some long-forgotten saint in a glass-topped niche. Beyond here is the right turn to Amári village. In the fork stand the graceful, though crumbling

Venetian buildings of Asomáton Monastery. Monastiráki on the Amári road has a beautiful small Venetian church. Amári itself has the lovely Ayía Ánna, signposted off to the right on entering the village. Forlorn-looking saints in the apse are dated to 1225, the oldest in Crete.

Returning past Thrónos, turn left down the west side of the valley. In the three-aisled Panayía church at Méronas (key with the priest at the second large white house on the left after the church) are beautiful, faded 14th-century frescoes including Christ washing the disciples' feet and the Virgin and St John comforting each other, as well as a locally venerated 14th-century icon of a sweetly sad Virgin.

The villages down this western side were razed by the Germans, and dozens of men summarily shot, in revenge for the abduction by partisans of General Kreipe, the officer in command of Crete. Memorials in Yerakári, Kardháki, Vríses and Áno Méros carry the names of the dead and the date of their execution, 22 August 1944. A sombre succession, relieved just to the south of Yerakári by the weather-worn but vivid late 13th-century frescoes in the ruined church of Ayíos Ioánnis Theológos.

▶▶▶ Anóyia 165D2

The sloping village street is lined with the usual tavernas. You could be in and out of Anóyia in a couple of minutes, but take a closer look. Almost all the buildings postdate 1944, when the village was subjected to one of the war's most atrocious reprisals. In retaliation for the capture and removal from Crete of the German commanding officer, General Heinrich Kreipe, soldiers were sent to Anóyia to raze the town. On 15 August 1944 every house in the village was burned to the ground and every male was killed.

A museum in the lower, older part of the village shows the work of the primitive sculptor and painter Alkibíades Skoúlas. His vivid painting of the sack of Anóyia shows lines of villagers waiting to be shot, German mountain troops and the corpses of dead partisans. Other paintings depict the German landings at Máleme in 1941, the Turkish siege of Arkádhi Monastery in 1866, and scenes from Cretan mythology. There are also strange, monolithic, stylised carvings of men and women, animals and birds. *[continued on page 171]*

War stories
Take time to strike up conversations with the elderly men and women of Anóyia and the Amári villages. All have vivid memories of wartime. Many of the older men were partisans and can tell you astonishing tales, most undoubtedly true.

Snow block
If you are planning to visit Anóyia in the depths of winter, check on the local weather forecast first. If heavy snow is expected, you could find yourself marooned in the mountains for several days or weeks if the snowfall is deep and prolonged as it can be occasionally.

The naïve paintings and sculpture of Alkibíades Skoúlas

■ If one word sums up Cretan history and character, that word is resistance. And if one image encapsulates the reality behind the word, it is a photograph in the wartime exhibition on the first floor of Iráklio's Historical Museum. A father and son stand tight-lipped against a wall, unshaven and bare-headed in the sunlight. The dark-haired young man's face is averted; his grizzled father stares straight ahead with slitted eyes, facing the gun muzzles of an execution squad lined up out of camera shot. These are their last few moments of defiance. In a few seconds more, both will be dead.....■

The proud face of resistance

The Cretan Runner
The Cretan Runner, by George Psychoundákis, a highly personal account of the author's experiences as a member of the resistance during World War II, is a wonderful read and a rightly acclaimed bestseller. The pages are thick with hundreds of remarkable incidents recalled by Psychoundákis, a semi-literate shepherd who became a Laureate of the Academy of Athens – a story worth telling in its own right.

This grim scene has been played out countless times down the centuries. Minoan islanders may well have been the first Cretan resisters, perhaps burning the palaces and towns taken over by the invading Mycenaeans. Ierápetrans held out against the Romans in 67BC. Byzantines battled the incoming Saracens nearly eight centuries later. Cretans from Lasíthiou and Sfakiá harried the Venetians from their mountain strongholds. Daskaloyiánnis whipped up rebellion against the Turks in 1770. Throughout the 19th century the *palikáres* fought the Turks in one uprising after another, in 1821, 1841, 1858, 1866, 1889 and 1896. Elefthérios Venizélos held out for *enosis* in 1897 and 1905. For four years during World War II the partisans were a constant thorn in the flesh of the German forces of occupation. During the late 1960s and early 1970s, Cretans were among the Greeks who most actively opposed the military coup by the Greek colonels, refusing as far as possible to abide by martial law.

The cost of armed resistance by the militant few has been borne throughout the years by the civilian population of Crete, a cost measured in wholesale massacres, in burned villages, in women taken away to lives of prostitution, and in orphaned children. The battle-cry of the *palikáres*, 'Freedom or death!', truly and succinctly tells the long tale of Cretan resistance.

A barred cell window at Arkhádi

The Venetian façade of Arkádhi Monastery

[continued from page 169]

Around the square near the museum are craft workshops selling brightly coloured and patterned home-woven rugs. Up in the main street of the new village, the Old Anóyian House Museum displays a mass of utensils, tools, furniture and decorations typical of the traditional life that still goes on in this mountain village that can be cut off for months from the outside world by winter snows. Little English is spoken in the village, but the hospitality is instant, and freely and proudly offered.

▶▶▶ Arkádhi Monastery *164C2*

The buildings of Arkádhi Monastery appear as a great jumble of orange stone walls, pierced by ranks of windows and overlooked by a bell turret. In the 16th century the Venetians completely rebuilt on a much older foundation. The remaining glory of this reconstruction is the church, built in 1587 of deep yellow stone ornately carved and decorated, which is now crumbling into dignified decay. It stands beyond the gateway in a cool, cloistered courtyard shaded by vines. Inside the church are some striking religious paintings: a half-naked suffering Christ in Glory, a wonderful exploding Burning Bush, a pitiful Adam and Eve being expelled in misery from Eden. Around the courtyard stand the monastery buildings that have become the prime symbol of the *'Freedom or Death'* slogan of the Cretan resistance movement.

1866 was a year of turmoil in Crete, as the islanders once more took up arms against their Turkish rulers. Arkádhi Monastery was a centre of resistance, and thousands of partisans and their families were inside the monastery in November when Turkish troops arrived to demand their surrender. Abbot Gabriel's refusal was followed by a two-day siege, culminating on 9 November in an all-out attack by the Turks. The surviving defenders gathered in the wine storeroom where they had been keeping their gunpowder, and as the attackers broke in,

Fireworks
There are great celebrations at Arkádhi, and down on the coast at Réthimnon, between 7 and 9 November every year, when fire-works, processions and other junketings commemorate the heroic explosion caused by Abbot Gabriel and Kostís Yiampoudákis.

The nightlights of the village of Ayía Galíni

Map fiction
It is technically possible to drive from Fódhele via Savvathanon Monastery (see page 189) to the Tílisos road. So the map tells you. But only a four-wheel-drive vehicle could happily negotiate this cratered, half-drowned dirt road. Cretan maps may not lie, but they are often economical with the truth.

Handmade lace and embroidery for sale in Fódhele

Abbot Gabriel ordered Kostís Yiampoudákis to fire his pistol into the powder barrels. The store exploded, killing hundreds of Cretans and Turks.

The roofless shell of the vaulted store stands in one corner of the courtyard. Orange, grey and black wrinkles on the surface of the walls show where the heat of the explosion was sufficient to bake and carbonise the stonework. In the nearby refectory, where a handful of survivors hid and were quickly butchered, you can still see wooden tables scored with sword cuts and a doorway pitted with bullet holes.

▶ Ayía Galíni *164C1*

The name means serenity, a holy calm. That might have been the case a hundred years ago when this beautiful site on the cliffs, looking out into the Gulf of Mesarás, was all but uninhabited. Fifty years ago it was still a tiny fishing village, known only to a privileged band of freewheeling foreigners. But tourism has worked on Ayía Galíni since then. Most guide books say the place has been ruined, but the truth is that it has simply come into its own as a thriving seaside holiday village, crammed with rooms to rent, car hire agents, tavernas, hotels and cafés. There are fine cliffs to east and west, clear green water beyond the little strip of a beach, and boats to other beaches, to the grottoes along the coast and to Sfakiá and Palaiókhora. Very little is ugly in Ayía Galíni, and very little is memorable. You take it for what it offers – sun, sand, sea and facilities.

▶▶ Fódhele *165D3*

Fódhele is charmingly sited among orange groves in a valley about 19km northeast of Iráklio. This is a quiet place of tumbled houses, a tree-shaded square, and small bridges across a river, that claims to be the birthplace of Doménico Theotokópoulos, better known as the painter El Greco (1541–1614). You can see what is claimed to be the house of his birth, a plaque to him in the village square, and copies of his paintings in the church. A strong imagination may be a better guide here than established fact, which advances equal claims for Iráklio.

▶▶▶ Frangokástello 164A1

Frangokástello is one of the most celebrated buildings in Crete: a great Venetian fortress, standing proud and foursquare on a lonely coastal site, that ought to deliver a sense of might and majesty, something more, at any rate, than the overwhelming feeling of emptiness and desolation one experiences inside its hollow, weed-grown and litter-strewn walls. The best view of the fort is from the mountain roads inland. Approaching it across the flat, dry coastal plain, Frangokástello looks unexpectedly small and two dimensional, rather like an abandoned film set.

Imagination is stirred, however, by the weather-eroded lion of St Mark that stands over the southern entrance. The Venetians built the fort in 1340, to dissuade the pirates then attacking Crete from the African coast, and as a symbol of the domination they wanted to exercise over the Sfakiot fighters in the hills behind.

Under Turkish rule the fort saw many bloody events. In 1770 the revolutionary leader Daskaloyiánnis, who had vainly trusted Russian promises to help him in his struggle, surrendered to the Turks at Frangokástello, and was taken to Iráklio where he was flayed alive. In the spring of 1828, during the War of Independence between the mainland Greeks and the Turks, the Greek leader Hatzimicháli Daliánis landed in Crete and barricaded himself in Frangokástello with 700 Cretans. Here he and his followers were wiped out to the last man. But in Crete history and myth are inextricably intertwined. Frangokástello still remembers these long-dead heroes. Every year, on a misty morning between 17 and 20 May, a ghostly procession of *drosoulítes* (dewy ones), marches a circuit of the walls. Some say these are the shades of fallen fighters, others that they are the souls of sinners not yet purged for heaven.

It is worth spending an hour walking over the plain around Frangokástello. The prickly bushes and scrub are home to a huge variety of wildlife including lizards, songbirds, burrowing beetles, cicadas and snails.

Scientific fact?
Scientists, unromantic fellows that they are, say that the *drosoulítes* are in fact mirages of people walking around on the coast of Libya, created under certain atmospheric conditions peculiar to mid-May, magnified and distorted by their journey across the sea.

The mighty Venetian fortress of Frangokástello

Walk Kamáres Cave

Of all Crete's well-known Minoan sites, none is more remote and difficult to reach than the great cave of Kamáres (marked Kamáres Spilia on the map, pages 164–5). For scores of miles along the Mesarás plain the mouth of the cave is visible, more than 1,000m above the plain, sited under a saddle-shaped ridge towards the uppermost heights of Psiloritis. It looks a straightforward if steep climb, an impression also given by the short line of the path shown on maps. But the cave lies 1,525m above sea level, and to reach it involves a climb of up to four hours on a poorly-marked track that dodges about from one half-concealed paint splash to the next. The descent is even more tricky, especially in the low cloud or mist which can swirl across with little warning on even the clearest of days. The rewards of this all-day expedition, however, are great, with the echoing,

The country around Kamáres

atmospheric depths of the cave itself, the weight of history and religious ceremony attached to it, and the stupendous view from the heights over Mesarás, spread like a promised land at the feet of the mountains.

Only make this climb by yourself if you are an experienced hill walker and properly equipped with weather-proof gear, hot drink, food and emergency equipment in case of difficulties. For most walkers, a better though fairly expensive alternative is to hire a guide in Kamáres village. Arrangements are informal, and the price negotiable. If you leave the village church and turn right, the *kafeníon* 200m along the street on the left will be able to help. Ask for Yióryio Saidákis. Allow at least six to eight hours for the round trip.

The track starts as you enter Kamáres, a small village of tightly bunched houses 12km west of Zarós, striking uphill as a narrow lane from the right side of the road opposite the village graveyard. The bed of a stream, usually dry, takes you high up above Kamáres to some cisterns. Bear to the right, east, above the treeline and continue the steep climb to the cave.

The cave, when you reach it, is enormous. The vast entrance is 40m across, the roof 20m high, and the dark interior runs back some 80m. A torch is essential if you want to investigate the furrowed recesses of the cave. The first intrepid explorer into the Kamáres cave in modern times was a local shepherd back in 1890. In 1904 Italian archaeologists came to the cave at the height of the first great era of Cretan excavations and discovered enormous numbers of pottery fragments, so exquisitely shaped and coloured that they were given their own designation, Kamáres ware. Further excavations by a British team in 1913 brought more antiquities to light, and the cave's significance as a centre of religious activity since earliest Minoan times was established.

The Kamáres cave had been a dwelling-place since neolithic times. From 1900 to 1700BC, around the time that the Old Palaces were being built at Knosós, Faistós, Mália and Zákros, it was used for burials and religious ceremonies that included fertility rites. The ceremonial vessels used here were made in the work-shops at Faistós and Ayía Triádha, 10km to the south. They were of two sorts: an early style of dark pottery decorated with red and white linear designs, and a far more delicate and elaborate type made later when the hand-turned potter's wheel had been supplanted by a faster and more sophisticated model. These designs are a superb artistic achievement, with floral motifs and mouldings, in beautiful flowing lines that complement the shapes of the vessels, using white, orange, yellow and black. Some of this later Kamáres ware is as thin as porcelain, and has been aptly christened 'eggshell' pottery. Examples are displayed in Rooms II and III of the Iráklio Archaeological Museum.

Kamáres, at the start of the walk

Cretan caves

■ There are an enormous number of caves in Crete. Well over 2,000 have been explored, but very many more must lie as yet unvisited. The limestone of which the island is largely composed has been eaten away by the chemical reaction of rainwater and by the flow of streams, riddling the interior structure of the mountains with subterranean passages and caverns to which a cave is only the front door.....■

Cave caution
Don't go in if you can't get out. Few caves on Crete have been fully explored, and most go back, and down, a lot further than they appear to.

Cretans have lived, died, worshipped and hidden in these caves since earliest times. The caves have yielded a high proportion of the archaeological finds of the island. Legends have accrued thickly around them, many developing into Cretan mythology. Yet only the Dhíktaean cave above Psikhró on the edge of the Lasíthiou plateau (see pages 118–19) has become a big tourist attraction, undoubtedly because it is comparatively easy to reach. The Ídaean cave on Psiloritis where Zeus was reared (see pages 178–9), and the caves of Artemis and of St John the Hermit, beyond Gouvernéto Monastery on the Akrotíri peninsula (see pages 220–1), are visited only by those prepared to walk some distance. The Kamáres cave above the Mesarás plain (see pages 174–5), though famous for the exquisite Minoan pottery found there, is too much of a climb for all but the hardiest visitor. The rest lie all but unvisited, guarding their secrets. A few are described here, but with a little local enquiry you can hunt down many more.

Birthplaces of the gods The cave of Profítas Ilías, the Prophet Elias, near Arkalokhóri, 32km south of Iráklion, makes a counterclaim with the Dhíktaean cave as the birthplace of Zeus. Here there must have been a cult of the *kourétes*, the shield-clashing guardians of the infant Zeus, for bronze sword blades have been excavated, along with miniature versions in gold, silver and bronze of the Minoans' sacred *labrys* or double-headed axe. Zeus, like the Cretan god of fertility, died and was reborn. On Mount Yioúchtas near Arkhánes, 15km south of Iráklio, a cave on the summit ridge is said to have been his deathbed.

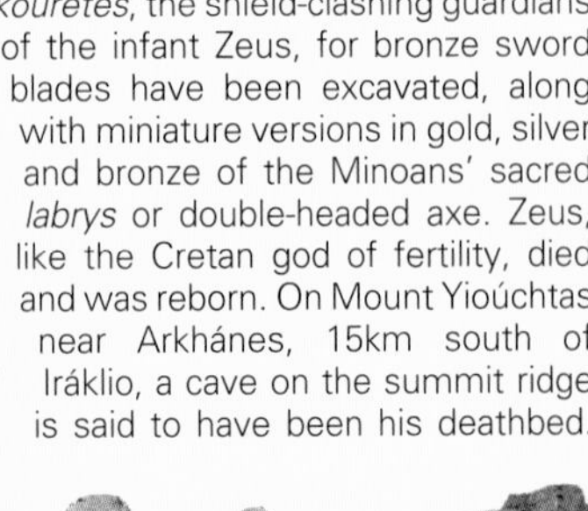

Formations that inspire legends

Caves are powerful symbols of fertility. The Ilíthia cave near Episkopí, southeast of Iráklio, has yielded several idols of pregnant women from the Stone Age. Two stalagmites have walled bases, perhaps enshrining them as phallic symbols. Ilíthia was born in the cave, daughter of Zeus's sister and wife Hera. She was also the centre of a fertility cult in a cave at Ínatos, in the beach cliff at Tsoútsouros (pages 104–5), from which came the earthenware totems of copulating couples and pregnant women now in Case 149 in the Iráklio Archaeological Museum.

Artemis was a fertility goddess in Graeco–Roman times, and was worshipped in the huge Skotinó cave, 5km southeast of Goúrnes. 160m deep and descending through four levels, the cave contained three Minoan bronze statues of worshipping men, the backs of their hands pressed to their foreheads. At a later date worship was taking place in the cave of the 99 Holy Fathers at Souré, out in the wilds about 15km northeast of Palaiókhora, a cold and dark climb down ladders.

The caves were places of concealment in difficult times, but they could also be death traps. In the Melidhóni cave, 4km east of Pérama, 370 Cretans were suffocated in 1824 by the smoke from brushwood fires lit at the mouth by Turkish soldiers. The previous year at the Mílatos cave, 7km north of Neápoli, the Turks had killed or sold into slavery 2,700 people to whom they had promised safe passage from their hiding place.

And to this day the caves attract myths, tales and legends. Did Bob Dylan once hang out with the hippie colony in the Mátala caves? If so, he has never owned up.

Honeypot
The unvisited, go-it-alone and do-it-yourself nature of most of Crete's caves is shown up in painful contrast by the cluster of touts, guides and donkey-drivers around the Dhíktaean cave's car park above Psikhró. This is Crete's only popular tourist cave, a honeypot that leaves all the others free.

Caving essentials
A torch with batteries that are not about to run out; a warm sweater; shoes with non-slip soles; a camera with flash; a ready imagination for matching fact with myth, legend and outright tall story. And always tell someone where you are going.

The cave of Ayía Sofía

Cape Drapanon from Yeoryióupoli

Watching the potter
In Margarítes you are welcome to visit the potteries and watch the process. Firing time is especially enjoyable, when the little kilns puff smoke and their interiors glow white-hot.

Margarítes potter at work

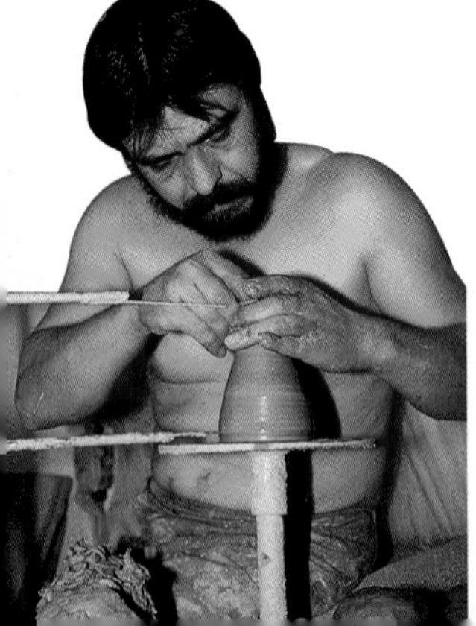

▶ Georgióupoli (Yeoryióupoli) *164A3*

Yeoryióupoli – the modern spelling – sits with its back to the north coast highway, overlooking the Gulf of Almiróu. It is a relaxed resort that retains some of the quiet atmosphere of a fishing village. There are a number of good and lively restaurants under the eucalyptus trees around the square, and hotels along the sandy beach that stretches several miles towards Réthimnon. The River Almiróu empties into the sea here, and several streams flow over the sands. The village was named in honour of Prince George of Greece who had a shooting lodge here. He became High Commissioner of Crete after Turkey had been forced to grant semi-independence to the island in 1898.

▶▶ Margarítes *164C2*

Margarítes lies just north of the foothills of the Psilorítis mountain range, and is a place where tourism has not yet seen off traditional industry. It is a pottery-making village, where you can buy anything from a tiny vase to one of the great *píthoi* or storage jars. Most of the potteries lie up the hill from the village in little stone-walled enclosures, each with a cylindrical kiln of plastered stone, crowned with a dome of firebricks. Some of the products are unashamed tourist tat, but the deep-bellied *píthoi* are direct descendants of the vessels made by the Minoans. In the village itself are colourwashed houses crowded along narrow streets, each bend revealing a new, differently coloured perspective (sky-blue is most popular). There are handsome stone archways in the walls of the lanes, and ancient frescoes in the church of Ayíos Ioánnis Prodrómos.

▶▶▶ Nídha Plateau and Ídaean Cave *165D2*

The road that runs south from Anóyia, climbing slowly into the foothills of the Psilorítis mountain range, is a long and winding one. Dotted along it are the stone huts or *mitáta* of the hill shepherds. Few are now occupied, but these humble structures were home in times past to men who spent the warm months of the year up here, making yoghurt and cheese from sheep's milk. It is rugged, bare terrain. All the more surprising and welcome, therefore, when you top the final rise and look down on the Nídha plateau, a flat circle of fertile grazing land nearly 1,400m up in the heart of the mountains. Despite the modern hotel at the foot of the road to the Ídaean cave (marked Ídhaiki Spilia on the map, pages 164–5), and the new ski resort not far away, this oasis in the dry, rocky hills is still the territory of the sheep and goat herd, an elemental place covered many feet deep with snow in winter when the animals are taken down to lower and safer ground.

Beyond the hotel a rocky track, the first stage just about negotiable by car, climbs to the mouth of the Ídaean cave, a wide black slit in the side of the mountain. Archaeologists have been carrying out excavations here for many years. A narrow-gauge railway plunges down into the cave, and an ugly fence with a locked gate seals the entrance. Enquiries in Anóyia (contact Yeóryios Sbókos, the mayor) *may* yield a guide who can unlock the gate and admit you to the great dark cave, 60m high, filled with snow in winter, always chilly and echoing, with stalactites dripping from the fissured roof, and mosses and ferns clinging to the walls.

Zeus, god of gods, was raised here from babyhood, his infant yells drowned out by his guardian warriors or *kourétes* with a constant clashing of their bronze shields. It was a necessary precaution. Rhea, the mother of Zeus, had hidden her baby here to protect him from his baleful father, Kronos, who had the unsociable habit of eating his children. Cretans believed that Zeus died and was reborn each year, as the Minoans believed of their god of vegetation who was also worshipped here.

The Minoans erected two enormous statues near the cave to act as landmarks for pilgrims from Faistós and Knosós. Just beside the cave mouth is an ancient stone altar, a solid slab of rock roughly shaped into a rectangle. Excavations have brought to light evidence of at least 3,000 years of worship here with finds including vases, utensils, gold jewellery, figurines and rings. Also unearthed late in the last century were a number of thick bronze ornamental shields, perhaps the core of fact around which was woven the legend of the *kourétes* and their sacred charge.

Kronos soap

There is another twist to the Zeus story, making Kronos out to be a very nasty piece of work. According to this version, Kronos is the result of an incestuous union between his mother, Gaea, and her son Uranus, the ruler of the world. Kronos castrates his father/brother Uranus so that he can take over control of the world. Then he marries his own sister, Rhea, and begets five children that he promptly eats. This is pure soap opera.

The pastures of the Nídha plateau

The atmospheric ruins of Káto Préveli

White and red
Cretan priests and villagers take pride in keeping their churches, however remote, brilliantly whitewashed. Topped with deep scarlet domes, the little white cubes stand out sharply in the landscape, especially so when dominated by an immense backdrop of mountainside. One or two of the most-visited churches, however, look as if they have not had a lick of paint in decades. Whitewash turns grey and shabby in a very short time under the Cretan sun.

▶▶▶ Préveli Monastery *164B1*

Káto Préveli, although it is now in ruins, is certainly worth half an hour's exploration. This is often a strange and muted experience, for it is a seldom-visited place which was stripped almost bare during the 1821 sacking by the Turks. There is an intimate tangle of ruined alleyways, flights of steps and shaded courtyards, in the middle of which stands the abandoned church with its carved abbot's chair, stalls for 21 monks, curiously unfinished iconostasis carvings and a rather crude, half-completed icon of Christ.

Píso Préveli, by contrast, is justly famed and popular with visitors with its handsome jumble of walls, pinnacles and turrets set on a saddle of ground overlooking the sea (open 9–7). Dating from the 16th century, the monastery was richer than Arkádhi in its heyday when, due to the unwillingness of the Cretans to allow their Turkish overlords to enjoy the fruits of their industry, the monastery benefited from gifts of olives, corn, farm produce, wine and animals. The plastered rubble walls of the monks' quarters look rather shabby, but the true glory of the monastery is the 19th-century church, which contains one of the finest examples of iconostasis in Crete. The great panel fills the end of the building, fantastically carved and filled with gilded icons. Also displayed is a golden crucifix set with diamonds, said to contain a fragment of the True Cross. Legend says that the Germans tried three times to take it to the Fatherland during the war, but the aeroplane's engines failed to start each time.

Outside the church, plaques record the gratitude of Allied soldiers from all over the world who were hidden here in Préveli after the fall of Crete, until they could be spirited away from nearby beaches by submarine. In the monastery's museum there are photographs of the abbots and monks who aided resistance fighters against the Germans and the Turks. Other treasures include richly worked monastic stoles and vestments, delicate silver holy water stoups, and pilgrims' offerings of rings, necklaces and crucifixes, all testimony to the power and glory of bygone Préveli.

Prayer and gunpowder
In the museum at Préveli there is a black-and-white photograph, obviously taken some time in the last century, of a fierce-looking brigand, swathed in belts of bullets, clutching a gun. Just the sort of ruffian you wouldn't care to meet on a mountain path. A closer look discloses a crucifix hanging around his neck. This ferocious outlaw turns out to be a 19th-century Préveli monk, Manassis Papadákis, who alternated prayer and gunpowder as his weapons against the Turks.

Píso Préveli is a place of pilgrimage for World War II veterans

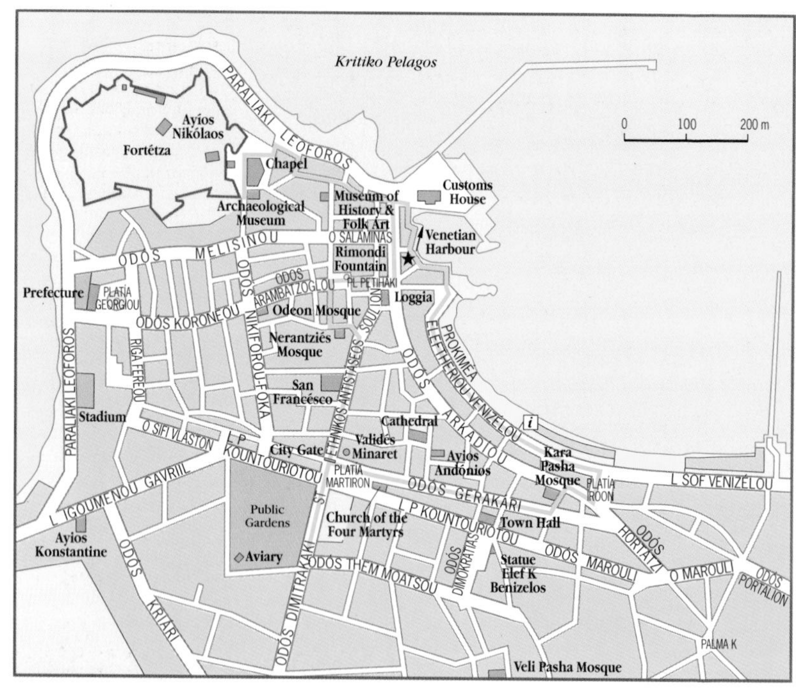

Pandelís Prevelákis
The writer Pandelís Prevelákis (1909–86) is Crete's overlooked man of letters, perhaps because of the giant shadow cast by Níkos Kazantzákis. Prevelákis, a native of Réthimnon, never achieved international status, maybe because his mixture of history, myth and fiction proved indigestible to non-Cretans. His *Tale of a Town*, written when a young man, was a big success when it was first published and is his homage to his upbringing in Réthimnon. The English translation is out of print, but it is worth enquiring at secondhand bookshops.

▶▶▶ Réthimnon 164B3

Early history and the Venetians A Late Minoan settlement and the cities of both Doric Greeks and Romans underlie present-day Réthimnon. Byzantium ruled the town for nearly 1,000 years. Then, early in the 13th century, four hundred years of Venetian domination began in Réthimnon. These were turbulent years when pirates, most notably Khaireddin Barbarossa, the Turkish admiral and buccaneer, sacked the port, and the Venetians responded by strengthening the walls of Réthimnon and building a mighty fortress. They were also civilised years of great prosperity, when the Venetians constructed breakwaters and a harbour, fine churches and houses, a splendid *loggia* where the town's aristocracy gathered, and public amenities such as fountains and gardens.

Turkish rule In 1646 Husein Pasha captured Réthimnon in one swift pounce and began a 250-year period of Turkish occupation. This era of domination lasted only half as long as that of the Venetians, but was just as influential on the life of the town. The minarets and domes of Islam sprouted from the churches and public buildings of Réthimnon, and the waterfront spawned a mass of cafés where the Turkish men gathered to gossip over sweet coffee and the smoke of their *narghiles*. With Muslims the dominant community, there were many cruel and bloody episodes as

Christian townspeople resisted conversion to Islam. In 1821, as mainland Greeks fought their epic War of Independence against the Ottoman Empire, the Réthimnon Turks reacted in fear and anger by massacring their Christian fellows.

German occupation When mainland Greek fought Turk again in 1896, the Russians took control of Réthimnon as part of the agreement between the Four Great Powers. After 1913 the town, along with the rest of Crete, enjoyed a taste of independence before World War II. During May 1941 much of the Battle of Crete was fought around Réthimnon. The town was one of the last to surrender, and became a centre of fierce resistance to the German occupation.

Réthimnon today Réthimnon is a noted seaside resort, with good bathing from the long central beach and those to either side of the town. The old town huddles below the Venetian *Fortétza*, and there are many fish restaurants and tavernas in the tall, ramshackle buildings around the curve of the Venetian harbour. Visitors, and Réthimnon's smart young set, sit here to watch sun or moon glowing on the pale stone of the breakwater and the lighthouse.

Away from the waterfront you catch the living and working town of Réthimnon. This is a tight maze of streets and lanes, darkly shaded between the walls of Venetian stone houses with elaborate Turkish wooden balconies. Greek Orthodox churches sport slender minarets and there are popular, crowded squares such as Platía Pétihaki with the famous Rimondi fountain. Other streets are less frequented, like those that run up from the harbour to the *Fortétza*, where the houses are low and cool, lacking the elegance of Venetian architecture, but exuding an individual charm. What Réthimnon has to offer is a dreamy, gentle dignity to go with the warmth and spontaneity of its inhabitants.

Réthimnon has always had a reputation for intellectual life, and today it boasts a Faculty of Philosophy with students adding to the lively atmosphere. In the fortnight before Lent there is a spectacular street carnival, and around Easter a flower festival, held in Réthimnon's city park just outside the old walls. Mid-July sees the town's Wine Festival (with free sampling included in the price of a ticket) which is then followed by a week of Cretan and Greek music.

Little *-ákis*
Much the most common ending for a Cretan surname is *-ákis*, as in Prevelákis or Kazantzákis. It is a diminutive, a fond way of saying 'little' – little Prévelis, little Kázantzis – and is probably derived from the Turkish. Some Cretans say it demonstrates how fondly the Turks regarded their Cretan co-citizens; others, that the rulers used it as a way of patronising, and therefore diminishing, their subjects.

Music at the mosque
In the early evening young boys gather in the anteroom of the Mosque of Nerantziés, *lýra* and bow in hand, to be taught the first steps in playing this most Cretan of instruments.

The belltower of the castle church

Walk Réthimnon

A Venetian doorway in Réthimnon

Allow about two hours. See map on page 182.

The walk starts on the waterfront, by the circular **Venetian harbour▶▶**, fortified between 1540 and 1570 at the same time as the city walls, after Barbarossa had sacked the town. Fix your sights on the castle, and make for it up narrow Odós Makedónias. Half-way up, turn right and then left up Odós Argyrópoulon, climbing to emerge under the walls of the ***Fortétza*▶▶▶**, a magnificent stronghold built on the promontory between 1573 and 1586, its great walls pierced for guns. Formidable it may look, but the Turks captured it easily in 1646, and roofed in the cathedral church of Ayíos Nikólaos in the centre of the fort with a dome of rough stone slabs. Various other ruinous buildings stand inside the walls, and outside the gateway is a former Turkish garrison building, later a prison, which now houses an **Archaeological Museum▶▶**. There is a superb view over Réthimnon, the coast and the hills behind from the vantage point of the walls.

Return to the waterfront by way of Odós Argyrópoulon and Odós Makedónias. Sidestep from Odós Makedónias into Mesolongíou Street. Just around the corner is the excellent **Museum of History and Folk Art▶▶▶**. Two rooms are crammed full of traditional, everyday items from the houses of local people: clothes, tools, lyres, furniture, pottery, agricultural equipment and evocative old photographs. At the harbour the road bends sharp right. Go immediately right after the bend down Arkadíou Street, unmarked here, to find the handsome ***Loggia*▶▶** of 1600, where Venetian nobles gathered. Tall stone columns support an old and beautiful carved timber roof. The building was derelict at the time of writing, but there are plans for renovation.

Turn right by the *loggia* into Odós K. Paleológou to find the vivid and noisy **Platía Petiháki▶▶** at the top. Here among the pavement tables and chatter of customers at cafés and restaurants stands the notable **Rimondi fountain▶▶** of 1623, with three spouting lions' heads still showing their Venetian dignity through the blurred, weather-eroded stonework. After the Turkish takeover of Réthimnon in 1646 the fountain, which was named after its builder, was covered in and domed over. Most of these additions have now fallen away.

The town beach in Réthimnon; there are better beaches further out

From Platía Petiháki continue up Theod. Arambatzoglou Street, and turn immediately left into the narrow Haril Trikoupi Street, with a strikingly slender and graceful minaret ahead. It was attached by the Turks to a former Venetian church, which they converted into the **Mosque of Nerantziés**▶▶, a tall, cool building, which is now a concert hall. You used to be able to climb to the minaret for a head-spinning view over Réthimnon, but it was closed for safety reasons at the time of writing. Turn left in front of the mosque, then right into the bustling, stimulating commerciality of **Ethníkos Antistáseos,** a street of shops that sound, smell and feel more like an open-air market. At the far end you pass through the old **city gate**▶, out of the thronged small streets of the old town onto busy Gerakári Street.

Opposite are the **public gardens**▶▶, the setting each July for the drinking, dancing and socialising of the Réthimnon Wine Festival. At other times the gardens are a haven of peace, surprisingly quiet in spite of the traffic roaring past, laid out with geometrical precision but pleasantly lush, where you can stroll under mimosa, acacia and exotic pines to the soothing sound of splashing and trickling water.

Back on Gerakári Street, turn right towards the big modern church of the Four Martyrs, and pass the heroic **statue of Kostís Yiampoudákis**▶ (see pages 171–2), his sword half-drawn, two pistols in his belt and another in his fist, the picture of defiance. Continue along Gerakári to turn left by the old **Mosque of Kara Pasha**▶ and pass through Platiá Iróon to the seafront. Turn left here to return to the harbour.

Venetian arches hang over the streets of the old town

Drive The old road from Réthimnon to Iráklio

You are sure to pass some of Crete's ubiquitous goats on this drive

This leisurely 72km drive passes through peaceful back country, along the old high road through the hills between Réthimnon and Iráklio.

If you arrive in Iráklio at the start of your holiday, you will probably be impatient to get to Réthimnon or Khaniá, and will take the new road along the coast. It is a good, fast highway, but the new road does not compare with the older parallel route that runs inland and offers a slow-paced way to see the landscape and villages of the north Cretan coast with a little taste of their atmosphere. This drive, if you can plan your departure by plane or boat from Iráklio around it, makes an excellent *au revoir* to Crete, a leisurely three-hour saunter from Réthimnon, or four hours from Khaniá, with plenty of time to linger over lunch on the way. See map on pages 164–5.

From **Réthimnon** you drive east along the coast for 5km to **Plátanias**, where the old road, signposted to 'Mon. Arkadíou', turns inland from the busy new highway. Follow this and the landscape begins to rise into rolling country with olive groves. These wonderfully gnarled and stubby trees that shade sheep and goats are often hundreds of years old. People ride along the roadside on donkeys laden with bundles of firewood, vegetables and fruit, and there are plenty of produce stalls and wayside cafés. The road winds east through **Loutrá** and **Áno Viran Episkopí** to come to **Pérama**, a large and thriving town that owes very little of its activity to tourism. Pérama is the commercial and social centre for this coastward country below the foothills of the Psiloritis mountain range, which rises in great pale peaks and ridges behind the town. It is a good place to stop, stretch your legs and idle over a drink while soaking up the atmosphere of a Cretan town where life centres around local trade and conversation. It may be a bit dusty and ramshackle, but it is lively and friendly.

The road turns left to leave Pérama and enters the long east–west valley of the River Yeropótamos. The lengthy range of the Kouloúkonas Mountains stands between the road and the coast. These are stark, impressive hills of pink and white rock flayed by the sun, their tops bare even of scrub. The two highest peaks of Kouloúkonas and Koutsotróulis rise to well over 900m. The road runs through more olive groves and orchards through the outskirts of small villages where time seems to have stopped since the opening of the new road deprived them of much of the passing trade they once enjoyed.

East of **Martzaná** you cross the river and a tributary, and come to **Apladianá**, where the Oasis café-restaurant stands on the right of the road. This was a busy halt before the new road was built, but these days it is a genuine oasis, a refuelling and watering hole where the owner greets each customer like an old friend. This is the perfect place to spend an hour or so on the vine-shaded terrace among tubs of flowers, munching your way through well-cooked lamb cutlets, potatoes and salad, watching the bicycles, donkeys and fruit trucks trickle sleepily by between the limewashed trunks of the trees.

Beyond Apladianá the road runs past **Doxaroú** and begins to climb over the eastward neck of the Kouloúkonas Mountains, passing through **Dhamásta** and curving round the base of the range to **Márathos**, where locals claim the honey is the best in Crete. From here it passes below the 760m peak of Stróumboulas to join the new road for the final 5km into **Iráklio.**

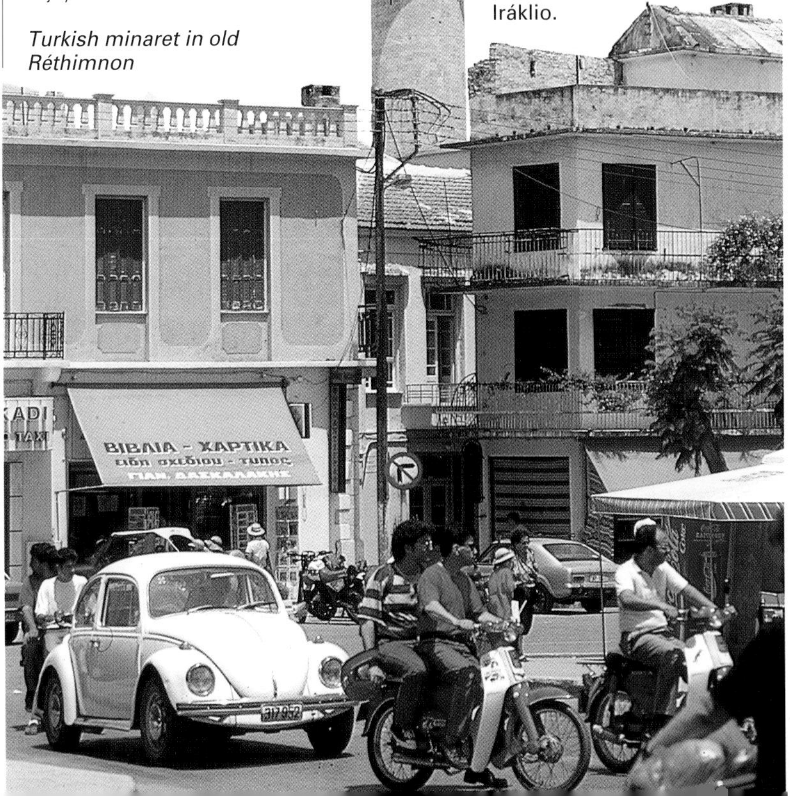

Turkish minaret in old Réthimnon

Fighting grandfather
In *Report to Greco* Níkos Kazantzákis records how his grandfather went to fight the Turks in the rebellion of 1878, and was lassoed and put to death outside the monastery at Savathianá. Kazantzákis went to see the old man's skull in the monastery sanctuary 'polished, anointed with sanctified oil from the watch lamp, deeply incised by sword blows'.

Mementi amori
According to Kazantzákis's mother, his grandfather spent his life either fighting or smoking his *chibouk* and gazing at the mountains. However, he must have had other pastimes. When the family opened his coffer after his death, they discovered a cushion stuffed with black and brown tresses of women's hair.

▶ Rodhákino *164A1*

Rodhákino is a pleasant, little-visited village on the south coast road, 27 km east of Sfakiá. It is divided into two neighbouring but distinct settlements: Áno Rodhákino perches on the mountainside, Káto Rodhákino stands further down the valley. Both are backed by the steep rise of the grey mountain slope. There are little-frequented tavernas and a few rooms to rent here, and there is the attraction of a rough walk down the cleft of the watercourse to the beach below.

The coast here is indented with little coves and beaches with no motor access, a perfect stretch for clandestine landings. During World War II many an undercover agent came to the beach below Rodhákino to be met by Cretan resistance fighters and taken away into the mountains with whatever he had brought: supplies, a wireless, gold sovereigns or simply a new set of instructions for some partisan group.

Rodhákino was an important staging post for this constant, stealthy movement of men and equipment into the island, and for traffic going the other way as well. In the spring of 1944, the German commander of Crete, General Kreipe, was taken from Rodhákino beach to Egypt aboard a Royal Navy submarine, after he had been captured by partisans and force-marched across Psiloritis. This was one of the most daring episodes of the war in Crete, and it resulted in a terrible backlash when the former commander, the ferocious General Müller, returned to the island as a replacement for General Kreipe. Müller burned several villages and executed scores of Cretans in reprisal.

▶ Rogdhiá *165E3*

To reach the beautifully sited village of Rogdhiá, take the old road towards Réthimnon from Iráklio and pass under the new road. After 2 km turn right, signposted, and climb steadily for 6km to reach the village, tucked into the flanks of the hills 300m above the sea. There is a splendid view out to the east over the Gulf of Iráklio and the Cretan capital, an especially striking prospect at night, when the dark coast below twinkles with thousands of lights. The village itself is a fairly quiet place with just a couple of tavernas.

The pleasant hillside village of Rogdhiá

There are a couple of reminders of Rogdhiá's more glorious past. The still impressive stonework of the façade of a big Venetian *palazzo* or country house is near the church, and outside the village, on a crag, are the ruins of a fort, the Palaiókastro, built in 1206 by the Genoese. At the time Genoa was contesting mastery of Crete with Venice, after the sack of Constantinople by the Crusaders had forced the Byzantine occupiers to leave the island. Three and a half centuries later the Palaiókastro saw the final humbling of the Venetians when they met the invading Turks here to negotiate a Venetian withdrawal from Crete. What makes Rogdhiá a particularly pleasant place to stop for a while is its setting in vineyards, backed by hills and far from the noise of traffic.

The carefully tended gardens of Savvathanon

▶▶ Savvathanon Monastery *165E3*

Savvathanon Monastery is in fact a nunnery. About 6km above Rogdhiá, it is made up of a cluster of bright white buildings in a remote upland valley at the end of a rough road, signposted from Rogdhiá. About 20 nuns live here, a surprising number when compared with the two or three inhabitants one usually finds in such isolated Cretan religious houses. The nuns pride themselves on the beauty of their gardens, the quality of their weaving and needlework which is on sale to visitors, and the palatable flavour of their *rakí*!

The nunnery was established in Venetian times and the big Panayía church dates from 1635. A smaller and older church, Ayíos Antónios, is built over the sacred grotto that inspired the founding of Savvathanon.

The imposing, four-square Savvathanon Monastery

The quiet village of Spíli nevertheless caters for visitors

Car blindness
The motor car has been a great liberating agent for visitors to Crete, enabling them to go almost anywhere they want. At the same time it has drastically reduced the pleasures of discovery along the way. Driving through villages such as Spíli, one cannot possibly guess at the delights of local life and architecture that lie just off the main road. These are only to be reached on foot.

The Venetian lion's-head fountain in Spíli

►► Spíli *164B2*

Spíli is one of those places it is very easy to miss altogether as you drive through. But this mountain village is a place where you should stop, a place which hides its character and charm around corners and up narrow alleys. Take time to wander in the maze of tangled alleyways on the hillside above the village square where you will find donkeys tethered to fig trees, quails in cages hung on house walls, tiny courtyards shaded by orange trees, balconied houses clinging like swallows' nests to the mountainside, smothered in brilliantly coloured flowers. You cannot properly appreciate Spíli until you have walked here and savoured this distinctly Cretan way of mountain living which has remained virtually unchanged for centuries.

Down below on the road, Spíli's village square is a delightful place with big plane trees, flowers in pots, vine leaves shifting in the breeze, and the splashing of water from a row of Venetian stone lion heads.

►►► Varsamónero Monastery *165D1*

Only the church of Ayíos Fanóurios remains of Varsamónero Monastery, at the far end of 2km of very rough track from Voríza. Ask in Voríza for the key (*to klithi*) held either by the priest (*o papás*) or the custodian of the church (*o filakás*).

There is beautiful stonework around the doorways and windows of the church, signs that Varsamónero was a powerful and wealthy monastery. Once inside, and having given your eyes time to adjust to the gloom, you are faced with three naves, two running east–west, and a third crossing them, and some of the finest frescoes in Crete which glow with startling colours, especially a vivid, ochreous yellow. These paintings date from the 14th and 15th centuries. Some say that they were worked on by El Greco and Mikhaíl Dhamaskínos, Crete's two most celebrated painters of the late 16th century. It could just about be true, as Dhamaskínos was working at the nearby Vrondísion Monastery in the 1580s, but there is no hard evidence to support the story. It does not matter: the paintings speak for themselves.

The faces are brown, serene and expressive, some faded, others astonishingly clear. Lines of saints stand calmly along the lower levels of the walls. Above, a 14th-century Life of the Virgin fills the ceiling. Scenes from the Life of Christ adorn the upper walls: the Three Kings follow an enormous star in a craggy landscape; St Peter walks on the water; angels hover over the stable; angels with huge wings surround a tomb; and angels with their feet drawn up support Christ on an orb of glory.

▶▶ Vrondísion Monastery *165D1*

Vrondísion Monastery stands in a superb location above the Zarós–Kamáres road, tucked in under steep, scrubby mountainsides alive with the sound of goat bells. Enormous plane trees shade the 15th-century Venetian fountain outside the gatehouse, where water pours from the silently howling mouths of the Four Sources of Paradise. From the monastery terrace there is a stunning view south over crumpled foothills to the Mesarás Plain. The church of Ayíos Antónios has some finely executed 14th-century frescoes, but the chief treasures of the monastery are six icons painted in the 1580s by Mikhaíl Dhamaskínos. These were removed to the church of Ayía Aikateríni in Iráklio in 1800. A wise precaution, as Turkish troops sacked Vrondísion in 1821.

The smaller and lesser-known monastery of **Ayíos Nikólaos▶** lies 3km nearer Zarós. It is a hospitable place, peacefully sited at the foot of a gorge, where you may be asked to sit down and eat and drink before being shown the church with its 14th- and 15th-century frescoes.

Fizzing monk
Visting Ayíos Nikólaos monastery, you may be fortunate enough to be served a snack by Brother Christodoúlos. This elderly monk was an active supporter of the resistance during the war. He fizzes with enthusiasm, tosses back his wine and encourages you to do the same, and spits his pomegranate seeds as accurately as the stones he throws at his sheep to stop them nibbling the olive trees.

A guide may take you to Ayíos Fanóurios at Varsamónero Monastery

■ Many thousands of visitors see the Psilorítis (Ída) mountain range from the waterfront at Iráklio, but only a few make the long and difficult trek to its highest peaks. For those with the time and stamina, the effort is repaid with a never-to-be-forgotten view over the whole of the island of Crete.....■

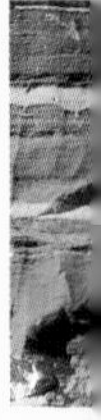

Oasis villages
The mountain villages of Crete, seen from afar amid the bright green of the fields and orchards cultivated so laboriously from the hillsides, look like wonderfully fresh, well-watered oases in a dull-coloured desert of bare rock and scrub.

For the majority of visitors to Crete, the island's four great mountain ranges are attractions they admire from afar. The Thriptís Mountains towards the eastern end of the island are virtually unknown, well off the central tourist beat. Lefká Óri, the White Mountains of the west, are often braved for the Samariá Gorge, but are otherwise left untasted. The Dhíkti range probably sees the greatest number of visitors, thanks to the fame of the Lasíthiou plateau and the easily accessible Dhíktaean cave above Psikhró. The Ída Mountains, or Psilorítis as the whole range is generally now known, see very few explorers. Yet it is the rearing peaks of Psilorítis that one notices from the waterfront at Iráklio. It is Psilorítis to which attaches the most celebrated incident of World War II in Crete. And it is Psilorítis that rises to the highest peak on the island, the absolute summit of Crete.

Looking to the Ída Mountains from the Amári valley

As a range of mountains, Psilorítis is far less impressive than the solid block of Dhíkti to the east, or the extensive, craggy upthrust of Levká Óri to the west. Most of the high land of Psiloritis, mountainous country from 1500m to over 2,000m, is confined to a lozenge-shaped area midway between Réthimnon and Iráklio towards the centre of the island. This high land lies from northwest to southeast, and measures only about 12km by 5km. It centres on Mount Ída, the peak also known as Psiloritis, the highest point of Crete at 2,456m.

The walk to the summit of Psiloritis, not an especially spectacular route in itself, is nevertheless one that only a very experienced walker should undertake alone. It is usually cold at such altitudes, very often cloudy, and the excursion may involve spending a night out on the mountain. A guide on this walk is a necessity, unless you are a very well-seasoned mountain hiker. You can make arrangements in Anóyia for a knowledgeable guide to accompany you from the Ídaean cave (see pages 178–9). It is a round trip of 7–8 hours to the summit. Alternatively you can ask for a guide in the village of Fourfourás in the Amári valley on the west side of Psiloritis (about the same time for the round trip), or in Kamáres village on the south of the range. It is a two-day round trip from the village, and about 6–8 hours' round walk from the Kamáres cave (see pages 174–5). Even better is to plan ahead and arrange a guide in advance through the Greek Mountaineering Club (EOS) office in Iráklio (tel: 081–227609).

The reward for all this planning and physical exertion is the view from the chapel of Tímios Stavrós at the summit of Psíloritis. There is a really breathtaking panorama to all quarters of the compass in which the whole of the island lies at your feet. Seen on a clear day at sunrise, this a prospect that will be embedded in your memory for a lifetime.

The Nídha plateau, high in the eastern flanks of Psiloritis and reached by a long mountain road from Anóyia (see page 169–71), still sustains a summer economy of shepherding and beekeeping. A modern ski resort a short way to the west is gearing up to provide winter sports on snow-covered Psiloritis.

As for the epic of World War II, it was across Psiloritis that Patrick Leigh Fermor, Manólis Paterákis and other resistance members ushered the German commander of Crete, General Heinrich Kreipe, after they had captured him on 26 April 1944. For nearly two weeks the party evaded a tight German cordon around the mountains. After many close scrapes they managed to reach the south coast at Rodhákino and their rendezvous with a Royal Navy submarine.

Working the terraces on the steep slopes of the Ída Mountains

Mountain bells

Only one sound pervades all the Cretan mountains, the solemn, low, musical clonking of the bells strapped round the necks of goats and sheep. There is no more welcome sound to the lost walker, who can hope to find the shepherd not far away. And there is no more seductive melody to soothe one to sleep under a tree. Some shepherds claim to have their teeth set on edge if one of the bells is badly tuned. Rather a nice judgement, if it is true.

Mountain walking

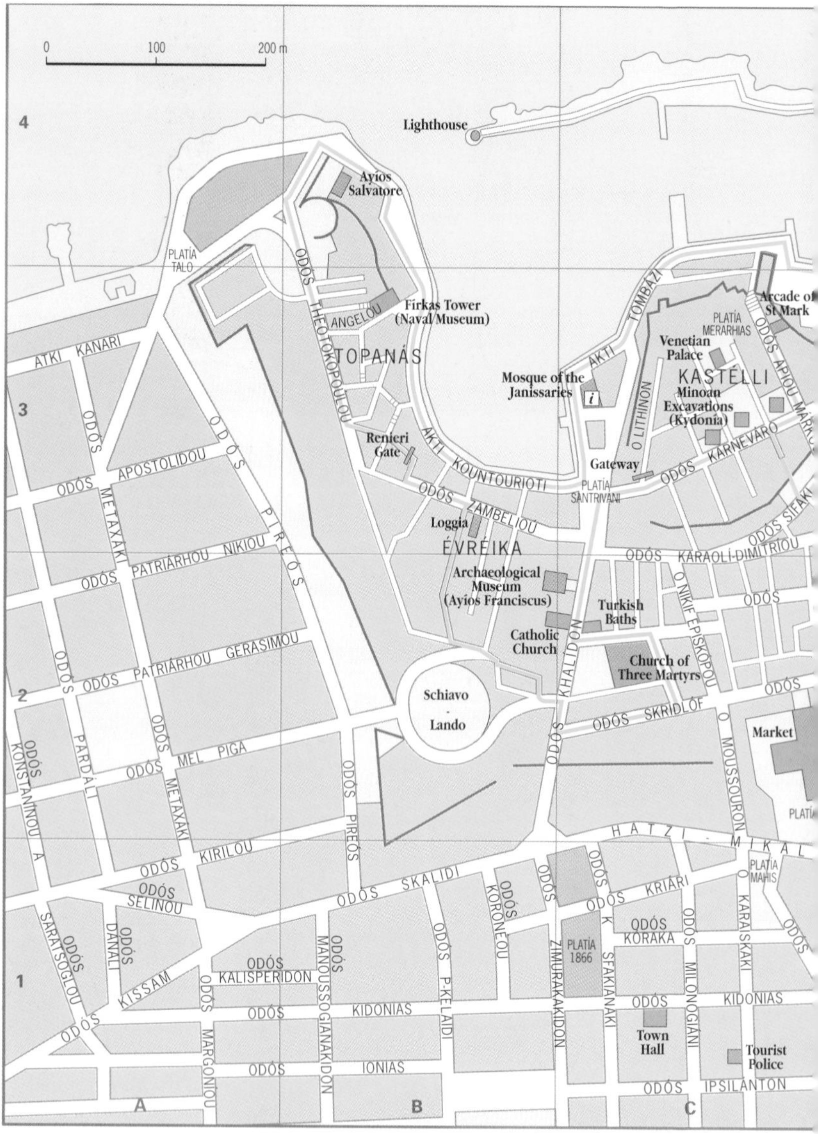
0
100
200 m
4
3
2
1
A
B
C
Lighthouse
Ayíos Salvatore
Fírkas Tower (Naval Museum)
PLATÍA TALO
ODÓS THEOTOKÓPOULOU
ANGELOU
TOPANÁS
AKTI KANARI
ODÓS APOSTOLIDOU
ODÓS PIREÓS
ODÓS METAXÁKI
ODÓS PATRIÁRHOU NIKIOU
ODÓS PATRIÁRHOU GERASIMOU
Renieri Gate
AKTI KOUNTOURIOTI
ODÓS ZAMBELIOU
Loggia
ÉVRÉIKA
Archaeological Museum (Ayíos Franciscus)
Catholic Church
Schiavo - Lando
Mosque of the Janissaries
AKTI TOMBAZI
O LITHINON
Gateway
PLATÍA SANTRIVANI
PLATÍA MERARHIAS
Venetian Palace
KASTÉLLI
Minoan Excavations (Kydonía)
Arcade of St Mark
ODÓS APIOU MÁRKOU
ODÓS KARNEVÁRO
ODÓS SIFAKI
ODÓS KARAOLÍ-DIMITRÍOU
O NIKIF EPISKÓPOU
Turkish Baths
Church of Three Martyrs
ODÓS KHALIDON
ODÓS SKRIDLÓF
O MOUSSOURON
Market
PLATÍA
ODÓS KONSTANTÍNOU A
ODÓS PARDÁLI
ODÓS MEL PIGA
ODÓS KIRILOU
ODÓS SELINOU
ODÓS PIREÓS
HATZI MIKAL
ODÓS SKALIDI
ODÓS KORONEOU
PLATÍA MAHIS
ODÓS KRIÁRI
ODÓS KORAKA
PLATÍA 1866
ZIMURAKAKIDON
SFAKIANAKI
ODÓS MILONOGIANI
O KARAISKAKI
ODÓS SARATSOGLOU
ODÓS DANALI
ODÓS KISSAM
ODÓS KALISPERIDON
ODÓS MANOUSSOGIANAKIDON
ODÓS P-KELAIDI
ODÓS KIDONIAS
KIDONIAS
Town Hall
Tourist Police
ODÓS MARGONIOU
ODÓS IONIAS
ODÓS IPSILÁNTON

194

Right: Khaniá harbour
Far right: distinctive blue Khaniá ware

RESTAURANT SELINI
HOLSTEN

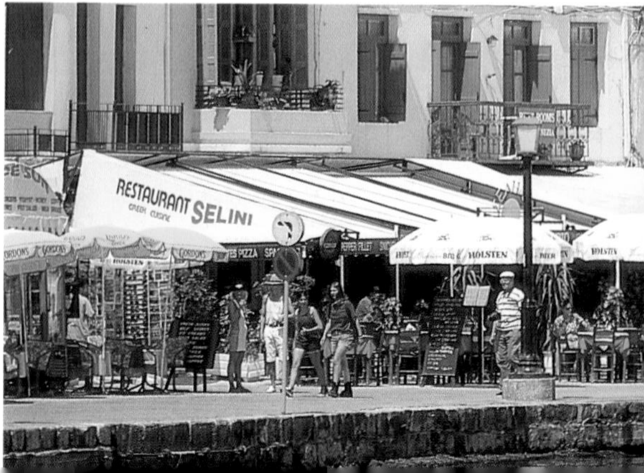

KHANIÁ

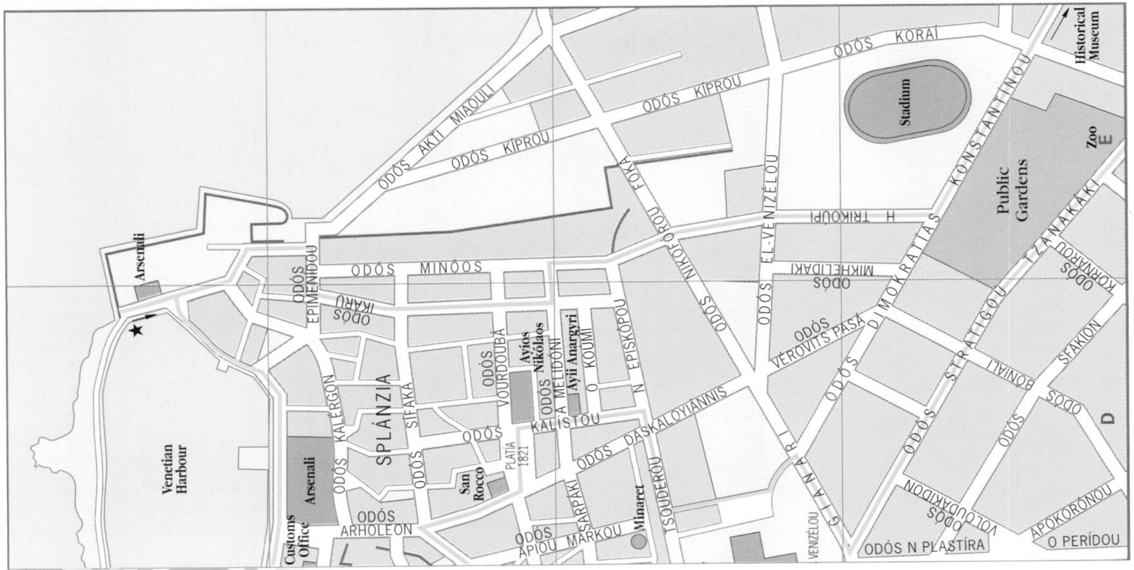

Venetian Harbour
Arsenali
Customs Office
Arsenali
ODÓS KALÉRGON
ODÓS ARHOLEON
SPLÁNZIA
ODÓS SÍFAKA
ODÓS IKARU
ODÓS EPIMENÍDOU
ODÓS MINÓOS
ODÓS AKTI MIAOULI
ODÓS KÍPROU
ODÓS KÍPROU
San Rocco
PLATÍA 1821
ODÓS VOURDOUBÁ
Ayíos Nikólaos
ODÓS KALÍSTOU
ODÓS A MELIDÓNI
Ayii Anargyri
O KOÚMI
ODÓS APÍOU MARKOU
SARPÁKI
ODÓS DASKALOYIÁNNIS
N EPISKÓPOU
Minaret
TSOUDERÓU
ODÓS NIKOFÓROU FOKÁ
ODÓS EL-VENIZÉLOU
VENIZÉLOU
GIANARI
ODÓS VÉROVITS PASÁ
ODÓS MIKHELIDAKI
H TRIKOÚPI
ODÓS KORAÍ
Stadium
ODÓS DIMOKRATÍAS
KONSTANTÍNOU
ODÓS STRATIGOÚ TZANAKÁKI
Public Gardens
Zoo
E
ODÓS N PLASTÍRA
ODÓS VOLOUDAKIDON
ODÓS BONIALI
ODÓS SFAKION
ODÓS KORNAROU
APOKORÓNOU
O PERÍDOU
ODÓS
D
Historical Museum

RESTAURANT
'KORALI'
GREEK CUISINE
Cafe Bar
Snack

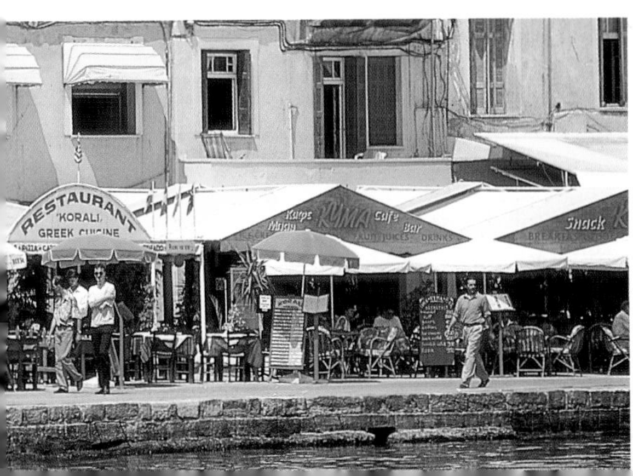

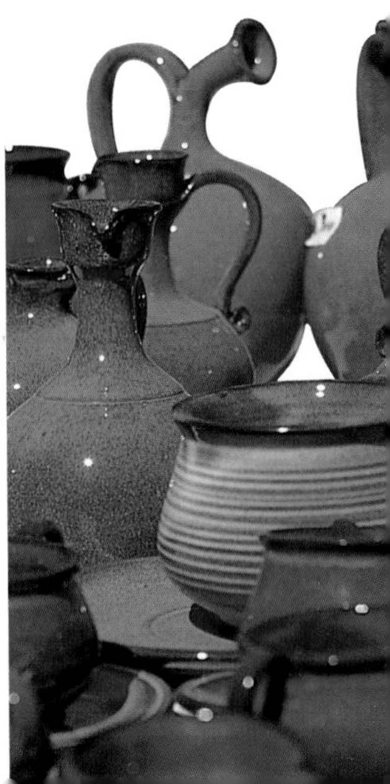

Looking over Khaniá rooftops to the break-water lighthouse – seemingly in the shape of a minaret

Lottery
On street corners, in shop doorways, around queues in public offices, on the waterfront, in cafés, along the beach – there's no part of Khaniá, nor of Crete's other big towns, not penetrated by the hoarse cries of the lottery ticket sellers. A few drachmas in exchange for a fortune – maybe.

Beggars
Beggars are a feature of Cretan towns, as they are in all European cities these days. Life can still be extremely tough for a disabled or handicapped Cretan. Hence the occasional display of infirmities and a hand outstretched for alms.

Khaniá Khaniá is, for most visitors, the most attractive and stimulating town in Crete. There is something special about the town, a warm and positive atmosphere allied to tremendous elegance and dignity, albeit somewhat crumbling and shabby in places. Khaniá owes this strong yet subtle flavour partly to its architecture: huddled streets of Byzantine, Venetian and Turkish remnants, some substantial, all of pale, honey-coloured stone. Then there is its undisputed position as social and emotional capital of the island. Iráklio, which became the official capital in 1971, may be more prosperous, but it lacks the wit and charm of Khaniá. And there is also its incomparable site, facing a lovely bay and the distant hills of the Rodhopoú peninsula, overshadowed by the peaks of the White Mountains that stand 2,500m above and behind the city, snow-capped or sun-baked according to season.

Provincial city Khaniá wears two hats: one as a popular tourist resort, thanks to its sandy beaches and wide range of facilities, and the other as a self-confident city of 60,000 independent-minded inhabitants which dominates the life of western Crete as capital of the nome of Khaniá. The town is small enough to retain an easy-going, provincial atmosphere, but it is also large enough to offer something to everyone who visits or stays here. It is an ideal size to explore on foot. Across the harbour and down the maze of narrow streets and alleys are fascinating glimpses of towers, walls, minarets, domes, balconies and archways spanning at least seven or eight centuries of history. Many are in disrepair. Khaniá suffered absolute devastation at the hands of both the Turks and the Germans, and those attempting to dislodge them. The modern town built since the war has sprawled out in both directions along the coast, parts of it stark concrete, other parts eddying around splendid 19th-century houses where consuls and merchants once lived.

The old town Away from the colourful, always thronged Venetian harbour and the tight warren of streets behind it, the old town still has the little shops and workplaces of knifemakers, cobblers, leather-sellers, wood-carvers, and potters, all working and shouting among the tavernas, souvenir hawkers, restaurants and rooms to let. These thread-like alleyways and streets are always packed to the walls with strolling visitors and locals. Of Crete's four main north coast towns, Khaniá gives off the strongest savour, and the most positive and optimistic.

Minoan to Roman The city's naturally advantageous site, near the deepwater inlet of Soúdha Bay, backed by fertile plains and sheltered by the White Mountains, has been occupied since neolithic times. The grandson of King Minos, the famously hospitable Kydon, founded the Minoan settlement of Kydoniá here. After earthquakes had devastated Knosós, Kydoniá became the powerbase of the Mycenaean rulers of Crete. Homer mentions the city as the place where King Menelaus lost his fleet, wrecked during its return from the siege of Troy. The Romans took Kydoniá in 67BC, in the face of fierce resistance from the always intransigent locals. The conquerors built a theatre on the centrally placed knoll of Kastélli, and had established a flourishing city by the time Byzantine invaders ousted them in AD352.

Byzantine to Venetian The new rulers, using Crete as a garrison to enforce their dominance in the Aegean, fortified Kydoniá and held it for nearly 500 years. Saracens arrived from Arabia in 826, captured the city and laid it waste, completing the downfall of Kydoniá by neglect. In 961 the Byzantines returned, retook Kydoniá and occupied it until Constantinople fell to the Crusaders in 1204 and the island was sold to the Venetians. The Genoese, keen to have Crete as a cornerstone in their rivalry with Venice, took Kydoniá in 1266. But they made little headway in the rest of the island, and their capitulation in 1290 launched the city on almost 350 years of growing prosperity and influence.

Quality gifts from the quiet back street shops?

Flowers for the lady?
Dark, young girls, often with a baby in the crook of one arm, prowl in and out of restaurants with buckets of tulips or roses to sell, usually targeting romantic-looking couples.

Khaniá's cathedral is set back from Khalídon

Low lights
The medieval feel to the narrow streets of Khaniá's old quarters is due as much as anything to the lighting. Dim lamps seem to cast shadows rather than illumination.

La Canea Merchants, traders and other rich and confident incomers from Venice and elsewhere poured into La Canea, as the city was renamed by the Venetians. They built well and handsomely around the harbour. They walled in the knoll of Kastélli, and successfully saw off the threat from the rapacious buccaneers that cruised the Cretan coasts looking for weak points. After the determined and ruthless pirate admiral Khaireddin Barbarossa had penetrated the defences and sacked the city in the 1530s, new walls were built round the expanded town, and the harbour was fortified and provided with *arsenali,* great ship-building sheds vaulted in stone. Continued prosperity seemed assured for the wealthy trading town known as the Venice of the East. But then the wind of Islam began to blow from ancient Byzantium. The Turks, strengthening as the 17th century got under way, came storming down from the north in 1645. Yussuf Pasha and his troops made for La Canea, and after suffering many thousands of losses during a bloody siege lasting 55 days took the city and entered on a period of dominance half as long as that of the enemy they had driven out.

Turkish takeover Physically La Canea, or Khaniá, as it came to be known, changed little. The Turks signalled the ascendancy of Islam over Christianity by grafting domes and slender minarets onto old churches in the city and converting them to mosques. One of Khaniá's mosques still bears the name of the Janissaries, fanatically anti-Christian soldiers who had started life as Christians themselves before undergoing conversion as children. The religious and ideological balance of the city's population changed as the numbers of Muslims increased throughout the 18th century. Some were born to Turkish parents, some were willing converts, others were forcibly brought to the new allegiance.

Headdress
Khaniá is the town where you will spot the greatest number of men wearing the traditional black headdress, a close-fitting woven cloth wound around the temples, with a fringe of tassels bobbing on the forehead. It gives a dashing and martial air to the wearer, almost certainly in town for the day from one of the more remot White Mountain villages, where this headgear is still standard among the older men.

The façade of the covered market – always a hive of activity inside

Gold and silver jewellery is a good buy in Khaniá

Turkish tyrants It is tempting to cast the Turks in the rôle of bogeymen, and the Venetians as peaceful merchants. Venetians certainly perpetrated their share of atrocities against insurgent Cretans, but there is no doubt that the Turkish rulers of Khaniá outdid them. Rebellion was put down with ferocity. In 1770 the uprising under Daskaloyiánnis was crushed after the rebels reached the gates of the city, and Daskaloyiánnis was taken to Iráklio where he was flayed alive. In the 19th century it was the same story. Khaniá was an impregnable Turkish garrison from which attacks were made on revolutionaries in the hills behind. In 1821 reports in Khaniá told of Janissaries casually shooting passers-by for fun after laying bets as to whether they would drop on their faces or on their backs.

Enosis The mainland war of 1896 between Greece and Turkey brought new hope to the beleaguered city. In 1898 the Four Great Powers of Europe, France, Italy, Russia and Britain, took over Crete, stationing soldiers in Khaniá. The city was designated the capital of Crete, and the Turks left the island under protest. But the desire for autonomy could not be denied. Elefthérios Venizélos, the charismatic and revolutionary politician, led insurrection against the administration from his base in Khaniá, and succeeded in uniting Crete with mainland Greece in 1913.

World War II The city saw some of the fiercest fighting of the Battle of Crete in May 1941. Allied troops, dug in around Khaniá and the Máleme airstrip to the west, shot the invaders, many of them little more than teenagers, as they parachuted in. Khaniá was bombed on 20 May, and much of the old town was burned to the ground. After the fall of Crete, resistance flourished in the city until the spring of 1945, when the Germans were driven out of Khaniá long after the rest of Crete had been recaptured.

Spot the locals
An excellent tip, if you want to eat well-prepared Cretan food, is to assess the proportion of fair to dark heads in the restaurant. The greater the number of locals, the better and more authentic the food and wine is likely to be.

Walk Around Khaniá

Khaniá is small enough to explore on foot, and half a day sauntering around the harbour and the old town will show you just about everything. But you are bound to be led astray, up side alleys, into shops and cafés, into conversations and offers of coffee and *rakí*. Khaniá is a convivial and friendly town, one that still has time and explanations for the inquisitive stranger. Don't expect to start in mid-morning and finish in time for lunch. It is far better to give up the whole day, lingering where the mood or conversation bids you, returning at night to the harbour to reflect on all you have seen over a meal and a few drinks. The Venetian walls which were built around the old town during the 16th century now stand in only a few places, but the area covered by this walk is roughly that which they enclosed. The square of Platía 1866 and the public gardens on Tzanakáki Street lie further south, but on a hot day you will be grateful to sit down for a few minutes under the trees in comparative peace and quiet. The sights listed on pages 202–5 are in the order in which you will encounter them on this walk.

The walk begins at the **Venetian harbour** where all visitors to Khaniá naturally congregate. Start at the eastern or inner end of the harbour, where the breakwater joins the harbour wall. Continue around the harbour to pass on your left the **Mosque of the Janissaries**. Walk on around the curve of the waterfront to the west side of the outer harbour, to reach the **Fírkas Tower**. From the Fírkas Tower, continue round the curve of the outer harbour walkway until you come to the opening into Theotokopoúlou Street at the top of the **Topanás quarter** of the old city.

A maze of streets backs the harbour

Looking out to the breakwater from the Firkas Tower

The **Renieri gate** is on your right before you reach Zambelioú Street. Continuing down Zambelioú, you are now in the **Evréika quarter**. On your right is the **Venetian loggia**. Turn right down Kondiláki Street to reach the **Schiavo-Lando bastion**. Turn left here to reach **Khalídon**. Odós Skridlóf is directly across Khalídon.

From Skridlóf turn left down Episkopou Dorotheou, and second left to reach a little square on Khalídon with the **Church of Trimartyre**. Turn right down Khalídon, to reach the **Archaeological Museum**. From Platía Santriváni, the square at the bottom of Khalídon, turn right into Karneváro Street and you will come to the **Kastélli quarter**. Immediately on your left, at the far end of Lithínon Street, is the gateway to the old Venetian **archive**. The Venetian **arcade of St Mark** is on your left down Ayía Marku. Turn right up any of the narrow, mazy streets of Kastélli to emerge on Karaolí Dimitríou Street. Along the north side of the street stands a tall section of the Venetian city walls. Turn left and continue along Odós Sífaki, past the tourist information office, to reach Daskaloyiánnis Street.

Turn right up Daskaloyiánnis and left into Platía 1821, at the heart of the **Splánzia quarter**. From Ayíi Anargýri church walk south to turn right along Episkópou and on across Daskaloyiánnis Street into Tsouderoú. On your left you'll spot a slender minaret, standing in Hadzimiháli Daliáni Street. Turn left opposite this, down the east side of the **covered market**. Turn right into Nikofórou Foká to reach the market entrance. **Platía 1897** is the square to the front of the main market entrance. Tzanakáki Street runs southeast; halfway along on the left you will come to the **public gardens**. Go up Tzanakáki Street, over the crossroads and on into Sfakianáki Street, and the Historical Museum is on your right.

Beyond the museum take first left, then left again down Dimokratías Street past the stadium. Turn right down Trikoúpi to cross Nikofórou Foká. From here you can continue down Minóos Street, or weave your way through Splánzia, to return to the waterfront where you started.

Landing swordfish on the quay

Mending the nets can be sociable

Sounds and smells
By night music, chatter and the smell of cooking fill the streets of the old quarters. But walk into the dark, sloping residential areas, and a different Khaniá will engage your senses with a cackle of laughter or the rumble of an argument from an open window, a whiff of sewage, a waft of perfume, the crackle of a motorbike, the distant barking of a dog, and the tang of dust, sweat and sea salt.

▶▶▶ Venetian harbour *195D4*

This protective arm of golden stone runs west, enclosing both inner and outer harbours, to end in an attractive stone lighthouse which is an obvious target for an evening stroll. At the junction of breakwater and harbour wall stand the great stone sheds of the ***arsenali***▶, built by the Venetians for the construction and maintenance of their big fleet of galleys after the sacking of the town by Barbarossa. Originally there were about 25 of these impressive buildings around the harbour, but only nine now remain. Fishing boats and yachts lie on one side of the sheltered inner harbour, and on the other is a run of restaurants and cafés which continues unbroken all the way round the harbour. The harbour walkway is of stone, always thronged at night with visitors and Khaniá residents out on their ritual *voltá* or promenade.

▶▶ Mosque of the Janissaries and Santriváni Square *194C3*

The Mosque of the Janissaries, domed and solid, was built in 1645 immediately after the Turks had captured Khaniá from the Venetians. Just south, at the innermost point of the harbour, is Santriváni Square, a popular meeting and eating place, named after the Turkish word for fountain, and there is a fountain, tucked away behind the open staircase of the Plaza Hotel. All around rise the old Venetian waterfront palaces and fine houses of the Kastélli, Evréika and Topanás quarters, many with their ground floors converted to restaurants and local craft shops.

The Mosque of the Janissaries beside the old harbour

▶▶ Fírkas Tower *194B3*

The tower's Venetian bastion houses the Naval Museum (see pages 206–7) and hosts dancing displays. Each Sunday and on public holidays the Greek flag flies from the tower, as it did on 1 December 1913 to celebrate the long-desired union between Crete and mainland Greece.

▶▶▶ Topanás quarter *194B3*

Theotokopoúlou Street▶▶▶ is a delight, the backbone of Topanás, packed with old Venetian houses with wrought-iron balconies. Many have given over their ground floors to good quality craft and souvenir shops. **Angelou Street▶▶** is lined with Venetian mansions. **Renieri gate▶▶**, at the top of Zambelioú Street, was built in 1608 and still bears the arms of the Venetian family who paid for its construction.

Direct line
If you are self-catering in Khaniá, and have the confidence and the Greek, you can bargain directly with a fisherman for fresh fish that could have been swimming only an hour beforehand. Or try for one yourself with a line and hook off the harbour wall.

Theotokopoúlou passes through the heart of Topanás

▶▶▶ Evréika quarter *194B3*

Evréika is a maze of streets with tottering, colourwashed houses, cafés and scraps of garden in sheltered courtyards. **Zambelioú Street▶▶** runs between needle's-eye alleyways and flights of steps, with Venetian houses and the Venetian **Loggia▶** to enjoy. The **Schiavo-Lando bastion▶** is a round 16th-century tower built to defend the old city walls. **Khalídon▶▶** is the spinal route of the Evréika quarter and the tourist heart of Khaniá, where souvenir shops stand shoulder to shoulder. **Odós Skridlóf▶▶▶**, directly across Khalídon, is narrow and jam-packed, the traditional street of leather-sellers, where you can buy belts, bags, sandals and purses, some made on the premises.

Harbour view
One of the best of Khaniá's many breathtaking views is from the seafront promenade east of the harbour, looking west to the great Venetian wall standing massively into the sea. It is especially atmospheric at night, when the lights bring a warm, yellow-orange glow out of the stonework.

Haggling
The agreeable, if uncertain, Mediterranean custom of haggling over prices is not entirely dead in Khaniá's market, though more prices are fixed nowadays than hitherto. Treat this as an enjoyable game rather than with stony-faced persistence. You will probably not strike much of a bargain, but the right mixture of cheek and nonchalance will bring a smile and some extra conversation from your adversary.

Caged birds
By day, the sound of the apartment blocks is the sound of bird-song, not from wild birds, but from the sweetly singing occupants of cages hung up on the balconies.

► Church of Trimartyre *194C2*

The 19th-century **Church of Trimartyre►**, or Three Martyrs, stands near a rather neglected, domed **Turkish bath►**. Trimartyre is the Greek Orthodox cathedral of Khaniá, an undistinguished church built by a Turk in thanksgiving for a miracle performed by the Virgin Mary that saved the life of his son. The **Archaeological Museum►►►** (see page 206) is to be found in the Venetian church of St Francis.

►►► Kastélli quarter *194C3*

The Kastélli quarter is under the knoll where the original city of Kydoniá was founded. At the entrance to Lithínon Street is the gateway to the old Venetian **archive►**, dated 1624, and a little further along the site of an ongoing excavation of Minoan **Kydoniá►**, where tombs, pavements and artefacts have been uncovered. As yet this is closed to the public. Nearby you will find the handsome Venetian **arcade of St Mark►►** and a tall section of the **Venetian city walls►►**, great pink and yellow sandstone blocks interspersed with cylindrical fragments of Greek and Roman columns.

►►► Splánzia quarter *195D3*

Platía 1821 is the square at the centre of the Splánzia quarter, a tightly woven, characterful warren of constricted lanes and alleys full of tiny shops and half-hidden restaurants with wooden balconies and overarching upper storeys. A plaque in the middle of **Platía 1821►►►** records the hanging of an Orthodox bishop here in that year. The plane-shaded square is surrounded by cafés where you can sit and rest, before visiting its three churches. **Ayíos Nikólaos►►**, originally a monastery church, was converted into the mosque of Sultan Ibrahim under the Turks before becoming an Orthodox church in 1912, hence its twin minaret and tower. The 1630 Venetian church of **San Rocco►** stands on the north side of the square, and to the south is **Ayíi Anargýri►►**, the Holy Poor, a 16th-century Venetian church rich in ancient icons, that somehow continued to hold Orthodox services under both Venetians and Turks.

Groceries and hardware in Splánzia

▶▶▶ The covered market 194C2

Khaniá's **covered market** is one of the most compelling attractions of the town. Plunge into the cool, tall, crowded and vibrant hall where all Khaniá and surrounding districts come to buy, sell and chat. The Turks had their own market which was covered when this building was put up in 1911, closely copying the market in Marseilles on a cruciform plan with bays and quiet corners. Your eyes may take time to adjust from the sunlight outside to the darkness within, but your ears will register the bustle immediately, with the shouting of stallholders, laughter and argument, and indignant reactions from customers who think they are being overcharged. The stalls, many painted with scenes of sea, land, garden and field, offer a heaped selection of just about everything that sustains everyday life: fruit, vegetables, cuts of meat, links of spicy sausages, nuts, herbs and spices, olives, myriad different cheeses and fish of every shape and size. Though you'll be invited to stop, taste and buy, there's no obligation. You can saunter around soaking up the atmosphere, then sit at a coffee stall or in one of the little restaurants tucked away at the side of the hall to enjoy the noise, smell and incessant movement. The market is one of the best free shows in Khaniá, and should not be missed. Apart from anything else, this is the best place in town to buy ingredients for your picnic.

Platía 1897▶ is a wide open space roaring with traffic. Its name commemorates the year when the revolutionary committee, under the leadership of the Cretan politician and hero Elefthérios Venizélos, met on the hill of Profítas Ilías on the Akrotíri peninsula east of the city to raise the Greek flag in defiance of both Turks and the occupying Great Powers of Europe. The square is dotted with a large choice of *kafenía,* their customers largely locals rather than tourists, where you can sit to watch a very specifically Cretan world pass by.

The covered market

Shade of Islam
In the public gardens you will find the elements so prized in Islamic culture and so often depicted in Islamic art: water, shade, greenery, and a harmonious and formal balance between nature and artifice.

▶▶ The public gardens 195E1

Tzanakáki Street is a modern thoroughfare lined with modern institutions. The Bank of Greece is on the corner, then Khaniá's main post office and the national telephone company headquarters, offices, clothes shops and newsagents. The street itself has none of the attractions of the old town down by the harbour, but the public gardens are a wonderfully cool, quiet and relaxed place to spend an idle hour or so, especially if you have children with you. The Turkish ruler Reouf Pasha had the gardens laid out for himself in 1870. Now there are cafés under the trees, a children's playground and a zoo with monkeys, birds and a collection of Cretan ibex. You are unlikely to see these in the wild, outside their sanctuary island of Día off Iráklio, or in the Samariá Gorge. Khaniá people come to the gardens for the folk dancing displays, evening concerts, film shows and plays put on in the open-air auditorium.

Khaniá's museums

■ **Khaniá's museums put the city into context. The Archaeological Museum brings alive the ancient sites of the area; the Naval Museum illustrates the close relationship between trade and warfare; and the Historical Museum celebrates two of Khaniá's greatest heroes.....■**

Plaster saint
Mementoes of Elefthérios Venizélos are not hard to come by. Almost every souvenir shop sells plaster statuettes of the great man, myopically peering through his round-rimmed spectacles.

Labels
In Khaniá the museums are not well labelled. Common sense, enquiry where necessary and assiduous use of guide books will tell you most of what you want to know, but the tourist and municipal authorities are surely missing a trick here and in just about every other museum in Crete.

The Archaeological Museum (open 8:30–3, Tuesday to Sunday). Most exhibits are from sites around Khaniá and the western end of Crete. They give a good general idea of the development of Cretan culture from the Stone Age through Minoan, Mycenaean, Greek and Roman times. Starting on the left, the first exhibits display crude pottery, both in shards and in reconstructed vessels, and tools from the late Stone Age (c. 3400–2800BC). Then come the Minoan cases, dating from c. 2800 to 1200BC. Basic zigzag and banded decoration gives way to delicate floral and swirling designs. A marine style of decoration then appears with water weeds and octopuses, before a decline from the high peak of Minoan artistry to more geometric and formal designs of giant spotted waves curled over feathery fronds and shrimp-like motifs in reds, ochres and browns.

Dorian artefacts include a clumsy child's toy terracotta animal on four thick wheels. Hellenic mosaic pavements feature Dionysius discovering Ariadne, and Poseidon rescuing Amymone with his trident perched on his shoulder. There is a 5th-century BC guitar-player finely drawn in red and black on a slender-necked *lekythos* or vase. Roman statuary incudes a delicately carved naked boy, and Aphrodite teaching Eros how to play the guitar.

The Naval Museum (open 10–2, and 7–9 on Tuesday, Thursday and Saturday, closed Monday). In the Firkás Tower above the harbour, the Naval Museum houses a fascinating exhibition on the history of sea trade and naval

The Archaeological Museum is housed in a former church

The Maritime Museum has displays on World War II

warfare in and around Crete. There are ship models, photographs of 20th-century wartime episodes, including some of the terrible World War II bombing of Allied shipping in Soúdha Bay, maps and prints of historic sea engagements, and a collection of naval weapons ranging from unreliable-looking early cannon to seafarers' side arms. One room contains a superb collection of sea shells.

The Historical Museum, 20 Odós Sfakianáki (open Monday to Friday, 9–1). The theme here is once again 'Freedom or Death', naturally epitomised by the two local heroes, Elefthérios Venizélos and Daskaloyíannis. The Venizélos room (ground floor), with its photographs of revolutionary meetings, grave portrait of the international statesman and more informal portraits of Venizélos as fiery local leader, along with his furniture and writing desk, gives a powerful impression of his importance in Crete's history, both practical and symbolic. Upstairs, Daskaloyiánnis stares nobly from his frame, the picture of defiance. Other relics of revolution include a bristling array of rebel weapons, and portraits of the leaders of some of the more famous 19th-century uprisings against the Turks.

Walk Khaniá breakwater by night

This walk takes rather longer than might appear during the daytime, owing to the roughness of the breakwater's stone surface, but it is undoubtedly one of the most rewarding that Khaniá can offer. It is best to allow nearer two hours than one, as you will certainly want to stop and admire the view from many points along the stone arm that encloses both inner and outer harbours. Watch your step – darkness adds greatly to the possibility of twisting an ankle in the dips and hollows of the great stone blocks that form the breakwater, and there are unexpected steps up and down, as well as the mooring chains and ropes of boats to step over. This is not a walk to be undertaken after one too many *rakís*!

Start from the innermost end of the inner harbour, setting your back to the Venetian *arsenali* and walking out along the narrow pathway that runs inside the length of the breakwater. It is founded on thousands of rocks tipped around the edge of the harbour in the 1530s and 1540s, when the Venetians were strengthening Khaniá in response to the violent raids of the Ottoman pirate Khaireddin Barbarossa. Halfway along, where the breakwater thickens, stand the ruins of a fort where both Venetians and Turks would hang malefactors and rebels as a very visible example to the townspeople.

The hum of the waterfront cafés and restaurants fades to a faint murmur as you approach the slender lighthouse at the western tip of the breakwater. This was a Venetian structure rebuilt by Egyptian forces when they had stationed themselves in Khaniá between 1832 and 1840 to help their Turkish allies govern Crete after the 1821–3 uprising. From the lighthouse you can enjoy a wonderful prospect. This is not the view of the city and White Mountains that daylight shows, but the thousands of coloured lights of the waterfront reflected in the rippling water of the outer harbour.

The breakwater ends with an elegant lighthouse

Khaniá outskirts

The entire coastline west of Khaniá is one long sandy beach, right to the base of the Rodhopoú peninsula. The first beach west of the harbour is Néa Chóra which is sandy, with plenty of facilities, but it is often crowded and messy with litter in the high season. Kalamáki beach is a twenty-minute bus ride from Khaniá, and is quieter and far less crowded, particularly if you walk on west for a few minutes. Further still you will come to Ayía Marína, 8km from Khaniá, and Platanías, 10km away, which has notable views out to the island of Agioi Theódhoroi and across to the Rodhopoú hills. Generally, though, this ribbon development west of Khaniá is a touch grim.

To the east of Khaniá there is a good beach at Kaláthas on the eastern flank of the Akrotíri peninsula, and a better and more spectacular one near the big taverna at Stávros, up at the northwesternmost tip of Akrotíri.

Probably the most interesting suburb of Khaniá is out to the east, an area of elegant old villas and little tree-shaded squares known as Khalépa. This was where George, Prince of Greece, came to live in 1898 after his appointment as High Commissioner in Crete following the departure of the Turks. The houses here, tall and solid, balconied and shuttered, most with architectural preservation orders on them, stand over secluded gardens dense with trees, looking out over the waterfront road to the sea. It is a grand and poignant part of town.

Where Avenue Elefthérios Venizélos dips northwards to meet the sea, you will pass the Hotel Doma on your right. The road forks, the airport being to the right. Turn left here and you shortly pass the walled French convent on your left, before reaching a large, immaculate house, on the same side, where Prince George once lived. Opposite, on a little square, is the beautifully proportioned house where Venizélos lived as a young lawyer and politician.

Get rhythm

There's nothing complicated about modern disco beat, but the rhythms of the traditional music of Crete are something entirely different. Time signatures can seem impossibly complicated to the unaccustomed ear, reducing the whole tune to a formless string of notes. Watch the players' shoes as they tap out the rhythm, and follow them with your own feet or fingertips. Suddenly, and magically, it all falls into place, and order emerges out of chaos.

The modern hotels lie on the outskirts of Khaniá

Accommodation

Real jam
A welcome sight on the breakfast table at the Doma Hotel is a selection of homemade jams and marmalade. A small detail, perhaps, but one that sets up the day as no plastic square of synthetic strawberry – the norm at many establishments – can ever manage to do.

Khaniá has responded to its popularity with visitors by sprouting a really remarkable number of rooms to rent, many of them cheap. You cannot wander in the old quarters of the town, and especially inland of the outer or western end of the harbour, without seeing literally hundreds of signs offering rooms to rent. It makes sense to book in advance during the high season, if you want something in the hotel line. Booking is also advisable between 20 and 27 May, the anniversary of the 1941 Battle of Crete.

Everyone wants a room with a harbour view, but few want the continuous noise that pervades the Khaniá waterfront. If you are sensitive to noise but want to rent somewhere very central, try the narrow thoroughfares of Angelou and Theotokópoulos in the Topanás quarter, and Zambelioú in Evréika, and their side lanes. Your views may be of the street, but you will have more peace and quiet in these old Turkish and Venetian townhouses and decent C and D class hotels.

Further east, around the curve of the harbour, Odós Lithínon and Odós Kandanóleon in the Kastélli quarter offer more of the same; as do the tangle of streets inland of Sífaka and eastward in the line of north–south streets behind the Splánzia waterfront. The atmosphere here is shabbier but much more authentic and less touristy, with fewer restaurants and souvenir shops.

Going upmarket a little, the drab-looking, modern Hotel Xénia is comfortable, and well positioned around the Fírkas headland west of the harbour. Out to the east hotels become larger, more expensive and more comfortable, particularly around the Khalépa suburb where the Hotel Doma is the finest, though not the most expensive. This is a truly elegant building on the right of Avenue Elefthérios Venizélos. About 20 minutes walk from the harbour. It is warm, friendly and very comfortable.

The old town and harbour hotels can often be cheaper

Food and drink

It would be a pity to leave Khaniá without trying some of the local delicacies, such as roast lamb with honey glaze and the little fried cheese pies called *kalitsounia* or *tiropitákia*, filled with either sweet or salty cheese. Around Easter time these are sprinkled with mint. Sausages from the region are especially spicy. In autumn the chestnuts for which the west is famous will have ripened. Chestnut bread and cakes are very delicious. Khaniots with strong stomachs enjoy *cochlioí,* baked snails served with potatoes, helping them down with Kissámou wine.

As usual with Cretan harbour towns, Khaniá's waterfront is lined with restaurants, but these can be on the expensive side. The futher east you go, towards the inner harbour and the Kastélli and Splánzia quarters, the better the quality and the greater the number of local customers. It may be a better idea to plunge into the maze of alleyways and canyon-like streets of the old quarters behind the waterfront, and follow your nose to make your own discoveries. The *Tamám* on Zambelioú is excellent; Odós Kondiláki, running north from Zambelioú, has several good places; east of Khálidon are the *Taverna Apovrada* on Odós Eisothion, and there is a pieshop-cum-café called *Tsedáki* on Odós Skridlóf. A highly recommended patisserie is *Boúgatsa* at 4 Odós Sífaka, not far from the municipal tourist office. It is named after the sweet and cheesy pastries which it sells with coffee and water from the shop next door.

There are plenty of Cretan-style fast-food stalls in Khaniá selling *souvláki* with a lick of lettuce. These are mostly around Platía Santriváni on the harbour and at the junctions of minor with major streets near the water. Odós Daskaloyiánnis, that climbs to form the boundary between Kastélli and Splánzia, is good for cheese pie and sweet pastry shops.

For elegance and an ambience beyond the range of these, go east to Khalépa and the wide Avenue Iróon Polytechníou.

Smoky bacon
Don't expect consideration in the matter of smoking in restaurants. Cretans smoke where and when they want to. So if you don't want the drift of tobacco smoke across your *stifádo*, choose a table outside, away from any local customers! Furthermore, smokers should note that a cigar is *to poóro*; a cigarette, confusingly, is *to tsigáro*.

Courtyard restaurants are quiet and atmospheric – and this one off Odós Zambelioú has the distinction of being in the shell of an old building

Local cheeses come in many shapes and sizes

Shopping

Khaniá ware

Made in Crete
In the souvenir shops you will find cheaply produced reproductions of Minoan vases, classical statues, over-excited satyrs, icons, embroidery and so on. The backstreet workshops are a better bet for a more genuine memento of Crete such as a huge-bladed knife fit for skinning a sheep (though you might have trouble with customs officers), or a pair of hand-made shoes, or a hand-tooled leather purse at half the price of anything for sale in Odós Skridlóf.

Leather sandals

In Khaniá you can buy just about everything, from *haute couture* dresses to a murderous-looking shepherd's knife. One of the great charms of the city is window shopping: staring into a dark little bootmaker's shop next door to a bridal emporium, which is flanked by a trashy souvenir kiosk with a blood-and-sawdust butcher on the other side, while next to that is a knifemaker's and a vegetable shop spilling out onto the street.

Odós Tzanakáki, which runs southeast from the covered market, has some modern clothes shops, and everyday shops can be found in a strip just south of the west–east Skalídi–Hatzimicháli Yiannári–Nikifórou Foká road. The covered market itself is the main focus for food shopping, with a huge variety of fresh food at very reasonable prices, and you get a free cabaret-of-life thrown in.

Khalídon is the chief tourist trap, and the souvenirs here are no worse than anywhere else. On Odós Skridlóf, at right-angles to Khalídon, you will find leatherwork of excellent quality at reasonable prices, if not rock-bottom bargains by Cretan standards. Leather boots are specially good value. Sfakiot shepherds buy them, and you can't get a higher recommendation than that! Handcrafted knives and tools of all kinds are well worth buying, as is the beautiful Khaniá pottery with its characteristic turquoise-blue glaze (see above), and glassware.

Local handicraft producers have banded together to form a co-operative, partly to increase their sales outlets, partly to help with quality control in a market flooded with poor products. They have an exhibition by the harbour, beside the Mosque of the Janissaries, with items for sale. Better than average craft and souvenir shops are now to be found along Odós Theotokópoulou and Odós Angelou, in the Topanás quarter; Odós Zambelioú in Evréika; and along Kaneváro in the heart of Kastélli.

Nightlife

Khaniá is a magnet for the large population of the west of Crete, as well as for thousands of tourists, and it is well provided with nightlife. There are some sophisticated cocktail and piano bars on Odós Angelou and along the waterfront going east from Platía Santrivání: for example, the *Four Seasons* or *Tésseres Épohes*. The disco bars hereabouts are quite pricey, but they represent your best chance of catching some live dance music of the modern variety. Try *Ariádni* and the *Canale Club*. The modern hotels often run their own rather stilted and soulless discos, and there are more holiday-party discos out in the beach resorts to the west.

Live traditional dance music can be found at various venues around the town and in the bigger hotels out along the beach developments to the west of town. Fly posters of traditional musicians clutching *lýra* and *bouzoúki* will appear around the streets, especially near the covered market, advertising venues. One excellent spot is the *Lyríkia*, by the waterfront, a bare little bar with nothing particularly to recommend it until the musicians strike up. Then the whole place and its Khaniot clientele come alive. Tables will be pushed back and dancing will begin, or perhaps the audience will be in the mood to sit and sing along. Another similar place is the *Café Kríti* at 22 Odós Kalergón, inland of the Venetian *arsenali* in the Splánzia quarter.

But it is the *voltá* or traditional evening ritual of strolling and mutual sizing-up that really unites Khaniots, and the harbour is the place to be seen, either walking from the *arsenali* to the Fírkas Tower and back, or the extremely enjoyable and scenic stroll to the lighthouse at the tip of the Venetian breakwater (see page 208). Afterwards you repair to the terraces of the restaurants along Iróon Polytechníou for a drink, well away from the hurly-burly of the harbour.

Thrills, not frills
Often the more elaborate the décor, the less Cretan the atmosphere. *Lyríkia* has a plain concrete floor, stark lighting and basic tables and chairs, but you don't notice these rather functional surroundings once the *lýra* and *bouzoúki* get going.

Impromptu music after dinner

Practical points

Coffee talk
Unless you ask specifically for nescafé, the coffee you order will be the thick, fragrant brew known to the non-Greek world as Turkish coffee, but in these parts called Greek coffee, *ellenikós kafés*. It comes in a tiny cup, and the contents are usually at least one-third sludgy grounds. You'll know when you've reached them! *Métrio* is medium sweet, *glikó* is tooth-meltingly sweet, *skéto* is without sugar. A glass of water usually accompanies each cup.

News from home
If you crave news from your own country, there are foreign newspapers on sale at many kiosks and bookshops in Khaniá. These are usually out of date by only one day, and will probably cost you about three times what you would pay at home.

Airport The airport is 13km east of Khaniá, on the Akrotíri peninsula. Frequent buses connect with Platía 1866 in the centre of town, one minute's walk from the top of Khálidon. Olympic Airways run buses to and from their office at 88 Odós Tzanakáki (tel: 0821–27701), 15 minutes walk from the harbour. Fixed-price taxis run between the airport and Khaniá. The route by car is well signposted.

Banks The National Bank of Greece is on the lower end of Odós Tzanakáki, opposite the covered market. There are many money changers along Khálidon.

Beaches To the east: Kaláthas and Stávros on Akrotíri peninsula. To the west: Kalamáki (4km), Ayía Marína (8km), Platanías (10km).

Buses Buses leave from Odós Kidoniás, at the southern end of Platía 1866. Blue buses operate within the city; green are long-distance.

Car hire Odós Tzanakáki is the street to find the major firms. Budget are at 39 Odós Karaiskáki (tel: 0821–92778/96880); Hermes at 52 Odós Tzanakáki (tel: 0821–54418), and there is a selection at the airport.

Car parking Simply put – don't drive into the old town! There is parking around Platía 1866, and unrestricted streets south of Skalídi–Hatzimicháli Yiannári–Nikifórou Foká. The best place to park is at the western end of the harbour between Akti Kanari and the Firkas Tower. Approach via Odós Metahaki.

Ferries To Piraeus from Soúdha, 10km to the east. Minoan Lines, 8 Khálidon (tel: 0821–23939); ANEK, Platía Sophoklís Venizélos, opposite covered market (tel: 0821–23636).

Festival 20 to 27 May is Battle of Crete week. Veterans gather and the city celebrates and commemorates heroism in 1941.

Foreign newspapers and books Newspapers are on sale around Khaniá at pavement kiosks and newsagents. For books try the shops in Platía Santriváni on the left as you leave Khálidon.

Gardens There are public gardens on Odós Tzanakáki, with summer evening events and a small zoo.

Hospital 6–8 Odós Dragoúmi (tel: 0821–27231).

Layout of the city The Old City is divided into four quarters: **Topanás**, **Evréika**, **Kastélli** and **Splánzia**. They are a mass of atmospheric, cramped and winding lanes with plenty of restaurants and cheap rooms, ripe for *ad lib* exploration. The main social focus of Khaniá, where it all happens and where everyone meets at night, is the Venetian harbour and breakwater – a striking semicircle of mellow Venetian architecture. Boat trips around Akrotíri peninsula into Soúdha Bay; to Rodhopoú peninsula and secluded beaches start from here.

Launderette 38 Odós Kaneváro, the main west–east thoroughfare of the Kastélli quarter. Open 9 till late.

Mountaineering Club (EOS) at 90 Odós Tzanakáki (tel: 0821–24647). Open 7pm–10pm.

Post office Odós Tzanakáki, opposite covered market. Open 7am–8pm, Monday–Saturday; money exchange 8–2). In the holiday season there is a Mobile Post Office by the Cathedral off Khálidon, in Platía Mitrópolis.

Police 5 Odós Sólomou (tel: 0821–51058).

Roman Catholic Church Platía Mitrópolis, off Khálidon.

Swimming pool On the headland west of the harbour, between Fírkas Tower and Néa Chóra beach.

Taxis Mostly around Platía 1866.

Telephones (OTE) Area code is 0821. Main OTE office is next to Post Office on Odós Tzanakáki (7am–11pm).

Tourist information National Tourist Organisation of Greece (EOT) office is at 40 Odós Kriári (tel: 0821–26426). Open 8–2. Municipal tourist office at 22 Odós Sífaka (tel: 0821–59990).

Tourist police 44 Odós Karaiskáki (tel: 0821–24477). Open all day.

Tour operators Canea Travel, 28 Odós Tzanakáki (tel: 0821–24780); Kydonia Travel, 10 Odós Karaiskáki (tel: 0821–57412).

Love the oil
One thing you can depend on when eating out in Khaniá is the rich taste of olive oil. Anything fried or grilled, plates of chips, salads and *mezédes* will be well doused. Khaniá people like their olive oil even more than other Cretans, which is saying something. Whatever your previous attitude to this Greek water of life, you'll learn to love it, or starve!

Khaniá is small enough to allow easy orientation

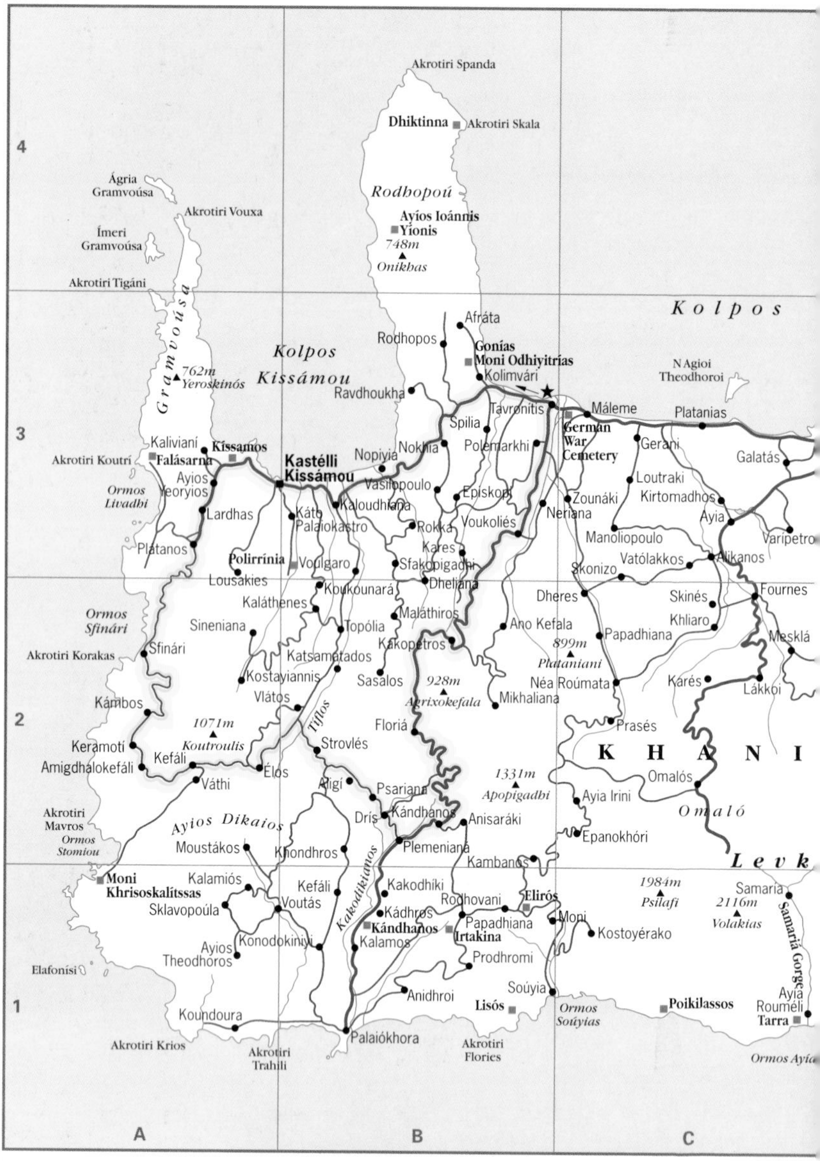

Looking south over the Askífos Plateau towards the Ímvros Gorge (from the route of the drive on pages 240–1)

THE WHITE MOUNTAINS AND THE WEST

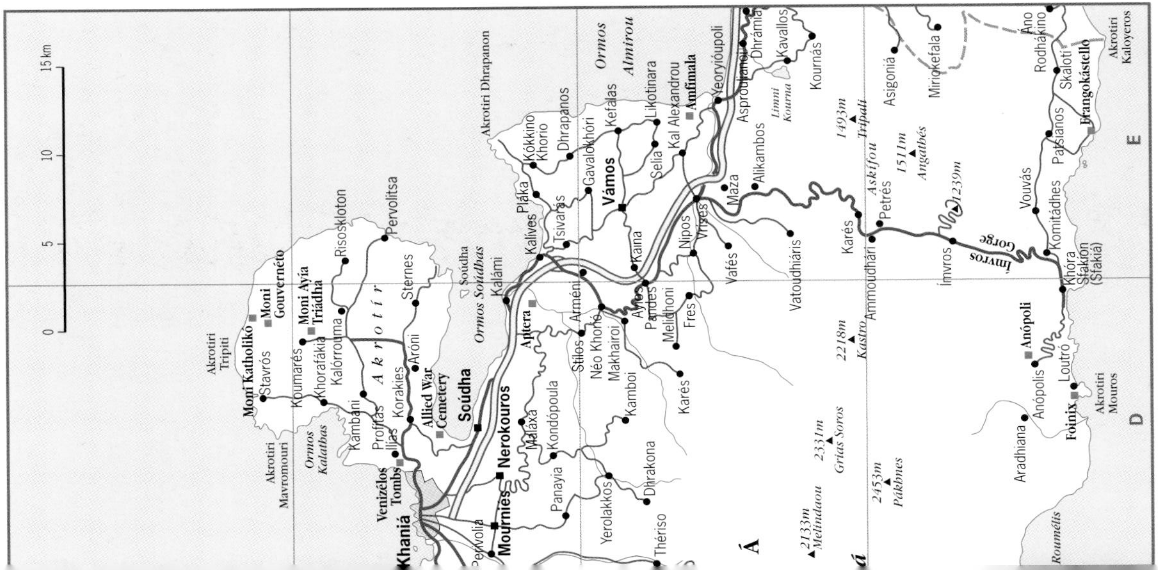

0 5 10 15 km

Akrotiri Tripiti
Moni Katholikó
Stavrós
Moni Gouvernéto
Akrotiri Mavromouri
Koumarés
Moni Ayía Triádha
Ormos Kalathas
Khorafákia
Kalórrouma
Risoskloton
Kambani
Profítas Ilías
Akrotír
Pervolitsa
Venizélos Tombs
Khaniá
Korakies
Aróni
Sternes
Allied War Cemetery
Soúdha
Soúdha
Ormos Soúdhas
Perivolia
Mournies
Nerokouros
Kalámi
Akrotiri Dhrapanon
Aptera
Malaxa
Kalíves
Pláka
Kókkino Khorio
Panayia
Kondópoula
Tsivarás
Dhrapanos
Stílos
Arméni
Gavalokhóri
Yerolakkos
Néo Khorió
Makhairoi
Vámos
Kefalas
Ormos Almirou
Kamboi
Kaina
Ayios Pandes
Selia
Likotinara
Thériso
Dhrakona
Melidhoni
Kal Alexandrou
Karés
Fres
Nipos
Vrises
Amfimala
Yeoryióupoli
Vafés
Maza
Asproulianoi
Dhrámia
Á
Alikambos
Limni Kourna
Kavallos
Vatoudhiáris
Kournás
2133m Melindaou
2331m Grias Soros
2218m Kastro
Karés
1493m Tripali
á
Ammoudhári
Askífou
2453m Pákhnes
Petrés
Asigoniá
1511m Angathés
Miriokefala
Ímvros
1239m
Ímvros Gorge
Aradhiana
Anópoli
Vouvás
Áno Rodhákino
Anópolis
Komitádhes
Roumélis
Loutró
Khóra Sfakíon (Sfakiá)
Patsianos
Skalotí
Foinix
Frangokástello
Akrotiri Mouros
Akrotiri Kaloyeros
D
E

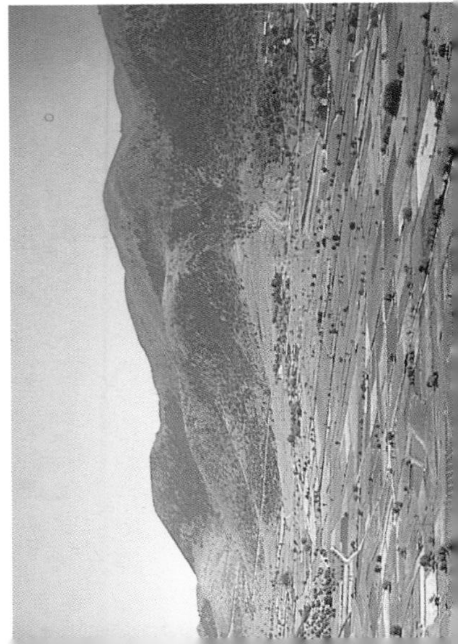

Looking from Maláxa to the Levká Óri

The White Mountains and the West The western end of Crete is by far the most exciting for visitors keen to get off the main tourist routes and explore. This is not to say that this region is undiscovered by tourism. Khaniá is a honeypot for visitors, and the roads of westernmost Crete are seeing a steady increase in traffic as they are steadily improved. But there are more hidden villages, Byzantine churches, coves, beaches, hills and valleys than in any other part of the island. And the White Mountains, the Levká Óri, are Crete's most rugged and challenging range.

Khaniá dominates the northern part of the region; a lively, handsome old Venetian seaport which was, until quite recently, the capital of Crete and is still a place where discerning people choose to be based. Khaniá has music, dance, theatre, conversation, argument, a sense of the unpredictable, the stability of long history and the volatility of strong local temperaments. It has a confident and positive atmosphere and is a good place to wrangle with souvenir sellers by day, and sit out along the light-spangled waterfront and watch the promenaders by night.

Three peninsulas reach out toward mainland Greece from the low-lying, fertile coast. There is club-shaped Akrotíri immediately to the east of Khaniá, and the long fingers of Rodhopoú and Gramvoúsa at the northwestern tip. Akrotíri offers a fine walk that connects three historic monasteries. Rodhopoú and Gramvoúsa are deserted, barren places where ramblers can stretch their legs with only birds of prey, mountain flowers and sea breezes for company. From Gramvoúsa one of Crete's most spectacular roads climbs and plunges south above a coastline of little-visited bays and steep slopes, winding among villages scattered on the mountainsides, branching further south into Selínou province, the least-explored corner of Crete. There are Byzantine churches with frescoes tucked away among

West is best
The topography of Crete dictates the island's road pattern. Most roads go north to south, threading their way through the mountain ranges. All are exciting to drive, but those in the far west are by far the most spectacular, with the best coastal views and craggiest mountains – and, it might also seem to the visiting driver, the longest drops and sharpest hairpin bends.

olive groves; capes and headlands where nobody goes; hilltop villages that give no thought to tourism; the sheltered harbours and thriving resorts of Palaiókhora and Soúyia below great mountain slopes; and the blue-roofed monastery of Krisoskalítissas where the two elderly inmates dispense rough and open-handed hospitality.

Blocking the way from north to south coasts stands the truly breathtaking mountain range of Levká Óri, the White Mountains, well named for the bare, pale limestone of which they are made. Though the summit of Mount Pákhnes, the highest peak of Levká Óri, is a couple of metres short of the top of Mount Psiloritis, the White Mountains are more impressive than the Psiloritis range with a mass of close-packed, plunging valleys and slopes.

Here, as around Psiloritis, you will hear stories of partisan refuge, revenge and struggle, not only against historic invaders, but during internecine warfare that has still not quite died out. The White Mountains are the stronghold of the famously fierce and implacable race of Cretans known as Sfakiots, people reputed to carry arms at all times and never to forget or leave unavenged an insult or injury.

A single road penetrates the heart of the White Mountains. This snaking track brings coachloads of walkers from Khaniá across the fertile plain of Omalós to the head of Crete's most famous natural feature, the 16km-long, dramatic gorge of Samariá. The sheer descent into this slit in the mountains and the walk along its rocky bottom to the sea makes a trek that will rank among your most memorable, no matter where you have walked.

Southeast of the mountains crouches the Sfakiot capital of Khóra Sfakíon, better known as Sfakiá, from which Allied troops were desperately evacuated after the German invasion of Crete in 1941, and from where a bus will take you on a switchback mountain road to Khaniá.

On the edge
A frequent and potentially lethal hazard of the mountain roads is the erosion of tarmac by frost, rain and weight of traffic. Chunks are bitten out of the road edge, often on the outside of a bend, directly over a drop of several hundred metres. Some, but by no means all, are outlined with a border of stones. Keep a wary eye out for these.

The isolated Gramvoúsa peninsula

The Venetian façade of Ayía Triádha Monastery

Chapel of the bear
The little chapel at the entrance to the cave of the bear stalagmite is dedicated to Panayía Arkhoudiótissa, Our Lady of the Bear. *Arkhoúda* means bear.

Zorba country
If the shape of the landscape looks familiar to you when you arrive in Stavrós, it is probably a case of cinematic *déja vu*. The rugged ridge overlooking the village was the setting for the climactic scene in the film of *Zorba the Greek*, when the pylons and cables bringing the felled trees down to the shore so dramatically collapsed. One of the classic spectacles of the cinema.

▶▶▶ Akrotíri Peninsula *217D3*

The club-shaped peninsula of Akrotíri, some 15km in diameter, sticks out into the sea immediately to the east of Khaniá, a place with a remote, island-like atmosphere.

As you enter the peninsula, signs point to the hill of Profítas Ilías, where the **tombs▶▶** of Elefthérios Venizélos (1864–1936, see pages 56–7) and his son Sophoklés (1896–1964) overlook a superb view of Khaniá, the sea and the White Mountains. There is no more fitting place for Venizélos, Crete's greatest revolutionary statesman, to be buried. In 1897, while Crete was under the control of the Four Great Powers (France, Italy, Russia and Britain), Venizélos convened secret meetings here which led to the raising of the Greek flag in defiance of both Turkish and European powers. The flag's standard was shot away by gunfire from the Four Powers' fleet, but the partisans continued to fly it by hand. This heroic gesture brought spontaneous applause from the naval gunners below.

The coastal village of **Stavrós▶** is half an hour's drive to the north, and is not well signposted. Here you will find a perfect, circular bathing beach overshadowed by a crumpled ridge of red rock that rises abruptly from the coast, and a big taverna with a fiercely friendly owner.

Return to Khorafákia, bear left by the taverna, and after 5km turn left again to **Ayía Triádha Monastery▶▶▶**. The road sign to Ayía Triádha is just *beyond* the turning, and faces the wrong way! It is not known when the monastery was founded, but some of the buildings date from the 17th century, and it presents a long Venetian façade to the road. In the church across the courtyard is a wonderful iconostasis covered in faded icons and writhing with gilt foliage. The frescoes are modern, but of agelessly traditional character. A Transfiguration with the disciples being knocked head over heels is especially striking. A museum in a side room contains treasures that survived destruction by the Turks in 1821, including crucifixes, inlaid boxes, beautifully worked 17th-century silk stoles, ancient books and icons, and medals awarded to the monks for their resistance work during World War II.

Either pick your way carefully by car, or leave it here and walk north for 5km up a stony road lined with beehives, among olive groves where every gnarled tree shades a goat, and up into the scrub-covered hills where **Gouvernétou Monastery▶▶** stands on a saddle of ground. The Turks came here, too, in 1821, and left only a smoking ruin, burned books and icons, and a pile of murdered monks. These days Gouvernétou is a haven of peace, home to a handful of monks and an army of cats. The façade of the domed church is carved with strange, snub-nosed, howling faces. Inside is another superb iconostasis. A thick fringe of silver *taxímata* or votary plaques, stamped with the afflicted noses, eyes and limbs of the sufferers who offered them, surrounds an icon of St John.

The rough path to **Katholikó Monastery▶▶▶** drops from the saddle to pass a cave on the right with a chapel at the entrance and a great stalagmite in the centre. This is Artemis transformed into a bear, according to legend. Continue downhill from the cave until the path turns sharp left and you see far below you the ruined walls of Katholikó Monastery, astonishingly sited in a narrow ravine spanned by a bridge. This was Crete's first monastery, founded in the 11th century by the hermit, St John, whose cave lies on your left as you go down. This dark, stalactite-hung hole runs 120m into the hillside, and at the far end you can worm on your belly to touch the rocky ledge where the hermit had his altar. Pirates sacked Katholikó in the 17th century, and the monks moved uphill to Gouvernétou where their successors met their fate at the hands of the Turks.

Weathered gargoyle at Gouvernétou

Gouvernétou Monastery

Wave dodging
If there is a rough sea running while you wait for your boat on the waterfront at Ayía Rouméli, you can while away the time watching children at their favourite game of wave-dodging. They wait until the last possible moment, then run back shrieking as the incoming wave bursts over the quay and showers them with spray.

▶▶▶ Anisaráki 216B2

The village of Anisaráki lies just off the mountain road from Kándhanos to Soúyia. You might easily miss it, for Anisaráki lies sunk deep in shady olive groves, and, like most mountain villages in the extreme west of Crete, it only shows a small portion of itself to the road. The houses are dotted around among the groves, dappled with shade as if covered with a net. The churches that are the treasure of the village are just as hard to find, standing away from the road and half hidden among the olive trees. If you leave your car, however, and walk down through the groves to knock on any door, someone will be pleased to show you around.

There are four churches in Anisaráki, each with marvellous 14th- and 15th-century Byzantine frescoes, blackened with age, in the humble shell of unremarkable stone walls. In the church of Panayía there are saints in medallion-shaped frames, a fierce red beast and a fine Archangel Michael, while outside stands a gaunt wooden gallows where an effigy of Judas is burned each Easter Saturday. In Ayía Paraskeví a sorrowing Christ looks down from the roof of the apse, and there is also a wonderful Dormition of the Virgin. Christ cradles his mother's soul in the form of a baby, and a demon who has attempted to snatch the Virgin's soul holds up the severed stumps of his hands while Archangel Michael the Smiter stands by with drawn and bloody sword. More tracery and beautifully coloured figures can be found in Ayía Ána, and in Ayíos Giórgios there is a figure of the saint riding a fine horse among other very old frescoes, some of which date back to the late 13th century.

▶ Ayía Rouméli 216C1

Ayía Rouméli is spectacularly sited at the foot of the Samariá Gorge, hunched down on the shore in a cleft of the tremendous mountains that rear away skyward at its back. There are plenty of places to eat, drink and stay here, as the village is the only embarkation point to Sfakiá or Soúyia for walkers who have just completed the Samariá trail. After the fall of Crete in 1941, King George of Greece

A relatively modern (but most appealing) screen from the church of Ayía Paraskeví in the village of Anisaráki

Deadly hollow
In one of the Anisaráki olive groves stands a mighty olive tree with an enormous girth, knotted and swollen, several hundred years old and still productive, its trunk hollowed with age. When a file of German soldiers came through the grove in May 1941, a local man and his brother emerged from their hiding place inside the hollow tree and shot the soldiers down with their machine gun, an incident still recounted in the village.

Elafonísi beach, despite appearances to the contrary, can be busy in season

was evacuated by British submarine from the beach here, after an epic journey on foot across the White Mountains during which he and his party were shot at by friend and foe alike. Ayía Rouméli is a stronghold of the Sfakiots, the men of these mountains who have always resisted invaders and suffered countermeasures, as witness the ruins of a Turkish fort glowering down on the village from its ridge. A mosaic pavement that probably predates Christianity surrounds the church of Panayía Rouméli, itself standing over a temple to Apollo built when the ancient settlement of Tárrha flourished here.

▶ Elafonísi *216A1*

Out of season it is well worth making the extremely rough and dusty 6.5km journey south from Khrisoskalítissas Monastery to the beach and island of Elafonísi. The beach is of white sand, and you can wade out to the low-backed island just offshore to enjoy perfect peace and quiet, if you can put out of mind the events of Easter 1824, when Turkish soldiers slaughtered 850 women and children who were hiding on the island to escape being transported to the harems of Constantinople.

The beach, which only a few years ago was an undiscovered paradise, is now a magnet in high season, crammed with jeeps, buses and motorbikes, while more unsightly concrete apartments and tavernas are springing up inland.

▶ Élos *216A2*

Élos lies sprawled along a series of S-bends on the mountain road to Palaiókhora, a couple of tavernas, a string of whitewashed houses smothered in flowers, all overshadowed and enclosed by olive groves and tall chestnut trees. The village is famous for its chestnut festival in October, when locals and visitors mingle to eat chestnut cake and sweets, and to dance.

Sign of intent
Bundles of metal rods poking up from flat concrete roofs are a feature of modern Cretan buildings, both finished and unfinished. They are left in place as a sign of the builder's intention to add a further storey, if and when finances allow, and to escape a government tax on finished buildings.

■ Several remote islands lie around the coast of western Crete with their own myths and legends. Most poignant is Gávdos, where the nymph Calypso entertained Odysseus for seven years, and died of grief when he left. Today it is still inhabited, but only just.....■

Gramvoúsa rebels
The Khainides, a resistance group dedicated to the overthrow of the Turks, used Ímeri Gramvoúsa as one of their island bases during the early years of the Turkish occupation, before the Turks themselves got hold of the fort and turned its impregnable position to their own advantage.

Paximádia and Gávdos The two islands of Paximádia lie 12km offshore in the Gulf of Mesarás. *Paximádia* is the name for the hard-baked bread that is softened with water before eating, and seen from the shore near Timbáki, the islands do look like two hunks of bread floating in the sea.

Forty kilometres west of the Paximádia islands, and about the same distance off the south coast, Gávdos lies isolated in the Libyan Sea. This is the southernmost landfall in Europe, a lonely chunk of rock with only the neighbouring islet of Gavdopoúla for company. A few families still cling on here, in increasing hardship despite television and radio communications. The silence, the isolation, the hard beauty of the island, the threadbare but genuine - hospitality of the islanders, make a visit to Gávdos an unforgettable experience. There are a few rooms to rent, a post office and a handful of shops. A ferry plies from Palaiókhora all year round, and from Sfakiá in summer. Exact timings depend on the state of the weather, and the journey can take several hours. It can also be rough.

The island rises to a ridge nearly 400m high that falls to an inaccessible west coast. From the landing place a rough road leads inland to the village of Kastrí, with shops and post office, and the remains of a prison in which political dissenters were held between the world wars. Here the road splits, running north to the settlement of Ámbelos and south to Vatsianá. Beyond Vatsianá you can get down to the excellent, unfrequented beach of Tripití. Beyond Ámbelos there is another beach on the north coast, and just east of this lies sheltered Sarakíniko beach which is about a half hour walk from the landing place and is where most of the few visitors go. There are one or two basic tavernas.

The shallow waters of Gramvoúsa beach and peninsula

Gávdos has been inhabited since neolithic times. Odysseus is said to have stayed seven years here, under the spell of the nymph Calypso. The ship carrying St Paul was blown past the 'island of Clauda' on its way to shipwreck on Malta. When the Byzantines first ruled in Crete there were 8,000 people living on Gávdos. Today there are fewer than 50. The young people have almost all gone, unwilling to face life with no mains electricity, an uncertain water supply, no job prospects, the hard labour of shepherding, and a complete absence of bright lights and fun. Mainland girls don't want to marry Gávdos boys and be obliged to live here. The crumbling, abandoned houses, the uncultivated land, the sparse supplies in the shops are all witness to a population coming to the end of its tether. Maybe modern tourism will save the day and open a new and entirely different chapter in the life of Gávdos…

Other islands Towards the top of Crete's western coast the islet of Petálidha lies off the ancient port of Falásarna. From here the Gramvoúsa peninsula points north. Off the west side of its outermost tip lie the twin islands of Agría (wild) Gramvoúsa to the north, and closer in Iméri (tame) Gramvoúsa, with a superb Venetian fortress clinging dramatically to its 157m crest. The island saw exciting times as a Venetian stronghold against the Turks, as a Turkish stronghold against the pirates, and as a pirate stronghold against all comers . Boats occasionally leave from Kastélli Kissámou.

Off Plataniás, west of Khaniá, lies Agioi Theódhoroi, a whale turned to stone for trying to swallow Crete. You can see the cavernous mouth from the shore. It is now an *égagros* reserve. And, finally, we reach Soúdha Bay in the shelter of the Akrotíri peninsula. Three nymphs lie in the narrows, having had their wings pulled off after losing a musical contest with the Muses. You may recognise them as the White Islands.

Weather warning
An essential precaution when planning a trip to Gávdos out of the summer season is to check on the local weather forecast in Palaiókhora or Sfakiá, and with the boat skipper. If the weather blows up you may be marooned on the island for a day or two, so don't make hard and fast plans that depend on getting back to Crete at any particular time. By the same token, it is wise to take enough essential supplies, for example medical items, to cater for an unexpectedly prolonged stay.

Cyclists take a rest from the heat of the day to look across towards Gramvoúsa island

The dome of Gonías Monastery

►► Falásarna 216A3

A turning on the main coast road at Plátanos (see pages 243) leads in 8km to a beautiful, curved beach of white sand, south of the headland of Cape Koutrí, where lie the remains of Falásarna, once the port for the ancient Graeco–Roman city of Polirrínia in the hills behind. An artificial channel runs north from where the cape curves out from the shore to reach a wide, shallow bowl in the rock, now levelled. This was Falásarna's man-made harbour, with towers and fortified walls to guard it. The city's acropolis stood on the back of the headland, with a temple to Artemis near the present day church of Ayíos Yióryios. The city lay between the acropolis and the harbour, and remains include house walls, water cisterns, tombs and a mysterious, square lump of stone, known as the throne.

Subterranean geological upheavals stranded the old port by raising it some 6m above the sea. They also caused the earthquake that destroyed Falásarna.

►► Gonías Monastery 216B3

Panayía Gonías Monastery, or Odhiyitrías ('Our Lady Guide'), lies just north of Kolimvári village at the south-eastern corner of the Rodhopoú peninsula. It was founded in 1618, and the Turks battered but did not destroy it when they invaded Crete in 1645. In the 1866 rebellion, put down with ferocity by the Pasha, Gonías Monastery had its precious library burned, but many icons and other treasures survived. The monks who show you around point out with pride the Turkish cannonballs still embedded in the walls.

The church has fine icons, and a particular treasure in the museum is a moving figure of Christ Crucified, painted by one of Crete's most celebrated 17th-century artists, Konstantínos Palaiókapas. From the church terrace there is a wonderful view of Rodhopoú, the bay and Khaniá.

Priests and people
A short distance from Gonías Monastery is the Orthodox Academy of Crete, frequently visited by priests of all ages, on retreat or taking part in seminars or courses. The Cretan priest is part of his local community to a greater extent than in most European countries, which may explain why he is on the whole well regarded, and why young men are continuing to study for the priesthood here.

Walk Gramvoúsa Peninsula

This is a hot, demanding 16km walk along an uninhabited peninsula, one of the loneliest and most magical rambles anywhere in Crete. The peninsula of Gramvoúsa is the more westerly of the two that stick out northward like the horns of a bull from the extreme northwestern corner of Crete, enclosing the sheltered waters of the Gulf of Kissámou. The other is Rodhopoú (see page 245). Gramvoúsa is a unique place, lonely, rugged and bare. There is very little shade on Gramvoúsa, so a sunhat, sun cream and a full water bottle are essential. Allow at least five or six hours.

Start the walk in the little village of Kalivianí, reached by a right turn off the coast road 5km west of Kastélli Kissámou. Pass the *kafeníon* and the church, and continue along the track, out among the bare, sun-baked rocks of the peninsula. Great bluffs of grey rock overhang the track, from which you get a stunning view over the blue waters of the Gulf of Kissámou to the long, jagged spine of the Rodhopoú peninsula.

Halfway along, the rough road ends abruptly and you descend to join a hill-side track that runs north through prickly flowering bushes, past boulders marked with faded red waymarks, to round the peak of Yeroskinós and curve from north through west. The track dives into a valley, where a view suddenly opens on a milky green lagoon, shut off by a bar of rock from the semi-circular Tigáni Bay, with a chunky rock island offshore.

Walk to the right, round the cliff, and you will be faced with one of the most striking views in Crete, looking across clear water to the two flat-backed, block-like islands of Agría (wild) Gramvoúsa to the north, and closer to the shore Ímeri (tame) Gramvoúsa with a mighty Venetian fortress dizzily clinging to its seaward peak (see pages 224–5). At the bottom of the steep path you will find an excellent bathing beach, and, surprisingly, a small taverna. Boats from Kastélli Kissámou and Khaniá bring a small number of sun-worshippers to Tigáni Bay, but it is never crowded.

The return walk is either back the way you came, or on a tough, narrow pathway along the western edge of Gramvoúsa.

Rough tracks on Gramvoúsa

A dish of herbs
Hospitality from Father Nektários and Sister Theodóti may well run to lunch at their table, if you are visiting around midday and there are not too many visitors about. Olives, peppers, bread and potato chips with local wine may be humble fare, but 'better a dish of herbs in the company of friends than a fatted ox in the tents of the ungodly.'

►► Hóra Sfakíon (Sfakiá) *217D1*

The capital of the Sfakiot region of Crete lies handsomely around its harbour and is best seen from the sea at sunset when the flat-roofed white houses and hotels glow pink amid their palm trees, a scene that owes more to Africa than to Europe. These days Hóra Sfakíon (sometimes spelt Khóra Sfakíon, but usually called Sfakiá) is primarily a well-provided ferry port with a good number of tavernas, hotels and rooms to rent. Boats leave from here for Ayía Rouméli, Ayía Galíni and the island of Gávdos. Scars of the ferocious bombing that flattened much of the town during the war have healed, though elderly local people still recount their memories of those terrible few days when Sfakiá was the evacuation point for retreating Allied troops.

►►► Hrissoskalítissas Monastery *216A1*

The road to Hrissoskalítissas (or Khrisoskalítissas in modern spelling) is part stony and potholed, part immaculately tarmacked – more of the former than the latter, as yet. This has helped to preserve the peace of this unique old nunnery, though new building is beginning to appear nearby, none of it particularly easy on the eye. Khrisoskalítissas perches high on a rocky bluff above a dusty plain on the extreme southwestern tip of the island, its blue barrel roof a landmark for many miles. The nunnery takes its name, Golden Steps, from the 90 steps that wind up to the church and buildings on the rock. One of them is golden, but only those who have passed a sinless day can see which one. Khrisoskalítissas was founded in the 13th century, in a cave. The present-day church dates from the 19th century, and has nothing remarkable to see inside.

Two hundred sisters lived here in the nunnery's heyday. Now there is only one nun left, Sister Theodóti, along with the splendidly bearded Archimandrite, Father Nektários. They speak no English, but they are kind people, and they may offer you hospitality.

Khrisoskalítissas Monastery

Father Nektários of Khrisoskalítissas

Battle of Crete evacuations

■ The aftermath of the successful German airborne invasion of Crete in May 1941 was a state of near-chaos among the Allied troops as the Nazis advanced on their positions all along the north coast of the island.....■

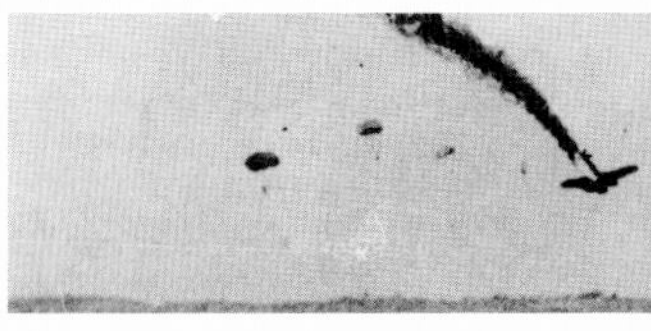

There were New Zealanders and British at Maléme and Khaniá, Australians and Greeks at Réthimnon, and Australians, Greeks and British at Iráklio. Crete's road system was primitive in those days, and soon it was choked with retreating men, all moving excruciatingly slowly and under constant threat of air attack.

Réthimnon held out for ten days before surrendering on 31 May, and those who could not make good their escape were captured. The Royal Navy evacuated thousands from the end of the mole at Iráklio, taking them off by night and sustaining terrible losses during the dash for the North African coast through the dawn. But the Navy could not get into Soúdha Bay to evacuate Khaniá. The troops here faced a hellish march across the White Mountains down to Sfakiá on the south coast, while brave and determined rearguard actions by separate forces of Greek and Australian soldiers held off the pursuing Germans. About 12,000 men retreated across the plain of Askífos and descended the narrow gorge of Ímvros (see page 231) in single file to reach Sfakiá.

There were appalling scenes at Sfakiá as exhausted and anxious soldiers jammed the little port. By day they had to find cover from the German bombers; for three nights running they queued to embark on Royal Navy ships whose own crews were tired and apprehensive. Again there were heavy losses as the ships ran the gauntlet of the Libyan Sea. A fourth night of evacuation was judged to be too dangerous, and thousands of troops were left behind to be captured or to hide in the hope of escape, including all the Greeks who had fought with the Allies, and the Australians who had been holding up the pursuit.

Waugh's war
Evelyn Waugh landed at Soúdha Bay in the last week of May 1941, when the Battle of Crete had already swung decisively in favour of the Germans. As brigade intelligence officer with a commando force, Waugh experienced at first hand the confusion, panic and desperation of the Allied evacuation, events he later recounted with characteristically cool insight and cynicism in *Officers and Gentlemen*, the second book in his *Sword of Honour* trilogy.

Soldiers retreating during the Battle of Crete

Ímvros mists
Fine weather cannot be guaranteed in Ímvros. Mountain and sea mists sometimes join forces to swathe the village, and at such times the *kafenía* are crowded with the elderly men who have been driven indoors from their customary roadside seats.

Practical partridges
Town-dwellers hang caged songbirds on their balconies to exorcise the traffic noise with sweet singing. Villagers hang caged partridges outside their houses, fattening in captivity, with a rather more practical end in mind.

► Ímvros *217E1*

The village stands at the top of the Ímvros Gorge (see opposite). Downgoing walkers are dropped here from buses, and those upcoming restore themselves at the end of their walk with pancakes, cheese and coffee at the big café on the main Sfakiá to Khaniá road.

Ímvros stands on a high plateau, surrounded by peaks of naked, dry rock. It is not a picturesque village, as many of the houses were rebuilt after the war with utility bricks, but it is an extremely characterful one, particularly if you can summon enough Greek to open a conversation with the Sfakiots, who have vivid memories of wartime and strong opinions on the modern world.

► Kádhros *216B1*

The village is reached by a left turn off the main Kándhanos–Palaiókhora road, a couple of kilometres south of Kakodhíki. At the top end of Kádhros, 100m past a *kafeníon,* a path on the right leads to the Byzantine church of the Nativity of the Virgin, with late 14th-century frescoes still sharp in colour and detail.

►► Kakodhíki *216B1*

Two churches near the village are worth seeing. Enquire at any house or in the *kafeníon* for the keys. Next to the modern Ayía Triádha church (up a track to the left off the Kándhanos–Palaiókhora road) is the Byzantine church of Mikhaíl Arkhángelos (Archangel Michael). The old iconostasis is beautifully carved in wood, and the frescoes were painted early in the 14th century. Further along the track, the church of Ayiós Isódhoros perches on a hill from which flow springs with celebrated healing power. The frescoes are finely drawn, though some have been defaced, reportedly by the Turks. They include scenes of the torture and death of St Isódhoros who is shown being dragged by galloping horses, though the saint seems serene enough about it.

14th-century church near Kakodhíki

Walk Ímvros Gorge

The scrubby slopes of Ímvros Gorge

The Ímvros Gorge is not quite as spectacular as the Samariá Gorge, but it is generally uncrowded and peaceful, a walk you can take at your own pace without being jostled or harried. You will get the best out of this walk if you do it early in the morning when there are very few people about, the light is clear, and fresh smells waft from the gorge vegetation and trees. Taking the walk uphill or inland is the recommended way. The slope is gradual, there is the sense of penetrating the mountains, and Ímvros village at the top has an excellent, if unprepossessing café on the main road where you can catch a bus down to Sfakiá or north across the island to Khaniá. Allow at least two-and-a-half hours for the 8km walk.

To reach the start of the gorge, leave Sfakiá on the Khaniá road, and after 3km turn off right through Komitádhes. The Ímvros Gorge runs inland on your left 0.5km beyond the village, from a sharp righthand bend in the road. The boulder-strewn river bed runs between bluffs dotted with caveholes, and becomes a torrent in winter. The rock walls soon narrow and rise, a chink in the mountainside studded with prickly bushes, figs and stunted trees among thick-leaved, water-retaining plants. The going underfoot is easy, a crunchy progress on small pebbles. Small birds call from the scrub and you might see blue rock thrushes which breed in the gorge. You will also hear the deep musical donging of goat bells, and catch glimpses of the goats cropping grass and plants on ledges and scree slopes that look impossible of access.

The path becomes paved with rock, a narrowing cleft shaded by cypresses and pines. At the narrowest point the gorge is a sinuous slit of black-banded rock, several hundred metres high, whose walls you can span with outstretched arms: a deep, echoing chamber which is very exciting to wriggle through. Near the top the sides widen, diminish and fall away, and you walk out of the gorge into Ímvros village and the mountains.

Kándhanos war memorial

▶▶ Kándhanos *216B1*

Kándhanos lies 20km north of Palaiókhora, on the main road to the northern coast and Khaniá. The village is the capital of the eparchy or province of Selínou, the most southwesterly and probably the least-visited corner of Crete. Warm winds pushing in from the sea give the province the highest rainfall in the island, and Kándhanos lies in the centre of a lush and fertile area dedicated to fruit and chestnut growing. Olives are the keynote here. Kándhanos and its many satellite villages are half hidden in the leafy, drab green groves.

The village takes its name from the ancient settlement of Kantánou, which stood just to the south and was wrecked by an earthquake. Kándhanos became a well-to-do Venetian town, and later a Turkish military centre after many of the inhabitants had converted to Islam. Down the centuries, the Kándhanos area has seen many ferocious battles as invaders have tried to subdue Cretan resistance. None has been as well documented, nor strikes quite such a grim note for present-day visitors, as the events of 23–25 May 1941, when Kándhanos was virtually removed from the map in one of the worst acts of reprisal of World War II.

After the capture on 20 May of the airfield at Máleme, German motor cycle troops were sent south to prevent Allied reinforcements from landing at Palaiókhora. On 23 May they were attacked in a narrow gorge to the north of Kándhanos by a force of partisans, men and women from Kándhanos and the surrounding villages. The Cretans managed to kill 25 soldiers in the ambush, and withdrew to their villages. Two days later bombers arrived over Kándhanos and flattened most of the village, killing many of the inhabitants. By the time German troops reached Kándhanos, several days later, the partisans had retreated into the hills. The soldiers killed everyone they could find, and then reduced the village to rubble.

Almost every house in Kándhanos today postdates this terrible event. In front of the church in the centre of the village is a commemorative garden, with marble plaques recording the destruction: 'Here stood Kándhanos. In

***Kafeníon* heroes**

The pictures that hang on the walls of the village *kafeníon* show how strongly elderly Cretans identify with the past – both national and personal. Heroes such as Venizélos and Daskaloyiánnis are flanked by fierce old *palikáres*, their sashes bristling with weapons; brides in 1920s wedding dresses; handsome young men in breeches, clutching rifles, circa 1941. Compare these last with the *kafeníon* owner and his cronies – they may well be one and the same.

retaliation for the bestial murder of German parachutists and pioneers by armed men and women of the area, Kándhanos was destroyed 3.6.41, razed to the ground, never to be built again.' Reading this stark declaration, one wonders why the Cretans should refer to their own resistance fighters as 'bestial murderers'. But remember that these plaques are replicas of those erected by the Germans in the ruins of Kándhanos. And the village did rise again.

► Káres *216C2*

Káres lies along the main Sfakiá–Khaniá road. Its main attraction lies in the view from the road above, looking down across the village's white houses and tremendous red and white church, crowned with turrets and dome, and away over the green and brown fields of the plateau beyond. All this is dominated by the pale grey heights of the White Mountains at their eastern edge.

► Kastélli Kissámou *216A3*

Kastélli Kissámou is the main centre for this remote northwestern tip of Crete. It lies along the coast road from Khaniá and commands a superb view out across the bay to the flanking peninsulas of Rodhopoú and Gramvoúsa. Kastélli Kissámou served the inland Doric settlement of Polirrínia (see page 244) as a port, and the Venetians fortified it as a prosperous harbour. But little remains of these former glories. It is a working town, concentrating on its local businesses and market. Its few streets are busy and not much concerned with tourism, though there are a number of hotels and rooms to rent, along with a sprinkling of tavernas around the little fishing harbour. This is a good place to base yourself for a couple of days if you are sated with the tourist clamour of the coastal strip and would like to taste an unaffected, bustling Cretan town.

Kafeníon cowards

Many visitors are reluctant to enter the *kafeníon*, especially the outwardly drab and nondescript version most often found in the villages. Reasons for this hesitancy vary: people may be unsure of their welcome as outsiders, handicapped by their lack of Greek, or simply unnerved by the stern stares of the customers. Be bold: a cheerful *khérete!* (hello!) will put everyone at ease. And if you want to talk, someone will probably have enough English (or German, French or even Italian in the east) to start up a conversation.

The main square of Kastélli Kissámou

Flowers adorn Kefáli's balconies

Early frescoes (and more modern votive offerings) at Kefáli

▶ Kefáli 216A2

Kefáli commands one of the best views on the straggling road that skirts the western coast of Crete. The village perches 5km inland in the neck of a tree-lined valley that plunges away to a distant sea 430m below. It is a rough, stony road in and out of the village, but worth pursuing as the church at Kefáli contains some of the best Byzantine frescoes in the area. Park your car near the *kafeníon* on the right as you come from the north, and follow a narrow path beside the *kafeníon* that drops through back alleys past tiny farmyards full of turkeys and cockerels. The path

winds around, but eventually brings you out in front of the little church of Metamórphosis tou Sotírou, Transfiguration of the Saviour. In the dark interior, haloes and eyes stand out startlingly from the faded figures in the early 14th-century frescoes, painted at a time when the resurgence of Byzantine culture under Crete's Venetian rulers was at its height. Visitors down the years have scratched their graffiti dates in the walls of the church; some date back 400 years.

▶▶ Khóra Sfakíon *217D1*

See Hóra Sfakíon, page 228.

▶▶▶ Khrisoskalítissas Monastery *216A1*

See Hrissoskalítissas Monastery, page 228.

▶ Lákkoi *216C2*

The village is spectacularly sited high in the mountains, where the road from Khaniá begins to zigzag and climb in earnest up the northwestern face of the White Mountains towards the Omalós plateau and the top of the Samariá Gorge. Lákkoi is famous for honey and for clear, aromatic mountain air. In winter it can be cut off for weeks by snow, but in summer a cool breeze blows over the red-roofed village. The road snakes tightly among the tavernas, but the best view is over to the left as you climb from Khaniá, a really breathtaking prospect of the red-and-white village church with its dome and minaret perched on the back of a knife-edge ridge, above dizzying drops to the valley below.

Ten kilometres towards Omalós there is a roadside plaque commemorating the death on 28 February 1944 of Sergeant Dudley Perkins, known to Cretan resistance fighters as Captain Vasilí, a formidable New Zealander who commanded a band of partisans in Sélinos province, in the southwestern corner of the island. Vasilí was said to have killed more than a hundred Germans. The ambush that killed him here robbed the partisans of a genuine hero, honoured as few others by the coveted title of Captain.

▶▶▶ Loutró *217D1*

A rough path connects Loutró with Sfakiá and the outside world. This charming coastal village retains the character of a place very much closed in upon itself, clinging to the theatre of rock at its back. Nowadays there are several tavernas and rooms to rent on the harbour which is Loutró's shop front, looking to the ferries from Sfakiá to the east and Ayía Rouméli to the west for its continued existence as a quiet holiday town under the huge slopes of the mountains behind it. Viewing Loutró from the sea, you can appreciate its past importance as a safe natural harbour, the only one on the entire southern coastline of Crete.

The ancient port of Foinix lay just beyond the western headland of the bay of Loutró. The Alexandrine ship carrying the captive St Paul to Rome could not enter this 'haven of Crete', and was driven on to shipwreck on Malta. Some Roman, early Byzantine and Venetian ruins stand on the headland, as does the church of Sotíros Khristós, Christ the Saviour, which contains 14th and 15th-century frescoes.

Foinix was the port for **Anópoli▶**, once a powerful Roman town, that sits high in the mountains above Loutró. There is a statue here to a famous son of Anópoli, the Cretan resistance hero Daskaloyiánnis (see page 57).

Nicknames
For reasons of security, and because foreign names sat awkwardly on Cretan tongues, Allied resistance workers in Crete were given nicknames. Sergeant Dudley Perkins was Vasilí and other well-known foreign agents were Yánni (Jack Smith-Hughes), Aléko (Xan Fielding), Aléxis (Sandy Rendel), Manóli (Geoffrey Barkham), O Tom (Tom Dunbabin), and Micháli (Patrick Leigh Fermor, later to become a celebrated and brilliant writer). Their exploits, along with those of the Cretan resistance fighters, have been detailed by George Psychoundákis in his notable book *The Cretan Runner*.

Ill wind
'And because the haven (*Kaloí Liménes*) was not commodious to winter in, the more part advised to depart thence also, if by any means they might attain to Phenice, and there to winter; which is an haven of Crete, and lieth towards the south west and north west.
'And when the south wind blew softly, supposing that they had obtained their purpose, loosing thence, they sailed close by Crete.
'But not long after there arose against it a tempestuous wind, called Euroclydon.
'And when the ship was caught, and could not bear up into the wind, we let her drive.'

(Acts of the Apostles, Ch. XXVII, v.12–15)

FOCUS ON *The White Mountains*

■ The White Mountains (or Levká Óri) are aptly named. The bare limestone heights stand out in pale magnificence against the blue Cretan sky in summer, truly white with snow in winter. The impression is always of bareness and whiteness, a pure and hard landscape, stunningly wild and beautiful from the sea or from the rooftops of Khaniá.....■

Sfakiots according to Sitiá
Natives of Sitiá at the other end of the island, styled as soft, easy-living and easy-going easterners, regard the Sfakiots with a mixture of admiration, fear and incomprehension. A Sitiá man, explaining the characteristics of Sfakiots, employs three gestures: a ferocious scowl, a clenched fist and a rotary movement of the index finger of his free hand against the side of his head.

This is the wildest country in Crete, the harshest and most primitive, where traditional ways of life and thinking cling on tenaciously in the face of tourism and the modern world. In spite of the fame of these mountains, they see far fewer visitors than the Psiloritis and Dhíkti ranges further east. This is partly due to the distance from Iráklio, partly to poor road access, partly to the lack of holiday towns around the extremely beautiful but forbiddingly steep coastline. Sfakiá is not much more than a small ferry port, and only Soúyia at the end of long and winding roads offers anything in the way of modern holidaymaking facilities.

The southern coastline of the White Mountains is the most isolated and dramatic in Crete. Between Soúyia and Sfakiá it soars from lonely beaches and craggy headlands up to the heights of the mountains, smooth slopes that tower magnificently above the Libyan Sea. This is 25km of roadless, virtually unvisited coastal splendour. Wandering by foot along the White Mountain coast you can follow dirt roads and tracks inland to remote villages.

Looking into the Samariá Gorge from Omalós

For example, in Ayíos Ioánnis above the harbour village of Loútro, or Prodhrómi northeast of Palaiókhora, you will be welcomed as a rare visitor. There are historic sites where no crowds gather such as the Hellenistic city-state of Lisós west of Soúyia (see page 251) and that of Arádhiana beyond Anópolis. There is Poikilássos, 6km east of Soúyia and only really accessible by boat, and the ancient port of Foinix just west of Loutró, which the ship carrying St Paul could not enter during the stormy voyage that saw the saint wrecked on Malta (see page 235).

The central massif of the White Mountains is the most extensive spread of high ground in Crete, a great barrier of mountains, 500 sq km at least, rising to the peak of the range, Mount Pákhnes. At 2,453m, Pákhnes is just three metres lower than Psiloritis, but even more difficult to reach. You can climb north from the tourist pavilion at the head of the Samariá Gorge for about an hour and a half to reach the climbers' hut of the Greek Mountaineering Club (EOS, tel: 081–227609), and continue from there on up to the central peaks. A guide is essential. Great gorges cut down to the coast through these mountains. There is celebrated Samariá, of course (see page 248–9), Ímvros (see page 231) and others. There are flat, fertile plateaux, too, such as Omalós (see page 239) and Askífos on the Khaniá to Sfakiá road.

The entire area is best known for its status as the homeland of the Sfakiots, proud and warlike people who have feuded, raided and resisted down the centuries. Daskaloyíannis, ill-fated leader of their 1770 revolt against the Turks (see page 57), stands as their symbol. But there is a dark, doomed side to their ferocity and independence of spirit. Feuding depopulated many Sfakiot villages during the 18th and 19th centuries, and their resistance during World War II exacted a fearful price in reprisals. Old men in the White Mountains still dress in full Sfakiot fig, though these days without a pistol in their belts (not a visible one, at any rate). This anecdote is telling: the Sfakiots went to God to complain that they had nothing but rocks to live on, only to be reminded that the rest of Crete was cultivating its softer lands just for them.

Shepherds' sticks
Shepherds' sticks are not used solely as crooks. Bags can be hung from them for ease of carrying, and edible plants can be dug up with their points. They can clean boots, thrash dogs, point out paths to strangers, support ruminative chins, poke fires, and kill scorpions. The best are made of iron-hard *prinos* wood. Many have sinuous or spiral shafts. When not in use, they are usually carried horizontally across the shoulders. A good stick, the shepherds say, is the best friend you can take to the mountains.

The road from Kares to Sfakiá winds over the plateau towards the Ímvros Gorge

Face of a fighter
In George Psychoundákis's book *The Cretan Runner* there is a photograph of Manólis Paterákis in his sheepfold near Kostoyérako, taken after the war. Paterákis wears a wartime battledress blouse. From under his beret an eagle's nose arches between deep-set eyes. The cheeks are hollowed and lean. The mouth, though smiling in the picture, can easily be imagined setting into a thin line of determination. It is a formidable face.

▶ Maláxa *217D3*

Maláxa sits about 8km southeast of Khaniá on the old mountain road that snakes inland to Néo Khorió and Vríses. One asset that distinguishes Maláxa is the excellent small taverna, run by Ioánnis, on the left in the village's single street as you come from Khaniá. 'Touristic Day Book' says the sign outside, and Ioánnis is more than happy to get you to inscribe your name and comments in the book, which is filled with inscriptions by visitors from all over the world, including many old soldiers returning to the scenes of World War II battles.

Ioánnis is a most hospitable man, quite likely to run out into the street, stop a visitor's car and urge the occupants inside to sign his book and enjoy a taste of his homemade *rakí*. His fare is plain, but entirely Cretan and good. Spicy Cretan sausages, eggs, bread, homegrown salad, fruit, wine, coffee and *rakí* will set you back less than the cost of a main course in any of Khaniá's modern restaurants, and will come salted with the cook's wit and wisdom.

▶ Máleme *216C3*

Máleme lies 16km west of Khaniá, along the coast road. Ribbon development has rather spoiled this low-lying coastline, though the road is fringed with thickets of a giant reed (*Arundo donax*) and orange groves that hide some of the recent building. To the right of the road on

The German War Cemetery at Máleme

Taverna-owner, Ioánnis (see Maláxa, opposite)

the western edge of Máleme lies the airfield, now operated by the Greek Air Force, that became the hinge on which turned the fortunes of the Battle of Crete in 1941.

When German paratroopers began landing on 20 May, a force of New Zealanders under Lieutenant-Colonel Andrew was in possession of Hill 107, overlooking Máleme airfield, an essential target for capture by the invaders. A lack of information led to the New Zealanders pulling back from the hill, which the Germans then occupied the following day. Now their airborne troops could land, though under fire and sustaining casualties. Within three days, German fighter planes were operating from Máleme, reinforcements were arriving, and the long Allied retreat to Sfakiá was under way.

Inland of the coast road is the immaculately tended **German War Cemetery**►► where nearly 4,500 young men lie, most of them killed as they parachuted in. An irony of fate saw two of the resistance's toughest fighters, George Psychoundákis and Manólis Paterákis, eventually appointed to take care of these graves.

►►► Omalós Plain *216C2*

Coming south from Khaniá to reach the head of the Samariá Gorge, the road passes across the dead flat Omalós plain, 1100m above sea level, a roughly triangular, fertile saucer of ground set among mountains that climb to 1830m and more. Local villagers stay up here each summer, tending their herds of goats and sheep, which have startling red fleeces coloured by the earth of the plain, and cultivating their patches of corn, potatoes, vegetables and tomatoes. In winter the plain is deep in snow, and in spring the meltwater sluices down off the hills, bringing with it the minerals that make the Omalós soil so fertile, flooding the whole plain until it drains off down an enormous plug-hole of a cavern.

In spite of the rash of ugly and out-of-place hotels and tavernas that have recently appeared along the road, Omalós has a remote feel to it. The plain, at the meeting point of many tracks across the White Mountains, was always a centre of insurgence against the island's foreign rulers. The little church to the left of the road was built by Khátzi Mihális Yiánnaris, a celebrated 19th-century leader of resistance against the Turks, in gratitude for his deliverance from a Khaniá prison. His simple house stands nearby, not far from his grave.

Cretan sausages
Cretan sausages or *loukánika* are generally delicious. You can have them *kapnistá* (smoked), *vrastá* (boiled) or *tiganitá* (fried). The spicy, heavy taste and slightly greasy texture are always good, and can be a gourmet's delight if you strike lucky.

Plain cold
Omalós can be genuinely cold, particularly at night and towards winter. Frosts and snow are commonplace here. Bring warm clothing with you if you intend to explore the plateau between September and May.

Grazing the Omalós plain

Drive or bus ride Sfakiá to Khaniá

After the thrills of the walk down the Samariá Gorge and the sea journey from Ayía Rouméli to Sfakiá, the prospect of returning by road to Khaniá may seem rather tame. But the mountain road from Sfakiá to Khaniá is no mundane route. This is one of the most exciting drives in Crete, and as you may well be in a coach you will also be able to take full advantage of the views – provided you can stay awake for the 70km...

The Sfakiá to Khaniá road is a wriggling succession of climbs, falls and hairpin bends, with superb views of the White Mountains and their high plateaux. The route is well engineered and maintained all the way, but will provide nervous drivers with some hair-raising moments. Not for nothing are the bends of the road liberally studded with the tin shrines that mark the sites of fatal accidents. Samariá Gorge walkers are spared the responsibilities of driving as they enjoy the dramatic scenery from the bus that plies regularly between Sfakiá and Khaniá – definitely the best way to travel this road.

Three kilometres east of **Sfakiá** the upward twists begin as the road doubles back and forth, climbing beside the open lips of the **Ímvros Gorge** (see page 231) on your right. Turn and look out of the back window of the bus for a wonderful view over the Libyan Sea to the distant island of Gávdos 37km offshore. The road climbs through thick stands of pine trees to reach **Ímvros** village (see page 230), a straggle of houses and tavernas surrounded by hills, a place famous for the resistance of its inhabitants to the many invaders of Crete down the centuries.

Now the driver's work begins in earnest as he hauls the bus round one sharp bend after another. As oncoming cars appear with Cretan suddenness and *insouciance* in the middle of the road, he swings over to place the bus wheels with cool precision right on the margin of tarmac and empty space, with tremendous drops below.

As the only good route providing north–south communication in this part of the island, the Sfakiá to Khaniá road has played a full part in Cretan history. Older people in the villages along the road well remember the interminable lines of exhausted Allied soldiers limping down to Sfakiá during the Battle of Crete, some of them lucky enough to be taken off by the ships of the Royal Navy, others destined to be left to face capture or months in hiding among the mountains or in the monasteries.

Roadside shrines may mark the sites of past accidents – so speed past them at your peril

At the highest point of the route, 760m above sea level, the villages of **Petrés**, **Ammoudhári** and **Káres** (see page 233) lie along the road, above the little square fields of the Askífos plateau, over which the grey heads of the mountains rise on all sides. The tightly packed houses are sheltered by fig and walnut trees. The bus squeezes round the hairpin bends between the buildings, the conductor standing amidships to talk the driver through the obstacle course. Free and frequent use of the blaring bus horn clears the road, eventually. Cretan bus drivers eschew reverse gear, with even greater tenacity than their car-driving cousins.

The road begins to fall from the summit, passing the Karé ravine where Turkish troops twice came to bloody grief at the hands of Sfakiot fighters: firstly, in 1821 during Crete's armed rising in sympathy with the mainland Greeks' War of Independence; and, secondly, in 1866 as an act of retribution against the Turkish soldiers who had captured Arkádhi Monastery and sparked the famous and terrible gunpowder explosion which claimed around 2,000 lives.

The bus makes its way down to flatter country, to reach the plane trees, waterfalls and slow-paced streets of **Vríses**, a pleasantly shady village famous for yoghurt and honey. Soon the excitement of the mountains is behind you as the bus driver swings west on to the coast road and puts his foot down for Khaniá.

Bees forage amongst the scented herbs on the hillsides

Fresh orange
The orange juice served for breakfast by many Cretan hotels and cafés is a noxious sweet liquid tasting more of chemicals and saccharine than of fruit. If you want the real thing, freshly squeezed, ask for *portokáli limós*, and you could back up your request with a mime if the waiter looks baffled.

▶▶▶ Palaiókhora 216B1

Winding down out of the mountains on the main road from Khaniá, you approach Palaiókhora, the Bride of the Libyan Sea, down a long avenue of eucalyptus trees, a rather splendid introduction to what is one of the most welcoming and enjoyable small resorts on Crete's south coast. Palaiókhora sits on the neck of a small peninsula that juts out a few miles east of the most southwesterly point in Crete, and if you come during the day there is still the feeling of having arrived in a bit of a backwater. The magnificent mountains behind, and the headlands east and west that hem in the town, contribute to this cosy, enclosed atmosphere.

At night along Venizélos Street, the main street of Palaiókhora, things come alive. Venizélos and the other small streets that run down to the sea are crammed with tavernas, bars and discos, nothing horribly loud or down-market, but with a real sense of fun and colour that is impossible to resist. Dionysius Restaurant on Venizélos Street offers a good choice of menu. Go into the kitchen and pick what looks good. Pork *stifádo* with a creamed aubergine salad is a speciality, but there are many other dishes. If you are sitting outside a restaurant, make sure you check which establishment actually owns the table. In Palaiókhora, as in many Cretan tourist resorts, the tables are jammed so close together along the pavements that only different patterns of tablecloth tell you which table belongs to which restaurant.

Waterside taverna in Palaiókhora

The rooftops of Palaiókhora

There are plenty of hotels in Palaiókhora and also inexpensive rooms to rent. Breakfast at one of the cafés along the east beach is a memorable experience if you are there in time to see the sun rise over the mountains and bay. This beach is pebbly, and not as popular or crowded as the wide beach of clean sand to the west of the promontory, crowning which is a square of golden stone walls, all that remains of Palaiókhora's Venetian fort. The fort was built in 1282 after a serious uprising in western Crete. Rebels captured it briefly fifty years later, and the admiral-corsair Khaireddin Barbarossa destroyed it in 1579 before the Turks finally took it after a siege in 1653. Nowadays there is nothing to see at the fort by way of architectural or historic interest, but the view over roofs, domes, peach and cream coloured walls and flowery courtyards to the mountains and sea is reason enough to climb up here. Below the fort is a maze of tiny streets bright with flowers and shaded with eucalyptus and tamarisk, where you can stroll at your leisure.

Palaiókhora's waterfront is the departure point for boats for Soúyia, Ayía Rouméli and Sfakiá, as well as to Elafonísi beach round to the northwest, and out to Gávdos Island, 37km to the southeast. There is a new, unfinished yacht marina towards the western side of the promontory, and a quay to the east side where the little fishing boats, pointed fore and aft, land their catch.

► Plátanos *216A3*

Plátanos is 11km west of Kastélli-Kissámou on the coast road, and is a good place to stop and refresh yourself before the long and spectacular climb across the mountainous coastline of western Crete. The Milos taverna by the watermill is well known for its good food and peaceful atmosphere. It is worth taking the side road that winds past the village houses where old men and women sit out under the trees, enjoying a wonderful view over the roofs of Plátanos to the roll and rise of the back of the Rodhopoú peninsula. In the village church there are faded frescoes and some icons.

Party line
The noisiest public telephone in Crete might well be the one in the middle of Venizélos Street, especially at night when Palaiókhora's unofficial street party takes place.

Shower shocks
The fittings of Cretan hotel showers may come as a shock to the unforewarned. There are rarely curtains; the user is trusted to direct the water in the general area of the tiles. A plastic stool is often provided so that you can make your ablutions while seated, a notion that makes up in pleasurable decadence what it lacks in practicality. Soap and towels are the responsibility of the guest in smaller establishments, so look before you lather!

The remains of Polirrínia

Get a hat
The sunhat is not only a practical necessity when walking in the Cretan countryside. It is also a powerful aid to social intercourse for gentlemen explorers. Raising the hat while intoning greetings always brings a smile from older people, not of hilarity, as might be the case elsewhere, but of genuine pleasure at the courtesy

▶▶▶ Polirrínia *216A3*

Polirrínia lies back in the hills 7km south of the coastal town of Kastélli Kissámou, which served as its port in Doric and Roman times over 2,000 years ago. A sign-posted road turns off left from the eastern end of Kastélli Kissámou's bypass to reach the village of Áno Palaiókastro. You have to leave your car here if you want to walk up through the paved streets of the village to the top of the rise. A track on the left brings you up to the Church of the 99 Martyrs, built largely of slabs retrieved from the ruins of the former settlement and fortifications, some with their inscriptions still legible. The church's foundations are four times as old as the building itself. These great cut stone blocks originally supported a Hellenistic temple built around 400BC.

The city was founded around the 6th century BC on this naturally fortified site, guarded by steep slopes falling to sheer rock walls and deep gullies. In Hellenistic times Polirrínia was fortified with massive walls strengthened by curved bastions. After the Roman invasion of 67BC the city entered a new phase of prosperity, was refortified and given a water supply by way of Hadrian's Aqueduct. The rock-cut channels can still be seen, along with cisterns, walls, houses cut into the rock one above another, and tombs hewn into the hillsides and rock faces.

After the Roman occupation the city entered a period of decline, and may have been sacked when the Saracens invaded Crete in AD824. But after the Byzantine reconquest in AD961 Polirrínia was revived, and when the Venetians took control of the island in 1204 they refortified parts of the site, notably the acropolis. A path, waymarked in red, leads from the church to the ruins of walls and towers on the peak, and a really spectacular prospect of both north and south coasts.

Walk Rodhopoú Peninsula

This is a long, tough and lonely walk in the mountainous interior of the uninhabited Rodhopoú peninsula, with an isolated church as the focal point. The twin peninsulas of Rodhopoú and Gramvoúsa (see page 227) frame the Gulf of Kissámou at the northwest corner of Crete. There is very little shade on this challenging circular walk on Rodhopoú, so it is vital to take a sunhat, sun cream and plenty of water. Wear strong boots, too, as the track is very rough. Allow a minimum of six hours for this strenuous 19km walk.

Rodhopoú is a quiet, end-of-the-road village where you will get both stares and greetings. Park by the church and walk north, climbing all the time on a stony road that gets steadily rougher, twisting through a baked, dusty landscape of grey rock, stubby prickly plants and dry gullies, everything absolutely quiet and lonely. The ridges and small peaks of Rodhopoú rise all around, with birds of prey floating above. Nobody lives out here. You have the long peninsula entirely to yourself.

After 6.5km the road forks by an old cistern, where a faded sign in Greek points left to Ayíos Ioánnis. You can see the way from here. The track changes colour from grey to red, and passes through a narrow gap between blasted-out bluffs in the hillside, to emerge with a breathtaking view over the rocky, crumpled western face of Rodhopoú. Far below, tiny against the immense backdrop of coast and sea, lies the little red-roofed church of Ayíos Ioánnis Yíonis, set among trees in a walled plot. Tens of thousands of people come here each 28 and 29 August, to witness the christening of boy babies with the name of the church's patron saint.

Zigzag down to the church, and then continue on a rough and steep footpath. Fork left after 4km to return over the neck of the peninsula to Rodhopoú and a welcome cold drink.

Rodhopoú village

The independent explorer, studying the map, will soon pick out the monasteries of the island. Where the roads shrink away to dirt tracks, descend to a lonely coast or come to a full stop among the mountains, there you are likely to see the prefix Moní, next to a church symbol, and almost certainly a good distance from the nearest settlement.....

Monastery rules
Monasteries vary in the behaviour they request from visitors. There is often a ban on shorts, and photography may be prohibited inside the church. Many of the monasteries close for a few hours in the middle of the day, and visitors are asked not to pry into the living quarters of the monks or nuns.

Forthright abbot
The current abbot of Préveli Monastery is a man very much in the mould of his predecessors: welcoming, forthright, hospitable and of wide interests. If you are treated to his views on Greek history and politics, be forewarned that they are strong ones and you may be listening for quite some time.

A life of prayer and contemplation demands isolatation and Crete is not short of this. Once the island supported over 1000 monasteries. Most were very small and fewer than 50 survived the first years of Turkish rule. Today only 40 monasteries of the Greek Orthodox faith are active, some enjoying prosperity, some in decline with only one or two inmates, some entirely deserted and converted to other uses or falling into ruin.

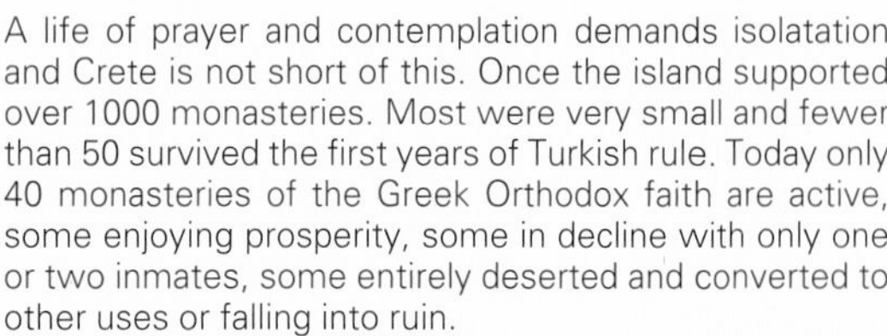

The monastic tradition in Crete is a long one. Well over a thousand years ago hermits were established in caves and remote corners of the island. There was an upsurge in the prosperity of the monasteries in Venetian times, with many Roman Catholic settlers converting to the Orthodox faith and building splendid churches and monastic quarters. A good number of these still stand. Arkádhi, in the hills southeast of Réthimnon, is probably the best known, thanks to the bloody drama of its history (see page 171). Others include the famous resistance centre of Préveli on the south coast (see page 180–1), Ayía Triádha on the Akrotíri peninsula (see page 220), Toploú in the northeast (see pages 154–5) and Vrondísion on the southern flanks of Psiloritis (see page 191).

These monasteries can face the future with a degree of confidence. Fewer young Cretan men and women are opting for a monastic way of life, as is the case all over the Christian world, but establishments such as Préveli and Ayía Triádha, with a steady stream of coach-borne visitors and museums filled with superb treasures of art and craft, have more than a toehold on financial security. The Abbot of Toploú is reputed to be one of the richest men in Crete, if holdings of land can be taken to represent actual wealth.

Monastic life is not easy

However, monastic life is seldom easy. It is at the more obscure and less frequently visited monasteries, tucked away on the coast or in the hills, that the inmates have a struggle to keep going. Such monks and nuns work hard. They can be seen in their working habits, sleeves rolled up, digging and cleaning or dressed in finely embroidered robes making their religious observances. Looking at the sparse furnishings, the rusty old pick-up trucks and the simple meals of monasteries like Faneroménis near Gourniá (see page 162), Arví on the coast south of Áno Viánnos (see page 127) or Kápsa to the east of

Ierápetra (see page 156), one sees evidence of a spartan lifestyle, lived in the hard light of reality. This is very much in accordance with Greek Orthodoxy, particularly the Cretan variety, demonstrating close practical links between the religious and the secular.

When it has come to fighting and resistance, the monasteries of Crete have never kept themselves above the strife. Arkádhi and Préveli were both eager to conceal and help evacuate Allied soldiers after the Battle of Crete. Abbot Silignákis of Toplóu was shot, along with a dozen of his monks, after the discovery of a radio transmitter in the monastery. Ayía Triádha was destroyed by the Turks in 1821, and Gonías Monastery on the Rodhopoú peninsula (see page 226) proudly shows off the Turkish cannon balls embedded in its walls.

Vidhianís on the Lasíthiou plateau, ancient Katholikó on Akrotíri (see page 221) and Káto Préveli, stand empty. But remote Koudhoumá on the south coast (see page 89) and Khrisoskalítissas in the west (see page 228), still dispense warm hospitality, and would never dream of turning away a benighted stranger.

Shaken, not stirred
Cretan monks, living as they do in some of the remotest parts of the island, face a long drive over rough roads whenever they venture abroad from their monasteries. Poverty and bad road conditions usually conspire to make early wrecks of the monastery's transport. It is not rare to see a couple of monks bouncing around in the cab of an old pick-up truck more dilapidated than any local farmer would tolerate.

Women, too, choose a contemplative life

Walk Samariá Gorge

This is the classic adventure walk of Crete, and one that hundreds of thousands of visitors take every year. It is a 16km linear hike in scenery unequalled anywhere else in Crete for sheer drama, and is a walk you will remember as long as you live. Five or six hours should see you through the Samariá Gorge in comfort, and leave time to dawdle along the way as you will certainly want to do. There are no particular difficulties, provided you wear strong boots and take the staple water, sunhat and suncream, but a few points must be borne in mind. There are no escape routes from the gorge. Once you are committed to the walk, you have either to see it through or return, painfully, to the start. From Ayía Rouméli at the foot of the gorge there are no roads out, so you must decide either to stay the night there,

Starting the descent into the Samariá Gorge

or to reach the village in time to catch the boat to Sfakiá or Sóuyia, from where buses will take you back to Khaniá. These run until quite late in the evening. Plan your timetable carefully. Khaniá to Samariá Gorge to Ayía Rouméli and back to Khaniá (see pages 240–1) makes a very long day. And note that the gorge at midday in the summer is one long procession of tourists and school parties, complaining or shouting according to type, certain to reduce your enjoyment of what ought to be an awe-inspiring experience. The gorge is usually open from 6am to sunset, and the earlier you set off the better. From November to April there is no access, as the river at the bottom becomes a dangerous torrent.

Start at the tourist pavilion at the head of the gorge. The initial descent is as breathtaking as you could wish, zigzagging 600m down a precipitous pathway known as the *xilóskala* or wooden stairway, which is what it was before the crowds began to come. The huge scree and rock faces of 2,080m Mount Gíiyilos stare down through gaps in the pines and cypresses, which scent the sharp mountain air with a delicious sappy smell. At the bottom is a picnic area where you will find the river, a trickle through dry boulders in summer but a rush of wild water in winter. A tiny plain stone church, Ayíos Nikólaos, stands beside the river, which you cross and recross under eucalyptus and chestnut trees. Stupendous grey corries curve away to the east as you approach the abandoned village of Samariá under giant cliffs near the halfway point. Its few houses were evacuated in 1962. It was always a resistance centre. The Turks never managed to take it, and it proved to be a nest of vipers for the Germans during World War II. There are fountains here and picnic tables under the trees, and across the gorge is the little white church of Óssia María, built in 1379, after which both village and gorge were named.

Now comes the drama. The gorge deepens and steepens into sheer rock walls, the sides falling together until you can almost feel them snap shut. Thick bands of white quartzite and black rock writhe along the cliffs, and the sky narrows to a chink overhead. Even the chatterers fall silent under the spell of this overwhelming place. At last the path, twisting over the pebbles, threads its way through the famed *sideróportes*, or iron doors, walls of rock less than 3m apart that tower well over 300m into the sky. Everyone spreads their arms as they go through here, but only those with a gorilla's stretch will be able to touch both walls at once.

The final few rocky kilometres are unimpressive compared with what has preceded them. They bring you out at the lower entrance gate, where freshly squeezed, ice-cold orange juice is for sale. This irresistible nectar will nerve you for the final 2km down to Ayía Rouméli and your boat.

The stream is this tame only in the summer months

Rough landing
A group of Allied resistance members who arrived by night on the beach near Soúyia on 27 November 1942 had a landing to remember. They had to swim to shore through storm waves from their wrecked boat, and most of their supplies were lost *en route*. They spent a miserable cold and wet night on the beach. At dawn they found themselves under the guns of the Paterákis clan from nearby Kostoyérako who had almost shot them by mistake during the night. The Greek submarine that had brought the new arrivals had omitted to tell anyone that they were coming.

► Sklavopoúla *216A1*

Sklavopoúla stands 640m above sea level, 16km miles back in the hills north of Palaiókhora, an all-but-unvisited village at the breezy summit of a very rough road. Slav mercenaries were granted land here by a 10th-century Byzantine emperor, and gave their name to the village. There are wonderful views over miles of plunging hill country where roads lie like coils of string. Sklavopoúla is utterly quiet and peaceful, its houses dotted around three churches: Ayíos Yióryios, Sotíros Khristós or Christ the Saviour, and the Panayía, Virgin Mary, contain Byzantine frescoes. Panayía's are particularly fine. Ask about keys at the *kafeníon* in the square.

To reach Sklavopoúla you turn off the road from Palaiókhora in the sleepy, tree-lined village of **Voutás►**, beside the first *kafeníon* on the left. About 2km up the Sklavopoúla road from the village, you pass a side track on the right into **Kalamiós►**. It is well worth turning aside for half an hour to enjoy this traditional and secluded hamlet of whitewashed houses scattered among olive trees with bulbous trunks and shading leaves. The women of Kalamiós still fetch their water from a stone trough. A path leads up to a tiny Byzantine church, its dark interior lined with cracked and faded frescoes.

►► Soúdha Bay *217D3*

Soúdha Bay is Crete's best natural harbour, a deepwater inlet 15km long and 3km wide that separates the southern shore of the Akrotíri peninsula from the north coast just east of Khaniá. The view of water, ships and the Akrotíri hills from the coast road is strikingly beautiful, but Soúdha Bay saw some of the bloodiest episodes of the Battle of Crete. In May 1941 the sky over the bay was black for days on end with the smoke of bombed and burning Allied ships. West of the port of Soúdha lies the big Allied War Cemetery, with 1,497 graves of those who died defending Crete.

Looking down on the Akrotíri peninsula and Soúdha Bay, still used by visiting naval vessels

Peaceful Soúyia Bay

▶ Soúyia

216B1

Soúyia is hidden away on the south coast, 70 km southwest of Khaniá at the end of a very long and winding road that skirts the westernmost flanks of the White Mountains. This little fishing port used to be one of the best-kept secret delights of Crete, visited only by those in the know, seekers after the simple pleasures of taverna, beach, coast and mountain walks, and a sight of one of the least-known Byzantine mosaics in the island. Nowadays, however, thanks to development of the settlement and an improved road, Soúyia has taken on the characteristics of a popular, if not yet too overcrowded, small resort. It is still an excellent bolthole for a couple of quiet days, and as a base for expeditions on foot.

The village lies beside the mouth of the Soúyanos River, fronted by a great double sweep of pebbly and partially sandy beach fringed with feathery tamarisk trees and backed by the rise of the mountains. Two thousand years ago Soúyia served as the port for the Graeco–Roman city of Elirós, 5km back in the hills to the north. A few shaped stones and slabs remain of the Roman port just to the east of the river mouth. The Byzantine mosaic, incorporating peacocks and deer, has recently been removed to Khaniá Archaeological Museum from its position under the fairly modern church just west of the village. The mosaic was discovered and the church built on the advice of a Soúyia man, who saw it all in a dream while sleeping on the site.

A short way to the west of Soúyia are the remains of the ancient city of **Lisós▶▶**. Foundations of a theatre, some tombs with barrel-vaulted roofs, a temple to Asklepios, the god of healing, and a fountain from which issued a curative spring can be reached by a walk of about one and a half hours on a waymarked track, or by a short boat trip.

Hard nut

The Venetian fort on the little island of Nísos Soúdha at the mouth of Soúdha Bay proved as hard a nut for the Turks to crack as did the other island fortresses around the shores of Crete. A garrison was still holding out here almost 50 years after Francesco Morini had surrendered Candia (Iráklio) to the Turks. The new rulers of Crete did not finally get their hands on this tiny symbol of Christian intransigence until 1715.

Drive West coast and mountains

This sometimes hair-raising, always thrilling, full day circuit is one of the most spectacular and least-travelled routes that Crete has to offer. It is a 320km circular drive from Tavronítis; add 40km each way to Khaniá.

The coastal road going west from **Khaniá** is pleasant enough as it runs straight and flat behind the shore to Tavronítis and on inland to regain the coast at **Kastélli Kissámou**. It is not until you reach **Plátanos**, 11km to the west, and see the mountains of westernmost Crete rise in front of you, apparently barring the way, that you begin to appreciate how the road from here on south might justify its fame as one of the prime scenic routes of Crete. Yet this is, as yet, a little-driven road. Its remoteness from the centres of tourism, and the enticing fact that it doesn't really go anywhere, both have something to do with its lack of traffic, as does the haphazard way its surfaces switch from tarmac to rough stone and back again. Going south the drops are mostly on the driver's side of the road, and the tarmac often does literally drop into space. As the few cars you meet will probably be well over in the middle of the road, and on a blind corner, great care and a moderate speed are essential. Cretan hire cars are fairly robust, and with careful driving there should be few problems. But do note the number of tin shrines beside the road, commemorating accident victims. Petrol stations are also few and far between, and even the most modern tyres can suffer punctures from sharp stones.

From Plátanos the road climbs to slumbrous **Sfinári**, perched among the hills above a pebbly beach. 'Fresh Fishes' says a notice by the road, and there are a couple of hopeful signs for rooms to rent. The road winds upwards on rock ledges, across the foothills of the mountains between olive groves and oleanders, past hillsides covered with vegetation either thick-leaved or covered with prickles, typical of dry country, even though this part of Crete is in fact one of the wettest. Villages such as **Kámbos**, **Keramotí** and **Kefáli** (see page 234)

You will pass tiny mountain villages, like Keramotí...

are small and mostly poor with goats, chestnut trees and olives on the outskirts, one store and a *kafeníon* in the narrow street of red-roofed, white-washed stone houses under the trees, men riding donkeys, and women tilling vegetable patches. The newer houses are along the road, and the older dwellings are tucked away down side tracks, in among the olives, all dwarfed by the huge slopes of the mountains, looking down to an undeveloped, unspoiled, secluded coastline a couple of kilometres below. Stop in these villages, try a couple of words of Greek, and you will be met with warm hospitality.

There is a good stretch of tarmac through **Élos**, and after 5km you turn off right across the River Tíflos to pass through **Strovlés**. Two kilometres further, and you take the roughest of dirt roads to the left to **Aligí** and **Drís**, and on through shady chestnut groves in steep, hidden valleys, zigzagging and switchbacking along the hillsides, at last descending to turn left on the Palaiókhora to Khaniá road at Plemenianá. From here it is a 40km drive north to the coast road at Tavronítis, but take your time. There are two neighbouring villages high in the mountains at **Floriá** to explore. Apáno Flório and Káto Flório both have Byzantine churches with frescoes. The road surface is better as you wind on down, sometimes with a distant sea view in front of you, to Voukoliés. The Saturday morning market here is a long-established tradition, but by the time you reach **Voukoliés** the traders will probably have packed up. The last few kilometres pass orange groves and roadside melon stalls, before you reach Tavronítis on the coast road to Khaniá.

...which can only be reached on foot

Boats and ferries

■ For thousands of years the islanders of Crete have recognised the many advantages of travelling by sea. Small coasters continue to provide an essential link between those communities, especially on the island's isolated south coast, which can only be reached by boat. Those visitors who are prepared to negotiate can often arrange to tag along with the crew.....■

Pay your way
If you miss your connection, it may be possible to negotiate a ride with a local fisherman. What you pay depends on whim. Sometimes a couple of drinks or even a present of cigarettes, for example, may be enough. At other times you may be charged well over the odds. If this happens, bear in mind that you are probably the only lucrative catch he will make all week.

Sea travel is an everyday fact of life for Crete. Only a few years ago the majority of visitors arrived by ferry from Piraeus. The south coast of the island between Palaiókhora and the Gulf of Mesarás, with almost no west–east road communications, still relies on the ferries. The harbours and coastal villages have not entirely given up fishing in favour of tourism. Indeed the two are complementary on an island surrounded by excellent fishing waters. And yachting, dinghy sailing and windsurfing are all on the increase in and around harbours such as Iráklio, Réthimnon, Khaniá, Ayíos Nikólaos, Sitiá and Palaiókhora.

The big ferries, to the mainland of Greece and those on the Palaiókhora–Soúyia–Ayía Rouméli–Sfakiá–Ayía Galíni run, operate to reasonably reliable timetables. If you are lucky at the end of your walk through the Samariá Gorge, you may sail from Ayía Rouméli with the splendidly theatrical skipper who has the habit, when upset, of dashing his cap in fury on the deck. Where the ferries cannot get passengers ashore, even with their modern let-down ramps, the *caïques* will sail. These boats vary in size and carry both passengers and supplies. Some have facilities, some are purpose-built, others are converted from fishing boats or double between the two rôles. The *caïques* have a more cavalier attitude to the clock. Prices on the whole are fixed by general agreement among the boat owners, and local competition keeps them reasonably low.

Where neither ferries nor *caïques* go, you can usually arrange to be dropped by a small private vessel or fishing boat. Try asking around on the waterfront. Take time to appreciate the beautiful lines of the traditionally built boats, brightly painted in primary colours, with pointed sterns and curved wooden tillers. This design has been essentially unchanged for thousands of years, in spite of the electronic fish-finding gear that some now carry.

Sun decks give unobstructed views of the coast

TRAVEL FACTS

By air

Flight time from Athens to Crete is a little under one hour. Olympic Airways, the Greek national airline, operates from Athens. Flights originating outside Greece usually involve a change in Athens, though many charter companies fly direct from other European countries. Olympic offer special economy rates to students and others. In winter their schedules are reduced. For flights in the high season from June to September early booking is essential.

Crete has three passenger airports: Iráklio, Khaniá and Sitiá. Iráklio handles 90 per cent or more of the holiday flights. The airport has an information desk (tel: 081–228426), the major car hire firms, and good bus and taxi connections with the capital. Unfavourable landing conditions occasionally divert flights to the small airfield at Khaniá (tel: 0821–63245) in the west; to the east Sitiá (tel: 0843–24666) is smaller still.

The neat building belies the chaos within Iráklio Airport

By sea

The two main shipping lines are Minoan (tel: 081–229602) and ANEK (tel: 081–221481). Most ferries depart from Piraeus, the port of Athens, sailing either to Iráklio or Khaniá. There are less frequent services to the smaller harbours at Ayíos Nikólaos and Sitiá, and to Réthimnon

The best and time-tested way to travel around the Aegean Sea

with the Rethimniáki company (tel: 831–29221/21518). Sailings usually leave Piraeus in the early evening, arriving 11 or 12 hours later depending on the exact route and weather conditions. Some sailings leave Piraeus early in the morning for an early evening arrival in Crete. As with air travel, it is Iráklio that sees most of the holiday traffic. The port of Khaniá is 10km east of the town, at Soúdha. Sailing into Khaniá early in the morning as the sun lights the snowy peaks of the White Mountains is a great scenic treat.

There are also sailings to Iráklio from the port of Yíthio on the south coast of the Peloponnese peninsula southwest of Athens, and from several ports in Italy: Venice, Brindisi, Ancona, Bari and others.

By car

You can drive to Piraeus and bring your car across to Crete on the ferry. The cross-Europe drive, however, makes for a tense and tiring start to your holiday. If you bring your own car, you will need an EC or international driving licence, your car registration documents and a nationality sticker. EC residents do not need Green Card insurance, but it is essential to have full, comprehensive insurance before driving on Crete. Most visitors hire transport on arrival, which is much simpler; all you need is your driving licence.

By train and coach

Taking the train to Piraeus or another port of embarkation, or to Athens airport, is a fairly relaxed way to travel. Package tour coach operators have beaten well-worn paths to the same destinations, but the long drive, as in a car, can be tiring.

Customs regulations

The usual restrictions apply to the import and export of dangerous goods, explosives, weapons, illegal drugs, etc. The current EC allowances apply to tobacco, alcohol, perfumes and gifts. In practice, there is very little harassment at customs, but two points in particular should be noted. Firstly, there are severe penalties, which include imprisonment, for possession of illegal drugs of any description, and much more severe ones for anyone who has supplied drugs, particularly to under-18s. And secondly, no antiques, including finds of ancient pottery from archaeological sites, can be taken out of Crete. Only constant vigilance has prevented most Minoan pieces finding their way to the salerooms of the world.

Passports and visas

EC visitors need an identity card. A valid passport is best. No visa is needed for a stay of up to three months by visitors from EC countries, Canada, New Zealand or Australia. Extended stays can be authorised by contacting the Iráklio Tourist Office (tel: 081–228225). Visitors whose passports contain a stamp from the Turkish part of Cyprus may be refused admission, so check with your travel agent.

Travel insurance

Hospital treatment is expensive in Crete. It is wise to take out comprehensive holiday insurance if it does not already form part of your package deal. Most banks and travel agencies at home can arrange this for you.

Begin your day early to avoid tour buses at the major sights

The higher you go, the later the Cretan spring starts

When to go

April and May are definitely the best months to be in Crete. It is springtime, the flowers are at their most spectacular, the crowds have not yet begun to arrive, and the islanders are slowly expanding from their winter insularity. The absolute zenith is probably the Greek Orthodox Easter celebrations and the weeks that follow.

June is a good time too, but it is getting hotter. The 'autumn spring' in September–October is also lovely with fewer visitors around, but some hotels and restaurants are beginning to close down for the winter by then.

Winter is a wonderful time for fluent Greek speakers who like a *triste solitude* and don't mind basic amenities. And there are always fine, clear days. The heat, dust, noise, crowds and general impatience of late July and August should be avoided, unless you have to dovetail plans with school holidays.

Climate

From January to mid-March there will be snow on the mountains, gales and rain, with some beautiful clear days. The average temperature is 12–13°C. The Cretan spring comes between mid-March and May, warm with coastal breezes and flowers everywhere. The temperature rises from 13–14°C in mid-March to 20–1°C in May. By June it is getting hotter (23–5°C) with still, dry days, but the flowers continuing to bloom in the mountains. July to September is the Cretan summer with a peak of heat in August (26–7°C, sometimes hotter). The rocks and sand are baking hot, and the powerful *meltémi* wind from the northwest raises sand on north coast beaches and dust on the roads. The island is very arid at this time, and crowded. The south coast is probably the best place to be. The temperatures begin to drop to around 24°C by the end of September.

From October to mid-November there is often a second flowering in the mountains. The island is tired and relaxed now and is looking brown and dry, with temperatures dropping to around 15°C. Mid-November to December sees the onset of gales and rain with snow later in the mountains. There will be a few wonderful fresh days, especially on the south coast, and the temperature falls to between 13 and 14°C.

National holidays

31 December and 1 January, New Year's Day. Cakes with lucky coins, midnight shooing of devils out of houses.

6 January, Epiphany. Youths dive for crosses blessed and thrown in sea. Fonts and springs are blessed, and demons exorcised.

25 March, Greek Independence Day. Town parades.

Carnivals take place during the two weeks before Lent in Iráklio and Réthimnon.

On Clean Monday (the last Monday before Lent), meat is foresworn and there is kite-flying.

Holy Week sees fasting.

Easter is between two and four weeks later than western Easter, and sees memorable, emotional celebrations (see pages 16–17).

Ascension Day. Parades with dancing and fireworks.

April. Khaniá Orange Festival.

1 May, Labour Day. Spring celebrations with picnics and flower gathering to make wreaths for house doors.

20–27 May. Battle of Crete commemorations at Máleme and Khaniá.

26–27 May. Anniversary of 1821 War of Independence at Sfakiá.

24 June. Feast of St John the

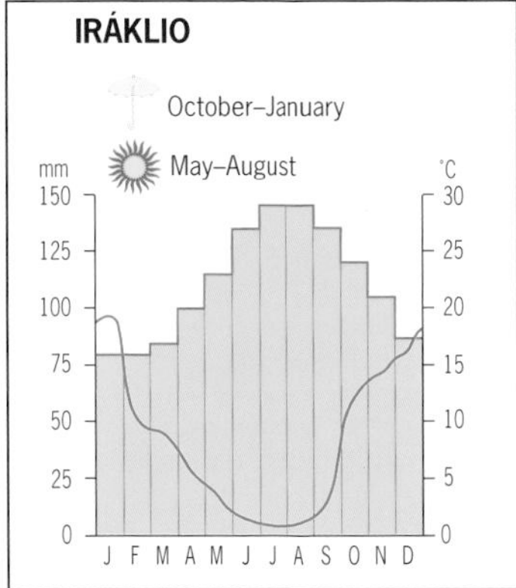

Baptist. Midsummer celebrations with fireworks. Wreaths from 1 May thrown onto bonfires, some Cretans leap the fires.

First week in July. Marine Week with events at ports, especially Soúdha.

Mid-July. Réthimnon Wine Festival.

July–August. Iráklio Festival with many cultural events.

Mid-August. Sitiá Sultana Festival.

15 August. Assumption of the Virgin Mary with services, music and dancing at churches, monasteries and villages.

29 August. Commemoration of the beheading of St John the Baptist. Christenings and gatherings of those named 'Ioánnis' at churches dedicated to the saint.

31 August. Consecration of the Virgin, festivities at Psikró, Lasíthiou.

Late October. Élos Chestnut Festival.

28 October. Óhi Day. Celebrating Greek pride in their 'No' to Mussolini in 1940.

7–9 November. Commemoration of the 1866 Arkádhi Monastery explosion. Fireworks and celebrations at Arkádhi and Réthimnon.

25–26 December. Christmas is a low-key affair, and demons abound.

Time differences

Greece is 2 hours ahead of Greenwich Mean Time (GMT). Greek summer time (GMT + 3 hours) starts on the last Sunday in March, winter time the last Sunday in September.

Money matters

Crete uses the Greek drachma. There are no limits for EC visitors on foreign currency and travellers' cheques entering the island, but declare cash in excess of £350/$500 so that you will be allowed to take it out again.

Banks

Banks are usually open Monday to Thursday 8–2, Friday 8–1:30. In big tourist resorts some may be open later, and on Saturdays. Most Greek and some foreign banks have branches on the island. It is advisable to change money and travellers' cheques at a bank, as commission is usually lower and rates better than in hotels, *bureaux de change* or travel agents. The EOT (Greek Tourist Organisation) offices will also change money, as will main post offices. Always take your passport as identification.

Credit Cards

Access, Visa and American Express are usually recognised in the larger souvenir outlets, car hire agencies and up-market restaurants at the coastal resorts, but you may find that other cards may well be treated with suspicion. In small villages and remote areas you will need to use cash. This is particularly important if you are driving as fuel stations away from the north coast very rarely accept credit cards of any kind. Small hotels and tavernas will also only accept cash.

Bank staff are helpful, and many speak English

Car rental

Most visitors to Crete hire transport when they arrive on the island. This obviates the need for a tedious drive across thousands of miles of mainland Europe, and is quick and easy to arrange. Car hire on Crete is not especially cheap, but savings can be made if hire is part of a package or fly-drive deal.

The major car hire firms are represented in the four big towns of Iráklio, Khaniá, Réthimnon and Ayíos Nikólaos, as well as in other large towns and at Iráklio airport. The better hotels will fix you up with a hire car on request. S. Kanákis Enterprises represent Holiday Autos at 38 Odós 25 Avgoústou, Iráklio (tel: 081–289497/284438), at Khaniá (tel: 0821–68711), Réthimnon (tel: 0831–25800), Ayíos Nikólaos (tel: 0841–25366/24343), Khersónisos (tel: 0897–23072) and Ierápetra (tel: 0842–25701). Other majors are Hertz at the airport and at 44 Odós 25 Avgoústou (tel: 081–229802); Budget at 34 Odós 25 Avgoústou (tel: 081–221315/243918); and Eurodollar at 24 Odós 25 Avgoústou (tel: 081–243237).

You will be asked to show, and even surrender, your driving licence, which must be a full licence held for at least a year. The lower age limit for hiring a car is 21, but some firms may require you to be 23. Hire prices are comparable to most other European countries. Out of season you can bargain for reductions. Do satisfy yourself that the deal you strike includes full, comprehensive insurance. Cretan roads are always

Four-wheel drives are fun, but mark the occupants as tourists...

Local companies compete with the big internationals

liable to spring nasty surprises, and it is far better to pay more and drive with peace of mind.

By the same token, check tyres for wear, windscreen washer bottles for water, battery and oil levels, and ask what that flashing red light on the dashboard means *before* you drive away. If you hire from a major company these checks should have been carried out already. Four-wheel-drive vehicles, although they cut a rugged dash, are not really necessary. Provided you hire a car with a reasonably-sized engine, over 1100cc, there are few dirt roads you will not be able to negotiate with care.

Petrol and diesel cost roughly the same as on mainland Europe, but trying to find petrol in remote districts of the island, which means anywhere away from the north coast holiday strip and the bigger towns, is a needle-in-a-haystack business. The golden rule is always to fill up when you have the opportunity, and not to set off with a nagging doubt about the car. Check it, or get it checked, first. Garages close at round 7pm, and sometimes earlier on Saturdays. On Sundays only the bigger garages in the main towns are open.

Driving tips

These are mostly covered on pages 102–3, Focus on Driving in Crete. The absolute basics that you need to remember are to: allow plenty of time and be patient; be prepared to turn back; and remember that place names in this guide, on your map and on the road signs may be spelt in three or more different ways. You will have to rely heavily upon your common sense.

Breakdown

ELPA is the Greek motorists' aid organisation. Several other motoring organisations, for example, the AA and RAC in the United Kingdom, are affiliated to ELPA. If you are a member of either of these, you will benefit from ELPA'S free breakdown service (tel: 157). They also offer free tourist information (tel: 01–174), and supply road maps. If you are not a member of an affiliated organisation dial 154 for assistance. Also call the car hire firm. Do remember to make a note of their number before you drive away from their premises!

Bus and coach travel

Bus travel on Crete is probably the best-value, drachma-per-kilometre, way of getting around the island. The buses, run under the loose organisation of the KTEL group, are inexpensive and reliable, though journeys can be hair-raising on the more frisky sections of road, particularly in the mountains. The service along the new road between the four main towns of Khaniá, Réthimnon, Iráklio and Ayíos Nikólaos is fast and frequent. From these big towns, local services are run to the smaller country towns and to most villages. Local tickets are bought on the bus. Long distance tickets are sold in an office at the bus station, usually marked *Praktoreíon*. On Sundays the service is reduced, and in winter the timetable changes. Local tourist information offices have details and timetables.

There are several bus stations in Iráklio (tel: 081–221765 for information). Station A is at the ferry port and operates services to the east. Station B is just outside the Khaniá Gate and serves the south and west. The station at the Venetian harbour operates services to the west, and services to the southeast leave from Platía Kíprou. Khaniá bus station is at Odós Kidonías, just south of Platía 1866, and information is available on 0821–93306/93052. Réthimnon bus station is at 44 Odós Moátsu, on the corner with Odós Dhimokratías. For information call 0831–22212/22659. Ayíos Nikólaos bus station is on the shore at the bottom of Odós Sofoklís Venizélos, telephone 0841–22234 for information.

Fires are a very real problem in the dry season

There are numerous coach tours to destinations all over the island, often with a cultural event thrown in: dancing, music, plate-smashing, waiter-smooching, and so on. These can be good fun if you're with the right people and in the mood. Some Iráklio operators are: Adamis (tel: 081–246202); Cretan Holidays (tel: 081–242106); Ikaros Travel (tel: 081–228602); Sbokos Tours (tel: 081–229712); Zeus (tel: 081–221103).

Flights

Domestic flights leave from Khaniá (tel: 0821–63245), Iráklio (tel: 081–228426) and Sitiá (tel: 0843–24666) airports. Destinations include Rhodes and other islands in the Dodecanese and Cyclades groups to the north of Crete.

Motorcycle and bicycle hire

To hire a motorcycle you must be 19 years old, and for anything over 50cc you will need a full driving licence. The same lower age limit applies to scooters and mopeds. Though these are cheaper by far, they won't be able to tackle the many steep ascents on dirt roads that you will meet if you want to explore the Cretan hills. But for tootling around the resorts, they're fine. Crash helmets may or may not come with the bike, most likely not. You should bring your own, or insist on the hire place producing one. It is not worth taking any risks on the poorer roads. If a helmet is not forthcoming, move along to the next hire place. There are plenty to choose from!

Bicycle hire is increasing in popularity with the advent of the mountain bike which can cope with the difficult roads and hilly landscape. There is no charge for bringing your own bicycle to the island, but if you want to hire, some Iráklio addresses are Nikos, 14 Bofor Street (tel: 081–226425); Horizon, 18 Idomeneos Street (tel: 081–286819); Candia Motor, 48 Odós 25 Avgoústou (tel: 081–221227).

Youth hostels are a cheap option

Sea travel

There is a lively trade in passengers and goods from most ports and harbours in Crete, both formally and informally. The island's main shipping companies are Minoan (78 Odós 25 Avgoústou, Iráklio, tel: 081–229602) and ANEK (also in Odós 25 Avgoústou, tel: 081– 221481).

Iráklio has services to Piraeus (Athens), Kós, Kálimnos, Íos, Náxos, Rhodes and other Aegean islands; also Ancona and other Italian ports. Contact the shipping lines direct; many have offices in Odós 25 Avgoústou above the Venetian harbour. Shipping agents, for example, Paleológos Shipping Agency, 5 Odós 25 Avgoústou, tel: 081–246185/246208.

Réthimnon also has sailings to Piraeus. Contact Cretan Travel on the waterfront on Sofoklí Venizélos, tel: 0831–22915.

Ayíos Nikólaos has ferries to Piraeus, the Dodecanese and the Cyclades. Try Massaros Travel, 29 Odós Koundoúrou, tel: 0841–22267.

Khaniá has a service to Piraeus from the port of Soúdha, 10km to the east with buses every 15 minutes. Contact Minoan on 0821–23939 or ANEK on 0821–23636.

Sitiá has sailings to Piraeus, Rhodes, Pátmos, Kos and Kálymnos. Try Tzortzákis Travel Agency on the harbour front, tel: 0843–28900.

Kastélli Kissámou is the departure point for the Peloponnese ports of Yíthio, Kalámata and Monemvássia, and the island of Kíthira.

There is also a good, regular south coast service between Palaiókhora–Soúyia-Ayía Rouméli–Sfakiá–Ayía Galíni. Details of this service can be obtained from local tourist offices.

Student and youth reductions

You can explore Crete very cheaply by staying in youth hostels. The number and locations vary, but they include Iráklio, Khaniá, Réthimnon, Ayíos Nikólaos and Sitiá, and some of the bigger resorts like Mália. International Youth Hostel membership cards are not often asked for, but rumour implies that things may be about to tighten up. Production of a student card will get you reductions on Olympic Airways flights into Greece, entrance fees to museums and archaeological sites, and on some tours. It is worth checking with tourist information offices.

Taxis

Taxis are widely available, and can get you to many of the parts the buses cannot reach. Town taxis operate fixed-price journeys within the towns. In other cases, agree both price and destination before you get in. You may be able to use a taxi to connect two ends of a walk, or to fill in a gap in the bus timetable.

The ubiquitous newsagent-cum-sweet seller; this one is in Iráklio

Media

Newspapers

Most of the major foreign newspapers and some magazines are available in the big seaside towns; buy them at street kiosks, big hotels, newsagents and bookstalls or the airport. The mark-up can be three or four times the cover price, and is stamped on the front page. In the Big Four towns they will be a day old, probably older in smaller places.

Television

Some concerts of traditional Cretan music are broadcast, along with a great many hoary American films, subtitled or dubbed to interesting effect. Do yourself a favour and choose a *kafeníon* without a television if you want to enjoy the atmosphere and chat.

Radio

Cretan and Greek music pours out of the radio; just twiddle the dial. Some local stations carry tourist information in English during the season. With perseverance you will pick up the BBC World Service, the Voice of America and US Forces radio.

Post offices

Post offices are open 7:30–2:30 weekdays, in Iráklio and Khaniá 7:30am–7:30pm. Other big towns may stay open later, and at weekends. The main post offices are: Platía Daskaloyiánni, Iráklio; Odós Tzanakáki, just up from the covered market in Khaniá; Odós

Don't rely upon post-boxes always being emptied every day

Moátsou in Réthimnon; Odós 28 Oktovrioú Ayíos Nikólaos; Platía Kothrí in Ierápetra; Odós Therissoú in Sitiá.

Post offices (*takhydromeíon)* sell stamps *(grammatósima)*, as do pavement kiosks and shops. Post offices will also change money and cheques. Parcels can only be collected from a parcels office, and should be sent from a main post office. Air mail letters take from three to seven days to reach European destinations, seven to ten days to the US, and 10–14 days to Australia and New Zealand. Postcards should be written as soon as you arrive if you want them to beat you home! *Poste restante* at main post offices will hold letters for up to a month. Take your passport when you collect, to identify yourself. Post boxes are yellow.

A recent and very welcome development is mobile post offices, an excellent initiative in an island that relies on pleasing its visitors. These bright yellow caravans park in the tourist resorts during the summer. They stay open late, and are often open on Saturday and Sunday.

Telephones

The Cretan telephone system works well, and people are generous with their offer of free use of their phones; but don't take this for granted. Phones in hotel lobbies may seem to be free, but check your bill on leaving! Most better-class hotels have telephones in the bedrooms, on which you can make local and international calls, at a price.

The big cities are well provided with telephone booths, and almost every town and substantial village has one. Those with a blue band painted round the top are for local calls only. Those banded in orange are for long-distance calls only. You can feed coins into these, but it is simpler to use a metered phone at a pavement kiosk. Some cafés display a sign: *tiléfono me metrití*. You make your call (to anywhere in the world), and the owner reads the cost from the meter.

You can also phone from Greek Telephone Organisation (OTE) offices. Main offices are in El Greco Park, Iráklio (7am–11pm); Odós Tzanakáki next to main post office, Khaniá (7am–midnight); Sfakianáki, Ayíos Nikólaos (7am–midnight); Odós Kondiláki, Sitiá; and Odós Koráka, Ierápetra.

Area Codes:

Iráklio:	081
Khaniá:	0821
Réthimnon:	0831
Ayíos Nikólaos:	0841
Sitiá:	0843
Ierápetra:	0842

Essential phrases

Yásoo	Hello
Kalí méra	Good morning
Kalí spéra	Good evening
Kalí níkhta	Good night
Adío	Good-bye
Né	Yes
Óhi	No
Parakaló	Please
Efharistó	Thank you
Póso káni?	How much?
Poú eené ...?	Where is...?
Parakaló, o drómos ya...?	Please can you tell me the way to...?
Meh léne ...	My name is...
Katalavéno	I don't understand
Iss-iyían!	Cheers!
Parakaló, mípos miláte...	Do you speak...
Angliká/Yermoniká	English/German/
Galiká/Olanthiká	French/Dutch
Ispaniká	Spanish?
Voíthia!	Help!

Keeping abreast of the news

Remember to take adequate supplies of water with you

Crime

Crete is a conservative, tight-knit society with strong moral standards, and there is very little crime on the island. Any perpetrator is much more likely to be a fellow-tourist than a Cretan. Almost all crime is restricted to petty pilfering from tents, hotel rooms and unlocked cars, so the usual precautions with regard to locking doors, and keeping tempting valuables out of sight, should ensure you a trouble-free stay. Lost property is almost certain to be where you left it, or being looked after by someone nearby. This especially applies to children. If you are really worried, contact the Tourist Police.

If you lose your passport, driver's licence or other important documents, tell the police as soon as possible, and also your consulate. If you will be making an insurance claim for stolen or lost property, be sure to ask for and keep a copy of any police report.

Be aware that drug dealers, even of small amounts, could face life imprisonment. The younger the person supplied with drugs, the stiffer the penalty for the supplier. People found in possession of small amounts for personal use can be jailed for a year. This applies to soft as well as hard drugs.

Sexual harassment is generally restricted to enthusiastic observation, but if you are really pestered, say '*Parátame!*' ('Go away!') as commandingly as you feel necessary.

Nude bathing, while technically punishable by a fine or even a short jail sentence, is not hotly pursued. There are many nudist beaches on Crete's coasts, usually remote from tourist centres. But you will certainly offend many Cretans if you appear before them only in Mother Nature's garb on a public beach.

Police

The regular police wear green uniforms, and deal, usually politely, with normal police business. The tourist police wear grey uniforms, which display national flags indicating the languages the wearer speaks. Their job is to advise visitors.

Consulates

Germany, 7 Odós Zografoú, Iráklio. tel: 081–226288;64 Odós Daskaloyiánni , Khaniá, tel: 0821–57944.
Great Britain, 16 Odós Papalexándrou, Iráklio, tel: 081–224012.
Netherlands, 23 Odós 25 Avgoústou, Iráklio, tel: 081–246202.
Norway, 24 Platía Agíos Dimítrou, Iráklio, tel: 081–220536.

Emergency telephone numbers

General emergency	100
First aid/ambulance	166
Police	171
Tourist Police	104
Breakdown	154

(157 if affiliated to ELPA)

Accidents and trouble

Keep as calm as possible; stay at the scene; don't make a statement unless you are sure that it is to a fluent speaker of your native tongue; telephone the tourist police or the regular police, depending on the circumstances. Be prepared to be detained for up to 24 hours, and make sure you contact your consulate.

Health

The only vital precautions to take are against sunburn, which can strike even on windy, cloudy days. Bring a sun hat, sun cream, dark glasses and after-sun lotion. Drink plenty of liquid at all times, particularly during a walk.

Crete has one variety of poisonous snake, one kind of poisonous spider and a population of scorpions. All three shun the limelight, and you are most unlikely to see any of them. Dogs bark a lot but rarely bite, and rabies has not been recorded. A stick deals with dogs; insect repellent with mosquitoes.

All tap and spring water is drinkable. Check that your polio and typhoid immunity is up to date, but vaccinations are not absolutely necessary.

Doctors and pharmacies

All big towns have English-speaking doctors. Pharmacies (*farmakí*) display a red, blue or green cross and have staff skilled in diagnosis and remedy. A 24-hour rota operates, details of which will be found on the pharmacy door.

Hospitals

There are hospitals at Iráklio, Khaniá, Réthimnon, Ayíos Nikólaos, Sitiá and Ierápetra.

There is very basic free care for EC nationals, but it is safer to have comprehensive health insurance which includes an immediate flight home.

Don't forget to wear sufficient skin protection to cope with the strength of the Mediterranean sun

Other information

Accommodation
For camping, youth hostelling and self-catering holidays between June and September, prior booking is essential. Out of season you may well strike an excellent bargain on the spot.

Camping

The main camp sites are at Iráklio, Ierápetra, Mália, Khersónisos, Mátala, Ayía Galíni and Palaiókhora. Others are scattered around the coast. Full details can be obtained from the Association of Greek Camping, 102 Solonos Street, 10680 Athens, Greece (tel: 010 30 1-3621560). Facilities are generally on the unadorned side, but the sites are clean and all basic requirements are present, usually along with a shop or taverna.

Camping on unofficial sites is technically forbidden and recently there have been attempts to tighten up this regulation, owing to the selfishness of a few campers who have fouled beaches and left litter behind. However, as with most aspects of life on Crete, what the official eye does not see the official heart does not grieve over. There are many wonderful beaches, headlands and flowery plateaux in Crete, far from prying eyes. The essentials are to ask permission at the nearest taverna, as they may well let you camp on their land if you eat your meals with them, and to clear up scrupulously after yourself.

Youth hostels

Youth hostelling is a good way to stay in Crete on the cheap. There are hostels in Iráklio at 5 Vironos between the bus station and Odós 25 Avgoústou, tel: 081-286281; at 33 Odós Drakoniánou, Khaniá, tel: 0821–53565; at Odós Pavloú Vlastoú, Réthimnon, tel: 0831-22848; at 3 Stratigoú Kóraka, Ayíos Nikólaos, tel: 0841–22823; on the former main Iráklio road at Mália, tel: 0897–31555; in the village centre at Mírthios, tel: 0832–31202; on the western edge of the village of Plakias, tel: 0832–31306; and at 4 Odós Therísou, Sitiá, tel: 0843-22693. For information contact the Greek Youth Hostel Association, 4 Odós Dragatsianoú, Athens, Greece (tel: 010 30 1-3234107/3237590).

Self-catering

There has recently been a great upsurge in provision for self-catering holidays. Villas and apartments can be found in all the main visitor centres, and in many other towns and villages. Local tourist information offices will have details. The travel pages of most major European newspapers carry advertisements for the large number of companies offering self-catering accommodation in Crete as well as private ads. NTOG offices in European cities can also help with suggestions and addresses.

Camping on Elafonísi beach

CONVERSION CHARTS

FROM	TO	MULTIPLY BY
Inches	Centimetres	2.54
Centimetres	Inches	0.3937
Feet	Metres	0.3048
Metres	Feet	3.2810
Yards	Metres	0.9144
Metres	Yards	1.0940
Miles	Kilometres	1.6090
Kilometres	Miles	0.6214
Acres	Hectares	0.4047
Hectares	Acres	2.4710
Gallons	Litres	4.5460
Litres	Gallons	0.2200
Ounces	Grams	28.35
Grams	Ounces	0.0353
Pounds	Grams	453.6
Grams	Pounds	0.0022
Pounds	Kilograms	0.4536
Kilograms	Pounds	2.205
Tons	Tonnes	1.0160
Tonnes	Tons	0.9842

MEN'S SUITS

UK	36	38	40	42	44	46	48
Rest of Europe	46	48	50	52	54	56	58
US	36	38	40	42	44	46	48

DRESS SIZES

UK	8	10	12	14	16	18
France	36	38	40	42	44	46
Italy	38	40	42	44	46	48
Rest of Europe	34	36	38	40	42	44
US	6	8	10	12	14	16

MEN'S SHIRTS

UK	14	14.5	15	15.5	16	16.5	17
Rest of Europe	36	37	38	39/40	41	42	43
US	14	14.5	15	15.5	16	16.5	17

MEN'S SHOES

UK	7	7.5	8.5	9.5	10.5	11
Rest of Europe	41	42	43	44	45	46
US	8	8.5	9.5	10.5	11.5	12

WOMEN'S SHOES

UK	4.5	5	5.5	6	6.5	7
Rest of Europe	38	38	39	39	40	41
US	6	6.5	7	7.5	8	8.5

Visitors with disabilities

Cretans are interested in other people and ready to help when needed, but the island is very short on provision for disabled people, islanders and visitors alike. You will find offices on upper floors, steps and staircases, hard-to-use lavatories and so on. Out and about in town, the pavements are often cracked, or non-existent, or blocked by parked vehicles, and cobblestones are a constant hazard. Zebra crossings are ignored by drivers. In the countryside roads are often steep and rough; paths are always lumpy with stones.

However, disabled visitors report that Crete can offer very enjoyable holidays, provided that as much as possible is planned before you arrive. This is the key to a successful trip, and is especially important in an island where not much information is available, even to native disabled people. Contact your own home country organisation. They will have information on holidays catering specifically for disabled people, and, if you prefer to explore independently, they may be able to put you in touch with someone who has first-hand experience of Crete and its challenges.

Among your other preparations, you will need to take all medicines and the equipment you require, a wheelchair servicing kit, and a thick skin – the more rural your wandering, the more penetrating the stares and murmurings. This is not rudeness, merely curiosity.

A Greek organisation recommended for being helpful is Mobility International Hellas, Egnatía 101, 8th Floor, Thessaloníki, GR54635, Greece, tel: 010 30 31–234489/206667.

Electricity

Electricity on Crete is at 220 volts A.C. Two-pin plugs are used, so bring an adaptor for three-pin appliances.

Etiquette and local customs

Greetings in Greek are always received with pleasure, and mark you out as someone who has taken some trouble. In Crete, courtesy breeds courtesy. A handshake on meeting and saying goodbye is good form, but do not wave your palm at a Cretan, as this can be taken as an insult.

Speak when entering a *kafeníon* or passing a seated person. It is good manners for the person on the move to start the exchange. *'Kalí méra'* will do very well.

You will not be permitted to pay back hospitality by buying your round. All that is required from you is a smile and some praise of Crete and your entertainment, in sign language if necessary. To be offered hospitality with a family is an honour. Taking them a present is acceptable if you are going to have a meal. If the woman of the house seems to be doing all the work and feeding everyone but herself, she is! Accept the custom, and eat what you are offered, individually or from a common dish.

Always ask permission before photographing people. Resentment can be caused by insensitive and patronising photographers.

Tipping is acceptable. Give a few drachmae to a taxi driver, 10 to 15 per cent at a restaurant, and what you judge for a hotel chambermaid.

Everyone displays curiosity, so answer back and be nosy yourself!

Opening times

EOT tourist offices are open Monday to Friday, 8am–2pm, 5pm–8pm; Saturday and Sunday, 8–2; high season 8am–10pm.

Post offices open Monday to Friday, 8–2, most places; 8–7, main towns and resorts. Mobile post offices in large resorts may be open later.

Banks open Monday to Thursday, 8–2, Fri 8–1:30. In high season one bank also opens 5pm–7pm, and on Saturdays, for changing money in Iráklio, Khaniá, Réthimnon and Ayíos Nikólaos.

OTE telephone offices mostly open 7:30am–10pm; 24-hour in Iráklio and Khaniá.

Shop hours vary widely according to place, season and inclination of the owner. Officially they are open Monday, Wednesday and Saturday, 8–2:30, and Tuesday, Thursday and Friday 8–2, 5:30–8. In high season, many resort shops are open all week to very late hours. Pavement kiosks are also often open from dawn to midnight.

Restaurants are open from 1–3 and from 8pm to the early hours.

Kafenía are open from when you arrive to when you depart.

Photography

All kinds of modern films are available on Crete. However, films brought from home will be cheaper and probably in better condition than those bought on the island. Unless you are very impatient to see your photographs, save processing until you get home. Again, it will probably be cheaper and better. You can hire video equipment in the bigger of the north coast resorts, but at a hefty price.

Photography is not permitted in churches, nor in the vicinity of the naval base at Soúdha, nor around the Síderos Peninsula in the northeast, site of another base. Large notices remind you of this. Most museums permit photography but charge a fee, which doubles or trebles if you use a tripod. Some exhibits may be off-limits to photographers, but these will be clearly labelled. Archaeological sites may or may not charge.

Places of worship

Almost all places of worship on Crete are Greek Orthodox. Anyone is welcome to attend a service, but be aware that in rural districts women with flimsy clothing, shorts or short skirts will undoubtedly offend local worshippers. If you have not attended a Greek Orthodox ceremony before, you are in for a treat, especially during the spectacular, often chaotic, celebrations around Easter time (see pages 16–17).

There are Roman Catholic masses on Saturday and Sunday, in the cathedrals at Iráklio, Khaniá, Réthimnon and Ayíos Nikólaos. No Nonconformist or Jewish services of worship are held.

Toilets *(toualéta)*

Public lavatories are usually sited in or near town parks or *platía*. These can be dark and smelly, of the big-drop variety, or, more rarely, a pleasant and reasonably modern surprise. Bring your own lavatory paper. *Kafenía*, restaurants, tavernas, and bus stations usually have facilities. The hotels almost invariably have a better standard, and all the better class hotels are en suite. A golden rule is to use the hotel lavatories before setting out for the day.

Crete's ageing plumbing system cannot cope with the demands made on it, especially in the high season. Conquer instinct and put lavatory paper, once you have used it, in the bin provided. Do not flush it down the lavatory pan unless you are of the Noah persuasion.

Women travellers and travelling alone

Crete is, on the whole, an easy place for women to travel around alone. Provided that you do not behave in a manner which invites attention, you will be treated with respect. There will always be the odd pushy character about, but you are more likely to meet with curiosity and concern. It is not usual for Cretan women to be unattached, either to their family or husband, so questions will be asked about why you are not married or where your children are. It is also unlikely that you will be allowed to eat alone in a local restaurant – you will be invited to join the family eating at the next table, and the questions will start all over again…

Topless sunbathing is widespread, but if you are alone it will be seen as an indication that you are somehow available and will, unfortunately, attract the beach wolves. It is best not to strip off unless you are happy with the company. Similarly, wearing very short shorts, or going sleeveless into churches, can cause tutting, particularly from the local women. Priests too will be dismissive; the men just stare. So the advice is to be aware of the cultural differences, and to respect Cretan values.

Colourful tie-dye and batik wraps

Tourist offices

The National Tourist Organisation of Greece (NTOG, known locally as EOT – *'áy-ot'*) has several offices in Crete, all overworked during the high season, and all helpful once your turn comes. They can arrange guides, tours and accommodation, provide information, brochures, maps and timetables, let you know what is going on in the way of festivals, celebrations and events. Make the EOT office your first port of call when arriving in a new town. There are several municipal offices, too, which are also well worth visiting. For example, there is one at 22 Odós Sifáka in Khaniá (tel: 0821–59990).

NTOG (EOT) offices in Crete: at the airports; at 1 Xanthoudídou Street, Platía Eleftherías (opposite the Archaeological Museum), Iráklio, tel: 081–228225/244462. 40 Kriári Street, Khaniá, tel: 0821–92943/92624. Avenue Eleftherios Venizélos (on the sea front east of the harbour), Réthimnon, tel: 0831–29148. 20 Aktí I Koundoúrou (by the bridge between Lake Voulisméni and the harbour), Ayíos Nikólaos, tel: 0841–22357. Platía Iróon Polytéchnichou, Sitiá, tel: 0843–24955. In high season, there is a mobile information office beside Hotel Ítanos on Platía Venizélos. Platía Kanoupáki, on the waterfront at Ierápetra, tel: 0842–28721.

There are NTOG offices overseas in: Athens, Amsterdam, the USA, the Republic of Ireland, Canada, Australia, New Zealand, Paris, Rome, Germany, Madrid, Copenhagen, Norway, Sweden, and in London at 4 Conduit Street, W1R 0DJ, tel: 0171–734 5997).

Khaniá's municipal tourist office

HOTELS AND RESTAURANTS

ACCOMMODATION

Hotels on Crete are classified into six categories: L (luxury), then A down to E. Luxury means what it says: international-style cossetting that is usually efficient, extremely comfortable and about as exciting and authentically Cretan as a milk pudding. Increasing numbers of such hotels are being built along the north coast holiday strip above private beaches. Prices could be five or six times as much as a decent D class hotel.

A and B hotels will be expensive, but not excessively so by general European standards, and have a little more character to them. They are often block-booked by tour operators, so previous booking is essential between July and September. C class probably represent the best vaue for money. These are, typically, solid family-run concerns, clean and friendly, with en suite accommodation, often with a restaurant attached to the hotel: D and E class can vary from basic but clean to pretty grim, but it is rare to find really unpleasant accommodation.

Most hotels will ask for your passport and keep it at least overnight. Prices for categories A to E are fixed by the National Tourist Organisation of Greece, who publish a yearly list of all L to C grade hotels in Crete, and another showing the current prices of each category.

Private rooms are classified from A to C. A class may often be a distinct cut above a moderate C class hotel, though only half the price. Private rooms are in private houses, all checked by the Tourist Organisation for cleanliness and comfort if they carry a classificaion. You may have to pay for a hot shower.

There are thousands of villas and furnished apartments in Crete which are not under the aegis of the Tourist Organisation. Travel agents will book you into these, but inevitably you take a little more pot luck.

General rules are always to inspect before you accept; ask to see another type or price of room if you do not like what you are offered; book several months ahead for July and August; out of season, bargain for reductions at both rooms and hotels.

If you are stuck without accommodation, ask at the nearest taverna or kafeníon; a little persistence will almost invariably procure you some sort of shelter for the night.

Since standards can vary within Greek Tourist Organisation categories, and these categories are revised year to year, a rough price guide is used below: £££ expensive; ££ moderate; £ inexpensive.

IRÁKLIO

The code for Iráklio is 081

Astoria (£££), Platía Elefthérias (tel: 229002). City centre location belies the quiet comfort of this well-appointed and long-established hotel. Service is friendly and very helpful, the hotel has recently been refurbished, and the social heart of Iráklio is right on the doorstep.

Iríni (££), 4 Odós Idomíneos (tel: 229703/226561). Modern and comfortable hotel at the northern end of the street that parallels Platiá Elefthérias and Odós Xanthoudídou. EOT office and Archaeological Museum just five minutes walk from this quiet backwater in the centre of the city.

Mediterranean (££), Platía Daskaloyiánnis (tel: 289331). Pleasant, solid, comfortable and welcoming. On a nice shady square just off the western edge of Platía Elefthérias, out of the main evening clamour but within a few minutes of the action and lots of eating places.

Xénia (£££), Sophoklís Venizélos (tel: 284000). A celebrated Iráklio hotel offering excellent service. Slightly staid, but always reliable. Just across the road from the Historical Museum and a little west of the harbour, a 10-minute stroll from Platía Elefthérias.

Youth Hostels (£). 5 Odós Víronos, just north of El Greco Park (tel: 286281), family-run; at 24 Odós Chándakos (tel: 280858). Both are clean and pleasant, and just a few minutes from the centre.

IRÁKLIO REGION

Arkhánes

Dias (££) (tel: 081–751810). A decent, quiet and friendly hotel in this nice, ordinary town. Free from tourist crowds, celebrated wine bottled by the Minos Co-operative in the town, and plenty of good tavernas and *kafenía* within a five minute walk.

Ayía Pelayía

15km northwest of Iráklio

Capsis Beach (£££) (tel: 081–811112). The place to come for a few nights of complete luxury. Everything you could expect or want from a very luxurious hotel, in a superb position overlooking a secluded bay to one side of this quite stylish small resort.

Limín Khersonísos

26km east of Iráklio

Pela Maria (££) (tel: 0897–22195). A small, clean and friendly family-run hotel near the beach, convenient for the fun of the resort but away from the loudest noise. Local people use the bar which is a good sign.

Mátala

Bamboo Sands (££) (tel: 0892–42370). Not the cheapest of the hotels in this lively south coast resort, but not the rowdiest either, and as decent as any.

Moirés

Little Inn (££) at Kókkinos Pírgos, 3km northwest of Timbáki (tel: 0892–52455). A good base for exploring Mesarás if you can't face the daunting shabbiness of Timbáki. Accommodation in plain but pleasant cubicles around an open-air swimming pool. Restaurant across the road just above the rather desolate beach.

Tsoútsouros

Ayíos Yióryios (££) (tel: 0895–51678). An agreeable place to hole up on this lonely corner of the coast. The hotel is longer-established than most on Tsoútsouros's strip of beach. But if development gets properly under way, the atmosphere may change.

Zarós

Idi (££) (tel: 0894–31302). Stunning views of Psiloritis from this comfortable modern hotel set among trees above Záros village. Swimming pool, own taverna above a millstream, Cretan music and dancing evenings, hardworking and obliging owners. A good base for Psiloritis excursions.

AYÍOS NIKÓLAOS

The code for Ayíos Nikólaos is 0841

Acratos (££), Odós 28 Októbriou (tel: 22721). Pleasant hotel in very central position, overlooking Lake Voulisméni. Clean and plain, but reliable.

Apollon (££) 9 Odós Minóos (tel: 23023). Clean and quiet; just south of Platía.

Hotel du Lac (££), Odós 28 Októbriou (tel: 22711). A decent hotel with excellent views over Lake Voulisméni. Front rooms on Odós 28 Októbriou can be noisy. Very conveniently placed in central Ayíos Nikólaos.

Minós (£££), follow Odós Filéllinon southwest from Lake Voulisméni. Not cheap, but its position, just ten minutes from the waterfront, is a recommendation if you do not want noise at night.

Minos Beach (£££), approximately 3km north of Ayíos Nikólaos (tel: 22345). A beautiful position on a private beach owned by the hotel. This is probably the place to spend an unruffled few days if money is not an issue, since the Minos Beach is just about as luxurious and exclusive as a Cretan hotel can get.

Mirabéllo (£££), approximately 4km north of Ayíos Nikólaos (tel: 28400/5). Another extremely luxurious and well-appointed hotel, spread over a cove and headland. Every kind of facility from a nightclub to sailboarding, outdoor and indoor pools with supervised games for children. Expensive, but not monstrously so considering the range of enticements on offer.

Pension Perla (£), 4 Odós Salamínos (tel: 23379). Pleasantly situated on the seafront promenade a little north of the harbour. One of the quieter pensions, clean and efficiently-managed.

AYÍOS NIKÓLAOS REGION

Ammoudára

1.5km south of Ayíos Nikólaos

Pension Polydóros (£) (tel: 0841–22623). A very friendly and relaxed pension not far from a good beach at Ammoudára. Well looked after and clean. Quieter location than Ayíos Nikólaos, but still handy for the town.

Arví

Ariadne (££) (tel: 0895–31200). The Ariadne looks on to the tamarisk-fringed beach, with hills rising behind and a great gorge just to the east. Superb, quiet location. A straightforward, pleasant, no-frills hotel in a holiday spot still mostly used by locals.

Eloúndha

Eloúndha Beach (£££) (tel: 0841–41812). One of Crete's most luxurious hotels. Accommodation either in hotel building or in bungalows on the private beach. A good place to splash out for an extravagant few nights, with every service and facility you would expect at top prices.

Keratókambos

Ve Rooms (£). Cook your own food and bring your own wine, or eat and drink cheaply at the couple of tavernas. This is a good place to base yourself for some lazy days in this beautifully quiet and un-hurried little hamlet where the bumpy road descends to the coast.

Kritsá

Pension Argýrou (£) (tel: 0841–51174). On the edge of the big, bustling and hospitable mountain village of Kritsá. Well-kept, clean rooms. Breakfast terrace under orange trees, and friendly owner who knows everything and everyone in Kritsá.

Mália

Pension Grammatikákis (££) (tel: 0897–31366). An upmarket pension on a good sandy beach with a view to the islets offshore. Comfortable and accommodating, with the atmosphere and salt smell of the beach.

Néapoli

Néapolis (£), 1 Odós Evangelistrias (tel: 0841–32268). An inexpensive hotel with nothing special about it, but it is clean and friendly and makes a good base for exploring this unpretentious town.

Tzermiádho

Pension Kourites (££) (tel: 0844–22194). Great views from this pricey pension, across the windmill-twirling Lasíthiou plateau to the mountains. Quiet location in big village on the far side of the plain from the Dhíktaean cave. Friendly and efficient management makes it worth the extra drachmae.

SITIÁ

The code for Sitiá is 0843

Arkhontikon (££), 16 Odós Kondiláki (tel: 28172). Near the Metiháki steps leading down to the waterfront, at the end of a shady back street artery of the town. Clean and quiet, but near the nightlife bars and restaurants on the front.
Itanos (££), Platía Elefthérios Venizélos, Sitiá (tel: 22146). On the opposite corner of the main square to the Pension Denis. Same remarks apply as to noise at night, but the rooms are somewhat sprucer.
Krystal (££), 17 Odós Kapetan Sífi (tel: 22284). Halfway up the hill that leads to the upper town. Quiet location, and very friendly, if rather old-fashioned, family run. Everyone pleasant and eager to please.
Mysson (£), 82 Odós Myssónos (tel: 22304). Second on the left up Odós Kapetan Sífi. Accommodating owner. A fair choice as a money-saver, plain but clean.
Pension Denis (££), 60 Platía Elefthérios Venizélos (tel: 28356). Just north of the *platía* and right behind the most popular restaurants and bars. Well-kept establishment in the midst of an evening atmosphere either lively or rowdy, according to your point of view.
Youth Hostel (£), 4 Odós Therísou (tel: 22693). A little way out of town along the Iráklio road. Friendly and lively; compares well with Crete's other youth hostels.

SITIÁ REGION

Ierápetra

El Greco (££), 42 Odós M Kothri, on the promenade (tel: 0842–28471/28472). Highly recommended seafront hotel, family owned and run. Exceptionally helpful and friendly staff, pleasant décor, comfortable. Own restaurant on the promenade.
Lygia (££), Odós Kyrva/Platía Kanoupáki (tel: 0842–28881). Absolutely central, right on the waterfront at start of promenade. Moderately priced, cheerful and decent.

Koutsounári

7km east of Ierápetra
Koutsounari Traditional Cottages (£££) (tel: 0842–61291). Beautifully set up reconstructions of traditional Cretan homes with bed slabs, furnishings, beams and gardens. Self-catering, or use of Koutsounari's own taverna. Run by owners of Eloúnda Beach, with same success. An unusual option, and a change from customary hotel accommodation.

Kató Khório

Istron Bay (£££), Ístro (tel: 0841–61303). Large, expensive and luxurious. Everything you could want from a modern top hotel: superb position on cliff over sandy bay which is nominally for the use of residents only; nightclubs; shops; children's and adults' swimming pools; watersports; tennis; bars; discos; Cretan evenings.

Mókhlos

Sofía (££) (tel: 0843–94179). Unfussy hotel in a quiet position down on the Bay of Mirambéllou, with a good view out to Mókhlos Island from the seafront rooms. A pleasant base for exploring this craggy coast between Pakhiá Ámmos and Sitiá.

Palaikastro

Marina Village (££), near Angathiá on road to sea (tel: 0843–61284). A couple of kilometres east of Palaikastro in a quiet spot. A short walk down a track to the beach at Khiona.
Pension Hellas (££), on the village *platía* (tel: 0843–61240). A first-rate pension in this large, rather back-of-beyond village at the eastern tip of Crete. Clean, welcoming and comfortable.

Xerókambos

Liviko View (tel: 0843–91473), provides information on request about availability of rooms to rent in this little haven of peace and quiet on the easternmost coast, above a wonderful sandy beach where few venture.

Zákros

Pension Poseidon (£), Káto Zákros (tel: 0843–93385/93316). Plain, inexpensive rooms overlooking the beach of this beautifully sited and unfrequented single-strip hamlet below the Minoan palace.

Hotel Zákros (££), Áno Zákros (tel: 0843–93379). On the main *platía* on the way to Zákros Minoan palace. Bed and breakfast only, but good tavernas nearby. Very plain from outside, but friendly and quite comfortable.

RÉTHIMNON

The code for Réthimnon is 0831

Adele Mare (£££), Platanes (tel: 71345). This is a good, expensive international beach hotel about 4km east of Réthimnon, with its own sandy beach, apartment houses set in landscaped grounds and a big hotel building fronting the swimming pool.

Brascos (£££), 1 Odós Daskaláki (tel: 23721). A very comfortable hotel on the corner of Daskaláki and Moátsou, just inland of the old city, a two minute walk from the public gardens, ten minutes from the harbour. Not the most fashionable of locations, but quieter than many.

Réthimnon Haus (£), 1 Vinzétzos Kornárou (tel: 23923). Often recommended and rightly so. Clean and pleasant, a friendly welcome, and conveniently near the town centre and the harbour.

Seeblick (££), 17 Plastíra (tel: 22478). Excellent central position just north of the harbour, near enough to be in touch with all the action, far enough away to miss the worst of the noise. Clean and comfortable, and good value.

Youth Hostel (£), 41 Odós Tombázi (tel: 22848). In a street running south from the old city gate. A big, well-run and welcoming hostel, with all the basic facilities. One of Crete's best.

RÉTHIMNON REGION

Anóyia

Dimótikos Xenónas Rooms (£). Make a booking here through the tourist office. These cheap apartment rooms, with basic facilities, are situated just off the main street of this hospitable and traditional Psiloritis village.

Ayía Galíni

Acropol Rooms (£), on the western edge of the town. Excellent views, clean and decent. A good place to try your luck, but there are dozens of such rooms in the village, though not many of this standard.

Soulia (££), Elefthérios Venizélos (0832–91307). A reasonable choice out of many hotels in the village. A very central position just off the main square near the harbour where everyone gathers, day and night. Not particularly quiet, therefore, but a pleasant place and good value.

Ayíos Pávlos

Ayíos Pávlos (££). This is one of those Cretan secrets, trembling on the brink of development. For the moment the hotel and apartments look out on a perfect, pristine little bay.

Balí

Balí Beach (£££) (tel: 0834–94210. The part-pebble, part-sand beach of Balí is 32km east of Réthimnon, overlooked by this comfortable and modern hotel: All facilities, including a private stretch of beach, and prices that compare favourably with other upmarket hotels.

Georgióupoli

Gorgona (££) (tel: 0825–22378). On the beach but away from the centre and noise, this is a clean and comfortable hotel, with its own good taverna fronting the sea.

Pánormo

Pánormo Beach (££) (tel: 0834–51321). The hotel is 23km east of Réthimnon, on a sheltered and sandy cove tucked below the new road. Easy-paced and comfortable, with a good view over the village and bay. Especially enjoyable early or late season.

Plakiás

Lamon (££) (tel: 0832–31205). Set a little way up the road from the beach at this fast-growing south coast resort west of Ayía Galíni. Quieter location, though not as picturesque, as the waterfront. A very clean, pleasant, moderately priced hotel.

Spíli

Green (££) (tel: 0832–22225). The Green Hotel, like this mountain village, is a delight. Extremely well-run and friendly bed and breakfast place, clean and comfortable, and furnished with eccentric reading matter. An excellent base for exploring the mountains and coasts of the Kédros range.

KHANIÁ

The code for Khaniá is 0821

Doma (£££), 124 Elefthérios Venizélos (tel: 51772/3). This handsome old building on the edge of the elegant Khalépa quarter to the east of Khaniá has in previous incarnations housed the

British Consulate, the Austrian Embassy and the wartime German *kommandantur*. Everything at the Doma is unfussily spot-on.

El Greco (££), 49 Odós Theotokópoulou (tel: 90432). Tucked away just inland of the waterfront on atmospheric Theotokópoulou Street. An older hotel with wrought-iron Turkish balconies, a roof garden and central access to the restaurants and clubs in the Topanás quarter of the old town. A contrast to the magnetically popular harbour front.

Pension Theréza (£), 8 Odós Angelou (tel: 92798). An up-market pension in a charming narrow old street. Superb view over the town and harbour from the terrace which is on the roof. Well-appointed, friendly and clean. A real find, which is becoming increasingly, and deservedly, popular.

Piraeus (£), 10 Odós Zambelíou (tel: 94665). This is a cheap, cheerful and atmospherically rather shabby hotel. The basic rooms are clean enough, and Zambelíou is the characterful artery of the Evréika quarter. Provided you are aware of what you are getting, the Piraeus makes a decent enough night stop.

Porto Veneziano (£££), Aktíi Enoseos Palaio Limani (tel: 59311/3). An excellent position right next to the Venetian *arsenali* at the eastern end of the inner harbour, with views from the balconied rooms, over fishing boats to the lights and bustle of the waterfront, but little of the noise.

KHANIÁ REGION

Kalíves

Koralli (££) (tel: 0825–31356). Apartments in an excellent quiet location at the southern end of Soúdha Bay. Just outside the village, and right above the sandy beach.

Kastélli Kissámou

Castelli (££), on the town square (tel: 0822–22140). If you are going to stay and enjoy the self-contained, busy atmosphere of this western town, the Castelli Hotel puts you right at the heart of the action. Good value, clean accommodation at better prices than most coastal towns.

Kolimbári

Rose-Marie (££) (tel: 0824–21220). Recently upgraded, but still no frills. A pleasant place to stay in this uncrowded seaside village at the foot of the Rodhopoú peninsula, with a wonderful view north and out over the Gulf of Khaniá.

Loutró

Porto Loutró (££). Call the Blue House Restaurant in Loutró (tel: 0825–91127) and ask to be connected to the hotel. Wonderful central position in the curve of houses, and as clean and fresh as you could wish, though by no means *grande luxe*.

Máleme

Máleme Chandris (£££) (tel: 0821–61221). This hotel is expensive and big, but has everything laid on for you: sea views over flower gardens and own beach, swimming pool, children's activities, Cretan dancing displays, sports.

Palaiókhora

Pension Lissos (££) (tel: 0823–41266). A better-class pension. On the main street, which means it can be lively at night.

Rooms (£), on the right as you enter town (tel: 0823–41589/41250). Very basic but clean rooms above the Palaiókhora Travel Agency and garage, run by Markos and Maria Xenákis.

Sfakiá

Pension Sofia (£), in the main town street parallel to the waterfront. Very clean and pleasant rooms, near to the practicalities and only a step away from the harbour eating places, the ferry boats and buses.

Vritomartis (£££), at Komitádhes, 3km east of Sfakiá (tel: 0825–91277). Efficient, plush hotel, much frequented by German visitors. Serve-yourself meals, chalet accommodation, own section of beach, swimming pool, acres of cool marble, pleasant staff.

Xenia (££), on the west side of the harbour in Sfakiá (0825–91206). A smallish hotel, one of the string of Xenia hotels established by the government. The usual good standard of cleanliness and comfort, and a handy position a little away from the waterfront with a good view up the town and over the harbour.

Soúyia

Pikilassos (££) (tel: 0823–51242). A comfortable and welcoming hotel, set back a little from the front in a quieter position. A pleasant atmosphere and its own good taverna. Worth paying a little extra for.

RESTAURANTS

The advent of mass tourism has seen both a huge increase in the number of places to eat out in Crete, and a separation into tourist restaurants and places where the locals go. Tourist restaurants offer roughly the same moderate-to-expensive prices and roughly the same Greek and international dishes from end to end of the island. Local restaurants are often a little cheaper, less attention is given to décor, and there is a more characterful approach to the cooking.

All the Big Four towns – Iráklio, Khaniá, Réthimnon and Ayíos Nikólaos – have expensive restaurants offering international cuisine which are often attached to the L, A and B class hotels. These can be excellent, or pretentious. Tourist restaurants often have coloured photographs of the dishes on offer displayed outside, and multilingual menus. You cannot really go wrong in these places, but after a while the unadventurous approach can pall. The local restaurants will be found up side streets, away from popular areas such as the harbour. Ask the hotel receptionist or owner where they would choose if they were going out to eat good Cretan food. Or assess the Cretan:tourist ratio of customers. These restaurants, like tavernas, will be only too happy to show you the dish of the day in the kitchen.

The good, plain tavernas are often a better bet than any of the foregoing if you are after a characterful, inexpensive meal of local cooking, cheerfully served with strong local wine from the barrel. There is at least one in all but the tiniest villages and they are always family-run. A *psarótaverna* specialises in fish dishes. Fish is often surprisingly expensive for an island so dependent on the sea for a living. An *ouzéri* is a small version of a taverna, often offering an astonishingly varied *mezédes* or hors d'oeuvres in lieu of a formal meal. And the *souvláki* stall, selling takeaway kebabs of meat or fish, is always a good cheap way to fill up the empty corners. Fast food restaurant chains selling burgers, fried chicken and pizzas can nowadays be found in all the main towns.

The following are widely available and reliable:
Tzatzíki: yoghurt, garlic and cucumber salad
Horiátiki saláta: Greek salad, almost a meal in itself, with *féta* cheese, red or green pepper, tomato, onion, olives, cucumber
Orektiká: mixed hors-d'oeuvres
Xifías: swordfish
Barboúni: red mullet
Bouréki: pie with potatoes, courgettes and cheese
Dolmádes: vine leaves stuffed with rice, meat and herbs
Kalamáres: squid fried in batter
Kleftídes: spiced meat balls
Kleftíko: lamb hotpot
Loukánika: spicy sausages
Paidhákia: lamb chops
Souvláki: kebabs of lamb, pork or fish
Stifádo: a spicy meat stew

IRÁKLIO

Áplo (£) Odós Milátou, in a narrow street off Odós Idomíneos and parallel with Odós Daidálos. This is the archetypal taverna, packed with young locals late at night, often loud with laughter, frequently with live music and singing on the tiny stage. Very few foreign visitors seem to find their way to this haven in the heart of the city.

Faros (££) 12 Odos Meteórou. Good fish restaurant, highly recommended around the town. Serves freshly caught local fish in a variety of styles, not all fried.

Giovanni's (££), Odós Kórai. Justly popular, which also accounts for slow service. Nice dark panelled interior, or eat outdoors on Odós Kórai's paved roadway. Imaginative cooking with touches of sophistication. Try their mouth-tingling *stifádo*. Talkative owner with excellent English.

Goody's (£), Odós Psaromílingou, parallel with Odós Chándakos, near the top of Market Street. A fast-food joint selling Greek food that locals will eat.

Kiriákos (£££), 45 Odós Dimokratías, just outside city walls to the southeast. Knowledgeable Irákliots come here to appreciate well-cooked *stifádo*, stuffed vine leaves, and cabbage in egg and lemon sauce, along with a characterful house red wine.

Klimátaria (££), Odós Daidálos. One of a number of restaurants along this pedestrian lane which connects Platía Elefthérias and Platía Venizélos. The place most frequented by Cretans on this very touristy road.

Ippokámpos (£), just west of the Venetian harbour. This is a highly recommended *ouzéri*.

Loúkoulos (£££), Odós Kórai. Very popular with a younger and better-heeled clientèle. Adventurous Italian cooking with a touch of Cretan character. Considered to be a smart place to see and be seen eating.

Mr Burger's (£), Odós Dimokratías. Outside the city walls to the south. The name describes the unexciting fare, but this is a place young Cretans like to hang out, so it becomes lively.

Ouzéri (£) on south side of Platía Daskaloyiánnis. Shaded tables on the pavement. Simple menu, but enormously varied *orektiká* (hors-d'oeuvres),

which are the best bet and make a complete meal in themselves. Good village wine, too.
Psária (££) at bottom of Odós 25 Avgoústou. Popular with locals and tourists alike for its fish specialities, but the real attraction is the wonderful view over the *voltá* strollers to the Venetian fort, and the fishing boats in the harbour.

IRÁKLIO REGION
Arkhánes
Snackbar Myriophytó (£), on the *platía* at the southern end of the village. Friendly owners serve unexceptional but well-cooked food on a very pleasant, leafy terrace overlooking the square. Dark red local wine by the carafe is the thing to drink here, and everywhere in Arkhánes. Key to superb frescoed church of Mikhaíl Arkhángelos kept here.

Kaloí Liménes
Panorama (£), on the beach. Does the usual taverna food well. Their *kalamáres* and other fish dishes have the sauce of a tranquil view out to the islets offshore (keep your eyes off the oil tanks). Out of season this is a notably peaceful place to eat.

Kapetanianá
Kafeníon (£). The *kafeníon* in this very remote Asteroúsia mountain village would not by itself be worth braving the bad dirt road from the Mesarás plain. But after your walk up Mount Kófinas, have at least a cup of coffee here. This is an entirely unmodernised, purely local village café where everyone stares their fill and exclaims with astonishment if you try out your Greek. These places are diminishing in number year by year, so enjoy this one while you can.

Limín Khersonísos
Taverna Pharos (££) stands on the headland to the northwest of the resort's crowded waterfront. The food, perfectly good though it is, takes second place to the wonderful view over the bay and evening lights.

Timbáki
The *kafenía* around the little *platía* just off the main street are worth lingering at for a quick snack and long *rakí*. None is especially recommended over any other. This is the most pleasant spot to eat or drink in this uncompromisingly non-tourist town.

Vóroi
Evangelina's Taverna (££). This taverna has a good reputation with discerning travellers for excellently cooked and varied menu of local food, good village wine and a friendly welcome. This is all on offer in a very picturesque small village just above the Mesarás plain on the hill road to Kamáres.

AYÍOS NIKÓLAOS
Ariadne (£££), Akti I Koundoúrou. This relatively expensive restaurant is on the east side of the harbour, one of the best in a scrum of eating places here. Justly popular, it is run by a friendly family whose cooking raises the fairly plain menu above the ordinary. Eat later rather than earlier to enjoy the atmosphere.
Harris (££), on the harbour. Well known for its excellent cooking of fish caught the same day. A lively location, and townsfolk eat here.
Ikaros (££) 25 Akti S. Koundoúrou. A couple of hundred metres north of the harbour, looking out over the bay. Away from the tourist clamour, but still lively and good-humoured. Good local food and wine.
Itanos (££), 1 Odós Kyprou, just southeast of Platía Venizélos. Off the tourist waterfront, and none the worse for that. Pleasant sevice and welcome. Plain local food cooked well, and eaten by more locals than visitors. Excellent value if you want a real Cretan atmosphere.
Ormos (£££), is a 20-minute walk north of the habour. Classy and expensive restaurant attached to Hotel Ormos. Highly praised cuisine with Greek food only one of the options.
Synantisi (££), on the right off the Eloúndha road, 50 metres from main traffic-light crossroads on the new road on northern edge of Ayíos Nikólaos. Good food and village wine, friendly waiters and expansive cook. Surprisingly quiet position. A popular local taverna beyond the normal visitor circuit.
Trata (££), at the bottom end of Odós Sfakianáki, just above Kitroplatía beach. Another local haunt. No bargain prices, but decent food on a rooftop terrace from which you can smell and hear the sea rustling up the beach.

AYÍOS NIKÓLAOS REGION
Keratókambos
Tavernas (£). There are a number of inexpensive tavernas here, where you can eat a good unsophisticated meal of Cretan food: fried squid, meat balls, lamb *souvláki* or whatever is on offer, with local wine and *rakí*, looking through the tamarisks and over the rather shabby beach, in wonderful seclusion.

Kritsá
Billy's Café (£), to the left just off the main street as

you climb up. Clean and friendly with conversation guaranteed.
Café under the Arch (£), just below the main street as it rises through the village. Excellent *mezédes* with your *rakí* or beer. Those who risk sitting out at tables in the lane have to pick up their chairs when a car comes by. Make all your contacts and arrangements here.

Límnes
Dionysos (£), just off the new road 3km east of Néapoli. Puts on Cretan music and dancing. On a poor night this place can be overfull of coach-borne whoopee-makers. On a good night, however, it has a wonderful lively atmosphere and plenty of local involvement.

Pláka
Manolis' Taverna (££). One of a number of tavernas in this tranquil spot. Try red mullet or other fish specialities, looking out from the bamboo-shaded terrace over the sparkling bay to Spinalónga Island. 'The people, they come here to be quiet', says Manolis.

Tértsa
Tavernas (£), one on each side of the single street, looking out over the water in this heavenly, remote hamlet at the end of a rough dirt road. Local wine, food and conversation: nothing whatsoever to do with tourism or the outside world.

Tzermiádho
Kronio (£), near where you wait for the bus that circumnavigates the Lasíthiou plateau. This is a friendly place with a young owner who enjoys a chin-wag and serves good Greek coffee.

SITIÁ
Kalí Kardiá (££), on Odós Emmanuel Foundalidóu. the next street up from and parallel with Odós Vinzétzos Kornárou. Locally caught fresh fish is a big speciality here, preceded by huge and varied hors d'oeuvres and lubricated with excellent local wine.
Mixos (££), on Odós Vinzétzos Kornárou. One of Sitiá's little gems, frequented by local people, either eating the good Cretan-style food or idling over the village red wine that seems darker, stronger and more irresistible here than elsewhere in the town. A real find, and very good value.
Neromílos (£££), a couple of kilometres east of the town. Very highly recommended as much for its stunning view, looking out over the Bay of Sitiá to the Dragonádha Islands, as for its local and adventurous food flavoured with spices and garlic. This one is certainly not for the shallow-pocketed.
Zorba's (££) on the water-front. If you are going to eat 'tourist' while watching the world strut by, then Zorba's is probably the place to do it. Acceptable Greek food served by dashing waiters. Not particularly good value for money, perhaps, but it is the lively hub of Sitiá's holiday nightlife and is a good place for lunch too. Patronised from time to time by Níkos and Pédros, the piratical pelicans.

SITIÁ REGION
Ierápetra
Bee House (££) on the promenade. Does a good spicey, biting *stifádo*. Just one of a long string of reasonably priced, reliable, unremarkable seafront restaurants along here.

Napoleon the Great (££), 20 Odós Samoúliou. An excellent, local restaurant, friendly and informal, whose plain décor belies the delicious food served here. Try their fish soup – fish and soup come separately – and ask for local wine.
Ouzéri Mános (£), on the corner of Odós Samoúliou and Odós Makedonómachon, at the seaward edge of the old Turkish quarter. Cheap, cheerful and good value. Try pumpkin balls fried in breadcrumbs, accompanied by pale wine from Mésa Moulianá.

Khandrás
Kafeníon (£), on the right of the *platía* as you go south through the village. Well worth a stop. Excellent *mezédes* with very inexpensive drinks. Locals play cards, chat and snooze in the dark interior, an archetypal Cretan village café.

Palaikastro
Elena's (££), next to the tourist information office. This is a very pleasant place for lunch if you have most of the afternoon to idle over your lamb cutlets, salad and wine. Definitely long on flavour and ambience, but short on speed and formality.

Triptí
Taverna (£), at the top of the walk from Episkopí (see pages 152–3). This is the first taverna you come to on the left. Locals come up from Ierápetra and Sitiá to sit on the terrace and eat cutlets, omelettes, chips and bread, all cooked by the genial owner. Wine is poured straight from its plastic container into your glass. Free and easy – a delight.

Xerókambos
Liviko View (£). Not only provides accommodation information, but also offers good and substantial cooking at very reasonable prices.

Áno Zákros
Erotókritos (££) on the main square in Áno Zákros. A pleasant establishment where you can enjoy well-prepared local food while watching the world fail to go by.
Maestro (£), where most of the village seems to eat. Another very ordinary, decent taverna, perhaps with a slight edge as regards the cooking.

Káto Zákros
Tavernas (£). A short line of tavernas offers the usual fare of grills, *souvláki* and salads, eaten whilst overlooking the little bay.
Taverna Maria (£). The reasonable food here is salted with some man-of-the-world conversation and advice from Níkos Daskalákis, a man with his finger in many pies.

RÉTHIMNON
Evangelia (££), **Battela** (££) and the **Zanfoti Café** (£), on Platía Petiháki. This is the square round the Rimondi Fountain, the less expensive and more spicy of Réthimnon's two dining centres. There is always bustle, shouting and laughter around here, a lively place to eat out on the pavement or under an awning. The restaurants and cafés here are always busy, most of them much of a muchness.
Gorgona (£££), on the corner of Odós Papanastásiou and Sofoklí Venizélos, on the beach road going east out of town. The Gorgona is well out of earshot of the harbourside noise. A pleasantly relaxed eating place offering a pricey selection of Greek food and international cuisine. Excellent cooking. A reliable treat.
Palazzo (£££), right on the Venetian harbour. The Palazzo is one among many restaurants here, and one of the most expensive, but it is a good bet if you want to eat imaginative food cooked with a bit more than the usual flair, in one of Réthimnon's prime positions.
Sunset Taverna (££), round the far side of the *Fortétza,* facing west. An unusual location for Réthimnon, and the sunset views can be spectacular. Enjoyment is enhanced by the comparative freedom from noise. Tables above the sea, decent food and service, which can be slow, comes with a smile.
Taverna Panagos (££), on the waterfront. With an excellent view of the coloured lights reflected in the harbour. Panagos is less expensive than most of its neighbours, and does Cretan food simply and well; hence it is patronised by townsfolk as well as visitors.

Around the curve of the harbour and in the streets just inland are the **pastry shops** (£) for which Réthimnon's old town is well known. The Turkish-inspired sweetmeats of *baklavá* (pastry with honey and nuts) and *kataífi* (shredded wheat, honey, nuts) are old favourites, but you might also try creamy *bougátsa* and *galaktoboúreko.*

RÉTHIMNON REGION
Anóyia
Taverna Areth (£), half way down the main street on the left. A typical, straightforward Cretan village taverna. The woman does the cooking (cutlets, *souvláki*, big Greek salads) and dishes up, while her husband clicks his worry beads and watches TV. Flustered and friendly, this is a good place to sit back and absorb the atmosphere of Anóyia.

Apladianá
Oasis (££), facing the old road between Réthimnon and Iráklio. Savoury Cretan food served by friendly proprietress. The local wine is strong and pale. Villagers and passing drivers drop in to sit and chat. A very peaceful place to idle away an afternoon on the vine-shaded terrace.

Ayía Galíni
Onar (££), toward the lower end of Odós Taverna. For a spectacular view and a not-quite-so-spectacular meal, but still palatable enough. Try to get a rooftop table if you can. You look from your seat in the gods right over the waterfront with all its bustle, light and noise.

Georgióupoli
Arkádi (££), out on the northwestern edge of the town, beyond the Almirós River. A very good spot to enjoy an evening meal looking across to the lights of Georgióupoli sparkling along their waterfront.

Mírthios
Taverna Giórgio (£), next door to the youth hostel, and certainly not the place for a quiet candlelit dinner *á deux*. This place can be a pretty rowdy taverna, depending upon the mood of the hostellers who frequent it. But the owners are accommodating, and they know their market well. The food is plentiful,

plain, well-cooked and cheap.

KHANIÁ

Aporathra (££) just south of Odós Karaoli. A smallish taverna patronised by locals as much as by visitors, with a widely varied menu. All dishes are well cooked and served in a friendly manner.

Dino's (£££). An excellent place for well-cooked and imaginative fish dishes. If your pockets are reasonably well lined, this restaurant is in a prime position on the inner harbour near the Venetian *arsenali*, away from the noisiest part.

Karnagio (££), 8 Platía Kateháki. Right in the very heart of the Kastélli quarter, but in a quiet location set a little way back from the place where inner and outer harbours join. This restaurant has very good food, a warm atmosphere and excellent jug wine; a long-established favourite.

Lyrikia (£), down behind the inner harbour. A basic, plain taverna where Cretan musicians and singers gather with *bouzoúki, lýra* and flute to play for their own amusement and the customers' huge enjoyment.

Nikterida (£££) at Korákies, just on the neck of the Akrotíri peninsula, a short taxi ride from Khaniá. A good restaurant recommended by locals in the know, serving well prepared Cretan food as well as a more pan-Mediterranean menu. Varied selection of sophisticated and village wines. Garden with wonderful views across Soúdha Bay. Sometimes has traditional music and is used by tour companies for Cretan evenings.

Tamam (££), Odós Zambelíou. This is another justly popular place. Tall, plain interior with tables on two levels, or alternatively cramped outside on the pavement of a narrow street. Really well-cooked local food is on offer. Try their sausages, lamb stew and local wine. Street cats may wander in and out. A relaxed restaurant where your meal can be spun out for hours.

Tsedaki (£), Odós Skridlóf. A cut above the other cafés, with some excellent sweet and savoury pies and pastries.

All along Odós Sífaka there are several good **pavement cafés** (£) selling cheese and sweet pies along with the usual Greek coffee and glass of water. These all face the ruins of the ancient city walls, in one of Khaniá's quieter streets.

KHANIÁ REGION

Ayía Rouméli

Páhnes (££). This is the first restaurant you come to as you complete the Samariá Gorge walk. Maybe this explains why its food, beer and *retsina* taste so wonderful!

Kaliviáni

Kafeníon (£) just above the church. This is an absolutely archetypal *kafeníon* with old men playing cards outside, very cheap drinks and nothing at all to do but sit back and stare at the shimmering rocks of the Gramvoúsa peninsula.

Kastélli Kissámou

Castelli Taverna (££), on the ground floor of the hotel. The food is undoubtedly good and the taverna is at the very heart of town activity.

Loutró

Blue House (££). Enthusiastically recommended for its well-cooked fare and pleasant service. And its good view over the peerless harbour.

Maláxa

Ioannis's Taverna (£), in the centre of this little village in the hills high above Khaniá. This really is a gem. There is a visitor's book with understandably fond inscriptions from all over the world, and it offers good unfussy Cretan food, such as spicy sausage, eggs, salad, bread, wine and home-brewed *rakí*. A delightful cheap eating place with a spectacular night view over the lights of Khaniá. Well worth seeking out.

Palaiókhora

Dionysos (££), on the main street. You are welcomed into the kitchen to inspect the day's choice of dishes. Try their excellent pork *stifádo* with creamed aubergine salad. You can eat on the pavement, along with the somewhat importunate street cats of Palaiókhora.

Pelican (££), on the water-front. A good place to eat and watch the fishing boats and strolling locals. Less crowded and noisy than the main street.

Platanías

Milos Taverna (££), 14km west of Khaniá. This has been popular for many years. Excellent food in a garden with ducks and peacocks and an old water mill.

Vríses

Many little **cafés** on the main street sell the famous local honey and yoghurt – mouthfuls of heaven.

Index

Acknowledgements

The Automobile Association would like to thank Kháris Kakoulákis for his assistance in the preparation of this book.

Picture credits

The Automobile Association would like to thank the following photographers, libraries and associations for their assistance in the preparation of this book.

MARY EVANS PICTURE LIBRARY 24a Icarus, 27 Palace of Knosós, Queen's Megaron, 33b Constantine the Great

T HARRIS 16b preparing lamb

HISTORY MUSEUM CRETE 36b Turkish attack on Candia, 60 *Deposition*

HULTON DEUTSCH COLLECTION LTD 229a German invasion of Crete, 229b Battle of Crete

MUSEUM OF IRÁKLIO 26a goddess with a sacred knot (*La Parisienne*) fresco from Knosós, 26b snake goddess from Knosós, 30/1 mosaic, 48 the dolphin fresco from Knosós, 81b harvester vase, 93 ladies in blue fresco from Knosós, 82 the Faistós disc, 133a Mália gold ornaments

NATURE PHOTOGRAPHERS LTD 96b golden eagle (W S Paton)

M REBANE 17 decorated church

SPECTRUM COLOUR LIBRARY 29 vase, Iráklio Museum, 73 Knosós, 151 Sitiá

THE MANSELL COLLECTION LTD 24b Theseus and the Minotaur, 25 Daedalus and Icarus

The remaining photographs are held in the Association's own photo library (AA PHOTO LIBRARY) and were taken by KEN PATERSON with the exception of the photographs on pages 5a, 56a and 265, which were taken by P ENTICKNAP, and those on pages 40/1, 41, 56b, 74, 108/9, 114, 122, 130, 166b, 167, 184a, 184b, 197b, 199, 201b, 207a, which were taken by W VOYSEY.

Contributors

Series advisor: Christopher Catling **Designer**: KAG
Joint series editor: Susi Bailey **Indexer**: Marie Lorimer
Copy editor: Hilary Hughes **Verifier**: Mick Rebane